# Surviving the Breakup

# SURVIVING THE BREAKUP

*How Children and Parents Cope with Divorce*

**Judith S. Wallerstein**

*and*

**Joan B. Kelly**

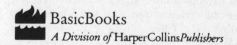

BasicBooks
*A Division of* HarperCollins*Publishers*

Library of Congress Cataloging in Publication Data

Wallerstein, Judith S.
  Surviving the breakup.

  Includes bibliographical references and index.
  1. Divorce—United States. 2. Children of
divorced parents—United States. 3. Divorcees—United
States—Family relationships. I. Kelly, Joan Berlin,
joint author. II. Title.
HQ834.W36      306.8'9'0973      79-5199
ISBN: 0-465-08345-5

96 97 98 RRD H 10 9 8 7 6 5 4 3 2 1

*To Bob and Jim*

# Contents

# PART 3

## *IN TRANSITION*

# PART 4

## *FIVE-YEAR FOLLOW-UP*

# Preface

This book is addressed to several audiences. It is addressed of course to our professional colleagues in many fields—in health and mental health, in law and education, in psychology and social work and family counseling—to all those whose professional lives bring them into contact with divorcing families and who, because of that, share our concern for the children of divorce. It is addressed as well to those individuals who are turning to divorce as the remedy to the failed marriage and who are seeking guidance on how best to mitigate the potentially harmful impact on their children. And in addition, it is addressed to those interested individuals concerned to know more about how social remedies to major societal problems can be kept from inflicting undue and unintended individual suffering.

Most of the early findings of the California Children of Divorce Project, together with the details of the project design and its methods, as well as the nature of the intervention services which we developed out of our experiences, have been published in the technical literature, in professional journals, and as chapters in professional books. Appendix B has the full listing of the project bibliography as published to date in the professional literature, and we are grateful to those journals and book editors, especially the American Journal of Orthopsychiatry and the Journal of the American Academy of Child Psychiatry, for permission to use material and case illustrations from those sources in telling our story here. But most of this book, the follow-up findings at a year and a half and again at five years, the story of the vicissitudes of the parent-child relationships during those years as well as the separate accounts of the experiences of the parents and of the children, the consequences even into early years of remarriages as well as in stabilized divorces, all these are presented here for the first time. Some of the more technical aspects of the data from these follow-up intervals and during our longitudinal time span will likewise appear in the professional journals.

This book itself represents the combined endeavors of a devoted interdisciplinary team held together by common purpose and commitment over many years. The initial members of the research team, Angela Homme, Ph.D., Susannah Roy, LCSW, Doris Juvinall Schwarz, LCSW, and Janet West, LCSW, continued to work with us throughout the life of the actual study from 1971 to 1977. Shauna Corbin, MA, joined our team at the second follow-up round and made a substantial contribution to its success. The loyalty and steadfast commitment of the whole initial group over the years to the project and their availability to make return visits to the parents and children at each of the follow-up points contributed substantially to the success of our follow-up endeavors, which were marked by an extraordinarily high response by these families to our continuing interest in them. We were actually able to obtain five-year follow-up data on fifty-eight of our initial sixty participating families. Moreover, our capacity to observe and to compare the changes and the continuities in both the children and their parents over the years of the study was immensely enhanced by the continuities provided by these same seasoned research observers.

We should especially emphasize here that our appreciation of the work of our project colleagues increased in growing measure as the project itself progressed and as we came to realize how much working with divorcing families, like all working with people under severe stress, is difficult and depleting of psychic and physical energy. The continued participation of the members of our interdisciplinary team has reflected therefore a level of commitment to the research goals, and more especially to the families and their children, which has been powerful enough to offset the distress of the work itself.

Throughout its duration, the project has been supported by the Zellerbach Family Fund of San Francisco. The Fund's remarkable executive director, Mr. Edward C. Nathan, as well as the members of the Board, had the vision to recognize that divorcing families, and particularly children of divorce, represented a significant and growing population whose circumstances were almost unexamined and whose needs—whatever they might be—were almost entirely unserved by the community. We are profoundly grateful to Mr. Nathan for his kindness, his wisdom, and his encouragement, and to the Fund for backing his leadership with its generous and unwavering support.

We are also indebted to others: to Ann Diamond, family attorney, whose sensitive concern with the unmet needs of her clients and their children led her to enthusiastically support the project and to help provide vital access to the legal community and the courts; to Margaret Baker, our statistical consultant; to David King Dunaway and to Amy Wallerstein for very helpful editorial suggestions; to our secretaries, Elza Burton, Patricia Sloan, and Carol Tara who so diligently and devotedly typed the several versions of this book; and to Midge Decter of Basic Books for welcome support and editorial ideas and excellent advice. And finally, we wish to acknowledge the Center for Advanced Study in the Behavioral Sciences at Stanford, California where the last writing and the final editing of this book took place. We are grateful for financial support provided at the Center by The Spencer Foundation, the Rockefeller Foundation, and the National Institute of Mental Health.

To Joan's children, Andrew and Sarah, who waited most patiently throughout their early years for their mother to finish, a fond note of appreciation. Our respective husbands, Robert Wallerstein and James Kelly, have encouraged us, comforted us, provided much excellent advice, and listened to us with almost unfailing patience. Therefore, this book is dedicated to the two of them with our love.

Judith S. Wallerstein, Ph.D.
Joan B. Kelly, Ph.D.

*November 1979*

# PART 1

*SEPARATION*

# Chapter 1

# The Beginning

When Dorothy walked along the yellow brick road in search of her home, which had been blown away by a tornado, she wisely selected as traveling companions a tin woodsman in search of a heart, a scarecrow in search of a brain, and a fearful lion in search of courage. But she finally succeeded in finding her way home by dint of her own efforts, plus a little help from her friends—and without the beguiling magic of the bogus Wizard.

The million American children whose homes were disrupted by the separation and impending divorce of their parents last year are in a similar situation, and to them may be added an additional million American children this year and, in all likelihood, next year as well. These children will need the full use of their intelligence, the full availability of their capacity for love and compassion, and all of their courage in order to face the many perils along the way until the continuity of their lives is reconstituted within a reasonably stable structure and a new family home. Beyond this, in addition to their own inner resources, the children will need the sensitive, understanding help and encouragement of parents, grandparents, teachers, and other adults whose professional and personal lives significantly touch theirs.

There is no wizard available to help, any more than there was for Dorothy, although there is hardly a child of divorce we came to know who did not cling to the fantasy of a magical reconciliation between his separating parents. Often these wishes for parental reconciliation lasted many years—sometimes long beyond the remarriage of one or both parents—variously disguised but still recognizable by the intense feelings with which the fantasy remained infused. Thus Danny, age seven, whose parents had been divorced for several years, softly confided to us his "best" fantasy. He had, he said, always wanted to fix up Hazel Street and Pine Street. "They all filled with mud and they don't join, but a long time ago they did, and I'd like to cut the two streets so they join, but this," he sighed, "will be a long time off."

Real lives, like fairy tales, are filled with tasks to be performed and journeys to be undertaken. The psychological and social obstacles that confront children and their divorcing parents are formidable, and the road to stability is much longer than many people realize. For the adult as for the child, divorce is not a single event. It is a chain of events—a series of legal, social, psychological, economic, and sexual changes, strung complexly together and extending over time. Divorce is a process which begins with the escalating distress of the marriage, often peaks at the separation and legal filing, and then ushers in several years of transition and disequilibrium before the adults are able to gain, or to regain, a sense of continuity and confidence in their new roles and relationships.

Change in adult life, as we have come to recognize, is gradual, painful, and hard-won, and it often extends over several years. Yet what may appear a reasonable expectation within the time sense of the adult has a different dimension and meaning in the life of a child. Two or three years of instability represent a significant part of the child's entire life experience—perhaps one-half the life of a kindergarten girl, or a third of the life of a nine-year-old boy. Nor is time the only issue. The child's unhappy awareness of a parent's distress may also extend over the early years of the newly divorced family.

Ann, who was not quite ten, tearfully told us a year after her parents separated, "I worry about my mom. I love her very much, but I have feelings. I'm afraid when mom takes a long time to come home. She once tried to commit suicide. I think of someone dying . . . how I'll be when I'm alone. She tried to commit suicide because of my dad. . . . It wasn't until long after the divorce that she stopped crying. I think of her jumping over the Golden Gate Bridge. Mom thinks no one worries about her—but I do."

The convergence of many factors led us to undertake a systematic investigation of the divorce-related experience of children and adolescents and their parents. Our study, which began in 1971 and ended in 1977, was designed to follow sixty divorcing families and their 131 children who were between three and eighteen years old at the time of the marital separation—following them from this beginning through their first five years within the divorced family.*

Initially, the plan had been to close the inquiry at the end of the first year. In accord with both conventional wisdom on these matters and crisis theory, we fully expected the transition period for most families

---

* For further particulars about both the design of the study and its population, see appendix A.

to have ended by that time, and we were eager to observe the process of the disruptions of divorce being resolved. We discovered that we were mistaken. Eighteen months after the separation many issues still remained unresolved in the lives of both parents and children. Feelings of anger, humiliation, and rejection were still running high; most adults had not yet reestablished stability and continuity in their lives, or order in their households. Moreover, an unexpected number of the children were on a downward course, compared with their overall functioning before the separation, and had not yet recovered their earlier developmental stride. For these reasons, our project was adjusted to conform to a more extended and realistic view of the postdivorce transition period, and redesigned to encompass the transition and the early years within the new family structure.

This book chronicles the experiences of sixty California divorcing families and their children. They granted us the singular privilege of significant access to their private lives, first during the difficult period of marital rupture, and then at specified intervals during the five years that followed. The project has no counterpart in the United States or in Europe because of the many years over which the cooperation of the divorcing families was sustained, the participation of so many children of different ages, and the kinds of questions which were posed. The findings provide the basis for this book: a detailed report of the continuity and discontinuity that occurred over the turbulent postdivorce years and insights into the consequences of these changes for children and adults, from which we derive certain conclusions and make certain proposals.

The study of divorce and children has been and remains a lonely field. As we end this decade the number of investigations, given the magnitude of the problem, is perilously low. Divorcing parents and their children have for some time been a population that is expanding explosively; yet its special needs are insufficiently recognized, little studied, and poorly served. Moreover, of those divorce-centered investigations that have been undertaken, only a fraction have examined the impact of divorce on children. One of the unhappy consequences is that the findings of this study in California, drawn primarily, but not entirely, from a white and middle-class population, must await comparison with those of families from other significant segments of the population whose experience may resemble or may diverge from these in important regards. For the present, we cannot know.

In the late 1960s and early 1970s a truly extraordinary rise in the incidence of divorce took place. With this trend continuing unabated during the years that followed—each year from 1972 to 1979 over a million new children below the age of eighteen experienced the divorce of their parents and the consequent disruption of their family—it has been estimated that 30 percent of all children growing up in the 1970s will experience the divorce of their parents.*

The state of California has for many years appeared at the top of the rising figures for divorce. In 1977 the rate of divorce for California was calculated at 6.0 per 1,000 population as compared with 5.0 per 1,000 population for the United States.† During the first months of 1979 there were almost as many divorces as marriages within the state, 79,403 estimated divorces as compared to 89,463 estimated marriages for the same seven-month period. ‡

This increasing instability of the American family was nowhere more visible than in the suburban counties in the San Francisco Bay area. In 1970, one year prior to the formal establishment of the study and intervention program described in this book, the number of people who applied for divorce in the particular county studied here exceeded those who applied for a marriage license. A coveted place in which to live, this county extends over 600 square miles of splendid Northern California countryside and contained in that year a relatively affluent, well-educated, and racially homogeneous population of 206,000. Of the families with children within the county, 11.6 percent were by 1970 already headed by a single parent, largely as a result of divorce.

Astonishingly little professional attention was being paid to the children in these families. The psychiatric literature at that time, for instance, consisted primarily of a limited number of case reports describing psychologically troubled children who had been brought to treatment several years after their parents had split up, or children originally brought as patients who were in continuing psychotherapy throughout the divorce experience. Although these psychiatric investigations did develop significant theoretical formulations, they failed to illuminate the expectable experience of the *normal* child at the time of the divorce. It seemed reasonable to suggest that clinical case reports from a disturbed population of children could not, without further study, be taken to represent the larger group of children in the community. Similarly, sociological research had only limited applicability. Several sociological studies reported findings from questionnaires which had been administered to classes of high school or college students, and to divorced mothers whose cooperation was elicited by interviewers in doorstep interviews. The reports from some of the surveys were encouraging in that they described relatively good functioning of many children of divorce on a number of social and psychological measures and greater intactness

---

* Mary Jo Bane, "Marital Disruption and the Lives of Children," in *Divorce and Separation*, ed. George Levinger and Oliver Moles (New York: Basic Books, Inc., 1979).

† Center for Health Statistics, California State Department of Health Services, Sacramento, Calif.

‡ *Monthly Vital Statistical Reports*, DHEW Pub. No. (phs 79–11–20) 28 September 1979.

overall compared to those children who had remained within unhappy, unbroken homes. Yet, by and large, the questionnaires were retrospectively directed, drawing on memory to elicit observations about events of a divorce that had occurred years earlier. Virtually none of the studies described the immediate experience at the time of divorce or addressed changes over time in the parent-child relationship.*

Our own program, which became known as the California Children of Divorce Project, was formally established as a Divorce Counseling Service and made available to divorcing families with children by the Community Mental Health Center of our county. It was designed to enable us to gain access to the perceptions, feelings, anxieties, and fantasies of the children and their parents. We were fully aware that these kinds of data are not available from observation or questionnaires alone, but that they must derive from mutual participation in an emotionally interactive process. The motivation for our respondents to unburden themselves to us, then, and to let us in this way become party to their inner psychological world, would have to be in their perception of us as persons worthy of their confidence, interested in them and giving promise of being helpful to them. In this sense, we knew that to succeed as a research study our program would also have to be perceived as a source of help. From the start, therefore, our project also included a broadly conceived, though necessarily brief, program of intervention designed to provide whatever psychological help and social and educational recommendations we could to alleviate acute distress and perhaps prevent, or at least diminish, poor outcomes.

The sixty families who participated in this project came to us voluntarily, out of their own wish for help in resolving the many problems that arise at the time of divorce in regard to the children, and not because of specifically identified needs for psychological help or clinical intervention. Allowing for human difference and complexity, the children in our project were a relatively normal group, having performed at age-appropriate levels in school, on the playground, and at home prior to

* Two studies influenced our conceptualization and planning. One of these had looked directly at the experiences of individual children in a normal, nonpatient population at the time of the divorce. This was a study of sixteen children observed in a nursery school after their parents separated, and it reported notable deterioration in over half of the children [John F. McDermott, "Parental Divorce in Early Childhood," *American Journal of Psychiatry* 124(10)(1968):1424–1432]. Soon thereafter, Hetherington [E. Mavis Hetherington, "Effects of Fathers' Absence on Personality Development in Adolescent Daughters," *Development of Psychology* 1(3)(1972):313–326] reported an experimental study of the behavioral responses to male interviewers of adolescent girls who had lost their fathers through earlier divorce, as compared with girls who had lost their fathers through death and girls from still intact families. The investigator found intensified seductive, and somewhat maladroit, behavior among the youngsters of divorced parents. This study pointed to the strong possibility that psychological effects of divorce could lie dormant for years and become visible at a much later stage of development, thereby underscoring the importance of long-term observations.

the divorce. Their part was to trust us with their thoughts and feelings. Our part was to listen, to offer what advice we could, when we could— and to learn. We struck an honest and enduring bargain. Of the original sixty families, fifty-eight were reached by us one year later, and then five years later as well. We have tried to do justice to our remarkable informants by quoting their own moving, and often eloquent, statements and by using many vignettes from their lives. At the same time, we have also exercised great caution in order to protect the confidentiality of the children and the parents. All names have been disguised, and identifying information which would be recognizable to anyone other than the subject has been removed.

We set off without any clear expectations of what we would find, and with as keen an interest in those children who were doing well as in those who seemed to be in trouble; our hope was to explore coping and growth as well as failure and retreat. We reasoned that precisely because most of these children were not stressed by chronic poverty or the pressures of racism, by overcrowding at home or school, or other similar inner-city problems, we would be able to study divorce at its most separable as a vector of change. Our goals were several and evolved more fully as we made our way. First of all, we were interested in understanding the youngsters' experience of divorce itself—capturing the nuances of the perceptions, the attitudes, the range of both intense and subtle feelings, and the underlying conflicts and anxieties at the time of the marital separation. From these we hoped to find the linkage, if any, between the early responses and such other factors as age, sex, family, parent-child relationship, marital unhappiness, and overt conflict in the predivorce family as well as, more broadly, support for the children in the social surroundings.

A second purpose was to follow children and adolescents over time in order to assess the impact of the divorce on their development and to gauge the extent to which the various developmental processes, taken individually and together, might be impeded or accelerated by family change. We wanted to find out whether the child's developmental march toward adulthood had been slowed, skewed, or interfered with by the marital rupture. Or, alternately, we wanted to ascertain whether the child's development had been accelerated or improved by release from the conflict-ridden marriage and the successful mastery of family rupture. It was our purpose to relate long-range findings to different factors and configurations within the child, in the parent-child relationships, in the family, in school, and in the social surround—and to tease out connections which might serve as predictors of good or poor outcome, and which would lead to the development of effective guidelines for parents and other helpers.

One difficulty encountered in assessing the condition of the partici- pants in the drama of divorce and its aftermath has been the absence of standards or norms against which to compare and contrast the various responses of the children and their parents. How to distinguish a serious developmental interference in a child from a temporary regression? How to separate the emergence of symptoms following the marital disruption—which are likely to be transitory and/or yield to help and support from the parents—from those symptoms which could indicate serious psychological difficulty requiring referral for psychological treatment? At what age and over what time span can one reasonably expect the child to comprehend the reality of parental separation and to accept it as a permanent change in the family structure? By contrast, at what age and at what temporal distance from the divorce would the child's continued unwillingness to accept it indicate the need for psychological intervention? In brief, what are the expectable ranges in attitudes, feelings, behavior, and responses in the wake of the divorce action and at various intervals later. What can one predictably say about the overall course of continued development? And, of course, to what extent can early signs of distress or regression serve the parent, the teacher, the clinician—all whose purpose is to help the child—as indicators of a current or emergent need or as likely predictors of some future intervention. Taken all together, we hoped that the experiences of the children and adolescents which we would observe over several years would offer the possibility of formulating a beginning set of standards and norms for psychological and social response to stress and in particular to divorce-induced stress, against which the responses of subsequent groups of children and adolescents might be measured.*

* These norms and standards need to be tested, modified, or affirmed, not only by the increased sophistication of method and accumulated knowledge, but by their applicability to the diversity of socioeconomic, ethnic, and geographical communities in this society. Because these hypotheses and these beginning norms have been derived from a California, suburban, predominantly (although not entirely) white, middle-class population, it would appear especially important to study divorcing families at several points in time and with perhaps related methodology in the different socioeconomic groups and with diverse ethnic backgrounds. One problem is the absence of any control group, in the usual sense, against which our own families can be highlighted. Short of a comparison group—families (with youngsters) equally conflicted and troubled who chose *not* to seek divorce as a solution, and yet made themselves equally accessible to intense and repetitive interview contact with our research group over a five-year span—no completely proper control group would exist. And, yet, aside from the obvious difficulty in assembling this kind of group (and one equivalent on the usual matching demographic and social criteria), we chose to pursue an avowedly hypothesis-generating search, one built on the fullest possible exploration of the "experience of divorce" for all its participants. The perspectives this study would generate could later, we trusted, become the subject of a more definitive hypothesis-testing study, one that paid attention to the specific controls necessary to test the hypotheses at issue.

We also want to note that, as a combined research and intervention study, our findings and their progress were inevitably confounded by the ameliorative impact of our interview method, both in its explicit and specific helpful intent, and also even in the nonspecific impact of a concerned and interested outsider seeking empathically to understand. We selected this course carefully. We decided there was no way to eliminate the effect of the interviewer, nor even to diminish that effect without vitiating

Our third major interest, which gathered momentum as we proceeded, was in the changes in parent-child relationships that take place at the time of separation and during the years that follow. Noting that the divorce-related changes in these relationships were at the core of both child and adult experience, we were particularly interested in what happened to the child's relationship with the visiting, noncustodial parent, because this relationship has no counterpart in the intact family. We were also interested in the relationship between the child and the custodial parent which, although it is not entirely unique, does present new and greater potential both for identification and closeness and for conflict than is generally the case in the intact family. Then the vicissitudes of parent-child relationships and stepparent-child relationships in postdivorce families began increasingly to excite our interest. For we came to realize how unexpected and far-reaching are the changes that occur in the child's relationship with both parents. And the implications of these changes apply not only to the evolution of the postdivorce family but to parent-child relationships in the intact family as well.

Finally, we were interested in the adults' experiences during the time of the failing marriage and the decision to divorce—in the hopes, disappointments, difficulties, and accomplishments that followed, with particular emphasis on the relationship of the divorced partners to each other, and as these affected their children in the period immediately after the divorce and during the years that followed.

The history of marriage and divorce in our society is replete with examples of the many unwarranted assumptions that adults have made about children, simply because such assumptions were congenial to the adults' needs or wishes at the time. Thus the conventional wisdom of yesteryear was that unhappily married people should remain married "for the good of the children." Today's conventional wisdom holds, with equal vigor, that a marriage that is unhappy for the adults is unhappy for the children and, furthermore, that a divorce that promotes the happiness of the adults will inevitably benefit the children as well. This presumed commonality of interests and perceptions between adults and children, along with the companion notion that the experience of the children can be subsumed under the experience of the adults, will be seen to be called into sharp question by our young subjects.

Only a few of the children in our study thought their parents were happily married, yet the overwhelming majority preferred the unhappy marriage to the divorce. As the children spoke with us, we found that

---

access to the lives of our participants in the study, thereby in effect vitiating the study itself. We can only assume, however, that our influence was more benign than not, and that the findings were more likely to be positive because of this brief intervention. Or put another way, any negative findings could be presumed to be more pervasive in a population that was entirely lacking even the brief and limited support which we offered in our three points of contact over the five years.

although many of them had lived for years in an unhappy home, they did not experience the divorce as a solution to their unhappiness, nor did they greet it with relief at the time, or for several years thereafter. To be sure, we also have evidence to report that years later, as the children matured, they often acquired a different perspective and regarded the accomplished divorce as a necessary or even useful solution to an impossibly conflict-ridden marriage. But at the time of the family disruption there were few who would have subscribed to this idea. Up until adolescence, we found little evidence in the children of any real capacity to identify with either parent's wish to escape an unhappy marriage. Many of the children, despite the unhappiness of their parents, were in fact relatively happy and considered their situation neither better nor worse than that of other families around them. They would, in fact, have been content to hobble along. The divorce was a bolt of lightning that struck them when they had not even been aware of the existence of a storm.

And yet as the adults talked with us—and they, too, spoke with intensity and sincerity, many out of a deep well of tragic feeling, long-standing loneliness, and emotional and sexual deprivation—the question that inevitably formed in our minds about their plight was, "What took you so long?" Many of these adults had been locked into marriages in which for a long time they had been demeaned, neglected, and abused, and the decision to divorce had by no means been taken lightly. Often it had been delayed long past the point when it seemed the proper and inevitable step to resolve their own life unhappiness. Several adults told us the long delay was caused by their still wretched memories of their own experiences as children when their parents divorced; they had resolved never to inflict similar suffering on their children.

We have surely not lacked for dilemmas in our generation, and this one cannot be resolved by denying its presence, by blurring the differences, the separate perceptions, and the experiences of each family member, or by insisting that what benefits the adult inevitably benefits the children. Only with a realistic and informed recognition of the individual as well as the shared experience during marriage, during the divorcing period, and in the postdivorce family does it become possible to address the many serious questions involved, and to make the decisions that will reflect a true consideration for all the family members—children and adults alike. Until this perspective is explicitly recognized—not only by the parents, but by the teachers, lawyers, judges, and mental health professionals as well—we will lack the basis for understanding and for developing ways to ease the impact of divorce on each of the differently affected parties, individual child as well as individual parent.

Finally, in our study we have not asked when divorce is the wise course of action, or whether society and its children are sometimes better served if the unhappily married pair remain together until the children reach adulthood. On the contrary, we have assumed divorce as a given, an appropriate social remedy and option that should be available to adults locked into unhappy marriages and as a legal recourse that is likely to become increasingly accessible to people in our society. Unfortunately, neither unhappy marriage nor divorce is especially rewarding for children. Each imposes its own set of stresses on the children and parents involved. We have asked instead how to divorce and what do we need to know to ease the experience on behalf of the children and their parents.

To end this chapter on a personal note, I remember walking across the university campus on the way to teach a class and seeing one of the youngsters from our project: Laughing in the sunshine, when she looks up, waves at me and smiles warmly. I find her delightful. I am also as aware as she is that we have shared a certain crossing together, she directly and I vicariously, and that each of us will never be the same. I am aware, as I see her, that six years ago, shortly after her parents separated, her first words to me were, "Thank God, they're not walking on eggs anymore. It's out in the open now." I recall, too, her shocked sense of disbelief and betrayal on encountering her father with an attractive strange woman at a local crafts fair. And I also recall four years later, after a national television documentary had portrayed a happy, smiling divorced family, that she called me in anger to say she and I knew there was no such thing as the "painless divorce" portrayed on the show, and that she had said to her mother that she and I both knew that it was not like that at all.

Yes, we know. And this book is about what we know, what we have learned from these children and parents whose lives have so enriched our own.

# Chapter 2

# The Ambiance
# of Divorce

The divorcing parents provided us with detailed accounts of the years of marriage, accounts infused with the intense emotion of their recent separation. As they reviewed their courtship, the evolution of the family, including the birth of the children and the course of the marital failure, we were struck with the diversity in the kind of marriages that eventually came to divorce. What was unexpected as well was that the divorcing families included not only those suffering from loneliness and isolation, with each family member going his or her own way, hardly communicating and rarely touching, but also families whose members shared a rich history, common recreational interests, and religious beliefs. Their conflicts were sometimes explosive and highly visible; other differences were muted and carefully concealed. A significant number of these families, however, were neither bleak nor overtly conflict ridden and were, to outward appearances, well-functioning, close-knit family groups which had been regarded as good, or at least good enough, by their children, friends, and neighbors. A full one-quarter of the divorcing families in our study had been close-knit and had engaged in many shared activities over the years. Some of these maintained careful constraint and reserve. Others, to be sure, were occasionally, or even frequently, afflicted with angry fighting and physical violence; but the web of family life had not been disrupted by such turbulence and the family's activities had included camping trips, shared vacations, holiday festivities, and birthday parties for the children.

About one-half of the families gave evidence of the kind of bleakness we expected. Among these, husbands and wives had lived together as strangers for many years. Sometimes both had lovers; more often, the husband had a steady lady friend with whom he spent most weekends and many evenings. Communication was poor or almost nonexistent. In one such family the adults refused to speak with each other for eighteen months and corresponded on little bits of paper when they needed to communicate. Not surprisingly, there was a good deal of anger, resulting in physical abuse—usually by men of their wives—or property destruction, accompanied by a good deal of fear. In addition, there were many cases of infidelity and an astonishing degree of long-standing sexual deprivation and loneliness. The women most often cited a feeling of being belittled and unloved, while for the men the complaint of feeling uncared for most often took the form of claiming an incompatibility of interests, goals, and values between them and their wives.

Many husbands and wives had been troubled with psychological problems during the marriage, of which the most common was chronic depression. Eight women in our study had made one or more suicide attempts during the marriage. Fewer men than women showed such severe depression, although one-third had been moderately depressed for several years, tending to withdraw, sometimes to a pathological extent, and appearing to be highly constricted and inhibited in their capacity to express feeling or respond to the give and take of relationship with their wives and children. Alcoholism and the violence which so often accompanied it were frequently reported by wives as chronic behavior.

But whether there were chronic psychological problems or not, men and women alike spoke sorrowfully of a pervasive sense of being uncared for. The most frequently mentioned complaint was the sense of having important and pressing needs which were unacknowledged, as well as unmet, by the marital partner. Beyond this shared and very frequent perception, men and women tended to regard their marriage differently.

Of course, they tended to blame one another for the failure of the marriage. But it was striking the extent to which others in general were blamed for difficulties in and outside the marriage: Besides the other partner, there were the lover, the school, the community, the employer, some extended family member, the women's liberation movement, the college, and the neighborhood crowd. No one, interestingly enough, blamed the children.

## The Child in the Failing Marriage

A complex balance of psychological forces governed the relationship between parents and children in the failing marriages. We soon learned that the parent-child relationship did not mirror the unhappy marital ties and that the stresses of the marriage did not necessarily spill over into parents' relationships with the children. In fact, it became evident that parenting can remain relatively unencumbered by marital unhappiness or, put more technically, parenting can be maintained as a relatively conflict-free sphere of behavior within a very deprived and unhappy marriage—though, of course, not always. We were interested, in this connection, to discover that men who readily resorted to violence in response to their wives did not necessarily beat, or even spank, their children. Parenting, in fact, could become a means of offsetting marital unhappiness by cultivating a special relationship with one or more of the children.

In a significant number of conflict-ridden households the parents were loving and supportive of the children's physical and emotional development. The quality of father-child relationships ranged from good enough to exceptionally good for at least one-fifth of the children. Similarly, the mother-child relationship was good enough or exceptionally good for one-third of the group. One-quarter of the children had two committed parents. Three-quarters of the children had a mother who was physically available to them when they needed her presence. One-half of the children had a physically available father. Furthermore, whereas only a tiny fraction (5 percent) of the married couples were able to communicate well with each other, at least one-quarter of the fathers and one-third of the mothers were able to communicate very well with their children.

Adults who disagreed strongly with each other on a great many issues were able to cooperate in the care of the children. Child-rearing issues were not a source of disagreement for over one-third of the parents. One-half of the children experienced relatively consistent handling by both parents. We were sometimes surprised to find, as a repeated occurrence, that two parents who related extremely poorly to each other were still able to share the parenting and caring function, and to maintain the other partner at his or her best as a parent. For a number of the couples in our study the highest point of adulthood they were able to achieve revolved around their relationship with their children. Thus a marriage experienced as impossible by the parents was not necessarily that stressful for the children, and many of the youngsters reflected good parenting in their overall adjustment and demeanor and in their trustful attitudes with us and other adults in their lives. They expected well of the world.

At the other end of the spectrum, over 40 percent of the children had relationships with their fathers which were exceedingly poor, marked by gross psychopathology or neglect. The attitudes of some of these men were severely corrosive of their children's self-esteem. Some were physically or sexually abusive of one or more of the children in the family. At least one-quarter of the mother-child relationships were also very poor, marked by serious neglect and threatened abuse. These relationships tended to reinforce each other. Parents who treated their children poorly were more likely to treat their marital partners badly as well.

Where physical violence occurred between the parents, children were usually not shielded and often witnessed the fighting. Sometimes we had the impression that the fighting only occurred when the children provided an audience. Physical abuse between the parents, mainly beating of the wife by the husband, was an ongoing expectable part of life for one-quarter of the children in this study and was witnessed on occasion by well over half the group. And even when such abuse occurred rarely, or even only once, it was long and vividly remembered by the frightened child. Several children in the families of habitual violence lived in terror, worried whether one or both parents would be hurt by the other, or when the police would next be called to separate the angry parents. Children also provided the audience for the accusations and counteraccusations of promiscuity.

It therefore appears that a complex psychology attaches to parent-child relationships in the failing, as well as in the intact, marriage. Many of our findings are paradoxical and reflect the tentativeness of much of the knowledge: There is evidence that the parent-child relationship is vulnerable to the tensions of the marital unhappiness; there is also evidence that the parent-child relationship may gain in closeness and intimacy because of the very frustrations of the unhappy marriage. Parenting appears to be a shared composite relationship through which each parent supplements the other to provide protection, or to further endanger the child. And, finally, it seems that parenting can sometimes be maintained relatively conflict-free by couples who are profoundly troubled within themselves and miserable with each other.

## The Decision to Divorce

People opt for divorce for complex motives, some of which have little, if any, relation to marital incompatibility. Unlike the decision to marry, the decision to divorce rarely occurs by mutual consent in families with children. Customarily, one partner wants to get out of the marriage with a great deal more passion than the other. Many times, only one partner wants to get out at all. For instance, in our study, women took the final step to terminate the marriage in three-fourths of the cases, while nearly half the husbands strongly opposed their decision. On the other hand, one-third of the women bitterly opposed the divorce, including some who had filed for the divorce originally themselves out of anger and hurt pride.

Whoever was the initiator, the differences between husband and wife over the decision to divorce set the tone for the interactions of the separation period. The parent who opted for the divorce, we found, tended to see the children as relatively well and adjusting to the crisis without difficulty. The parent who disapproved of the divorce, however, was more likely to perceive the children as suffering or in crisis. Such differences in regard to the decision to divorce and the aggrieved responses of the marital partner who opposed it usually lie at the root of litigation over child custody.

The nature and circumstances of the decision to divorce, in turn, become factors in the child's capacity to cope, immediately or eventually, with the family rupture. To set the general framework, there appears to be an important link between the child's success in coping and his or her capacity to understand and make good sense of the sequence of the disruptive events within the family. The child's efforts at mastery are strengthened when he understands the divorce as a serious and carefully considered remedy for an important problem, when the divorce appears purposeful and rationally undertaken, and indeed succeeds in bringing relief and a happier outcome for one or both parents. The child's understanding is reinforced by the perceived improvement in the condition of a parent, and thus, though the transition period may be difficult, the child's overall sense of coherence and order is not undermined. Moreover, under these circumstances, the child's very efforts at mastery may be additionally rewarded by a greater understanding of the nature of human relationships in general.

Conversely, where the divorce is unplanned, undertaken impulsively, pursued in anger or guilt over fancied or real misdeeds, or where the divorce coincides with other unrelated family crises, the child's capacity to cope is severely burdened. He is likely to be confused and bewildered and feel that his parents lack rational direction. If he feels they are driven by hate or mere impulse, he may perhaps conclude that there is no rational way to comprehend the distress that he and the other children have experienced. Thus, the basis on which the divorce decision is taken can have long-standing consequences for the child's capacity not only to integrate the experience, but also for his attitude and assessment of his parents and, through this, his view of the entire adult world.

*Divorce as a Rational Solution*

The decision to divorce was easiest for the children to comprehend when it represented the culmination of years of visible unhappiness and where the divorce itself had long been considered—the legal step reflecting a disengagement which had already been underway. Sometimes in cases of this kind the final resolve to divorce occurred within the context of psychotherapy, a new milieu, or the return to school. More often than not, there was no clear "last straw," only the accumulation of discomfort, combined with a growing awareness of the possibility of a better life and followed by a burst of courage.

Mrs. N., for example, filed for divorce after ten years of marriage during which her husband, a political figure, stayed out of the home four or five nights out of seven or staggered in drunk to creep into bed with his oldest child. He was often abusive and demeaning of his wife and children. Mrs. N. said, "We haven't lived together as man and wife for three years. I feel neutered." It had taken her several years to reach her decision. She was afraid of living alone, and she was especially, and not unrealistically, concerned about the financial burden of the children which, in consideration of her husband's anticipated unreliability, would fall on her shoulders. Finally, in utter despair, she decided to divorce him. Mr. N. opposed her decision, responded with hurt pride, and refused to leave the house. His anger was expressed in refusal to provide appropriately for the support of the children, which led to continued litigation over the years.

The children did not share in the relief Mrs. N. experienced following the divorce. They were worried about whether their mother would be able to take care of them, and whether they would lose contact with their father, and they were frightened about the disruption of their home. They could, however, understand the mother's decision and were eventually able to accept the wisdom and the courage of her long-delayed action.

Sometimes the decision to divorce occurs in the absence of overt conflict between man and wife and reflects one partner's mounting resentment instead, the sense of having been exploited during the marriage, and the yearning for a different, more gratifying relationship in marriage. Such divorces often reflect the personal growth of the partner who is seeking the change.

Mr. and Mrs. J. had been childhood sweethearts and were married four years when she decided on divorce. Almost from the start of the marriage, Mr. J. had refused to work, saying, "Your thing is money; mine is not." As a result, Mrs. J. supported them both, and during her pregnancies worked through her eighth month. By the time the first child was three years old, Mrs. J. had tired of supporting the family and asked that her husband help support the family and find work. He refused and felt aggrieved by his wife's complaints. He considered himself the children's primary caretaker, although his wife disputed this.

Their oldest child, who had been content and well cared for within the intact family despite the mother's growing unhappiness, was greatly distressed by the divorce, which disrupted her life and separated her from her beloved father who had been her constant companion during the mother's workday. Nevertheless, the mother's increased sense of well-being benefited the child. Continued visiting with the father (who did not want sole or joint custody) was helpful in restoring the child's prior good functioning.

Finally, in the group of divorces we call rational—that is, undertaken to undo an unhappy marriage considered unlikely to change—there were a few cases of people who struggled to break free of marriage to a mentally ill partner. Such a struggle was often an ordeal for the person seeking the divorce because of the psychological conflicts engendered, the gradual and exceedingly painful realization that the partner they married was indeed mentally ill, followed by the guilt associated with the decision to divorce and depart. But in such a divorce, as in the foregoing examples, the children could understand, or could be helped to understand, the basis for the parent's decision in ways that sooner or later came to make sense to them, and of which they eventually approved. These rational divorces took place in one-third of the families within our study.

Other kinds of divorces, because they seemed hardly addressed to the marital stress and brought in their wake no relief to the family, did pose serious difficulties to the children, however helpful they might have been to the parent who sought the divorce.

## Divorce as a Stress Related Response

Divorces occurred in families where marital unhappiness had not been a special source of concern to either partner. Rather, the decision to divorce followed upon some stressful experience outside the marriage which was profoundly upsetting to the person who then initiated the move towards divorce. The response to the external stress, in other words, ricocheted into the family arena. Experiences that induced such divorces in our sample included the unexpected death of a grandparent, the diagnosis of a mortal illness, or a crippling accident to a child. The psychological mechanisms that lead from such stress to divorce can be explained by the stressed person's need to take flight to ward off the depression that threatens to overwhelm him or her. Thus, the same tragedy that has the potential to mobilize some families, drawing the members closer together in mutual support, paradoxically has the potential to rupture other families, as one or both parents escape from each other and run from the marriage in a desperate effort to avoid the unbearable memory of the tragedy and so avert the threatened depression.

The decision to divorce at such an inopportune time, of course, only serves further to diminish the supports available in the family, just when supports are the most sorely needed all around. The children are burdened especially, since the divorce makes no sense, brings no relief to any identified family conflict, and the pain of the family disruption only adds to the awful pain of the family's initial unhappiness.

An example of this phenomenon is the case of Mrs. K. Mrs. K. filed for divorce shortly after her mother died. Her husband, a gentle, devoted family man, was startled and begged her to change her mind, or at least to permit him to remain within the family home, since he had no place to go. The children cried and implored their mother to change her mind. Her oldest child tried to comfort her and spent many evenings with the sorrowing woman, trying gently to cheer her. Four years later, Mrs. K. told us, "I wish I could marry him again. I was upset. My mother had died, and I felt that he wasn't sympathetic, and I filed for divorce. It was a terrible mistake, but there is nothing to do now. I have ruined the lives of four people."

Another form of divorce that must be seen as reflecting psychological stress and that also makes little sense to family members, especially the children, is a divorce that is linked to the severe psychological illness of the parent who files. Several adults in the study developed a sudden rash of symptomatic behaviors which included their decision to divorce as one of the new symptoms. Some of these decisions occurred within the context of an ongoing marriage that other family members assumed was satisfactory, even happy. These divorce requests, coming from persons in the throes of severe psychiatric illness, were often tragic because if the person who sought the divorce was successful, he or she was separated from family support exactly when it was most needed. An additional complication was the fact that the person who was decompensating often showed other bizarre behavior at the same time, and the children were therefore confronted simultaneously with a disturbed parent and a ruptured marriage.

Mrs. V. began to complain of telephone taps, of being followed, and of hearing voices. She denied any need for psychiatric treatment and attributed her difficulties entirely to stresses within the marriage, about which we were unable to elicit any coherent details. Her small children and her husband were frightened and worried by her changed behavior and by her unprecedented screaming and fighting in the household. While recognizing that her husband loved her, she filed for divorce in the face of his despairing opposition.

The families in which divorce was sought by an emotionally disturbed parent often did not identify the behavior as disturbed or psychiatrically ill. There was general recognition that the person was behaving irrationally, but most people failed to recognize the severity of the illness or its widening effects. Few of these troubled people were in psychiatric treatment, or sometimes, psychotherapy which focused on marital counseling did not identify the irrational basis for the divorce suit. The children in these families and the marital partner who opposed the decision were often bewildered and distraught. And moreover, as noted earlier, since the decision to divorce did not address any particular problems within the marriage, there was no subsequent relief or sense of closure.

## Impulsive Divorces

A third group of divorces were undertaken without reflection or planning or any real consideration of consequences. One example of divorces undertaken impulsively were those employed as a strategy by the aggrieved husband or wife to punish the partner involved in an extramarital affair and to try in this way to return him or her to the marriage. Several women sued for divorce in outrage and jealousy, yet secretly hoped to win back their husbands with this maneuver. Mostly, if not always, this strategy failed, and the husband was simply able to depart from the marriage more easily and with less guilt.

One consequence of the use of divorce as a weapon to punish the errant spouse is that the aggrieved partner may continue to rage for years. Furthermore, since the intent was to employ the divorce primarily as a strategy to restore the marital tie, the parent brought a lessened capacity and little motivation to the complex tasks of the divorcing period.

Another not unfamiliar configuration was a divorce which followed a sudden, unexpected revelation of one spouse's infidelity and announced intention of marrying a lover when there had been no explicit recognition of difficulty within the marriage. Such delinquency created bitter opposition, rage, and sometimes violence, severe depression, and threats of suicide in the spouse who felt scorned. The children were often coopted in the battle, and became the allies, confidants, and rescuers of the grieving parent.

## Decisions Encouraged By Others

Some of the divorce decisions were made within the context of psychotherapy and with the encouragement of a therapist. Several of these decisions were helpful in setting people free from marital relationships which exploited or abused them. Some decisions to divorce reflected the person's newly identified need for self-realization and the shared conviction of therapist and patient that the marital partner represented a hindrance to the patient's continued development as an adult. Occasionally, however, psychotherapist and patient shared the rhetoric of self-realization without recognizing the underlying depression or the regressive allure of the search for a vanished adolescence. Sometimes, the consulting physician, gynecologist, or internist, in finding severe psychosomatic symptomatology, directly advised the patient to divorce. Although little such advice, whether in psychotherapy or with the consulting physician, was offered without foundation, it sometimes took insufficient cognizance of the road ahead and assumed, without direct knowledge of the children involved, that a plan that would benefit the unhappy parent would inevitably benefit the children as well.

All of the varieties of divorce sketched here wrought significant changes not only in the family structure but in numerous other aspects of the children's lives. There were abrupt alterations in financial and economic stability, for example, and in the mothers' working hours and child-care arrangements. These were tangible changes, some of which the youngsters could at least observe, discuss, and react to. More important were the problems created by the parents' moods and attitudes after the separation, for in the majority of families conflict and bitterness between the parents escalated following the decision to divorce. The sudden external change in their circumstances was the skeleton of the child and adolescent postseparation responses.

## Economic Changes

Virtually every parent in our study was preoccupied with the change in family economics created by the divorce. This intense focus on family finances has several sources, the most obvious being the legal requirement that the divorcing spouses divide shared community property equally between them. What once supported one family unit must now support two families, forcing a decline in standard of living for every family member, regardless of level of affluence. While our own sympathies and concern quite naturally tended to be directed more to those whose standard of living moved toward or plummeted below the poverty level, the sudden reduction in available monies was as deeply affecting to women of middle-class means. While such women perhaps worried less about feeding their youngsters adequately or having their car repossessed, the stress of adjusting themselves and their children to living on substantially less money was nonetheless real. In addition to this decline and fear of financial instability, there was the psychological response of the parent to both these new conditions, including the perception of how he or she was faring relative to the other spouse.

Despite the legal requirement that community property accumulated during the marriage be equally divided, the women in our study were affected by severe economic changes more substantially and more permanently than were the men. This was especially true in the middle-

and lower-class families where, in fact, there was little, if any, shared property to divide.

Only about one-quarter of the women and two-fifths of the men did not experience any substantial change in their standard of living—with some men and a few women, this was because of their considerable wealth—but a notable decline in the standard of living was the experience of three-fifths of the men and three-quarters of the women. This decrease in the income available to mothers and children was true despite a very high percentage of fathers (87 percent) who paid child support on a more or less regular basis. For about one-quarter of the men and one-third of the women, their changed economic situation was an abrupt and very serious one for which there had been little if any preparation. Seven percent of these women moved onto welfare rolls.

But even without so drastic a slide as onto welfare, the decline in the standard of living was made more troublesome for some women by the way it brought them into a lower socioeconomic class. Women who had been in the highest and most prosperous socioeconomic group, in particular, faced an entirely changed life. For these women, all of them left by their husbands, the moorings of their identification with a certain social class, and with it the core of their self-esteem—formerly exclusively determined by the husband's education, occupation, and income—were shaken loose. (While the self-esteem of the men left by their wives was often as devastated as with these women, the men did not additionally have to contend with a change in status which upended their base of social operations.)

With respect to financial arrangements between divorcing spouses, the aggrieved parent, especially if he or she was the primary wage earner, not only felt "ripped off" by being left, but viewed his or her spouse's ability to take half of the family property as the final insult. In contrast, the parent who chose to terminate the marriage was more likely to ask for less, if it was the wife, or, in the husband's case, was more inclined to financial largesse in child support or alimony settlement. Such conduct represented attempts to deal with guilt and a concomitant wish to pacify the partner's rage or nullify bad feelings. (Once the guilt diminished, of course, the parent who had agreed to a lopsided arrangement was apt to become bitter about having "given everything away.")

## Mothers as New Heads of the Household

The abruptness of economic change and the instability that ensued pressured many women to make major life decisions precisely at the time of turmoil and depleted emotional reserve. Some who had not really begun to contemplate their futures felt the immediate need to choose a job or career. Some had the vision and competence to pursue responsible careers or professional lives but did not have adequate financial reserves. So they combined part- or full-time work with schooling in an exhausting schedule that continued three or four years.

Half the women in the study had worked part or full time prior to the separation. Within just a few months of the separation another 10 percent entered the work force, and the ratio of women employed part time to full time reversed, with the majority now taking on full-time responsibilities. Most of the younger women worked willingly and, as they experienced success, had a rising sense of self-esteem. But a small group bitterly resented the need to work and regarded their jobs as tedious and overly fatiguing. In all, of the working mothers, three-quarters enjoyed their work, whereas the remainder either hated it or accepted the necessity of working with resignation.

Looking for employment now became a necessary activity for an additional group of formerly unemployed women. For some, this was a new and rather exciting experience, whereas for others, particularly those with no prior work experience or marketable skills, there was a diminished self-esteem conjoined with hopelessness in job hunting.,

Among the women who did not work and remained at home full time were a group who suffered with moderate or serious depressions or other serious mental illnesses. Some were chronic, long-standing illnesses, others were newly precipitated by the divorce crisis. A few women spent most of their days in bed; several were alcoholics; some were intermittently preoccupied with suicidal thoughts. And a second smaller group that remained at home suffered with recurring physical ailments that immobilized them periodically. Thus, while these women remained behind to care for their children full time, the presence of psychological or physical illnesses constrained their caretaking capacities.

## Changes in Child Care

Changes in providing care for the children naturally accompanied these shifts in working patterns, particularly for those newly employed or those taking on full-time positions. Household help was rare and financially feasible for only a few professional women in the group. Only one family had a full-time housekeeper. More often, young children were carried to babysitters early in the morning and picked up by their mothers on their way home. Most fathers, even if their schedules permitted, refused to be considered a babysitting resource. Rather than welcoming the potential time with the child as an opportunity to continue or enrich their relationship, they viewed the mother's request as a manipulative exploitation. Some fathers refused, on principle, to be available for the mother's "convenience," even if, for example, she was taking weekly night classes to improve her career or vocational opportunities. This attitude, like that toward money, arose from the need to punish the mother for leaving the marriage by insisting that, in all things, the responsibility was hers alone.

A few fathers did participate in child-care arrangements. One father regularly took his children to live with him during his wife's exam week. Another was responsible for his preschool child three days of the working week. Whenever parents worked out such arrangements, the children proved the ultimate beneficiaries of the flexibility and love demonstrated toward them by both parents.

But by and large, child-care responsibilities belonged entirely to the mother. The pace was exhausting. Several mothers, newly working full time, described their need to work past midnight regularly to complete household chores too numerous or difficult for young children to help with. Except for a very few instances, grandmothers or other extended family members were not available for assistance, and household routines were rarely shared with friends or neighbors.

Older children, often first pleased with the mother's new ability to earn a living, were in turn sobered by her reduced availability. Younger children clamored for more attention, and often, of course, when the mother had the least energy available. Within six months of separation, one-quarter of the mothers interviewed judged themselves to be substantially less available to their children due directly to expanded work schedules and/or new educational demands. One of the ironies of the woman's move toward independence, increased self-esteem, and personal growth was that the children did not always share in the benefits, at least not in the first year. Certainly one of the most pressing dilemmas for the single parent is the difficulty in balancing financial and psychological needs of parent and child in the wake of the separation.

# Changed Neighborhoods

Moving to less expensive housing became the focus and symbol of the increased financial hardship for many families. Nearly one-fifth of the youngsters moved within the first six months following separation. Most parents tried to wait until the school year was completed if the move entailed changing schools. For the most part they were sensitive to their children's anxieties about making new friends. Only rarely was a move undertaken to wreak vengeance, in which case it appeared as a symbol of the chaotic, embittered parent's need to make a very strong statement to the offending spouse. Considerable talk of moving was in the air for many other children, and such anticipated moves tended to produce as much anxiety and sense of uncertainty as the actual event.

## Emotional Changes

The greatest disruptions in the children's lives were those that stemmed from pervasive changes in parental mood, attitude, and behavior. Bitter and explosive interactions between parents were, for most of the youngsters, the hallmark of the divorce experience. In divorce, the mutual ties that served sometimes to restrain the expression of hostility during the marriage are broken. Agitated by stress, by failure, by disappointment, by humiliation, the partners to divorce often finish off whatever last vestiges of good feeling might have remained in the marriage.

### The Angry Parent

Angry feelings associated with the failed marriage and divorce found their expression in an incredible array of behavior. Four-fifths of all the men and an even higher proportion of the women expressed anger and bitterness toward their spouses. Thus, in almost every family, there was at least one, if not two, angry parents. In the few rare cases where the parents were not, in some degree, angry at each other, the children were, of course, less stressed, and the parents were better able to attend the youngsters' distress.

The women were clearly the more hostile. Not only were more of them angry, but the intensity of their anger was greater. It may be that the same women who described marriages in which their competence had been demeaned and belittled began, with the separation, to recoup some self-esteem by uncapping the wells of intense hostility toward their husbands.

The majority of the angry men and women confined themselves to verbal assaults on the integrity and behavior of their divorcing spouses. As mentioned previously, money became a focus of intense hostility, not just regarding the division of community property, but over necessary expenditures that had not been spelled out and agreed upon explicitly in the separation agreement. There were enough gray areas left to enable any angry parent to take advantage of the other. Frequently, the children's needs were also involved.

Donna needed medical attention for a kidney infection. Her mother directed the physician's office to bill the father for the several visits involved, based on her understanding of the temporary agreement. The father refused to pay but did not so inform the mother. When Donna returned several months later with a recurrence of the infection, the office informed the mother that they could no longer treat Donna because no one was assuming responsibility for the bills. Embarrassed, Donna's mother agreed to pay the bill in small installments but angrily admitted to us her concern that now Donna is not getting adequate attention because the mother cannot afford frequent visits.

Three weeks before entry into college, Mary had no idea who, if anyone, would pay the tuition. Her father angrily insisted that he had given that "greedy bitch" more than enough to pay for college; Mary's mother, just as angry, held steadfastly to her claim that the father's responsibility for college expenses was spelled out in the divorce agreement. Anxious and confused, Mary wondered whether she should pack for college or give up.

Sometimes whole families would become embroiled in financial matters. Mrs. B.'s three children angrily accused her of squandering their father's money on things for herself. "You *never* have any money for the things *we* want! So when we ask Dad for shoes, or a jacket, he gets mad and yells at us that he gives you *plenty* of money." Mrs. B. responded by flying into a rage, accusing the father of lying, hiding income, and making erratic payments. In a joint session held between mother and children to review the monthly budget in minute detail, the youngsters began to understand their own role in exacerbating the hostilities between their parents.

Many parents' hostilities spilled into the arrangements for visiting, which provided a rich arena for struggles around the issue of who should be in control.

Mr. H. normally picked up his youngsters every Thursday at noon, during the summer months. Arriving twenty minutes late one day, he found no one at home. Mrs. H. had waited for ten minutes, then taken the children to the movies for an afternoon outing. Outraged, Mr. H. threatened to sue for custody of the youngsters. Mrs. H. frostily told us that if Mr. H. wanted the children during the day, then he would not be permitted to disappoint them by coming late. If there was a traffic jam, or he got held up at work, that was just his tough luck. In her intent to punish the father, she ignored the children's anxiety about father not finding them home.

Certainly the most common form of expressing postseparation hostility was denigration of the other spouse. One of the central complaints of the youngsters in our study was the "badmouthing" and "backbiting" of their parents. They had good reason to complain. More than half of the mothers, and almost as many fathers, were extremely critical and abusive in all their comments about the other parent. For the most part, children heard their parents describe each other in new terms. Men were "liars, bastards, terrible parents, unreliable, sleeping around with cheap women, disgusting, and crazy." Women were "whores, unfit mothers, drunken bitches, greedy and grasping, sexually inadequate, and crazy." Children were invited to participate in these hostilities. Some did, with alacrity; others felt anxious; some were disgusted.°

At the uppermost end of the spectrum of hostility was a group of men and women whose hatred was so intense, and their wish for righteous vindication so desperate, that nothing seemed to stop them from pursuing their goals. This group of parents, close to one-fifth of the women and slightly fewer men, shared an extreme and bitter opposition to the divorce. There was thus usually only one such parent in a given family, and for these individuals every aspect of the divorce process became an opportunity for the expression and consolidation of rage, particularly when the children were present as audience or Greek chorus. We have called such parents the "embittered-chaotic" father or mother, and found that their behavior was generated by a triad of psychological responses to the divorce. The intense anger was associated with a serious divorce-engendered depression and a severe, disorganizing disequilibrium. Yet it was the rage that was visible and seemed to function in part to ward off a potentially more devastating depression. Paradoxically, the raging tirades and complex angry behavior had an organizing influence on these shattered individuals. Thus, the anger was central to the parents' capacity to maintain a semblance of psychological inner order, and may explain why their rage was so easily refueled over the months and years by almost any action or word of the offending spouse. We were impressed by the tenacity of this psychological response triad and by its imperviousness to brief interventions.

The embittered-chaotic parent never shielded his or her child from divorce bitterness and chaos. More often, he pulled the child into the middle of the maelstrom in a desperate attempt to marshal psychological support and alliance. Where the father was embittered, there was a high likelihood of physical violence, and child-napping attempts were not uncommon. Embittered-chaotic fathers threatened custody battles, and

---

° One encouraging result of the counseling intervention was the ability of some parents to refrain from continued criticism of the other spouse when they understood what an assault this represented on the child's own self-esteem. They had not, of course, intended such a thing and were shocked at how this aggression affected their child. The youngsters' decreased trust in their parents after separation may have been related in part to each parent's attempt to undermine the other.

concentrated their efforts on convincing the children, and the court, that the mother was either morally bankrupt or emotionally unfit to continue mothering. Ironically, in our sample, none of these embittered-chaotic men had a predivorce relationship with his children that was particularly good. But in the postseparation period they hammered away at their children with a vision of the future happiness and safety that would result were the father to obtain custody. Often the underlying motive was a desperate wish for reconciliation.

Mr. G., a rigidly perfectionistic man, expected model behavior from his wife and children during a turbulent marriage. When they failed to live up to his exacting standards, he flew into cruel rages, beating them for various forms of misbehavior. For many months after Mrs. G. filed for divorce, Mr. G.'s rage continued as he berated the "wicked, fallen" mother for kicking him out and promised the children a new house and swimming pool if they could change her mind. The eldest boy became a carbon copy of the father, sharply criticizing the mother's behavior and dress, yet pleading with her to reconsider the divorce. Sounding so like his father in tone and words, the boy told us, "My mother has failed the family. She has left my father to remain hopeless and in despair for the rest of his life." Both father and son suddenly began to attend frequent meetings of a fundamentalist sect, praying regularly for the mother. Piety alternated with frightening and belligerent behavior in a turbulent period lasting more than a year.

With embittered-chaotic mothers, the shattered self-esteem led not so much to violence as to unending, bitter tirades against the father, delivered in the presence of the children. These women openly raged against their faithless, untrustworthy former husbands, trying to convince the children that their father did not care for them. "Your father doesn't love you! He doesn't love *any* of us, or he wouldn't have left!" The intent, vigorously denied, of such embittered-chaotic mothers was to punish the father by destroying the father-child relationship.

Sometimes children and fathers were simultaneously punished. Mrs. T., after throwing her husband out in a rage, was furious that he had left. The children came home from school one day to find the family dog gone. Mrs. T. had the dog destroyed because "your father doesn't give us enough money to feed it."

More often, the embittered-chaotic mother's rage focused on the father's continued efforts to see his children. Visits were portrayed to the children as bothersome, empty rituals. "If he didn't love you enough to stay here, then why would (should) he visit?" Sometimes more sinister intent was hinted, but the father's attempts to visit were always enormously disruptive to the mother. Most often, these women claimed to be supportive of their children's need to visit.

Mrs. T. yelled angrily at the interviewer: "I don't tell my children not to see him! I tell them that if they want to go, that's their business, and

I'll have their suitcases ready!" Despite her disclaimer, Mrs. T. continually created obstacles to the visiting.

The unspoken threat to many of the children was that their relationship with their mother might well be in danger if the youngsters retained some loyalty to the father. Even if the youngster aligned with the mother, we noted a deterioration in such mother's capacity to handle the day-to-day care and comforting of their children. Further, there was almost no sensitivity, with such embittered mothers and fathers, to the child's distress.

As for embittered-chaotic fathers, more than a quarter of them showed severely disorganized behavior, some over a period of many months, others for one episode lasting a few days or a week. Some of these men had had a history of well-controlled, circumspect behavior throughout their marriages; they were successful as businessmen or professionals and, in some instances, continued to function quite well in their occupations despite the eruption of primitive behavior out-of-hours. Now they had begun to engage in such things as spying, breaking down the door at night, obscene phone calls, physical beatings, vandalism, and attempts at child-napping. Their wives and children were understandably startled and frightened, and some of the women sought the protection of the courts and police.

It is estimated that 10 to 15 percent of divorcing families take their struggles over children to the court. There, the issues are defined in the socially-sanctioned arenas of custody, visitation, and financial support of the children. The adversary proceeding sharpens and consolidates the parents' differences, and once it was initiated, compromise, flexibility, and civilized exchange are neither valued nor possible. In our experience, the embittered-chaotic parent was significantly more likely to turn to the court than his less angry counterparts. The desperate need to salvage shattered self-esteem and wreak vengeance on the offending spouse was most often an underlying motive for such battles, now given status and legitimacy by court ritual. One particularly unfortunate aspect of such cases is the attorney's binding obligation to pursue and achieve his client's wish, regardless of whether this is compatible with the child's needs. These seem to be the cases which, ultimately, no one wins. There is also much evidence that such custody and visitation struggles, usually requiring several years to settle in court, have no end. They continue on within the family after the legal intervention has ended and are frequently back into court again within a year of what was to be the "final" judgment.

## The Depressed Parent

While angry interactions between parents were more common for the majority of children following separation, there were other youngsters whose experience was more vividly influenced by the obvious depression of a parent, and in our study an equal number of fathers and mothers (about 30 percent) were severely depressed following the separation. When a parent is seriously depressed, the routine, but still energy-draining, tasks of parenting leave him or her even more depleted. The withdrawal of attention from the child, which so often accompanies severe depression, exacerbates feelings of loneliness in young children and contributes to the older child's sense that nobody cares for his needs. In addition, a parent's severe depression can in itself be terrifying, particularly so when the parent confesses to suicidal impulses.

After her husband announced his intention to terminate the marriage, Mrs. L. became seriously depressed and curtailed all of her activities. She sat for weeks on end in her darkened house, shades drawn. Without extended family and almost no financial support, Mrs. L. became increasingly withdrawn, unable to get her children to school or to cope with their needs.

The more common experience among the younger children and adolescents was to be dealing with a parent who was mildly to moderately depressed. This larger group of parents—one-third of the men and three-fifths of the women—included both those who had wanted the divorce and those who had not. With some, the decision to divorce symbolized the lifting of more serious depression that had developed within a stifling or demeaning marriage; these were becoming less depressed. Others experienced a new divorce-engendered moderate depression that commonly accompanied the final acceptance of a failed relationship and its termination. These men and women generally continued to function adequately in jobs, at school, or as parents despite their depression, though the women in particular tended to feel overwhelmed by their new responsibilities as single heads of household.

## A Feeling of a New Beginning

The other side of the rage, the severe depression, and the regressive pull of the divorce is the feeling that the divorce presents a new chance to begin anew. This "new chance" phenomenon was expressed most by women who had actively sought divorce as a rational solution to an unhappy relationship. Many had, as well, felt uncomfortable about the effects such a marriage had on their children's well-being. One-fifth of all the women in the study described to us their hope that the divorce would enable them to improve the quality of life for their children and themselves.

Men who sought the divorce, particularly to marry a lover, also had a feeling of a "new chance," but primarily in relation to improving their own lives, rather than those of their children. As we later learned, some fathers, in fact, accomplished notable positive shifts in the relationships with their children over the first year, but they did not articulate this feeling of a new opportunity at the time of the divorce.

### Social and Sexual Lives after Separation

Because sexual deprivation and emotional unresponsiveness had characterized so many of the marriages, a number of men and women approached the postseparation period with the hope of enjoying the social and sexual gratifications long denied them. It was here, in the area of postmarital heterosexual activity, that strong sex differences emerged: Significantly more men than women dated frequently. Of the men who dated quite often, the majority moved very quickly after separation to establish an active social life. Among these, in about one-half of the entire group, we found at least two different underlying motivations for the high level of social and sexual activity. On the one hand there was the group of mostly affluent men who either had initiated the divorce or had felt relieved by their wives' move to do so. Their self-esteem was high. They were sought after as eligible males and welcomed in many groups and gatherings. They were quickly caught up in a social life that allowed little time for visiting their children. On the other hand were the men who, still embroiled in conflict with their former wives and motivated primarily by anger or a wish for revenge, entered quickly into a flurry of social and sexual activity. Some did so with a flamboyance that seemed calculated to bolster severely undermined self-esteem by calling public attention to their success in attracting women. They made sure that their former wives knew about their activity, either directly or via messages given to the children. In fact, some children were presented with the startling experience of finding former babysitters turning up as dates and lovers in their father's homes.

One-quarter of the men did not date at all in the first six months, and another one-quarter did so only sporadically. Among these men there were also two discernible groups. The first were men closely attached to their predivorce family, who remained on friendly terms with their former wives and felt no particular need to date, occupying their free time more often with their children. The second group included men suffering moderate to severe depression who seemed afraid to venture, and lacked the energy or motivation to establish new contacts.

Among the women, nearly one-third began at once to have an active social and sexual life, and about half of these began immediately after the separation. By and large, these women were younger and, unlike the socially active men, were among the lower socioeconomic groups. Again, in contrast to men, the self-esteem of women was not significantly related to dating frequency. Rather, it was the women not especially interested in parenting, who tended to view the children as a hindrance to their social activity, who seemed to have a greater opportunity for social and sexual experiences following divorce. A small number of these women, like their male counterparts, entered the sexual market in high excitement and engaged in frenetic sexual activities.

Mrs. L., a young and attractive woman, divorced her husband in part because she resented the amount of time he spent with his male friends, and in part because she had concluded that she had married too early and missed an opportunity for her own adolescence and young adulthood. Following the divorce, she embarked upon a hectic social life which included bringing men home several times a week to stay overnight. She became concerned about the effect of her behavior on her young daughter only after the child wrote a note on the kitchen door saying, "Fuck mother."

The largest group of women had no dates and no real social life. In this group were those who had suffered very much at the time of the marital separation, and whose self-esteem was shattered. In general, they tended to be the older women in our sample.

The loneliness of the initial postseparation period is not just a matter of dating, for it is the larger structure, which comes with marriage, that falls apart with the separation. Friends, for example, seemed conflicted about which spouse to call, and there also seemed to be a tendency, particularly for divorcing women, to allow this collapse of social relationships to occur. Women believed they were unwanted, or thought their married friends were threatened by the "contagious" nature of divorce, and so were hesitant to call. (Indeed, there is some evidence that old friends do shy away, perhaps out of some anxiety in relation to their own marriage, but more often because they feel uncomfortable and inadequate in providing solace.) Beyond close friendships, the majority of the men and women belonged to no clubs or community or active church groups, so the diminution of a social life with friends was especially painful.

It was, however, the onset of close relationships symbolized by dating that sometimes became a pivotal issue in the response to divorce and its eventual resolution. Sometimes the divorce only became real to one partner when the other began to develop a regular relationship with another man or women.

Mr. and Mrs. J. had communicated well since the separation, and Mr. J. had visited his children frequently, with the full cooperation of his divorcing wife during the first four months following the separation. Mr. J. was very angry at his wife for leaving the marriage, blamed her in discussions with friends for ruining the marriage, but essentially behaved in a fairly circumspect way. But when Mrs. J. started to date a man regularly, Mr. J. reacted furiously. He began to bring intense pressure on the children to reject their mother and taught them to call her names. She was "a whoring bitch, a Jezebel!" Unable to contain himself in his fury, Mr. J. next filed for custody of the children alleging alcoholism and immoral behavior in his former wife. Interestingly, throughout this entire time he had a woman living in his apartment with him, while Mrs. J. had limited her sexual experiences to overnights only when the children were visiting at the father's residence.

The advent of a regular woman friend in the divorced father's life can affect the mother, and also the child that is attuned to the mother's response.

Mary responded with some anger to her father's leaving and expressed wishes for his return, but otherwise seemed able to deal with the divorce in the first three months after separation. When the father acquired a steady girlfriend whom the little girl liked, she began to show new symptomatic behavior on returning home from her visits: Her mother complained that after each visit, the child regressed in her toilet training and became irritable and cranky. The mother's response was to forbid the father to bring his date to the visit. The child seemed caught in the crossfire of the mother's jealousy and, sensing her mother's anger, was conflicted and frightened in her own warm response to the father's new friend. The conflict for the child was more than she could bear, with her regression an expectable response.

The relationships of children, parents, and lovers presented central difficulties in the postseparation period. The custodial parent's problem was likely to be more complicated since the children resided in the same house. A mother's full-time parenting responsibilities created difficulties. If she went out too frequently, for example, she brooked the children's displeasure or risked being described by an angry spouse as a "bad mother" who was uninterested in her children. If she brought her friends home, she ran the risk of incurring the children's displeasure and jealousy. The children's responses often created anxiety and guilt in the mother.

It becomes evident that, for children, the transition from a married family to a postdivorce family is complicated because they have little control over the changes in their lives. Not only did many youngsters have to adjust to new locations, new and more stringent economic situations, and the changed availability of the mother, but there were the more difficult adjustments that they had to make to the changed attitudes and behavior of their parents. Accordingly, the youngsters' own initial response to their parents' divorce must be seen and understood in this context. They were not responding just to the structural change of the family itself, but to the whole of the complex, sometimes tragic drama precipitated and set in motion by the decision to divorce, and its often long-lasting aftermath.

# Chapter 3

# The Child's Experience During the Divorcing Period

For children and adolescents, the separation and its aftermath was the most stressful period of their lives. The family rupture evoked an acute sense of shock, intense fears, and grieving which the children found overwhelming. Over one half of the entire group were distraught, with a sense that their lives had been completely disrupted. Less than 10 percent of the children were relieved by their parents' decision to divorce despite the high incidence of exposure to physical violence during the marriage.

We have learned that a child's early response to divorce and separation is not governed by any balanced understanding of the issues that led to the parents' decision. Nor are children much affected, if at all, by living in a community with a high incidence of divorce. Instead, at the time of the parental separation the child's attention is riveted entirely on the disruption of his or her own family, and he is intensely worried about what is going to happen to him. Whatever its shortcomings, the family is perceived by the child at this time as having provided the support and protection he needs. The divorce signifies the collapse of that structure, and he feels alone and very frightened.

## Diminished Capacity to Parent

Adding significantly to the widespread distress of the children is the fact that many of them face the tensions and sorrows of divorce with little help from their parents, or anyone else, for during the critical months following the separation parental care often diminishes, not because parents are necessarily less loving or less concerned with their children during divorce, but because the radical alterations in their lives tend to focus their attention on their own troubles.

When a custodial mother was feeling humiliated, depressed and angry, there would be corresponding deterioration in her day-to-day handling of the child. Children who were accustomed to feeling comfortable and secure would suddenly be set adrift. The increased daydreaming among these youngsters, particularly the young boys, reflected their increased anxiety and preoccupation with the divorce.

A parent's depression also increased the child's anxiety by making it difficult for the parent to offer consolation. Sometimes in attempting to comfort the child, the parent would reexperience his own anguish and sob along with the grieving offspring. Children might then become alarmed at the impact of their distress on their parents, and learn to refrain from expressing their sadness or seeking solace. Parents who confessed to thoughts of suicide made their older youngsters acutely anxious and preoccupied with thoughts of the future. Feeling an urgent need to become the parent's caretaker, such a youngster would offer his or her presence and support in poignant efforts to alleviate the parent's depression. Severely depressed, noncustodial fathers worried children as much as depressed mothers; in these cases, the children's efforts concentrated on effecting a reconciliation in order to alleviate the father's distress.

Unlike stress that originates outside the family, the stress of divorce—and the child's difficulty in coping with it—is compounded by its involvement of one or both parents as its central source. In other traumatic events—say, a serious illness or a threatened natural disaster—experience shows that the comforting presence of the parent is enough to reassure a child under the most difficult conditions. But the particular and paradoxical import of divorce is that the disruption of the child's life is itself initiated by a parent, often by the parent whose inner turmoil renders him or her relatively insensitive to the child's needs at that time.

The central event in the divorce from the child's perspective is the physical separation of his parents. This is the step that children cannot fail to perceive, however much they may consciously or unconsciously deny the impending rupture. The actual physical separation forces the children to revise their perception of their parents as a unit and to confront the visible evidence of the splitting of their family. The child's efforts to cope with the divorce, therefore, usually begin with the reality of one parent's departure from the household.

The adult who sees divorce as the remedy to a conflict-ridden marriage and hopes for an improved family life expects, not unreasonably, that the child, too, will share the parent's relief and hope for a brighter future. This expectation collides head-on with the child's panic-driven need to reverse the divorce decision and to restore the unbroken family unit. As a result, in this way too, child and parent are driven further apart at a time when the child's need for the parent is sudden and great —and at a time when the parent also needs reassurance that the child will not be hurt.

When one parent opposed the divorce decision, the intensity of the youngsters' earliest response was significantly related to the degree and pervasiveness of parental turmoil in that first period following the separation. Aside from the distress created by the dismantling of familiar family structure, youngsters were most stressed by the bitterness expressed by their parents. Such bitterness, in turn, bore a measurable relation to threats of custody litigation. The greater the rage, the more likely that threats and litigation over custody and visitation would become a central feature of the divorcing period. Children of families in which this kind of rage was operative were most likely to be immensely anxious and preoccupied with details of the parents' battling, with their own future, and sometimes with the issue of maintaining fairness and loyalty to both parents. They perceived in sadness and with clarity that their relationship with at least one, or both, parents would henceforth be constrained by the parents' rage at one another. The task of dealing with these issues was so all-encompassing that the children were often unable to tackle the other tasks of their lives.

In families where custody and visitation battles were not a central issue, the degree of bitterness between divorcing parents nevertheless remained an important determinant of the child's stress. When a parent, and particularly a custodial parent, was bitter about the divorce, the children were less likely to be protected from the turmoil. A bitter mother was more likely to blame her child's anxiety and distress on the thoughtless father who abandoned the child, and to fail to understand how her own abusive tirades against the father might be just as stressful. And conversely, an angry, rejected father was likely to view his children's anxiety and sadness as a manifestation of poor mothering rather than as a reflection of the turbulence between him and their mother. The anger, the accusations, the primitive behaviors, all of these were part of the unsettling chaos of the divorce for many children and adolescents.

We did find some age and sex differences in the response of the children to bitterness expressed by parents. In general, the parents expressed their anger more openly with the older youngsters and tried to shield the youngest children from the worst of the bitterness. Thus, the older youngsters, the nine to eighteen year olds, were frequently more upset, and their distress continued, parallel to the parents' anger. A father's bitterness and extreme anger were found to be more anxiety-producing to children and adolescents than were the mother's. Because the most angry fathers also tended to be quite disorganized and in severe crisis, it may be that the youngsters feared the father's unpredictability and potential for violence, and identified as well with the mother's anxiety for her own safety. Older boys and girls sometimes identified with the parent of the same sex. The older girls were more distressed and upset by the anger and bitterness the mother expressed toward the father. They seemed to identify with the humiliation and feelings of rejection that were overwhelming their angry mothers. Older boys were especially upset and preoccupied with the divorce when they felt the father had been "thrown out." Their anxiety, as well as the pervasiveness of their wishes for a reconciliation, were significantly linked to the father's shattered self-esteem.

## What the Children Knew of the Divorce

Some writers maintain that children always have foreknowledge of the imminent dissolution of their parents' marriage. We found little evidence for this. As we tallied our observations we found that fully one-third of the children had only a brief awareness of their parent's unhappiness prior to the divorce decision. But divorce and threats of divorce were a chronic part of family living for another one-third of the children. Sometimes such children watched hawk-eyed for years for clues regarding the state of their parents' marriage. One nine-year-old girl told us she kept track of the positioning of the twin beds in her parents' bedroom. Her anxious guesses about the future of the marriage and about her own future depended on whether the beds had been pulled together or pushed apart.

Even when the children were aware of marital strife, there is no evidence in our study that this knowledge either prepared them psychologically for the divorce or diminished their distress when the separation occurred. Some were, perhaps, less surprised when the battling parents separated, but the divorce, when it finally arrived, represented for some youngsters the coming of an event long feared, like meeting a nightmare in waking life. Their response was not muted by years of anxious anticipation.

Jason, whose parents divorced when he was seven years old, vividly remembered his parents' quarrel and threats when he was three and a half and asleep in the back seat of a car. He kept this information as his own private, dreaded secret but told us, "I never forgot it." Very distressed when his parents separated, Jason remembered being sure that they would not reunite after their separation. He said, poignantly, "I wish that mom and dad could love each other the way grown-ups should."

It may well be that the notion that children have some foreknowledge of their parents' forthcoming divorce has gained in popularity because adults have so much difficulty discussing their decision to divorce with their children. Our findings in this regard are quite extraordinary: Four-fifths of the youngest children studied were not provided with either an adequate explanation or assurance of continued care. In effect, they awoke one morning to find one parent gone. Among this relatively educated and concerned group of parents, the hesitancy in explaining their divorce reflected a high level of anxiety and discomfort about discussing the family breakup with their young children. This omission of the parents may be a symbolic marker for what we have described as the diminished capacity to parent at the time of the divorce.

## Telling the Children

The parents' grave difficulty in telling their children about their decision to divorce involved not knowing how much to tell, or how many details of their intimacy to reveal, whether to elaborate on a partner's infidelity, frigidity, or indifference to sex. They did not know where or when to tell their children. Should they do so a day, a week, or a month before one parent departs from the household? Or should they tell their children all together, separately, or divide them by age?

In the main, these parents are apprehensive that their children may be unhappy, frightened, or angered by their decision and, feeling somewhat battered and depleted by their own ordeal, they are reluctant to take this on. And they are profoundly worried and sometimes heartsick about the psychological, social, and economic effect of their decision on their children in the present and for the future.

In much the same way, on their side the children sense that their parents are troubled and unhappy, and wish to ameliorate or at least not contribute to their distress. A crying parent is very upsetting to children, and parents at the time of the separation are not infrequently tearful. Hoping the storm will pass, most children feel a constraint about questioning their parents and wait for a parent to initiate discussion. The result in many families was a great awkwardness in communication, with the silence finally broken by the parents' announcement that they had, indeed, decided to divorce. This announcement, when it was finally made, was often brief and unaccompanied by any explanation of how the children would be affected: what future plans were being made for them to continue to see both parents, what the divorce was about, where the family would live, and all the many details of life which concerned the children and which were of central significance in helping them understand the divorce and its implications for them. When parents assured their children that henceforth things would get better, hoping that the children would agree, they were shocked in turn by the intensity of the distressed response they frequently encountered. Sometimes the announcement was made in such a way as to make it almost impossible for the children to express their feelings. A few men stressed that they would now have a swimming pool available when the children visited. Other parents emphasized, often with forced good cheer, that things would be the same or better, except that the children would now have two households instead of just one.

A few couples who had carefully planned how to tell the children entered into long postmortum discussions after their meeting, dissecting how each had erred in the technique of the presentation. No single family in our study was able to provide the children with an adequate opportunity to express their concerns, to recognize with them that the divorce was indeed a family crisis, and that while things were likely to be difficult for awhile, the expectation was that life would improve. Furthermore, no parent recognized that "telling" was not a pronouncement but should properly initiate a gradual process which would help the child both understand and integrate the important changes in his life. The parents' inability to be helpful to their children at this time undoubtedly contributed to the intensity of the children's response and, most particularly, to their fearfulness.

One encouraging aspect of this finding is that it opens the door to intervention and education of parents. Parents need help in understanding that telling the children about the divorce provides a signal opportunity to help the child cope with the crisis, and that the telling is not an act apart but a central component in the supportive role of the parent.

### The Children's Immediate Response

The response to the announcement of the divorce confirmed the parents' apprehensiveness. As we have noted, less than 10 percent of the children and adolescents in our study expressed relief or welcomed the decision. Mostly, whatever relief was expressed was by adolescents when there had been violence in the family. Joseph, age sixteen, had actively encouraged his mother to divorce. His father had humiliated her and the children for years. Following one violent episode where the father had beaten the boy and forcibly kept the mother from going for help, Joseph insisted, "Mother, you must leave him." She finally listened.

Most often, the children responded to the announcement with apprehensiveness or anger. Over three-quarters of the children opposed the divorce very strongly. Many burst into tears and pleaded with parents to reconsider. Some prayed for God's help. Sonia, age eight, first vomited, then hugged and kissed her mother, offering a new washing machine or a clothes dryer to placate her. Several children asked, "Will I ever see my daddy again?" A few children had delayed reactions. Five-year-old Fred watched TV silently when told of the decision and a few days later began to sob, "We don't have a daddy any more! I'll need a new daddy!"

Several children panicked. Everett, age twelve, ran screaming through the house, "You're trying to kill us all!" Jan, at nine years of age, dashed to the neighbor's house crying for help. Others appeared numb or initially uncaring. Betty, at age ten, said, "We were sitting in the dark with candles and they (the parents) told us suddenly about the divorce. We didn't have anything to say and so we watched TV." Jack, age eleven, told his parents, "I don't care," and then added, "Sometimes one can cry on the inside without crying on the outside."

Anger was the reaction of some children. Helen, age thirteen, screamed, yelled, and cursed at her parents. Sam, age eleven, yelled, "Why did you have to wait till I was so old? Now I'll remember all my life!" Gertrude, age nine, reproached her parents, "I don't believe it. You'd better not. You'd better not divorce." Some children withdrew into their own anger and sadness. David, age eight, retired to his darkened room and sat alone for a day. He confessed later that he kept thinking, "I wonder who she's got now."

Finally, a great many of the younger children, about one-third of the entire group, didn't really believe what they had been told. For these youngsters, the single announcement by the parents made it easier for them to pretend that the divorce would soon go away and to postpone their own response to the frightening changes in their lives.

## Where Do Children Turn for Support?

Although people at all ages need the affection and friendly, sustained support of others, children especially need the help of adults at a time of crisis. The almost absolute dependence of the human child on adult care and caring is well understood by children and contributes to their insecurity when the adults around them are troubled. Furthermore, in order to be truly helpful, the adult has to understand what the child is thinking and feeling. A child who is fearful of abandonment will not be comforted by a generous birthday present. Similarly, a child who is worried about his mother's capacity to manage without her husband is unlikely to calm down just because he is told to do so.

Our findings pointedly highlight the children's unmet needs. Over one-half the children felt that their father was entirely insensitive to their distress at this crucial time, and only 10 percent of the youngsters felt strongly that the father was sensitive and understanding. These findings were not entirely expectable because many of the men had participated actively in the care of their children. Some had been the primary caretakers; others who had not worked throughout the marriage had, as part of their daily routine, spent many hours with their children.

Mothers were more actively helpful and more in touch with their children's needs, although their efforts were experienced as insufficient by the children. Over one-third of the children felt that their mother was entirely unaware of their distress, and only 15 percent experienced her as very sensitive and in tune with their concerns. One-third of the children experienced moderate to severe deterioration in their mothers' day-to-day care for them.

By and large, parenting of the younger children was more sustained by both parents. Older children, from the age of nine upwards, were acutely aware of the lapses in parenting and felt aggrieved and neglected. Almost all of the nine- and ten-year-old boys felt their father to be entirely unavailable to them, and felt profoundly hurt by this experience. Similarly, the older girls felt emotionally abandoned by their mothers during this critical time. It is likely that the ease with which older children were coopted as allies in the marital battles was related to their fears of being left out in the cold unless they joined the battles and demonstrated their continuing usefulness to the parent.

In addition to the emotional remoteness of the parents and the high visibility of the marital conflict, children also experienced the diminished amount of time their parents had available for them. Very few young children were able to understand the changed economic conditions of the family and the mother's consequent need to work. Nor were they able to appreciate the many new preoccupations of both parents. Within a few months following the separation, one-third of the mothers were substantially less available to their children because of jobs, school commitments, engagements, or all three. Often these changes occurred abruptly. Parents who had been at home every afternoon to welcome the children after school took full-time jobs, and the house was lonely and empty. Some parents took jobs like selling real estate which occupied weekends and leisure hours. During the long weekends, parents who had previously stayed home or accompanied eager children for hamburgers or to a local movie were now busy, actively searching for a new social life or engaged in a new relationship. Children were now more likely to eat by themselves, to make their own lunches for school, to spend long hours in empty homes, and to put themselves to bed. The preschool children, particularly, experienced the greatest change in the lessened physical availability of the mother. They were left with new babysitters or child-care homes. Usually these different patterns of care were instituted quickly after the separation and without a transition period. To compound the loneliness, other mothers in the neighborhood sometimes did not permit their children to play with the newly lonely, forlorn children of divorce because they had so little supervision during the after-school hours.

As an example of the extraordinary shift in major support figures, Karen, who was not quite three, was spending four days a week at her mother's home shortly after the divorce, and three days a week at the father's. During the days at her mother's home she was cared for in a child-care home during the day because her mother worked full time. During the same period her father had moved into the home of a woman whom the child had not met before and who was introduced to her as "mommy." But before the separation Karen had been taken care of entirely by her father while her mother went to work every day.

Moreover, although most fathers continued to visit the family, their initial postseparation visits tended to be less frequent than they would subsequently become. This was partly due to the fact that fathers had not yet established residences where the children could spend time. Then, too, there was the newness of the visitation experience and the attendant difficulties in establishing a regular visiting pattern which, as we have learned, occurs frequently following the separation.

Contributing to the widening of the gulf between parents and children at the time of separation is the children's increased irritability and emotional lack. Two-thirds of the children became more difficult to manage; they were touchier, more cranky, and more unruly. The anger of the older children was disconcerting and discouraging to their preoccupied parents. And the neediness and the clinging of the younger children, and their unwillingness to let the custodial parent out of their sight for fear that he or she might not return, further depleted already fatigued parents.

*A Lack of Extrafamilial Resources*

Although most of the families had lived several years in the community and had maintained stable residence in one place, few resources outside the immediate family were of help to the children during the family crisis. Even within the families, approximately three-quarters of the children were not helped by grandparents, uncles, or aunts, many of whom lived in different parts of the country. Some grandparents living close by were very helpful and provided special treats and took children into their homes occasionally. These children appeared to benefit considerably from this special concern and care.

Outside of the school, however, few institutions touched these children's lives. Fewer than 5 percent of the children were counseled or sustained by a church congregation or minister. Occasionally a neighbor would be unexpectedly helpful. One child spent many hours in a neighbor's kitchen, engaged in long and serious conversations with a lively elderly lady who baked her cookies and comforted her. Other children reported later than they had been helped by parents of some of their friends and had spent long hours in their friends' homes.

Tina was asked four years later what had helped her at the time of the separation. She said, "Other people. My school counselors knew about it, and I adopted my girlfriend's parents. I slept over there as much as possible. My grandparents, also, were very helpful."

Yet, in all, less than 10 percent of the children received adult help from their community or family friends. And, although pediatricians regularly treated many of these children, none of these physicians was contacted at the time of crisis and none talked to the children. Few were even informed of the family crisis, nor were any of the children seen by the attorneys concerned.

The school was helpful to the distressed children, largely because of its continuing presence in their lives at a time of great discontinuity. The ongoing classes and the need to attend them regularly helped organize the children's lives. School also provided a refuge from family difficulties and sorrowing parents.

The children on the whole received less help than we expected from teachers. In fact, more than half the children had no support at all from this source. Many teachers knew nothing about the divorce, often learning about it from the child. School personnel frequently lacked knowledge of the family and hesitated to intrude on family privacy. Several elementary school teachers did demonstrate remarkable sensitivity by sharing their own lunch with children who came to school hungry. A few teachers in the early grades held angry and fretful children on their laps, recognizing the needs beneath their tantrums. But overall, nursery and kindergarten teachers were not able to provide sufficient nurturance to contain the anxiety of their young charges, and we found that many children could not be comforted by their ministrations, except very temporarily.

Children did not feel that turning to friends for comfort helped to ease their sadness or fears. Although at the time of the parents' separation half of the youngsters had good relationships with friends, they reported to us that their family troubles were not easily shared just then. Often the reverse was the case, and the distress at home spilled into the relationships with friends. Peers were useful not so much for sharing confidences as for providing activities and welcome distance from the household unhappiness. Older boys, particularly, made use of their peers to distance themselves from the turmoil.

The "only" child had greater exposure to parental conflicts and pressures than the child with brothers and sisters. Many children did not consider their siblings helpful, although their absence clearly made for greater loneliness and vulnerability. Although children didn't acknowledge the help of siblings, they huddled together with them and conferred frequently. The youngest of three children sometimes felt more protected by the older siblings because the older siblings acted as intermediaries and representatives to the parents.

## Central Themes of the Child's Divorce Experience

All in all, though each child and adolescent felt himself uniquely burdened, a range of feelings and concerns was held in common. These were complexly woven into themes that appeared over and over, in different configurations and varying intensities, in the play and behavioral symptoms of the very little children, up the developmental ladder to the often quite sophisticated reflections and comments of the adolescents.

### Divorce is Frightening

First of all, children and adolescents alike experienced a heightened sense of their own vulnerability. Their assurance of continued nurturance and protection, which had been implicit in an intact family, had been breached: They confronted a world which suddenly appeared to have become less reliable, less predictable, and less likely in their view to provide for their needs and expectations. Their fears were myriad. Some were realistic; others were not. The specific content of the worry varied with age and child and family, but the anxiety itself was a widespread phenomenon, and appeared as a central response.

All of the little children worried about who would take care of them. Some worried about who would feed them, others about who would protect them. Over three-quarters of the entire group was consciously preoccupied with the concern that needs—not only present but future—would go unattended.

We learned from the children about this sense of future jeopardy only gradually, and were at first taken aback to discover that children in economically comfortable homes were concerned about whether they could go on to college. And we were startled when a few mentioned their worry that as a result of the divorce they would be placed in foster homes.

The children's fears reflected confusion about their future relationship with their parents. Not unreasonably, they concluded that if the marital tie could dissolve, the parent-child relationship could dissolve also. About half the children in the study were intensely afraid of being abandoned by their father. Understanding little of the visiting relationship, their decreased trust in their parents' continued love for them, and in the reliability of human relationships as a whole, led them to fear that each visit might be the last. The erratic and, by their standards, infrequent pattern of much of the early visiting only served to reinforce these fears. Moreover, their awareness of parental anger led many, especially the younger ones, to expect that the outcome of the battle, which they only dimly understood, would be that the losing parent would be banished from the home and not permitted to return. And, as we have noted, they were not assured otherwise.

One-third of the children also worried that their mother would abandon them. The younger children were afraid that they would awaken in the morning and find their mother gone. The frequent sleeping disturbances which had their onset at this time were linked to the children's terrifying preoccupation with the thought of awakening to an empty house, abandoned by both parents. The notion of a parentless household as a real possibility was not uncommon among children at various ages. Little children repeatedly played dollhouse scenes in which adult dolls took care of other adult dolls, and little dolls took care of each other. Older children sometimes expressed their fears directly. Nine-year-old Marjorie addressed her mother: "If you don't love Daddy, how can I be sure what will happen? Maybe I'm next."

It is likely that the fear of abandonment is a common concern of all children at a time of high stress. The particular configuration of stress during divorce, because it splits the centrality of the family, may well call this fear into prominence.

### Divorce is a Time of Sadness and Yearning

Children were heavily burdened by their enormous sense of loss. Jay, age five, solemnly announced as he came into the consulting room, "I have come to talk about death." More than half of the youngsters were openly tearful, moody, and pervasively sad. One-third or more showed a variety of acute depressive symptoms, including sleeplessness, restlessness, difficulty in concentrating, deep sighing, feelings of emptiness, play inhibition, compulsive overeating, and somatic complaints of various kinds. Whereas the younger children were specifically concerned with the father's departure, older children and adolescents were preoccupied with the loss of the family as an ongoing presence, with the lost sense of continuity and structure the family had provided in their lives.

Two-thirds of the children, especially the younger children, yearned for the absent parent, one-half of these with an intensity which we found profoundly moving. "We need a daddy. We don't have a daddy," burst forth five-year-old Jack and other children close to him in age. This widespread yearning for the father did not appear to be rooted just in a good predivorce father-child relationship but drew its sustenance from the child's developmental needs and fantasies.

The poignant fantasies of reconciliation that preoccupied youngsters at every age can be understood as ways of restoring the family in order to help stave off the acute pain of loss. The hope, the wish, and sometimes the expectation that parents would reunite is at its height at the time of separation, and was a vivid fantasy for over half of the children. In their games, no single child in the entire group played separate homes or even separate bedrooms for the divorcing parents. Children happily restored the family in the playhouse by placing father and mother in one bed, together, with their arms tightly woven one around the other. Older children tried, sometimes directly, to bring about or even force the reconciliation they desired.

### Divorce is a Time of Worry

The children's sense of their own vulnerability overlapped with and was increased by, their perception of their parents' distress. Many children were concerned over one or both parents' emotional stability and their capacity to manage without the other's help. Boys and girls alike worried about their father and the details of his life and residence. "Where does he live?" they asked themselves and us. "Who will cook for him? Who will be his friends?"

The departure of the father from the household is an extraordinary event. Especially for the younger ones the departure was terrifying and the departed father acquired a somewhat disembodied quality; like the figure in the Chagall painting, he appeared to be hovering somewhere in space over the roof of the house, without fiddle and without joy. One seven-year-old, when told his father had moved to Oakland, looked worried for days and finally confessed his profound confusion, asking whether Oakland was in Mexico and where indeed was Mexico? For many children the visit to the father to establish where he was in space—that indeed he existed, and had a bed and a refrigerator—was immensely important in allaying the intense anxieties of the postseparation period.

Over half the children worried intensely about their mothers. They were aware of a new feeling of precariousness, of being dependent on one rather than both parents together, and they worried about the health and well-being of the remaining parent. Their fears of being left unparented merged with real concern for the parent's suffering, depression, and physical health. Children viewed with misgivings, and sometimes outright alarm, the hectic schedule of many of the women. They worried about their mothers' emotional upset and moodiness, and some worried about suicidal impulses, about possible accidents, about chronic illness. "If my mother smokes and gets cancer, what will happen to me?" asked nine-year-old Janice. Many children sat up on weekends waiting for parents to return home from social engagements and worrying about a tardy parent and a possible second loss.

In addition, the children worried about the changed economic and social realities of life, about which they became acutely aware. They were concerned about money, about changing schools, about moving to another house and neighborhood. And as parents acquired new friends, lovers, and fiancees, the children worried about being displaced by the new relationships, including remarriage, and of being forgotten in the shuffle. They worried about remarriage and its possible implications for them. Said Mary at age ten, "My daddy's girlfriend has two daughters. If he marries her, will I be Cinderella?"

## Divorce is a Time of Feeling Rejected

The children experienced a parent's departure from the home as indicative of a diminished interest in them. The parents' preoccupation with their own problems, the partial withdrawal of interest in them, and the interruption in their care seemed a further rejection. Young children particularly were unable to understand one parent's departure from the other as different from leaving them. As a result, over half the children suffered intensely from feelings of rejection by one or both parents during this critical time.

Sometimes children, especially boys, identified with the departed father and experienced every criticism directed at him by the remaining mother as though directed at them. Angry or grieving mothers contributed to the child's sense of rejection by exclaiming, "He left *us*. He no longer cares about *us*. He does not love *us*." The children's sad sense of rejection led them to nagging questions about their own loveability, or whether they were in some way unworthy of the departed parent's esteem and affection. In this, we found a significant age and sex difference. Six- to twelve-year-old boys, as a group, felt the most rejected by their fathers, regardless of their psychological condition.

## Divorce—a Lonely Time

The loneliness of the child at this time is profound. We have described the temporarily diminished capacity to fulfill the role of parent that occurs following the separation. The child feels that both his parents are slipping out of his life as the father departs from the household and the mother goes to work and engages in new and seemingly strange activities; one or both parents appears preoccupied or behaves in unfamiliar ways. The children's loneliness was acute, painful, and long remembered, especially when they waited long hours after school for the working parent to return home or waited all afternoon while a depressed parent slept through dinner or spent long weekend hours alone. Youngsters who were extremely lonely often experienced great longing for the father. It is sad and ironic that so many of these youngsters had not enjoyed especially gratifying relationships with their fathers during the marriage. It may be that their intense yearning reflected, in part, the fantasy of a more nourishing, fun-filled relationship with a father that they had hoped might someday be realized, or that they were reluctant or unable to disavow.

In general, the only youngsters not particularly lonely were those well-functioning adolescents whose capacity to rely upon peers for diversion and support was quite good, and who enjoyed the father's continued interest. The loneliness which most youngsters experienced was frequently wedded to the sense of rejection and to the yearning for the intact family or the departed parent. Loneliness was likely to be most intense following separation if the children and adolescents had a prior history of poor adjustment and low self-esteem.

### Divorce is a Time of Conflicted Loyalties

The marital battle is often conceptualized by children as a pitched battle between two opposing sides. They feel pulled by love and loyalty in both directions. Often the conflict is exacerbated by parents and, indeed, two-thirds of the parents openly competed for the children's love and allegiance. Even when this did not occur, the child had a sense of divided loyalties. School age children particularly appeared to conceptualize the divorce as a struggle in which each participant demanded one's primary loyalty, and this conception greatly increased the conflict and unhappiness of the child. For, by its logic, a step in the direction of one parent was experienced by the child (and sometimes by the angry parent as well) as a betrayal of the other, a move likely to evoke anger and further rejection. Some children refrained bravely from stepping in either direction, out of a sense of honor and love of both parents. They faced, instead, the consequences of aloneness, with a despairing sense of having no place to turn for comfort or parenting. Their conflict of loyalty placed them in a solitary position midway in the marital struggle. For most children this was a new position, one which they had not even been pressed to take during the conflicted marriage. Some youngsters resolved this unbearable dilemma by joining the battle in alignment with one parent, in bitter anger against the other.

### Divorce is a Time of Anger

Children and adolescents of all ages experienced a rise in aggression. Temper tantrums increased in the youngest children, as did the hitting of other children and siblings. Older children and adolescents expressed anger directly, sometimes in highly organized patterns of verbal attack.

A full quarter of the youngsters experienced an explosive anger which they directed at one or both parents. Beyond this, for over one-third of the children, especially but not exclusively among the older boys, anger was a major accompaniment of the separation experience. Although the father was more often the object of this anger, there was a significant rise across the board in general crankiness and rebelliousness with the custodial mother about household routines and discipline.

The strands of the children's anger were many and complexly woven. Some of the aggressive behavior was, doubtless, stimulated by witnessing parental fighting and the children's not illogical conclusion that direct expression of intense anger had become acceptable. Beyond this, the children considered the divorce an act of selfishness in which the parents had given primary consideration to their own needs and only secondary consideration to the children. Some youngsters bitterly resented the destruction of their family and their home, and they felt betrayed by what they considered the unbecoming, immoral behavior of a parent.

## The Question of Guilt

Unlike what has come to be the common belief, not all children feel responsible for the marital strife and family disruption. The eagerness of children to reunite their estranged parents does not necessarily reflect their wish to undo mischief for which they attribute responsibility to themselves. Nor is the children's sense that they may have contributed to family tension the same as taking responsibility for family rupture. We have, in fact, been impressed with the clarity of children's perceptions and their realistic, and sometimes sophisticated, assessment of the causes of marital failure.

Children who do feel responsible for the divorce are more likely to be found among the very young. One-third of the children in the study who were more likely to accept some significant amount of blame for the family rupture came particularly from the group aged eight and younger. When these young children did feel to blame, the divorce occupied their waking hours; they felt isolated and lonely and unable to achieve peace. They attributed the marital rift to some sin of omission or commission on their part.

Among the older children, those who were most likely to suffer with the guilt that they had triggered the divorce by their behavior were more often troubled in other ways and had symptoms which also reflected difficulties in other parts of their adjustment. This coexistence of symptomatic behavior with fantasies of responsibility may account for the frequency with which clinics and private practitioners report that children do feel almost universally guilty for having caused the disruption of their family.

## Differences in the Children's Responses

We have spelled out some common themes underlying the experience of children during the immediate postseparation period. Within this framework, factors of age and development influenced how the individual child responded to these concerns, and how he interpreted the events around him. And these responses, whether expressed in words or silences, or acted out in behavior, contributed significantly to the intense family interaction of the time.

### Developmental Influences

The psychological perspectives which governed our thinking were drawn from developmental and clinical psychology and were consonant with the notion that children move upward along a common developmental ladder that is shaped by biology, psychology, and culture and that the achievement of each rung on this ladder depends upon negotiating those below it. Although children differ widely among themselves from birth onward, each climbs this developmental ladder to reach adulthood. Each ascends at his own pace and in his own way within broad limits, but the progression is common to all.

Consistent with developmental theory, the major differences which we observed in the initial responses of the children were related to the child's psychological age and place along the continuum which we have described. For the children's perceptions of the divorce, their thoughts, their feelings about the marriage and the departed parent, their understanding of what has happened and what will happen, their fears and worries are, to a considerable degree, governed by their age and place along the developmental ladder at the time of the marital rupture. Similarly, children's attempts to cope with their own anxiety reflected age and developmental stage.

In addition to enabling us to see developmental and age-related patterns in the children's responses, the developmental perspective enabled us to conceptualize the effect or the potential effect of the divorce on the child. We have conceptualized family rupture as intersecting sharply with the child's progression or developmental pathway. In this view the particulars of the child's developmental agenda at the time of the parental separation, namely, the tasks which the child is engaged in mastering at that time, are central to understanding both the child's immediate response and what the eventual effect is likely to be. And our examination of each of these children asked not only the response of the child, but how that response affected the child's developmental progress.

We had expected a general correspondence between the child's initial behavioral response to the divorce and his or her age and developmental stage, but we were surprised at the extent to which these factors actually govern the initial responses. We were unprepared for the relative neatness of the broad bands of behavior that we were able to identify. Indeed, one major finding of this project is that the initial response to divorce (and perhaps children's responses to stress in general) are so closely age-related and seem to fall so reliably into broad and distinguishable categories that we have been able to mark them off: namely, preschool children (approximately three to five and one-half years old); young school-age children (six to eight years old); older school-age children (nine to twelve years old); and adolescents. We did not begin with these groupings but our observations dictated them.

## Pervasiveness and Intensity of Response

Unlike the patterning and content of the response which was so age related, the intensity of the child's or adolescent's response to the divorce varied widely, reflecting individual differences as well as differences of family style and culture. Expectably, the child whose family was constrained in emotional expression or who generally tended to mute feelings would also be less likely to express feelings openly about the divorce. Others were encouraged by family tradition to protest more loudly. The underlying feelings, however, might differ very little.

Beyond the issues of temperament or family culture, the intensity and pervasiveness of the children's responses reflected the individual child's psychological functioning. Of those children who had been in good psychological health prior to the divorce, those who had been functioning adequately, and those remaining who had been burdened by repeated failures in various aspects of their lives, all responded differently. Those children and adolescents who had psychological difficulties prior to the divorce were initially more stressed, as their unhappiness, anxiety, low self-esteem, or loneliness were exacerbated by the family rupture. The greater intensity of their responses, during the prolonged period of disequilibrium, in fact, magnified their earlier difficulties.

Thus, while many children became angry at the time of the divorce, the most intense, enduring, and explosive anger was that of the youngsters who felt aggrieved at the time they were faced with the divorce situation. The divorce also intensified feelings of being rejected, especially for those youngsters who already came to the divorce with nagging doubts about their parents' interest in them. And, although many intact children felt rejected at that time, the greater suffering was the lot of those with poor self-esteem.

Another group of children whose responses were more intense and more pervasive were those youngsters from close-knit families who had had little awareness of the marital unhappiness. These youngsters were bewildered and more likely to assume blame. Their shock affected them strongly and considerably diminished their capacity to mobilize ways of coping with the changes in their lives.

## Factors of Little Influence on Children's Responses

There were several aspects of the family life which, again to our surprise and contrary to our expectations, did *not* affect the children's responses at this time. For example, it seemed reasonable to expect that the children would experience a sense of relief in direct proportion to the amount of marital discord between parents. Yet, no such finding emerged. The intensity of the fighting between the parents and the amount of violence within the marriage that the child witnessed were not by themselves associated with the child's feelings of relief at the time of the divorce. Younger children experienced relief at the divorce only when they themselves had been frightened by the father's violence. Older youngsters were more likely to approve the divorce when they had long-standing awareness of the conflict between their parents. But the same tie did not hold for the younger children, for whom an awareness of the conflict appeared to make little difference in their distressed response to the divorce.

Furthermore, we had expected that the quality of the parent-child relationships prior to the separation might influence the amount of distress the children experienced. Such was not the case. The children's preoccupation with the divorce, and the intensity of their response, were not linked to the quality of their relationship with the departed parent. The intense longing for the father and the sadness precipitated by his departure occurred among youngsters whose prior experience with the father ranged from abusive and critically rejecting to warm and consistently caring. Similarly, except for young girls, the warmth and consistency of the predivorce mother-child relationship did not reassure the youngsters to the extent that it lessened their distress. Only among the young girls did a small, but significant, relationship appear between the intensity of the child's distress and preoccupation with the divorce and an emotionally impoverished predivorce mother-child relationship.

These little girls struggled anxiously with a double deprivation following the father's departure from the home, as they remained in the care of an emotionally unavailable mother.

The anger of the older youngsters that was generated by the divorce was not related to the quality of the parent-child relationship before separation. Often children turned angrily on parents who least expected or deserved it, and, conversely, some critical and abusive parents were suddenly showered with demonstrations of support and affection. Such rapid shifts were especially bewildering and painful to the devoted parent suddenly harangued and abused by his or her children. The youngsters' anger was related to their disapproval of the divorce and to the amount of stress they were experiencing about the dissolution of the family, and not to the earlier parent-child relationship. The greater their indignation and disapproval, the higher the likelihood of angry outbursts directed at both parents, but especially at the parent who sought the divorce.

Finally, too, it is important to distinguish the distress of the child at the time of parental separation from the effects on the various stages of development. The central hazard of divorce for the child is not his acute unhappiness, however tragic this may be, but the possibility that the family disruption will in some way discourage his progress along the developmental ladder—slow him down in ways hard to remedy, impede or interfere with his continued development, or move him perhaps prematurely into a phase for which he is not yet quite ready. Developmental interference is not unrelated to unhappiness, but it is clearly not the same. And it is important to distinguish the distress of the child from the finding of psychological harm to the child. Distress and anxiety are, after all, expectable and appropriate in the child's perception of the family breakup and in his recognition of distress in one or both of his parents. Temporary regression is an expectable part of the child's developmental progress, and unhappiness is a cause for providing comfort, but not for alarm. Developmental interference or depressions that endure beyond the acute phase are quite another matter. These are difficult to distinguish at the time of the breakup.

# Chapter 4

# How the Children Responded

The age and developmental groupings into which the children's responses fell, with a regularity which we had not fully anticipated, provided a congenial way of categorizing their concerns, feelings, and behaviors at the time of the marital breakup. Some of our cases illustrate the close similarities as well as the striking differences which emerged.

## The Preschool and Kindergarten Children (Three-to-Five-Year-Olds)

### Linda's Perspective

Linda, age four, appeared in our office, an attractive, blond, well-groomed child. When asked about what was happening at home, she solemnly explained that her father was living in the city because he didn't like Mommy, and that Mommy felt bad because she (Mommy) still liked Daddy. As was characteristic of many of the children, Linda accompanied her sober and dutiful recitation of the events of the household with play which belied her spoken words.

Linda played in an eerie silence. All the usual and familiar sounds with which children accompany their play were absent. She constructed a serene scene in which mother and father lay in bed together. The children played happily in an adjoining room as the baby slept peacefully in the crib. As the narrative developed, the mother arose to make a bountiful breakfast and the little boy generously brought a bowl of cereal to another child.

At the second meeting the child again arranged a happy family scene. The family members all watched television together. The father held the baby on his lap and the baby was comfortable in the father's arms. The children were seated on the floor in front of their parents. After the show, the family had dinner together and the father continued, tenderly, to hold the baby.

In the third hour with us the child went quickly to the now-familiar dollhouse and arranged the furniture to her satisfaction. The togetherness theme took over with new and rising intensity. Methodically and soberly, the child placed father, mother, and the three children in a bathtub together. She then removed the entire family to the roof and the father and mother and the children were all sitting, one on top of the other, on top of the house. Then, suddenly, her play ended, she jumbled the furniture and the dolls and began a wild puppet play in which large animals bit each other viciously. The whale bit the crocodile, and the crocodile bit the giraffe. And then, finally, apparently carried away by her play, the child broke through the play and bit the crocodile savagely and then pummeled it out of shape. All of this, including her final giving way to anger, attack, and loss of control, occurred in the total absence of any sound.

There is a very moving eloquence to Linda's wordless portrayal. First, there is togetherness and tenderness: parents care lovingly for happy children; the food is abundant; and the family never separates, not even in the bathtub. Suddenly, the peaceful scenes are disrupted and the family, which is perched precariously on the roof, but still together, comes crashing down and is overtaken by cascading aggression, attack, destruction. The child herself leaves her role as director and, caught up in the play, regresses and herself bites one of the main players. Her four-year-old capacity to distinguish between her play and reality is wiped out with the rise in aggression and the weakening of controls as her wish for the close and intact family becomes too painful for her.

The extraordinary silence which accompanies the play may express many feelings—perhaps the child's unexpressed and unexpressable grief, perhaps feelings which we can only guess at at this stage and which would require considerable skill to plumb. One needs, however, no special training to read Linda's agenda for restoring her family, or to follow her perspective on the divorce events.

## Fear

The youngest children who came to see us were, like Linda, frightened, bewildered, and very sad. Their immature grasp of the events swirling around them, together with their difficulty in sorting out their own fantasy and dream from reality, rendered them especially vulnerable. Having seen the central relationship between their parents come apart, they concluded, not without logic, that other relationships might similarly come undone, and they might well be left alone.

The routine separations of daily life were suddenly filled with dread. Some clung to the remaining parent, whimpering or crying when the parent left on a routine errand or departed for work at the usual time, or went out for the evening. Parents who returned from work or retrieved their children after school were greeted with angry tears, crankiness, and sometimes tantrums by children sufficiently relieved by the parent's return to express the anguish and frustration which they had suffered during the parental absence. Anxieties rose as darkness approached, and peaked at bedtime, which soon became a tense and unhappy battle of wills between an exhausted angry parent and a panic-stricken child. Throughout the night children became fretful, waking frequently, crying, and begging to be taken into the parent's bed.

Children who attended nursery school or kindergarten became anxious about leaving home to go to school. Like Hansel and Gretel in the fairy tale, they were fearful of not finding their way back home again. Or they feared that no one would be there to greet them. They refused to ride in familiar carpools unless mother came along; they objected to returning to kindergartens which they had previously enjoyed. Youngsters who had adjusted well to their mother's employment found their mother's departure very difficult and greeted her return with tears of relief and the accumulated crankiness of the worrisome day.

## Regression

Regression was a common response among the youngest children. Overwhelmed by their anxiety, very young children returned to their security blankets, to recently outgrown toys. Lapses in toilet training and increased masturbatory activity were noted. The difficulty in separating from the custodial parent also reflects regression to earlier modes of relationship, characteristic of the toddler who needs to keep the caregiver in full view or readily accessible. The child who regresses tells us by his behavior that it is all too much, that he must hold back in development, mark time or move backward, in order to gain strength for the next step forward. Although in most instances the regressions lasted a short time, a few weeks or a few months at most, the custodial parent found these particularly difficult because they disrupted household routines and increased the child's need for care at a time when the parent lacked both time and patience.

Karen, whose father left the household when she was not quite three, regressed in her toilet training and became whiney and demanding. Her father, who had been the primary caretaker, left in hurt and indignation and visited her irregularly. Karen clung desperately and tearfully to her mother every morning when the mother left for work although the mother had worked since the child's infancy and the child had been well adjusted to this routine.

### Macabre Fantasy

Children elaborated macabre fantasies to explain the father's departure and the marital disruption. These fantasies were shaped by their own limited capacity to understand the confusing events and their frightened perception of the parents' quarrels. The absence of suitable explanation and assurance from preoccupied parents added to their reliance on their own immature fantasy explanations. And indeed, the most frightened and regressed children were those who had not received any explanation of the events in the family and were at the mercy of their own conclusions. Moreover, seeing the tense mood of the parents, the children kept their ideas to themselves and in this way added to their own psychological burden.

John, a sturdy, handsome youngster of three, was brought to us by his young father. His mother had left suddenly after a bitter quarrel. The child was described as tearful, frightened, and very confused. He was sleeping fitfully, wetting his bed nightly, and hitting his baby sister. This behavior began after the mother's departure. John had been offered no explanation, in part because the young father had himself been overwhelmed by grief, and in part because the father considered the child too young to understand.

At our suggestion the father undertook to explain to the child that his parents had separated because of their unhappiness. He recalled the many quarrels which the child had witnessed and assured him that these would not continue and that the father was better able to care for John and would continue, reliably, to do so. John responded with many urgent questions which had preoccupied and worried him and which were the basis for his regressive behavior and changes of mood. One highly significant concern that John revealed was that he had been afraid that his mother had "burned up in a fire." (There had been a relatively minor fire in the household the week before the mother left.) John asked urgently whether his mother was well and begged to see her. After the visit was arranged and mother and child visited over cocoa and cookies, John returned home with his father and began to sob. His father took him in his arms and said, "I understand, son, that it's hard when mommy isn't coming back to live with us." John responded, tearfully, "Daddy, can we have another talk?" Gradually, within the next few weeks as the father's care and assurances continued, the child's regressions disappeared, and his mood began to restabilize.

One fairly common fantasy which children expressed in their play was their fear of being left hungry by their parents. This fear of hunger was associated with their fear of abandonment and with the consequences of aggression. Children constructed toy scenes of powerful animals with big teeth who snatched food away from hungry little animals who were helpless to defend themselves.

## Bewilderment

Children were painfully bewildered and trying anxiously to comprehend the present and future vicissitudes of their relationship with both parents. Their concept of the dependability of human relationships and personal ties had been profoundly shaken. Sometimes the fear of being hurt or betrayed in a relationship spread to the relationship with the teacher at school. Larry begged his teacher to hold him on her lap and then hollered, "Don't get too close to me!" and ran away. Recurrent playroom themes were those of aimless, woebegone searching, and trying dispiritedly to fit objects together. Sometimes they essayed to clarify boundaries and master distinctions and linkages by asking uncomprehendingly and repetitiously of familiar objects, "What's this?"

John explored the room, handling everything in sight. At the slightest rustle outside, however, he would look up apprehensively. "Who's that? Where has daddy gone?" He turned abruptly to the toys. "What's this?" he asked, "What's that?" He obviously knew and answered just a few of his own questions. Boxes intrigued him and he shook them open and scattered the objects, then rapidly moved on to the next box. The play that lasted consisted of poking objects into objects; fitting things together, sticks into clay, tinker toys, cars into boxes, puppets into a house. The central theme of the child's play was what belongs to what, and who belongs to whom.

Fred, age five, played endlessly with a magnet, bringing objects into its magnetic field and releasing them, silently playing out the coming together and the separation, and seemingly unable to integrate the experience or to move on from it.

Karen, age three, became preoccupied with staking out claims all over her house. Crossly and imperiously, she asserted about various objects that seemed selected at random, "That is mine, and that is mine." We observe here not only the child's preoccupation with what is indeed hers, but also her sad recognition of the limits of her claims by her bold, if futile, efforts to undo her loss by claiming dominion over everything.

### Replaceability

As the children made heroic efforts to encompass the disturbing events of the separation they reached explanations that caused them great anguish. One unhappy conclusion which the four-to-five-year-olds arrived at was that the departed parent had rejected them and left to replace them with another family elsewhere. It was almost impossible for these children to conceptualize the one parent's departure as being directed at the other parent and not at them.

First seen when he was four years old, Frank had been his mother's favorite child, and his self-esteem, although badly shaken by the divorce, was still high. He was, however, at the time that we saw him, very frightened and especially fearful of abandonment by both parents, and he was clinging, tearful, and petulant. He offered, with a conscious gallant effort to save face, "I don't miss my father. I see him all the time. It's just like always." On the way home, however, following his interview with us he began to question his mother for the first time. Poignantly, he asked her, "Is daddy going to get another wife? Another dog? Another little boy?"

### Fantasy Denial

Fantasy was employed extensively, especially by the little girls, to help them cope with their painful sense of rejection and loss. Some of the little girls denied their father's absence with a thousand wish-fulfilling fantasies. "When he grows up he'll come back; he promised." "He'll divorce her [his new wife] and marry me," or "I go see my daddy whenever I want to" [not true]. "I like it better this way" [not true]. These fantasies gradually came to occupy increasing amounts of the time and psychic energy of these children.

Wendy, age four, arrived and seated herself comfortably on the therapist's lap, saying, "You look like a mommy." Arranging the members of the flexible toy family, each in its own separate apartment, she said that her daddy lived in his apartment, and she loved to visit him there. Soon she placed the family all together, with the father's arm around the mother. Later, when drawing her family at the interviewer's request, Wendy said that she sees her father all the time; he has an apartment but, she said, "He lives with *me*. He sleeps in *my* bed every night." "You mean," said the interviewer, "You *wish* he slept with you and that he still lived at your house." Laughingly Wendy replied, "Yes, but someday he really will. He promised me that he would." Later Wendy reported that her sister was such a baby because she cried all the time. "*She* wants her daddy to come home," said the child with mild disdain.

Several little girls, referring to their absent fathers, confided, "He loves me the best." Whether reality or fantasy, or a mixture of both, the sense of having been loved "the best" appeared as a guiding fantasy in undoing the rejection and in maintaining the self-esteem and sense of their own lovability that was threatened by the father's departure. The children's loyalty and intense love for the father remained unchanged, despite repeated disappointments in the postseparation relationship. Several of these little girls remained nourished for many years by vivid fantasies about the father and his expected return. These fantasies clearly served to reverse the unbearable sense of rejection, of not having been loved sufficiently, if at all.

Fantasy was employed by little boys, as well, to undo the painful reality of the family rupture, but they appeared less able than the girls to deny the father's departure. Boys and girls were equally committed to fantasies of a restored family.

## Play

Children of both sexes gravitated to the dollhouse in the consulting room and played house. There they created anew a peaceful, bounty-laden, well-ordered family life in which mother doll and father doll sleep side by side in one bed while the children help themselves liberally and gloriously to the fantasy contents of the well-stocked toy refrigerator. One play theme we noted that began to appear around this time, and was to reappear many times later both in play and behavior, was the theme of children who solicitously take care of children while adult dolls only take care of each other.

Some of the children in this group suffered a temporary disruption in their ability to enjoy play. In the presence of an attractive array of toys, several shook their heads or sat quietly in a chair on the floor. In fact, no single child was able to relate joyfully to the array of toys with which he or she was presented in the playroom, and one immediate impact of the divorce can be considered a disruption in the pleasure of play. The youngest children, particularly, experienced play inhibition and appeared burdened and constricted as they constructed unsafe toy worlds populated by hungry, assaultive animals.

## Rise in Aggression

About half of these very young children also showed greater irritability and rising tempers which they expressed at home in relation to their younger brothers and sisters, or to the parent, or at school, and sometimes in both settings. Jane said angrily, tossing her head on being scolded by her mother, "You're not my mommy; I don't have a mommy anymore."

Children constructed toy scenes with menacing animals who fought each other to the death or pounced cruelly on little baby animals. Nora arranged crocodiles and other bigmouthed animals and had them bite each other. Then they all joined in pursuit of the baby lamb. As the baby lamb is captured by them, it cries to the mother for rescue but the mother's efforts to rescue it fail.

Since very few children were protected from witnessing parental quarrels, these scenes may have stimulated aggressive behavior. The children's play contained many scenes of people hitting each other, of houses burning, of wild, uncontrolled destruction or chaos.

### Inhibition of Aggression

While for some children the family rupture catalyzed a general rise of aggression, for others the response was the reverse. These children evidenced a massive inhibition of their own aggression and sometimes became acutely fearful of attacks. Nan, age three, assured us unsolicited, "I never, never break things." Tim was afraid to go to sleep at night because he might be killed while he was sleeping. Harold brought little clay balls into his play session to protect himself just in case somebody attacked him. And Edna fearfully approached the interviewer with the repeated admonition, "Don't hurt me, don't hurt me." Several children appeared to listen intently for sound outside the consulting room and to watch every motion as if it were potentially dangerous.

### Guilt

As we have said, preschool children were often given to self-blame. Kay told us that her father had left because her play was too noisy. Jennifer said her father objected to her messily trained dog and left for that reason. Max savagely beat the "naughty baby doll." These self-accusations, which severely troubled these children, were highly resistant to change by educational measures or by explanations undertaken by parents or teachers. These children clung to their self-accusations with great tenacity. Their feeling of helplessness on the one side, and of total responsibility for the disaster on the other, were both present in their thinking and they suffered from both.

### Emotional Need

Some of the behavior which we saw in these young children has no counterpart in clinical practice. Children are usually brought for help because of symptoms which disturb the adults in their life, or because they are not learning appropriately. In the course of time, however, we became concerned with the general emotional neediness in several of these youngsters. This behavior expressed itself in a random reaching out to new adults, climbing into strange laps, and other behavior reflecting a diffuse need for physical contact, nurturance, and protection. Teachers in nursery school and kindergarten reported the same phenomenon. This almost randomly expressed hunger for affection and physical contact appeared to endure long after some of the immediate responses which we have described had subsided.

### Mastery

Finally, these young children tried to cope successfully with the stress in a variety of mature ways. A few appeared able to keep their inner balance, their perspective, and their own distance from parental difficulties.

Harold told us, "You have to keep your anger in." He maintained this calmly and sagely at a time when his parents were threatening each other with guns, and violence was escalating all around him. His stance was sober and mature, and he, at age five, told us seriously about his responsibility to be a big brother to his younger sister. The wishes that Harold confided were for a helicopter and wings. These may well reflect his eagerness for escape and seemed prompted by his wish not to become enmeshed in the family struggles. Apparently he was succeeding: His teachers reported he was an excellent student as well as a cheerful youngster whose behavior had not changed.

A few of the little girls also displayed only moderate change at the time of the family rupture. Although saddened by the father's departure, after several days of greater restlessness, increased tension, and tears these children appeared busy with age-appropriate pursuits and were quickly occupied again with playmates, school, hamsters, and various group games.

Immediately following her father's departure, Nancy built an elaborate tree house which excluded all the other members of his family. Frances told us "The divorce is okay, cause mommy asked him to leave."

Viewed at close range, it is remarkable how some of these five-year-old children showed the capacity for perception in regard to their families and an ability to accept the family rupture with a minimum of subterfuge and self-blame. How much of this reflected a conscious, studied scanning of the family landscape is hard to judge. We were often impressed with the acute social sensitivity of these children.

Harold, who drew himself with large eyes and enormous ears, reflected perhaps both the intensity and the strain of needing constantly to assess the world around him. Despite their own pain, these children seemed able to distinguish clearly their wishes for reconciliation from the reality they perceived. John told us how much he missed his father and how much he wished to live with him. He added with great sadness, "But he does not want to live with us anymore." The children worked hard at explaining the separation even when it made no sense to them. Frances insisted that her parents divorced because of fights about mail and taxes, although it was perfectly clear that, at age five, she had little comprehension of either.

Some children made heroic efforts to find or reestablish some meaning and order in the disarray of their lives. Throughout his four hours of interviews, Frank produced many drawings of animals, of flowers, sometimes a family portrait which always included both parents. Otherwise, he spent his time soberly straightening up the office, lining up pencils, pens, and toys in rows to his liking. Neither in conversation, play, or art did he express his worries, fears, or angers directly or indirectly. Instead, he used the office as a microcosm in which he could reestablish the order, the continuity, the familiarity, and the control which were clearly absent in his perception of his world at that time.

The anxieties that these children showed in the consulting room can be differentiated, in a general way, from the anxiety other children of the same age show when they are brought to psychiatric clinics for evaluation or treatment. These youngsters had a relatively intact ability to relate to adults and, in fact, their search for adults led them to make very quick contact with us. These were children who had neither been rejected by their parents nor had they been given poor care, but rather they were children whose lives had been disrupted and who therefore expected to be received well by adults and to be treated with kindness and consideration. They did not appear as psychologically disturbed children, but as children responding to severe stress whose life experiences with adults had not been poor until the sudden disruption of their families which, for that very reason, left them unprepared and bewildered. Ease in their relations and a hunger for contact appeared in many of the children.

The interviewer reported, "At the end of the hour John heard a voice in the waiting room and wanted to leave. He panicked as I said, "Just a minute," and he dashed to the door, yelling, "I want Daddy! I want Daddy!" I had been leaning against the door while playing with him and he tried to get out, running over me before I could get up. After this first hour and despite this rather unceremonious leave-taking, he came back and was reluctant to say goodbye, and as I knelt down to say we would see each other again next week, he walked slowly up to me with his head bowed. I repeated several times for him the hour and day that we would see each other. Once up to my face, John broke into a wide grin and kissed me."

## The Young School-Age Children
## (Six-to-Eight-Year-Olds)

I asked the child "if you had three wishes, what would they be?" Ben said, "I only have one. It's to have a happy life." "You sound sad when you say that," I said. The child nodded. "Is there something that might make you happy or change the sadness?" "I don't know," said the child. "I've heard some children say that things could be better if their divorced parents would get back together." Ben looked up, briefly, and then bowed his head. "I wish my parents would be together again. I think about that a lot. But there isn't any chance. There's nothing to do about that."

Drawings of children in first and second grade differ considerably from those of younger children and reflect the extraordinary maturation that has occurred within a very compressed time span. The new intellectual and emotional advances increase the capacity of children at this age to understand the meaning of the divorce, as well as some of its specific implications for them. A more adult, although still immature, sense of time enables them to distinguish immediate from distant future, to grasp in a general way how long a week is, and more specifically to estimate the waiting period between visits. At the same time, their ability to grasp true cause and effect in human relationships remains very limited, and their capacity to understand the needs of their parents as separate from their own is not yet within their emotional reach. Children during these years are more aware than their younger brothers and sisters of their separate relationships with each parent. They are intensely preoccupied with taking the giant step that leads them from the contained world of the family into the wider world of school and playground, and they are in emotional and intellectual transition between these two very different worlds. Their precarious sense of being in transition between home and community, and their fear of retreating from their most recently acquired and still shaky gains in independence are increased by the family rupture and particularly by the father's departure from the family.

### Grief

As with Ben, the most striking response among the six-to-eight-year-old children was their pervasive sadness. The impact of the separation appeared to be so strong that the children's usual defenses and coping strategies did not hold sufficiently under the stress. Crying and sobbing were not uncommon, especially among the boys, and many children were on the brink of tears as they spoke with us. Unlike the preschool children who made extensive use of fantasy to deny the separation and loss and who held fast to the idea that someday their family would be reunited, these children, more intensely conscious of their sorrow than any other group in the study, had great difficulty in obtaining relief. Sometimes the intensity of the child's distress was directly related to the amount of turmoil generated between the parents, but some children suffered acutely where there was no overt or apparent parental upset.

More than half of these young children expressed their sorrow directly to us, at the time we first saw them.

Roger, age seven, began his first appointment by asking if the interviewer had heard "the bad news" about the divorce. He felt "very, very sad about the split" but maintained that he couldn't cry. "I have to hold it in, 'cause I'd be crying all the time." He observed that it would be very embarrassing to cry at school. Roger related mournfully how he gets his own breakfast and lunch because his mother doesn't get up in the morning like she used to. "She must be sick." Roger knew there was trouble from the beginning: "They only knew each other two days, and they should have known each other at least nine days before getting married." He sadly recounted his unsuccessful efforts to interrupt his parents' fighting.

Some children perceived the whole world to be filled with symbols of loss.

Jenny was tense and reluctant to talk, remembering at first only that she told her parents "over and over," long before the divorce, "You'd better *not* get a divorce." Her near despair was poignantly conveyed by her inability to think of three wishes, stating instead she didn't have any favorite things "in school, at home, or anything." Jenny's mother had told her divorce was better because she would have *two* places to live and visit. Jenny, doubtful, said, "I'll wait and see." In the second interview, she wondered sadly why children usually live with their mothers, expressing again the wish to live with both parents. After a tired sigh, Jenny talked worriedly of a dog's heart attack, then the therapist's doll: "Poor little thing, she doesn't have any eyes." In the last interview, Jenny volunteered that she had finally thought of her three wishes: "First, that my daddy would come home. Second, that my parents would get back together. And third, that they would never, ever divorce again." Sadly she said, "It will never happen, I won't get any of my wishes."

Mary, seven years old when her parents separated, sadly described her vision of divorce as, "It's when people go away."

Some children kept their feelings in careful check and fell back on complicated coping maneuvers which enabled them to maintain their surface composure.

Dan, age eight, stoutly maintained he didn't have too many problems about the divorce, and he was glad it was over. When asked to draw his family, Dan instead spent the entire hour on a compulsively elaborated drawing of his many-roomed house that had a place for everyone, and he talked lovingly of each added architectural detail. Dan anxiously asked if he should put *everyone* in his family in the drawing, including his kitten, now dead of leukemia. Eventually, he declined to draw any people. Only at the end of the last session did this child admit to a "tiny problem" of wanting to see his dad more. Several months later, Dan requested an interview "to talk of the awful bad problems I'm having at night."

### Fear Leading to Disorganization

Like the younger children, these children were also very frightened by the collapse of their family, and they had many unrealistic fantasies, including the fear of being left without a family or of being sent to live with strangers. Several of them showed severely disorganized behavior and panic on occasion.

Greg's father came back to the family home shortly after the separation and chased his estranged wife through the house with a shotgun. Greg ran into his mother's closet and, seemingly out of control, wildly pulled down his mother's clothing. Found crying on the floor, Greg said, incoherently, "If Dad had shot you, I was going to wreck your closet." During the two months following the incident, the child was sleepless and tearful, and showed increased irritability and problems in controlling impulse.

Sonia rushed into her classroom and announced to the class and teacher "with glee" that her father had moved out the night before. After a few days, she began to vomit her breakfast regularly and alternately clung to and angrily shouted at her mother. Anxiously and repeatedly she asked her bewildered mother, "Don't you love me?"

### Feelings of Deprivation

Fantasies of being deprived of food, of toys, of some other important aspect of their life pervaded the thinking of many children.

Carol's compulsive overeating and weight gain after the separation was reflected in her puppet play, as she directed the whale to say, "Please make me not eat this poor little girl." Later she warned the interviewer, "You'd better not ask me about the divorce or I'll get hungry."

Carol's preoccupation with going hungry is reminiscent of the hungry, needy animals who appeared so frequently in the play of the preschool children. Her compulsive overeating suggested that her efforts to deal with her sadness were unsuccessful. She confessed to us that whenever her parents began to fight, she ran to the kitchen to open the refrigerator.

Often, the children's fantasies were quite elaborate.

Jason, age seven, told us an almost convincing story of his mother's mean boyfriend who deprived him of breakfast every morning after his mother left for work. He also invented a fantasy of a benign figure of a nude man who bountifully fed him as much breakfast as he wanted.

Several children reacted to their fear of being deprived by begging and wheedling gifts—new and fancier bicycles, clothing, or toys—and trying to enlist the interviewer's support in persuading their parents to grant their frantic requests. Some wove elaborate fantasies of gratifying vacations, of being an indulged only child, of having not one but two homes, of having several swimming pools.

Barbara, who was neglected by her agitated and depressed mother, played a remarkable fantasy of an almost Biblical peace in which lion and lamb lie contentedly side by side, and life is bountiful for all. Appointing the interviewer as Mother, and instructing her strictly to say only "yes, my dear," Barbara began to play out a series of scenes. In the first scene, the children return from school, request a generous snack, and the mother happily grants this saying (as instructed), "Yes, my dear." The second scene finds the child asking whether she can bring all the children in the neighborhood for snacks, to which the mother responds, "Yes, my dear." Emboldened, the child now asks whether she can invite all the animals in the zoo, the big and the small, the wild and the tame, and once again the bountiful mother says, on cue, "Yes, my dear." In ever widening circles, Barbara finally created a world exactly the reverse of her own forlorn and lonely life to undo in the only way that she could the emotional hunger which she was unable otherwise to assuage.

### Yearning for the Departed Parent

Particularly striking in this age group was the yearning for the father. More than half of these children missed their father acutely. Many felt abandoned and rejected by him and expressed their longing in ways reminiscent of grief for a dead parent.

Jack appeared unable to play without interrupting himself frequently and turning disconsolately from one activity to another. He told us "Nothing feels right because daddy isn't home," adding that before he goes to sleep nightly he prays for his father's return and that he cries in his sleep.

While it is not surprising that most children missed their fathers, the intensity of the response in this age group, especially among the boys, was notable—and again, it had no relation to the degree of closeness between the father and child during marriage.

It seemed clear to us in confronting the despair and sadness of these children and their intense, almost physical, longing for the father, that inner psychological needs of great power and intensity were being expressed. Separation from the father, at this crucial age, may threaten to disrupt the process of identification with the father. Moreover, the threat of regression may be particularly frightening for these children, especially for the little boys who have newly resolved oedipal conflicts and who now experience the anxiety of being alone with the mother, without the father's reassuring and constraining presence.

Some of these little boys urgently requested their mothers to remarry. Soon after the separation, Jack asked his mother to remarry, stating that he needed to have a daddy of his own, for himself. Ray told the interviewer he would like his mother to remarry, because "I'm just used to having a father around the house."

Not unexpectedly, some children idealized their father following his departure and talked continually about the father as if to invoke his presence by their words.

Nathan told us, "My daddy is smart; he is making a new motor for his truck," and added, with emphasis, "I said *make,* not buy." The child told us how much he loves his father and enjoys going with him to the ball games. When he, Nathan, grows up he is going to be a smart man, just like his dad, because his dad has taught him everything he knows.

Some children undertook, directly, to restore the father's departure by representing him and his continuing presence within the family.

Robbie took to wearing his father's tie to school and at home. He began methodically to plan his own life so that he could follow his father's career choices in every particular, including even the changes in them. Robbie's father had attended law school and left after one year, and Robbie told us he planned to do exactly the same.

### Inhibition of Aggression at Father

Related to this intense yearning, we found that very few children expressed anger at their father. Jack, who appeared quiet and withdrawn following his father's departure, commented, sighing heavily, "I just can't help thinking about my BB gun. I don't even care to shoot my BB gun any more." This comment may reflect his sense that the father's leaving had inhibited his expression of certain kinds of aggressive activity. Generally, we found that children whose aggressive behavior was of grave concern to their mother and who fought a lot with playmates and hit their younger siblings were subdued in the presence of the father. Few children in this age group criticized the fathers at any time during the immediate aftermath of the separation.

### Anger at the Custodial Mother

In contrast with the difficulty in expressing anger at the father, there were some children in our study, mostly boys, who expressed considerable anger at their mother for either causing the divorce or driving the father away. Those children most profoundly hurt or made anxious by the loss of the father tended to be those most enraged at their mother. Anger was expressed directly in several instances.

Soon after his father departed, Don's behavior began to mirror the father's abusive treatment of the mother. In addition to his demanding and degrading remarks, Don began to compile an angry list of complaints about his mother, presented it to his father weekly, and then enjoyed his father's ensuing tirades at his mother.

More often, anger was expressed by means of such displacements as teachers, friends, brothers, and sisters, or in temper tantrums.

## Fantasies of Responsibility and Reconciliation

A few children openly admitted to the thoughts and worries that they had caused the divorce, and in two cases, both girls, the children seemed to assume primary responsibility.

Eight-year-old Debbie was saddened and bewildered by her mother's decision to divorce and anxiously admitted that her failure to relay an important message from one parent to the other had precipitated the intensely heated argument which had led to the divorce. The interviewer's efforts to explore the parents' divorce with Debbie and to provide some reassurance of her innocence were met with considerable skepticism.

Feeling responsibility for the divorce was not the predominant response in this group, however. Most of these children denied any feelings of responsibility, nor did this emerge in their fantasy or play. Wishes for reconciliation between the parents, by contrast, were widespread and enduring. Some children even held tenaciously to the fantasy of reconciliation after the remarriage of one or both parents.

Nathan confided that his first and his only wish in the whole world was that his father would return to live with them. Moreover, he knew that his father would return. He knew it because his parents didn't fight any more; they were friends; "They don't turn their heads away from each other." As the child left the office, he added with emphasis, "Don't think I lost anyone. I now have two daddies and one mommy. It's great."

## Conflicts in Loyalty

Unlike the preschool children, these boys and girls were of sufficient age to be enlisted actively, by one or both parents, in their waging of hostile confrontations. In most of the divorces in this age group, there was a considerable amount of turmoil, bitterness, and accusations from which the children were not shielded. One quarter of these children were under heavy pressure from their mothers to reject their fathers. Tugs and pulls for loyalty caused some children to feel that they were being physically torn apart. Unlike the older children, the youngsters in this age group seemed not to have ways of avoiding the pain of feeling pulled in both directions by love and loyalty.

Jason described his parents' divorce by saying, "It's splitting me in two." To illustrate the point, Jason drew his hand, hatchet-style, down the middle of his forehead.

Such divided loyalties were experienced even when the parents were not pushing the child to take sides. But where there were parental pressures of this kind, children of this age group seemed unable to comply with the demand that they align with one parent against the other. These youngsters continued to be loyal to both parents, frequently in secret, and often at considerable psychological cost and suffering. Their capacity to do this, despite the pressure, and their courage were often moving and impressive.

## The Older School-Age Children (Nine-to-Twelve-Year-Olds)

The difference in response to stress in general and to the divorce in particular that we observed between those children in the six-to-eight-year-old group and the nine-to-twelve-year-olds took us by surprise, because psychological theory does not suggest a significant distinction between children in the primary grades and those in the fourth or fifth grades. We were therefore unprepared to find the distinguishing differences in response which we reported here, and which suggest that the stance of the child, vis-á-vis his parents and his need of the family undergo an important change: that there is, in fact, an important milestone in development that occurs somewhere in the eighth or ninth year.

While this requires replication in other studies as well as explanation in psychological theory, our findings point to the eighth to ninth year as a time of rapid growth and strengthening in ego as evidenced by a newly available repertoire of coping skills, a time of greatly enhanced capacity to understand a complex reality and to withstand stress without regression. There appear, also, to be very significant changes in relationships with parents.

### How They Looked When They Came

Many of the children in the nine-to-twelve group had presence, poise, and courage when they came to their initial interviews. They perceived the realities of their family's disruption and the parent's turbulence with a soberness and clarity we first found startling, particularly when compared with the younger children who so frequently appeared disorganized and immobilized by their worry and grief. These youngsters by comparison were actively struggling to master a host of conflicting feelings and fears, and trying to give coherence and continuity to the baffling disorder in which they now found themselves. Robert said, "I have to calm myself down. Everything is happening too fast."

With the fine perception of children in this age group, Gwen said that a long time ago when she was little she had thought that everything was fine. Her parents "really loved each other and nothing would happen to them until they were real, real old." Her mom and dad had been married eleven and a half years. They had known each other for sixteen and a half years. With tears filling her eyes, the child said, "I always thought love would last if they stayed together that long."

Some children came prepared with an agenda. Anna, after a few general comments from the interviewer which were designed to put her at ease, interrupted with a brisk, "Down to business," and went on immediately to describe the diffuse feelings of anxiety with which she suffered these days and which made her feel "sick to my stomach." Paula volunteered that she was "so glad" her mother had brought her to talk about the divorce because, "If I don't talk about it soon, I'll fall apart."

Some of these children tried immediately to establish a longer and continuing relationship with the interviewer. Janet begged to return the following week. She offered, "I like to talk about my problems," and drew a heart on the blackboard, writing under it, "I like Miss X," referring to the interviewer.

Others among these children found the interviews uncomfortable and barely kept their anxiety under control by keeping themselves or their extremities in continual motion, the rhythm of which motion accompanied and punctuated the subjects discussed. Thus, Robert's legs moved faster when his dad was mentioned. He tried bravely to maintain his calm and referred, with some disdain, to "Mother's divorce problem," adding with bitterness, "I wonder who she's got now." Others maintained their composure by denial and nonchalance, which enabled them to keep their emotional distance. Ken stated, "I keep my cool. It's difficult to know what I'm thinking."

## Layering of Response

Their various efforts to manage their upset—by trying to understand, refusing to believe the marital rupture, courage, bravado, reaching out to others for help, keeping in constant motion, consciously trying not to think about the divorce—all emerged as the age-available ways these youngsters had for coping with the profound underlying feelings of loss and rejection, of helplessness and fear of loneliness, that preoccupied them, and that in most of them only gradually became visible as we got to know them in the course of several successive interviews. They were, in fact, extraordinarily resourceful in their efforts to keep from being overwhelmed by their powerful feelings and fears. The efforts were in part attended by what we have come to think of as a layered response, involving simultaneous denial and distress. The denial was sometimes an effort to deceive the observer, but also helped the child deal with his own anguish.

After his father left the home, Robert sat for many hours sobbing in his darkened room. The father visited infrequently and continued to disappoint the child. When seen by us, Robert offered smilingly, "I have a grand time on his visits," and added, unsolicited and cheerily, "I see him enough." Only later, in the context of our third interview, would he shamefacedly admit that he missed his father intensely and longed to see him daily and was profoundly hurt by his father's inconstancy.

The children were ashamed of what was happening in their families and to them, and they tried to conceal the events and the accompanying feelings from the outside world. Their sense of being ashamed and different was not notably relieved by the high incidence of divorce in the community around them. Sally said, "I'm so ashamed when people call. I can't tell them that mom and dad are separated. I just tell folks to call back."

The way their parents were behaving was also a source of embarrassment and the children lied bravely to protect them and to camouflage their own hurt feelings.

George, for instance, proudly told us that his physician father had insisted that all of his shots be in his left arm in order to protect his pitching arm. Actually, the father had evinced no interest whatsoever in George's athletic career.

### Attempted Mastery by Activity and Play

Unlike the younger children, so many of whom became depressed or regressed in response to the family disruption, the unhappiness which these children experienced often galvanized them into vigorous activity. Such activity represented a composite of coping and defensive strategies designed to help overcome those feelings of powerlessness which the children in this age group experienced as so humiliating and so threatening to their equilibrium. Sorely shaken by their recognition that they had so little influence on their parents in the divorce decision, of which they disapproved, several youngsters undertook directly to undo the parental separation. They addressed this task with energy and often with a high sense of drama. Although they failed to bring about the reconciliation, they more than succeeded in the psychological purpose of undoing their sense of powerlessness and passivity which they found so oppressive.

Marian embarked on a frenzied sequence of activities designed to intimidate her mother and force her to return to the marriage. Marian scolded, yelled, demanded, and berated her mother, often making it impossible for her mother to have dates, and indeed almost succeeding in reversing the divorce decision by mobilizing all her mother's guilt in relation to herself and the other children.

Several children in this group energetically developed a variety of new, exciting, and intrinsically pleasurable activities that seemed to be on the borderline between play and reality, and to overlap both domains. These activities required not only fantasy production but the enterprise and skill of children in this age group.

Robin, whose father was a successful advertising man, designed and issued a magazine filled with articles, drawings, and cartoons heralding the impending divorce of her parents and announcing other interesting happenings in the neighborhood. She distributed and sold the magazine in her school and the community.

By writing, publishing, and selling a newspaper about her parents' divorce, Robin had achieved a remarkable (and appealing) solution to several psychological problems set off by the divorce, in a way that would not be possible for younger children. The activity clearly identified her with her father, and thus in effect brought him back into her life. By publishing the news of the divorce, she was proclaiming her acceptance of it and forcing herself to master it. But central to the maneuver (and central to our outstanding of the responses of all these children) was her ability to recapture the center stage, to undo the humiliation of being pushed aside and, most of all, to transform her pain and unhappiness into the pleasure of achievement.

Other children stood on this same narrow borderline between play and reality in their efforts at mastery.

Bill spent many hours after school in the empty office of his uninterested father, sitting alone in his father's chair, answering the telephone, playing out the role of executive, and calling his mother at regular intervals to tell her, with emphasis and conviction, that he was having "a grand time."

It was hard in many of these instances to know whether the audience for such a play was the child himself, or the parent, or the imagined world of public opinion.

## Anger

The single feeling that most clearly distinguished this group from all the younger children was a fully conscious, intense anger. It had many sources, but clearly a major determinant was its role in temporarily obliterating, or at least obscuring, the other even more painful affective responses we have noted, especially feelings of sadness and helplessness. Although we have described a rise in aggression and irritability in the younger children following parental separation, the anger experienced by these older children was different in being both well organized and clearly object-directed; indeed, their capacity to articulate their anger directly was striking.

John volunteered that most of the families of the kids on his block were getting a divorce. When asked how the children felt, he said, "They're so angry they're almost going crazy."

Approximately half of the children in this group were angry at their mothers, the other half at their fathers, and a goodly number were angry at both. In the main children were angry at the parent whom they blamed for the divorce.

Amy said she was angry at Mom for kicking dad out and ruining their lives. "She's acting *just* like a college student, at age thirty-one—dancing and dating and having to be with her friends." One adopted child screamed at his mother, "If you knew you were going to divorce, why did you adopt us?"

For some, anger against the parents was wedded to a sense of moral indignation and outrage that the parent who had been correcting their conduct was behaving in what they considered to be an immoral and ir-responsible fashion.

Robert said that, "Three days before my dad left, he was telling me all these things about 'be good.' That hurt the most," he said, to think that his dad did that and knew all along that he was going to leave.

The intense anger of these children was variously expressed. Some-times it took the form of rising crescendoes calculated to create a nuisance when the mother's dates arrived.

Shortly after the divorce, Joe's abusive father disappeared, leaving no address. The mother reported that now she had to ask the boy, instead of the husband, for permission to go out. Joe reproached her if she drank, and he monitored her telephone calls. Furthermore, when she purchased something for herself, he screamingly demanded that the same amount of money be spent on him. Joe used his sessions with us primarily to express his anger at his mother for not purchasing a BB gun for him.

Adding to the dictatorial posturing and swaggering expressions that these children enjoyed playing out following the departure of their fathers was the fact that in many of these households the father had been responsible for harsh and frightening discipline. His departure thus signaled a new freedom to express impulses that had been carefully held in check during his presence, a freedom to do so with impunity and with pleasure.

### Shaken Sense of Identity

Children experienced a sense of a shaken world in which the usual indicators had changed place or disappeared. These changed markers were particularly related to their sense of who they were in the present and who they were likely to become in the future. Generally, during this developmental stage, the child's conception of his own identity was closely tied to the external family structure. They depend on the presence of parental figures, not only for nurture, protection, and control but also for the consolidation of age-appropriate identifications. Children in this age group referred characteristically to "my neighborhood," "my house," "my school." Their self-image and identity was organized around "I am the son of John and Mary Smith."

These youngsters experienced confusion and a threat of ruptured identity at the time of the parental separation. They raised anxious questions and compared their physical characteristics with those of their parents, as if trying in this way to reassemble broken pieces into an important whole. The children brought this to our attention in both comments and questions.

Neal, unsolicited, volunteered a long discussion of his physical features. "My eyes change color, just like my mom's. My hair is going to change to light brown, just like my dad's. Other people say I'm like my dad. My dad says I'm like my mom. I say I'm like a combination."

Part of the threat, which the children experienced as directed against their sense of integrity and identity was posed even more specifically to their sense of right and wrong and to their conscience, which is very much in formation at this time of life. Children felt that their conscience had been weakened by their disenchantment with the parents' behavior, and with the departure of the very parent who had more often than not acted as their moral authority. Several children became involved in petty stealing and lying immediately following the parental separation. The threat seen by the children to their sense of moral and social obligation, as well as their worry about having to take care of themselves, was movingly conveyed by Ken's story of his two rabbits.

Ken volunteered, as he entered the office, "I think I want to talk to you today." He told us in detail the story of the two rabbits he had bought several years before, and cared for in an elaborate highrise hutch which he had carefully constructed. One day, he said, despite his protective watchfulness, two vicious neighborhood dogs ripped the cage apart, and the rabbits disappeared or were dragged off. The two rabbits, who he had named Ragged Ear and Gray Face, may have escaped, he thinks, because recently he came upon two rabbits playing in the woods. They were wild rabbits now, but they resembled the two he had lost.

The two rabbits of this rich fantasy may well refer to the child and his brother, and his story may reflect his fear of the primitive angers (the two vicious dogs who may also represent the fighting parents) let loose at the time of divorce, and the child's fear that he would be destroyed. In the solution arrived at in the child's fantasy, the rabbits take care of themselves, but at the price of returning to their presocialized, wild state. Clearly, the little wild rabbits who survive by dint of their own efforts had a different identity and a different conscience from the rabbits who had been cared for so lovingly by the child in the elaborately built hutch. And if we make the assumption that the child equates with the rabbit in this fantasy, we can appreciate Ken's apprehensiveness about what may become of him in the absence of adequate parental care, and his expectation that he may become an unsocialized, vulnerable child. It is perhaps presumptuous to say that this story was prophetic, but Ken did become seriously involved in delinquent activities during the years that followed.

## Somatic Symptoms

Finally, somatic symptoms of different kinds and degrees of severity, such as headaches and stomachaches, were reported by these youngsters. These exacerbated symptoms were often linked by the children to parental conflict and parental visits.

Tony had cramps in his legs which he said were only relieved when his father massaged them. Several children in this group who suffered with chronic asthma experienced intensified attacks occurring more frequently.

## Alignment with One Parent

A very important aspect of the response of the youngsters in this age group was the dramatic change in the relationship between parents and children. These young people were particularly vulnerable to being swept up into the anger of one parent against the other. They were faithful and valuable battle allies in efforts to hurt the other parent. Not infrequently, they turned on the parent they had loved and been very close to prior to the marital separation.

The most extreme identification with the parent's cause we have called an "alignment"—a divorce-specific relationship that occurs when a parent and one or more children join in a vigorous attack on the other parent. It is the embattled parent, often the one who opposes the divorce in the first place, who initiates and fuels the alignment, not infrequently as he or she discovers the involvement of the other partner in a new relationship. In our sample of 131 children, 25 formed strong, and often long-lasting, alignments with one parent against the other. Nearly twice as many united with their mothers as with their fathers.

Parents who initiated the alignment often felt betrayed by the divorce-seeking partner. Women who had worked to support their husband's professional training were in this category. Many felt used as stepping stones towards a financially remunerative position. Now that their husbands had achieved this goal, they were cast aside for younger, more attractive women. Alternatively, some men perceived their wives as wantonly rejecting them and the morality which they represented for young, lusty, more abandoned, and less virtuous lovers. When these fears led to a parent-child alignment, the common denominator was often moral outrage and the conviction of having been shamelessly used and discarded. Sometimes the reality of these feelings was hard to assess. The angers which parent and child (or children) shared soon became the basis for a complexly organized strategy, aimed at harassing the former spouse and sometimes at shaming him or her into returning to the marriage. Mostly, the open agenda of the alignment was to reconstitute the marriage; the unspoken agenda was revenge.

Our findings suggest strongly that children, as well as adults, who joined in these endeavors were less psychologically stable than their brothers and sisters who refused to do so and that these youngsters who did join one parent against the other were highly distressed at the time of the separation and felt especially vulnerable from the divorce. Children who are emotionally hungry are likely to find the parental seduction dazzling and irresistible. Certainly the child in such an alignment feels more important and more needed as he plays an active role in the divorce.

By and large, these alignments appeared to be both age and sex-related. The most useful allies in the divorce-related fighting were the nine-to-twelve-year-old boys and girls. We found that the child at this age has the capacity to be an unswervingly loyal friend or team member, and exceeds in his reliability his sometimes more capricious, more self-preoccupied adolescent brother or sister. He or she is, therefore, a valuable ally in the battle. Within this age group, mothers did better at courting their sons as allies, and fathers succeeded better with their daughters.

The life span of these alignments appeared related to custodial arrangements. The alignments with the father, or the noncustodial parent, do not appear to last past the first postseparation year. Only a very few children continued in an alignment with the father beyond that time. Almost all these children had chronically poor relationships with their mothers prior to the separation. Maternal alignments, or alignments with the custodial parent, on the other hand, included almost a fifth of the children and remained strikingly stable at the first year and a half after separation. When aligned with the custodial parent, these divorce-inspired relationships appeared to have surprising staying power which may reflect not just the intensity of the underlying feelings but also their daily reinforcement. Parents who maintained alignments after the first year were disturbed, angry people, who had yet to reestablish their equilibrium or to respond constructively to the divorce. It is reasonable to suppose that for many parents these anger-driven campaigns warded off impending depressions. It is therefore no surprise that their intensity remained undiminished for a long time after separation.

### The Case of Paul

Paul was eleven years old and the oldest of three children when his father decided on a divorce. Paul's father was informally referred to us by the court after complaining of his wife's vindictive blocking of his visits with his three children. A successful chemical engineer, the father expressed sadness and longing for his children and concern that his children were being systematically turned against him by their mother's unremitting attacks. The children had rebuffed their father in his repeated efforts to visit them. They received him coldly or not at all. The mother had told the children of her exploitation by the father. She told them they would be unable to get a new pet to replace the father's dog because the father was not providing sufficient money to purchase its food. (At that time, the family was receiving over $1,000.00 a month in support.) To us, Paul's mother expressed astonishment at the father for unilaterally deciding to divorce her, describing her many years of love and hard work which supported the father's graduate education. Because she was a devout Catholic woman, she insisted that she would never harbor anger. Yet, she said, "My son, Paul, will never forgive his father, nor forget."

Paul's initial response to the parental separation was regression to sobbing in a dark closet which alternated with telephone pleas to his father to return. Later, in recalling this time, the child said to us, "I felt I was being torn into two pieces." By the time we saw Paul, several months following the separation, he had consolidated an unshakable alignment with his mother. He extolled her as small but powerful, possessed of ESP, and knowledgeable in six languages. Of his father, he stated, "He'll never find another family like us."

Among Paul's activities during the year following our initial contact was his continuing reporting to his mother about his father's social life and presumed delinquencies, and his continued rejection of his father's increasingly desperate overtures, including gifts and expression of wishes to maintain visitation. Paul also maintained a coercive control over his younger sisters who were eager to see their father, and he made sure, by his monitoring of them, that they would not respond with affection, at least in his presence. At follow-up, he told us, "We are a team now. We used to have an extra guy and he broke us up into little pieces." His anger, and his mother's anger, seemed undiminished at this time.

We have suggested that the 9- to 12-year-old children who are standing on the threshold of adolescence are especially vulnerable to participation in alignments. There are many reasons which suggest that this behavior is especially congenial to the developmental needs of children in this age group. The immediate achievement of this alignment relationship, when viewed as a coping behavior at the time of the divorce, is that it serves to reduce symptomatic responses among these children, to ward off loneliness, sadness, and more serious depression. These youngsters are galvanized into exciting activity; they speak with new and ringing authority; they are given permission to express hostility and to engage in mischief; and they experience very gratifying closeness with one parent. The alignment enables them to split the ambivalent relationship with both parents into a clear and simple good parent and a bad one.

This rending of the parental relationship into good and bad reflects the harsh, unmodulated, immature conscience of youngsters at this age. The good parent is conceptualized as all virtuous and powerful and the bad parent conveniently becomes the repository of sin, starkly conceived. These youngsters not only enjoy their sense of righteousness and the permission they receive from the "good" parent to inflict punishment on the other, they especially enjoy their enhanced sense of power and their capacity to humiliate the vulnerable adult. It was clear that these youngsters were notably successful in wounding the parent they attacked, in part because of the particular interdependence of parent and child at this stage of the child's development and the very significant role which the child is so often pressured to play in restoring, or further diminishing, the parent's self-esteem at this critical time. We may also conjecture that youngsters in this age group may sense a need for a protective structure for the adolescent years ahead. Their search for stability during the coming years may lead them to hold tightly to the one parent they feel will maintain them.

## The Adolescents
## (Thirteen-to-Eighteen-Year-Olds)

A few days before her parents separated, Tina, age sixteen, dreamed that both of them had died but remained alive. They stood together in a darkened room facing a man who was writing at a brightly lit desk surrounded by total darkness. Behind them were two dark hallways and, as the dream ended, each parent walked alone, slowly, away from the other down the long, narrow, dark corridors until both figures disappeared.

Tina's dream conveyed her loneliness, her fear of being isolated, and her unconscious equation of her parents' divorce with death. Kafkaesque in its landscape of isolated institutional structures, narrow darkened corridors, and lonely figures, Tina's dream accurately represents the mood of many adolescents at the time of the family rupture. The central theme of her dream, namely the adults who walked away from each other and gradually disappeared, represents what we have found to be a common thread in the adolescent response to divorce, namely that these young people experienced the divorcing parents as leaving them in lieu of their own adolescent leave-taking of their parents and of the parental home.

Fearing loneliness and depression, Tina, like her peers, was preoccupied with the survival of relationships, wondering with great trepidation whether her family relationships would remain alive or would die with the dying marriage.

We were not surprised to find many adolescents like Tina shaken by the marital rupture. We were, however, unprepared for the quality of their anguish and, particularly, for their frantic appeals to us to restore the parents' marriage.

Jack, age fourteen, told us "I felt that the rug had been pulled out from under me. I cried and I begged and begged. I tried to talk sense to my mom until I was almost mute." Jack had even explained to his parents that a reconciliation would save the family a great deal of money. He appealed to us. Could we do something to effect a reconciliation on his behalf?

## Changes in Parent-Child Relationships

In order to understand the often overwhelming experience of these young people, it is necessary first to spell out the extraordinary changes which were precipitated in their relationships with their parents following the divorce decision. Although children of all ages experienced important changes in the relationship with their parents at this time, the adolescent response is so inextricably interwoven with their relationship with their parents that the two have to be considered together. The key issues for the adolescents' response to the divorce derive from the particular impact of the divorce on the normal developmental processes. The threat the divorce poses to adolescent development occurs because of the changes it has precipitated—namely, the changed perception of the parents, the changed relationship with the parents, and the diminished availability of the family as a supportive structure.

It may be useful to review the adolescent experience within the intact family, to compare it with the experience of the young person in the

newly divorced or divorcing family. Within the intact family, a change
in the direction of psychological disengagement from the parents takes
place gradually over several years. In the more usual course of events,
the youngster advances several steps toward maturity and, as soon as
this is welcomed by parents and teachers, he or she is likely to fall back
into more childish behavior, only to advance again in a continued back
and forth over the several years of adolescence. The back-and-forth rocking motion of the adolescent towards greater independence and maturity, followed by retreat to more childish behavior and dependence, is an
essential part of the gradual emancipation of the youngster from the parents. Although the incongruity of this behavior is often baffling to the
adult, only in this way, by advance and retreat, does the young person
gradually, over the several years of adolescence, let go of the parents and
venture into the independence of the young adult who is ready to
move on.

Accompanying this fluctuation in behavior, the adolescent youngster's
perceptions of his or her parents also undergo many changes. These perceptions also alternate between the young child's exaggerated view of
the parents as powerful, idealized figures and the somewhat cocky, familiar, equally exaggerated view that parents are fallen idols. Gradually,
in accord with his or her own timetable of change, the young person
acquires a more realistic view of his or her parents. The alteration between the two poles of dependence and independence, between the perception of the parents as powerful or weak are the leitmotifs of the normal adolescent process.

Yet precisely because the adolescent characteristically seesaws back
and forth over several years between the safety of the family home base
and the exciting but still chancy world of his or her contemporaries, the
need for a stable family structure is very great. An important purpose of
the family during these adolescent years is to provide the youngster
with the opportunity to return to base, to replenish emotional supplies
that have been depleted, to restore battered self-esteem, to regress
briefly, to retreat temporarily, and finally to gather courage for the next
venture into independence.

The toppling of the family structure at this time burdens these normal
developmental processes and threatens to derail them. The adolescents
who came to us felt that the change in the family had limited or entirely
removed the family as a safe base for refueling. The parents who were
newly preoccupied with their own needs and decisions were not available or able to concentrate their efforts on the problems of the adolescent.
The parents' needs, in effect, had preempted the center of attention
within the family. Moreover, the adults were felt to be changing more
rapidly than the youngsters, and to be disengaging from their earlier,
more familiar, more reliable roles. Hence Tina's dream about the adults
who walk away from the center (of her life?) and gradually disappear

was so representative of the feelings and concerns of her age mates. It was Ann, at age thirteen, who said, "I felt like I was being thrown out into the world before I was ready!"

As one consequence of these divorce-induced family changes these youngsters felt that the time available to them for growing up had been drastically foreshortened. They felt hurried and pressed to achieve quickly the independence which is usually achieved over several years. They felt deprived of playtime and a sense of leisure. In accord with these formulations, one potential major impact of divorce is either to drive adolescent development forward at a greatly accelerated tempo, or to bring it to a grinding halt. Some youngsters found the challenge congenial and rewarding, and matured rapidly. Others were unable to make it without the family supports and fell behind.

Other family functions crucial to maintaining adolescent development were also weakened by the divorce. These included providing discipline, external structure, and controls. The shaky family structure of the newly divorced family and the loosened discipline of the transition period combined with parental self-absorption or distress to diminish the available controls. Some of the youngsters lacked inner controls, the consolidated conscience and independent capacity to make judgments that they needed to maintain themselves without strong parental support and guidance. The divorce left them feeling vulnerable to their own newly strengthened sexual and aggressive impulses, and surrounded by the temptations of the adolescent world without the supports that would hold them to a straight course. Although many youngsters were able to maintain their own course, their efforts to do so were costly.

Contributing to the adolescents' anxiety was their divorce-related perception of their parents as sexual persons. This was often a startling discovery for them. Adolescents generally find it comforting to regard their parents as old and sexless. The relative invisibility of sex in the intact family reinforces their capacity to deny that their parents have sexual needs. Family rupture tends to change this situation abruptly. Parents who accuse each other of infidelity and who engage in the pursuit of new sexual liaisons present inescapable evidence of having sexual desires.

The distress of the youngsters was frequently increased by the youthfulness of many of the parents' lovers. Some of these relationships came dangerously close to crossing generational lines. Thus, the mother of one adolescent girl had a twenty-seven-year-old lover. The girl described her panic when, hearing about the mother's liaison, her own boyfriend quipped teasingly, "Hey, maybe I should date your mom." And several of the fathers took as lovers young women who were close in age to their adolescent daughters.

This newly visible behavior of the parents evoked vivid sexual fantasies about them in their adolescent children. The children's feelings were intense and included sexual excitement, acute anxiety, anger, outrage, embarrassment, dismay, and envy. Some youngsters curtailed their visits in order to avoid contact with the sexually active parent. Others openly and cruelly castigated the parent. A few of the adolescent girls became sexually active when they discovered a parent's involvement in an extramarital affair. One adolescent boy harassed his father's mistress, let the air out of the tires of her car, and tried to break the windows in her house.

The psychological and social changes in the lives of many parents led them to preoccupations and behavior which closely paralleled those of their adolescent children, and threatened to narrow the generation gap. Pushed by their own turmoil and their need to reshape their lives, parents were newly taken up with such questions as "Who am I and where am I going?" They felt pressed to rethink sexual, vocational, and lifestyle choices, not unlike their adolescent youngsters. Furthermore, many parents found themselves back in the sexual marketplace, which closely resembles the world of the older adolescent. Some parents at the time of the divorce actually regressed to adolescent or pseudoadolescent behaviors. Men and women bought themselves new wardrobes and changed their hairstyles in order to look younger. They adopted new ways of talking which they thought resembled those of younger people. These changes brought great discomfort to their youngsters.

The most distressing aspect of such change from the child's perspective was the conscious or unconscious competition from their parents they now experienced. This competition was exceedingly painful for the adolescents who felt deserted and betrayed by the parents they had fully expected to support their own growth towards adulthood.

Mrs. B., thirty-three years old, depressed and anxious following her husband's departure, brought home a succession of young men in their early twenties. She wore her skirts very short, her clothing very tight, and her hair loose in the style of a teenager. Her manner was flippant, bright, and hard. She complained that her thirteen-year-old daughter Valerie was chronically peevish and disobedient. She admitted that she felt little closeness with Valerie these days. One of her friends had observed, she told us, that "Valerie competes with me." The week before a twenty-six-year-old man had invited her out for a drink and, as she had left the house with him, Valerie had inquired sharply, "Where are you going, Mom?" Probably, said Mrs. B., smilingly stroking her own thigh, "She is jealous of me." Valerie, for her part, complained bitterly to us that her mother was selfish and bought pretty clothes only for herself. With sudden wistfulness, the girl stated, "What I want most in the world is for my mom to understand—but she won't."

Finally, the parents' psychological distress was very disturbing to adolescent youngsters. They felt the need for stable and strong adults who could provide a steady, reliable, and supportive presence during the many crises of growing up. Instead they felt that the tables had turned and they needed to take responsibility for the needy parent. They were fearful of being caught in the net of the parent's unhappiness. "Marriage ruins so many lives," concluded John.

Selecting his words carefully and slowly, Gary, age sixteen, described his mother's excessive drinking since the father's departure. He explained how he knew when his mother had been drinking because her eyes took on a glazed look and she became sullen. "She cries a lot," he said. Then gravely and carefully choosing his words, he said in quiet resignation, "There's nothing I can do."

As a consequence of this extraordinary cogwheeling of the divorce-related changes in the parent-child relationship with those issues which cause adolescents intense concern in the normal course of events, the impact of the divorce was magnified many times. The adolescents as a group often experienced anxiety greater than the reality of their predicament might dictate but which was nonetheless profound and pervasive. And because of their feeling of being exposed and vulnerable, each of the ordinary, expectable adolescent worries was intensified. They worried about their present and their future, about who would support them and who would send them to school, about whether they would succeed or fail as sexual partners, and about whether they would achieve a better marriage than their parents. Sometimes this anxiety bordered on panic.

## Worry About Sex and Marriage

Because the marital rupture occurred at an age when the adolescent would have been preoccupied anyway with sex and marriage and the search for a partner, these issues became centers of anxiety.

Karen, age fourteen, asked, "Tell me, is it so that kids will have trouble in the future when their parents get divorced? Does this mean that my marriage will break up? I need to know."

Many youngsters like Karen were terribly vulnerable to the fear that their parents' divorce foreshadowed their own future failure in love and marriage and many responded to the parents' divorce as if it were a direct message about their own future.

Rhonda, age fourteen, doubted that she would ever marry. She said, "I would like to travel a lot and live with a man. If we had a child, then I suppose we would have to take some appropriate action. I just don't know whether I will ever get married." Asked whether all this planning had been triggered by her parents' divorce, Rhonda answered, "Of course!"

Gary, age fifteen, told us, "I'm going to be more careful than my par-

ents. I'm not sure I'll ever marry—certainly not until I'm in my thirties."
He added, "I never would have children, unless of course I get to be a
millionaire and need an heir."

These youngsters, as we have said, also experienced heightened
anxieties regarding their future competence as sexual partners. Although preoccupation with one's own sexual attractiveness and success or
failure in sexual performance is common during adolescence, the normal
anxiety levels were increased many fold. Sometimes parents contributed
to their youngster's anxiety by providing explicit lurid details of the other
parent's sexual inadequacies. Even without such contributions, the
adolescents were sufficiently identified with one or the other parent and
sufficiently anxious about their own emerging sexuality to assume
straightaway and unquestioningly the greater likelihood of their failure.
We were, in fact, shocked at some of their unquestioning acceptance of
their likely disappointment in the future. Two adolescent girls dramatically accused their mother of making them "frigid." These girls assumed
(with or without information from the parent) that the mother's frigidity
had been an important factor leading to the divorce. Their adolescent
anxiety converged with their identification with the mother and led them
individually to conclude, in deep despair, that they, too, were likely to
fail as sexual partners in the future.

## Mourning

These adolescents experienced a profound sense of loss. Some reacted
with profound grief, as if they had lost a beloved person. They reported
feelings of emptiness, tearfulness, difficulty in concentrating, chronic fatigue, and very troublesome dreams, all symptoms of mourning. Although no person had died, they nevertheless mourned the family of
their childhood. And as they mourned its passing, reviewing good memories and recalling separate incidents in detail, it was much as one
would recall events following the death of a friend or a family member.
Their sorrowful sense of loss because of the divorce joined with their
adolescent feelings of outgrowing the family of their childhood. Both
sets of feelings fused and magnified their grief for the family which
would no longer be available to them because of the one parent's departure, and for the family they were leaving because they were growing up.

Several youngsters reported a jagged sense of discontinuity. Here too
one may suppose that the sense of discontinuity consequent to the parental separation joined with the discontinuity that youngsters often feel at
this time in their lives. The family breakup dramatized their sense of
being psychologically in limbo, poised between the dependency of childhood and the independence of adulthood.

Years later, we were puzzled when several of these young people ques-

tioned us closely about details of their earlier remarks. "What did I say
then?" they asked us repeatedly. Gradually we understood that our
association with them over the years had enabled us to perform a special
service. In recalling for them their earlier remarks, we were turning the
pages of an imaginary album of family photographs for their benefit,
pointing out like loving relatives, "There you were at twelve years of
age, or here at age fourteen." By doing so, we were helping them
reestablish a sense of continuity which had been doubly disrupted, both
by their own adolescence and by the external changes within their
family.

## Anger

Karen said, "Mom and I hassle. My mom tries to get me to say criticizing things about my dad and I don't want to. So I yell at her and then
the fighting starts."

Anger was a common response, congenial with the age and temperament of many of these youngsters. Many scolded their parents, accusing
them of behaving childishly or immorally, and pointing out that the
divorce represented the adult's unwillingness or incapacity to address
marital problems with the maturity appropriate to their years. Occasionally they became physically violent. One well-bred fifteen-year-old
girl, while screaming at her mother to withdraw the divorce filing, put
her fist through the wall in the hallway of their elegant home. Sometimes
the youngster's anger was directed at the parent's lover and led to real
mischief.

The anger of these adolescents had many intertwined roots. Some of
the anger was age-related, given a new form, another voice, and new
permission for expression. Furthermore, it was highly useful in camou-
flaging their vulnerability and their sense of powerlessness. Tantrums
and threats undoubtedly served to shut out grief from the consciousness
of these youngsters, and were more congenial to their age and their pride
than grief.

The anger also served to express their resentment at one or the other
parent for presuming to give their own wishes and needs priority over
the needs of their adolescent children. We found it interesting that, although a few youngsters understood very well the serious considerations
behind their parents' decision to divorce, many of them, although intelligent and well informed, were still angry at their parents and considered
them selfish and insensitive for seeking divorce at this time.

## Perceptions in Flux

Changes in the relationships went hand in hand with rapid, often unpredictable, changes in the adolescent's view of each parent. It was not

uncommon for a parent to be newly perceived as vulnerable, distressed, or dependent. Nor was it uncommon, by contrast, for an adult to be newly perceived as strong and invincible. Moral judgments often attached to these perceptions. A previously admired parent could suddenly fall from grace in the eyes of the youngster or be catapulted into a very admired, even noble position. Typically, most young people were unaware of the changes in their own perspective.

The divorce often pressed the adolescent to separate out each parent as an individual and to regard them separately. Whereas the adolescent had earlier tended to think of his or her own interests as counterposed to theirs and to regard the parents as a unit, the youngster's perceptions now had room for several separate slots, and their differences no longer automatically divided along generational lines.

Especially in seeking to understand the divorce-related events of the family, each parent was assigned his or her place separately as the young person bent every effort towards understanding what had led to the divorce. And even where responsibility was given to both parents, the adolescent usually attempted to sort out the particular contribution of each adult and understand the individual's role in the interaction. Because of adolescent predilection to view issues in dichotomies and extremes, it was common for the youngster who perceived some flaw or frailty in one parent to deidealize that parent and to regard him or her as sinful, cruel, or self-seeking, and the other parent as aggrieved, mistreated, or even martyred.

### Loyalty Conflicts

In many of the divorcing families, one or both parents turned to their adolescent youngsters for support in their marital and postmarital struggles. More than half of the youngsters were profoundly conflicted by issues of allegiance and loyalty. These demands of the parents on the youngster frequently led to despair, depression, and guilt. Some of the youngsters angrily protested the role they felt was being forced on them.

Betty, age fourteen, began to sob, "I am in the middle. It is my struggle. I am loyal to my father and I love my mother. I want to help my mother and I know she needs it."

Unlike their younger brothers and sisters, whose alignments tended to be longer lasting, most of the adolescents who took the side of one parent or the other were likely to disengage from the battle by the end of the first year. Nevertheless, the struggle at its height was often bitter and long remembered. One not infrequent result of being embroiled in the battle between two parents was a pulling away from both, sometimes in scorn but sometimes with compassion and a sad acceptance of the parents' continued unhappiness and inability to resolve their differences.

*Greater Maturity and Moral Growth*

The emotional and intellectual growth that was catalyzed by the family crisis was impressive and sometimes moving. The youngsters of this age soberly considered their parents' experiences and drew thoughtful conclusions for their own futures. They were concerned with finding ways to avoid the mistakes their parents had made. How to make better and more informed choices in regard to lovers or marital partners was only one of many serious preoccupations: Many attempted thoughtfully to learn from their parents' failures how to become better, more mature adults, how to find appropriate ways to harmonize the needs of the individual and the needs of the family, and how to reconcile the conflicting needs and interests of family members who elect to remain together.

Sally, age sixteen, said thoughtfully, "I won't marry young because I want to develop my interests and my skills first. Love and respect are necessary, but companionship is the most important thing in a marriage. The trouble with my parents was that they didn't respect each other at all. Their only common interest was us kids."

Personal morality became a central issue for youngsters who felt pressed to assign blame and responsibility for the marital failure. Morality for these young people was not an abstract issue. Their disappointment in their parents' failure to behave in accord with their standards of proper conduct led them to worry about issues of right and wrong in general. Yet their purpose was serious and mature as they sought to determine standards to guide their own behavior in the present and the future. Their conclusions reflected ethical commitments which were sometimes very moving.

Mary, age fourteen, said that her code of conduct calls for more candor among people and also more kindness. All her life there has been a "Let's not talk about it" policy in her family. She found this burdensome and blamed her parents for the marital failure. She doubted that they had tried sufficiently and she suspected a lack of kindness to each other.

Some youngsters openly rejected the examples set by parents, which they considered deplorable, and attempted directly to substitute their own standards of conduct.

Valerie, age thirteen, volunteered, "Even though my mom and dad are dishonest and I used to be, I suddenly stopped lying. I don't know why, I just stopped lying last year. I decided that I didn't want to be like them and that I would tell the truth." She added that she had thought a lot about her parents recently cheating on each other (referring to extramarital sexual affairs), "And I think it's terrible!"

### More Realistic View of Money

Concern about money was a frequent response of these youngsters that was not entirely anchored in the reality of family economics. Because money was one of the most common battlegrounds between divorcing parents, many of these youngsters became "moneywise" somewhat prematurely. Most of their anxiety about finances focused on their future needs. Some youngsters were sure that neither parent would finance their college education, despite the obvious fact that sufficient funds were available. Further, they were disinclined to settle the matter by discussing this with the parents separately for fear of starting new arguments and bitterness between them. Other adolescents were told by their mothers that no money would be available at that time, and that their fathers were insisting that college support was part of the final settlement given to the mother.

Gradually, even those adolescents who had been accustomed to affluence adopted a more realistic stance toward the availability of money and tended to be less demanding. In general, the divorce appeared to create a more mature attitude toward financial matters in the long range, despite their initial anger and anxiety about being deprived.

### Changed Participation Within the Family

The recognition of the parents' unhappiness and need for help catalyzed increased maturity in approximately one-third of these youngsters. These boys and girls, as we have described elsewhere in these pages, moved quickly into protective and helpful roles and took on the sharing of household responsibility and care of young children with competence, sensitivity, and pride. Parents were able to depend on these youngsters for companionship, for advice, for sharing of major decisions, and for their very real help.

At the other end of the spectrum, an equal number of youngsters responded by attempting to increase their distance from the family crisis and their parents. These youngsters entered actively into a variety of activities which kept them away from home. Some took advantage of the diminished supervision. Perhaps stimulated by the divorce, they became quickly involved in a very hectic social life which included increased sexual activity. The accelerated social activity or staying away from home was especially threatening to parents who had been apprehensive initially about the acting out of their adolescent children pursuant to the divorce, and whose apprehensiveness may have increased by virtue of their own new found sexual freedom and temptations.

Some of the young people who kept their distance were those who had, in the main, already led emotionally and socially detached lives and were ready for independence. These youngsters had already set their own course.

## Strategic Withdrawal

A small group of adolescents held steadfastly to detachment and distance verging on aloofness at the time of the separation and immediately thereafter, although their lives had not been detached from their families earlier. Their "cool" manner was a source of some initial concern to us, the question being whether the central developmental impact of the divorce would be an increase in self-interest verging on selfishness and a diminution in empathic response. We were therefore much interested to find that these particular youngsters measured up well indeed at the end of the first year, not only in terms of their having matured considerably during the intervening year, but also in terms of a now greater capacity for empathy, and a willingness to help within the household.

Ann, who had been spending most of her time out of the home at the time of the separation, seemed to have mellowed considerably. She was less defensive and less angry. Whereas earlier she had said, "I don't care about them," in relation to her parents, she now expressed her concern about her father's problems. When reminded of her statements of the year before, and her fighting with her sisters and strong criticisms of her family, Ann laughed freely and said, "Was I like that—wow, I really was a brat then!"

We understand these youngsters' behavior at the time of the separation as a strategic withdrawal that helped them maintain their intactness and separation from parental fighting, and the crisis at that time. Creating distance from the parents at the height of the struggle saved these youngsters from overwhelming anguish, humiliation, and emotional depletion, and enabled them at a later date—at a time appropriate to their own time table and when the external turmoil had subsided somewhat—to be supportive, empathic, and sensitive to needy parents. Thus their withdrawal served to maintain the integrity of their development. Nor is there any reason to assume that such capacities for compassion and protectiveness will not endure into adulthood. These observations add evidence on the usefulness of defensive withdrawal and denial in the normal development of children and adolescents.

## Failure to Cope

Although many youngsters rose to the challenge and moved more quickly into psychological independence and maturity, and some had concurred in the parental decision to divorce and welcomed relief from conflict-ridden families, others responded to the greater pressure by hanging back and turning toward childhood or toward a pseudoadolescent adjustment.

TEMPORARY INTERFERENCE WITH ENTRY INTO ADOLESCENCE. Temporary regressions were not uncommon. The forms of regressive behavior were various and included turning to much younger children as playmates for a period of several months and withdrawal from age-appropriate activities at school, spending increasing amounts of time at home, either alone or in the company of one or the other parent. Where the retreat toward more childish relationships and behavior was temporary, the effect on development was minimal, although parents were sometimes alarmed by temporary disruptions in school attendance and slipping grades. And, of course, diminished school achievement, even if temporary, was more serious in the higher grades, where failing grades could adversely affect admission to college.

Helen, who was thirteen years old when her parents separated, had a close relationship with her father, who had held her on his lap until she was eleven years old. He was a violent and abusive man to his wife and two sons, but never to his daughter. After the mother filed for divorce, the father refused to leave the house and returned nightly in a towering rage. When the divorce was granted, he disappeared for a period of time, although he continued to send child support regularly.

Helen was apprehensive, depressed, and inarticulate when she was first seen. Her sadness, her sense of loss, her worry about her father, her forlorn hope that he still loved her despite his disappearance, and her tattered self-esteem emerged gradually, but without bringing relief or a diminution of her depression. In the three months following the mother's decision to file for divorce Helen gained twenty pounds. During this period she dropped her relationships with her friends at school and began to engage in doll play with younger children in her neighborhood. Her regression lasted approximately a year, after which she gradually began to regain age-appropriate performance at school and to resume her friendships with youngsters within her age group. Although she was still somewhat subdued and stolid in her responses, she seemed to have moved back into age-appropriate adolescent development. Her recovery had coincided with the mother's remarriage and Helen's good relationship with her stepfather.

PROLONGED INTERFERENCE WITH ENTRY INTO ADOLESCENCE. Regressions were more likely to become consolidated when one parent relied heavily on the adolescent child and consciously or unconsciously encouraged the son or daughter to give up customary activities and interests in order to devote increasing amounts of time, energy, and affection to the care of the parent. This kind of intense emotional dependence of the adult on the youngster is not at all the same thing as cooperation between parent and adolescent. The latter was usually temporary, promoted maturity, and was undertaken to help the troubled parent to regain his or her customary ability to function. The regression detrimental to the adolescent was that which returned parent and child to an earlier and more infantile attachment, to a sense of exclusiveness and a shutting out of other relationships. Whether regressions of this kind were transient or became more permanent depended in large measure on the vulnerability of the adolescent at the time of the divorce and the psychological disturbance in the parent. The capacity of the parent to refrain from actively pulling the youngster into his or her emotional orbit was critical to the duration of the youngster's response.

Tom, at age fourteen, was one of several boys who in their efforts to rescue the custodial mother from a chronic depression became enmeshed in a gratifying relationship from which they could not extricate themselves. Immediately following the father's departure from the household, Tom began to assume the role of a protective adult in his mother's troubled life. Soon he began to check on her social activities, to monitor her telephone calls, to sit in his father's place at the dinner table, and, on occasion, to lie down on the sofa beside her to comfort her. Gradually he became increasingly preoccupied with his mother's mental and physical health. He was jealous of her other relationships, and his worry about her reached phobic proportions as he began to stay up at night to await her return. At the same time, his attachments to his friends and his interest in his school activities lessened.

We were very concerned about Tom and other youngsters like him who, in their wish to rescue a troubled parent, found that their wishes exceeded their capacities and drained needed energies away from developmentally appropriate tasks.

REGRESSION FOLLOWING LOSS OF EXTERNAL VALUES AND CONTROLS. The sudden discovery of a parent's infidelity could trigger severe regression. Adolescents, as we have seen, felt betrayed by the parent's "immoral" conduct. Needing the external presence of the parent, often the father, to reinforce and organize still insufficiently consolidated conscience and control, these youngsters sometimes became overwhelmed with anxiety in the face of their own heightened sexual and aggressive impulses, and in the absence of the familiar external limits. The response of these young people was sometimes dramatic, and the changed behavior included delinquent acting out, flight, and acute depression.

Priscilla accidentally discovered that her father was having a sexual liaison with a young woman before this information was known to her mother. The discovery caused her intense anguish. "I began to feel a lot of anxiety. Should I tell my mom? Should I have a talk with my dad?" She concluded that her father had betrayed *her* as well as his own value system. "It was rare that you could go to my dad with any kind of a problem and not have him say, 'You have to stick with it.' This time my father was ducking away from the philosophy that he had taught me. It meant to me that maybe my point of view was wrong, since my dad was throwing it away." Priscilla developed somatic symptoms, including sweating, dizzy spells, sleeplessness, and fear of being alone. Eventually she became acutely depressed, suicidal, and required brief hospitalization. Central to her breakdown was her statement, "The beliefs which gave me the ability to deal effectively with life were blown apart for me by my dad's behavior. I felt like I was taking a leaking boat, namely me, into the storm."

PSEUDOADOLESCENT BEHAVIOR. The incidence of sexual acting out increased following the parental separation. This behavior, although sometimes transient, had the potential for an enduringly grave effect on the youngster's life since it sometimes led to dropping out of school and other such major decisions which would be difficult to reverse. We had noted that the general weakening of the family structure burdened many youngsters because it imposed on them the responsibilities for controls on their own behavior for which they were not ready.

The relative absence or diminution of parental injunctions, the increased visibility of the parents' sexual behavior, and the greater anger within the family led to a rise in sexual activity, especially among the girls, which had no counterpart in inner growth of conscience or greater ego controls. One danger specific to adolescents is entry into heterosexual activity prematurely, before having acquired the conscience and capacity for love and intimacy as preconditions for truly loving heterosexual relationships. To the extent that the sexual activity occurred under the dominance of the tie to the parents, or as an extension of the parents' conscious or unconscious needs or impulses, or primarily as reactive to the behavior of the parents, then the adolescent can be said to be living out a pseudoadolescence, rather than a true, emancipating, adolescent experience.

Jean began her sexual activity at age fourteen, coincident with her discovery of her father's extramarital affair. She was verbally abusive of her father, loudly castigating him as an adulterer, and described her fantasies about his sexual performance in obscene language. These fantasies regarding the father's sexual activities were shared at length and in detail with the mother. Together Jean and her mother elaborated complex and sometimes bizarre strategies for punishing the father and his lover. The judgment of both mother and daughter seemed clearly impaired as they plotted revenge and shared erotic fantasies about the father's sexual activities.

Jean continued on a course of sexual involvement with a succession of lovers in the year that followed the divorce. Her primary interest at school at the time of the separation seemed to be flirting with her male teachers. She was aimless, not motivated to develop plans for her own future, preoccupied with anger at her father and with her own sexual activities. Shortly thereafter, she became involved in drinking and drug abuse—in short, a severely disturbed youngster urgently in need of psychotherapeutic intervention.

## Summing Up

Adolescents who were already in psychological difficulty at the time of divorce were naturally severely burdened by the rupture at this vulnerable stage in their lives. Although they sometimes affected to view the parental conflict with boredom, they were left without role models at a critical stage in their development, yet were driven by their wish to achieve relief from the conflict and unhappiness at home, and by the need to find gratification somewhere and somehow. But they lacked the inner integration necessary to successfully face the complex and exacting demands of adolescence.

On the other hand, some youngsters increased in maturity and independence through their need to take greater responsibility, not only for themselves but also, at least temporarily, for their troubled parents. Some adolescents who appeared to do well were those who from the outset had been able to maintain some distance from the parental crisis, and whose parents had permitted them to do so without intruding on them. Many of these youngsters developed a remarkable capacity to assess their parents realistically at the same time as they showed them compassionate concern. This, combined with independence of spirit, appeared to augur well for their future.

# PART 2

## PARENTS AND CHILDREN AFTER SEPARATION

# Chapter 5

# Changes in Parent-Child Relationships

## The Early Changes in Parent-Child Relationships

One major legacy of divorce is discontinuity in many parent-child relationships, in which the changes of separation, divorce, and its extended aftermath are reflected in unexpected and far-reaching alternations in the child's relationship with both parents. As the family breaks apart, each parent-child relationship essentially swings free of the structure that has held it in place. The chain of reactions so abruptly set off may reverberate for several years and lead to new relationships greatly at variance with those that obtained when the family was together—relationships, indeed, that have no real counterpart in the intact family. These include the relationships based on visiting, the hostile alignment of child and one parent against the other parent, and the various combinations of custody.

In the course of time some relationships slowly but markedly improved. This was true of cases where parents were strengthened and made more hopeful by the divorce, and were thus freed to become more sensitive and nurturant toward their children. The new mastery of the parental role took time and practice and was often hard won.

The unfamiliar structure of the postdivorce family naturally contributed to the anxiety of both parents and children at this time. Parents were often aware of the changes taking place in their relationships with their children and were acutely troubled by the absence of role models for a divorced family. They brought lists of questions to their meetings with us that reflected their doubts about roles and ground rules in the new family structure. In the main their questions were practical ones: how to tell the children about the divorce—how much of the marital unhappiness to explain and in what detail; how to introduce new and/or changing lovers; how to control rebellious children; and how to deal with children who continued to be critical of the divorce decision.

The transition being described here extended from several months to several years, but the changed attitudes which emerged during this transition lasted for various lengths of time. Sometimes the children temporarily took on new roles, and sometimes the relationships of the transitional period became consolidated and endured for many years. The introduction of new participants, such as lovers, stepparents and stepsiblings, naturally contributed to the shifting pattern of relationships of the postseparation period. The overall effect on the children of these rapidly changing patterns was similarly varied, but certain broad caterogies emerged. Sometimes, as we have said, the new relationships catalyzed intellectual and emotional growth in the child, giving them greater capacity for compassionate responses to sorrowful parents. Sometimes the children were pushed ahead by their greater closeness to agitated parents into a variety of pseudomature, sexually precocious behavior which affected their development adversely. Some children were captured by depression and the anger of the parent and lost ground. Others committed themselves to a futile effort to rescue a psychologically ill parent or were unable to break out of the orbit of a vengeful or depressed parent.

## Changed Parental Perceptions

How the parents saw their children during this postseparation period was often impossible to separate from their overriding need to justify their own role in the divorce. We soon discovered, as we have indicated, that the parent who was eager to dissolve the marriage tended to perceive the child to be adjusting well and, conversely, that the parent who opposed the divorce was likely to regard the same child as sorely distressed or even psychologically impaired. Not surprisingly, we found that neither view was reliable.

Parents' perceptions of their different children could also reflect the continuing angers of the marital disruption. Occasionally, one child in the family was thought to bear a real (or fantasied) physical or characterological resemblance to the other partner. Whereas in a happy family such resemblance might earn the child special favor, at this time the real or fantasied resemblance was, for some of these children, a severe handicap. Such a child was sometimes singled out as the representative of the departed parent and made into a scapegoat. Ironically, the continuing presence of the victimized child as representative of the other parent also served as an ever-present reminder of the departed spouse and in this way symbolically reversed the departure. Also, as often happens with such complex interactions, the accusation or perception in time became a self-fulfilling prophecy. Such children not only wondered intensely about their shared identity with the vilified parent but sometimes took on that parent's behaviors as well.

The irrational and unresolved anger led one parent to perceive all children of the opposite sex as representative of the rejected spouse. There is evidence in our findings that many mothers were more responsive to their daughters than to their sons, and that there was a significant preference for their daughters in their parenting at this time. Similarly, fathers sometimes visited their sons and ignored their daughters. Several fathers expressed their disdain for all women when the children visited them, and their little girls cried all the way home after each visit.

A related and more exaggerated change in perception was the parent's sudden marking off of the children as "his" or "hers," as if one were setting up competing teams. Children were treated differently in accord with these differing, relatively new perceptions. The preferred child was treated well; the rejected child, shabbily. The children whose attachments to the parents did not reflect these preferences or choices were bewildered. Often they all suffered intensely—those who were elected felt guilty, those who were rejected were acutely unhappy.

Sam told us with evident distress that his father had invited him and not his sister to live with him. He added that his father had sent him a Christmas card which he had inscribed "With all my love," but had only sent his sister a formal card. "I guess it made her feel pretty bad," said the boy sadly.

Although such divisions and the choice of a favorite child by one or both parents also occurs in the intact family, where it also causes a great deal of distress, in that setting at least the parent's attitude rarely changes suddenly and the children have a long-standing familiarity with the parental preferences. We were surprised, however, to observe how little anxiety divorcing parents sometimes experienced in abruptly and openly rejecting a child who was so obviously grieved at that rejection by the parent he or she loved dearly. A variation of this was thoughtlessness and insensitivity for their own children, and often open preference for children of the new lover or the new marriage in the very same age group. One father told his eight-year-old boy that his stepson had a beautiful, lean, and graceful dog as compared with his own son's funny look-ing dog which had short and stubby legs. The son was heartbroken at his father's cruel observation. It may be that the usual structure of the intact family serves in most instances to hold the hostility of a parent to a child in careful check and to preserve the facade of harmony under pretense that all children are equally valued by both parents. As the family structure breaks apart, these hostile feelings toward one child may move into the open and no longer be inhibited. Or it may be that these children were newly rejected under the impact of the divorcing process.

The most unusual disturbance in the parental perception of children at separation were those instances in which the distressed parent addressed the child, even the very young child, as if he or she were adult and able to comprehend the complex confessions which the parents made. Several such children were brought into the parental bedroom at the separation to provide the lonely parent with companionship. These parents, who were usually socially isolated and in profound psychological turmoil, maintained stoutly that their young children were fully able to under-stand them and endowed with unusual capacity to provide wise counsel. Children who were cast in this role sometimes became profoundly wor-ried about issues they hardly understood—financial worries particularly, which led some young children to devise elaborate fantasy plans for making contributions to the family income.

Mrs. N. extolled the wisdom of a seven-year-old son, explaining that she treated him as an equal and that since the separation they discussed everything together. When asked whether the child ever had difficulty understanding the issues which the mother discussed, she responded, "He understands everything that I say." She offered as an example that the child had recently advised her to remarry.

The confusion that some parents experienced at this time, in their per-ceptions of themselves and in distinguishing their own needs from those of their children, was of considerable concern and also contributed to the diminished care these children received.

Mrs. A. assured us that her young son who was clearly grieving did not miss his father. She said, "He's the kind of person who doesn't get at-tached to people. Just like me."

## The Children's New Roles

Children acquired new emotional meanings for their parents within the divorced family. Whereas in an intact, loving marriage children represent the continuity and the expectation of a shared future, the mutual caring and responsibility, the love and sexual commitment of the parents to each other, these psychological meanings are destroyed by the divorce. Moreover, many of the adults in our study had had few emotionally significant relationships with other adults during the marriage. Therefore, at the collapse of the marriage, they turned to their children, who became new sources of support and love. At both younger and older ages, they were pressed into being advisors, practical helpers, buffers against loneliness and despair, replacements for other adults—in other words, parents for their own parents.

A major role conferred on children was that of bolstering the parent's sagging self-esteem. In this capacity children acted to ward off a threatened depression or even the psychological disintegration of a parent. The child's absence was feared because it was regarded as confirming the diminished importance, if not expendability, of the parent.

Mr. G. told us that he absolutely depended upon the physical presence of his eight-year-old daughter. "She's a mood elevator for me. I need her. Without her I go down!"

Children were also needed by parents to confirm the correctness of one or the other's behavior in the divorcing process, or to confirm their femininity, their masculinity, their attractiveness, or their youthfulness. Visiting fathers who treated their little girls as dates and took them to elegant restaurants during visits did so in part to reaffirm their own attractiveness, which had been threatened by the divorce. Mothers needed to hear from their children that they were young-looking and still sexually attractive. Fighting between parents for the child's loyalty and affection at the time of the divorce is often related to each parent's need for that child's presence to maintain self-esteem and to ward off self-criticism and depression. Litigation over custody thus may reflect the dependence of the adult on the child, and the adult's need to hold on to the child to maintain his or her psychic balance.

## Old and New Intimacies

Major changes occurred soon after the separation in parent-child relationships which had flourished in the unhappy marriage. Children who together with one parent had constituted a subgroup within the family, based on that parent's unhappiness in the marriage, suddenly found themselves displaced by a lover or other new-found interest, a discovery that often took them by surprise. While the parent felt happier and improved, the child suffered from a loss of the old intimacy, which compounded the stress of the divorcing process. For some children, the loss of the close relationship with the parent, which was sometimes part of the unhappy marriage for many years and had, in fact, made it bearable for both, was the more grievous one. Although such changes were ultimately advantageous to both parent and child, the child experienced the parent's new freedom to associate with adults as an unexpected, and very painful, rejection.

Bill had been particularly close to his mother prior to the parental separation, the partner in an intimate relationship which he and the mother had maintained for many years and from which the father and the other children had been excluded. The boy suffered with a chronic illness and mother and child spent many happy hours together, which also enabled the mother to maintain a close vigil. Although quiet and considered somewhat of a loner, the boy appeared relatively content, was doing well at school, and was not considered to be presenting any particular problems. Following the separation, his mother quickly found a lover whom she subsequently married. Her new companion had many active interests and hobbies that he expected her to share only with him, which she did gladly. The suddenly excluded boy was startled and dejected.

Sometimes the closeness between parent and child had reached pathological intensity. Such relationships were often brought to an abrupt end by the divorce, with little preparation for the change.

Mrs. K. and her oldest daughter, age ten, were inseparable during the wretched marriage. They slept in the same bed; they bathed together, and spent their leisure time together. The father worked at several demanding jobs and was rarely home. Following the divorce, the child's jealousy of her mother's new lover was intense. When the child turned to her father, she found that road blocked as well by her father's devotion to a girlfriend and by many years of noncommunication. Feeling cut off suddenly from both parents, the child was now lonely and depressed. She was characterized by her teacher as "a pathetic, pseudosophisticated girl, unable to concentrate, uninterested, and hardly learning."

The most unexpected changes in relationship patterns between parents and children, however, were those of the opposite kind, involving a parent's sudden discovery of affection for a child whose presence he had taken for granted, or minimally acknowledged, or even seemingly resented, during the years of marriage. The parent's new attitude toward the child was sometimes triggered by the shock of the impending loss of a relationship which had been insufficiently valued. As the parent experienced the sorrow of the impending loss, this sometimes resulted in the sobering realization of a long-standing, but unspoken and hardly expressed, love for the child.

Other relationships which changed radically with the separation were those where a more limited relationship was more congruent with the parents' emotional needs. This seemed to be especially the case with fathers of preschool children. Our findings are that 40 percent of the preschool children had improved relationships with their fathers following the marital disruption. Fathers who had barely acknowledged their preschool children, who during long weekends and evenings had characteristically hidden behind newspapers or retreated to television programs, felt considerable relief within the contraints of this new, more limited relationship. They were less anxious and less fearful of being overwhelmed by the demands of noisy, lively children within the new structure, which clearly demarcated and limited the interaction. These men paradoxically showed greater warmth and interest for their children than they had been able to express during the marriage.

## Increased Anxiety about Sex

Among the parents who sought our advice, it soon became clear to us that their requests for advice reflected not only their unfamiliarity with the new roles of the postdivorce family but also a feeling that they had lost inner balance and a sense of control over their emotional lives. They experienced a sudden absence of safeguards against sexual temptation and a loss of the external constraints against engaging in sexual behavior.

This preoccupation with sex on the part of the adults can spill into the parent-child relationship. The phenomenon of fluid boundaries between the psychological repercussions within the parent and the inappropriate involvement of the children occurs frequently at the time of divorce. So it is that sexual worries about the children reach new prominence at this time, reflecting this parental preoccupation with sexuality. Mothers, without discernible evidence for it, began to express anxiety about actual or potential sexual promiscuity in their teenage daughters. Sometimes concerns about the daughters' sexuality increased directly after some sexual encounter of the mother's which had left her feeling anxious.

Some parents had sexual fantasies about their children's relationship with the opposite parent. Mothers, particularly, became concerned with the child's continued contact with the father, which the mother suddenly perceived (without visible or new evidence of any kind) as dangerously seductive. Incest fantasies projected onto the divorcing partner were not uncommonly shared with the child. Children were asked, "Where did you sleep? Was daddy naked? Did you undress? What did you do about going through his bedroom when you had to go to the bathroom at night?" Such parental admonitions served to stimulate the children to regard the other parent as a sexual object. A few mothers instructed their children to search through the father's house for evidence of a sexual partner. Fathers made pointed inquiries about the sexual activity of the mother. These instructions and inquiries, and the fantasies which prompted them, undoubtedly contributed to a greater eroticizing of relationships between parent and child, which further reinforced the initial anxieties.

## Intensified Sexual Activity

The changed sexual behavior of the parents exercised an influence on their school-age and adolescent children, but especially the seven-through eleven-year-olds. Following the separation, a significant number of both mothers and fathers entered into an extended period of intense sexual activity. The frenetic patterning of this sexual behavior appeared as a divorce-specific response among adults whose behavior had so often been constrained and discreet during the marriage. Often the children found this new behavior striking and dismaying. Lovers appeared in rapid succession, sometimes during a very compressed time period. The sexual encounters often occurred at home with the full knowledge of the children.

Some of the children reacted with intense, even overwhelming excitement and jealousy. These youngsters were preoccupied with sexual thoughts and fantasies. They were sometimes privy to their parents' changing preferences and, not infrequently, a child's advice was solicited, or was sometimes offered unsolicited. The advisory role and the role of observer alternated with the role of providing comfort to the parent during the acute, sometimes suicidal, depression which followed the lover's departure or the parent's decision to terminate the affair. Several girls were propelled into a precocious adolescence. They acquired a veneer of sophistication, and they showed intense eagerness to grow up and become just as sexually active as soon as possible. Sometimes they combined this precocity with a fine disdain for adults who seemed to them to have so little control of impulses and to be so vulnerable to hurt. Some of the girls felt alienated from their peer group and began to seek out older companions.

Ann was ten years old when her parents separated. Her mother entered into an exciting social life in which she had numerous affairs with men both younger and older than she was. The father also soon acquired a comparable number of lady friends. Ann was acutely aware of her mother's and father's sexual activity and was preoccupied with fantasies and thoughts about sex. She began to dress seductively, to flirt with men twice her age, and she talked compulsively about her sexual fantasies. She said, "My mom is worried that a lot of people will want to have sex with me, but nothing can come of it. As long as they don't break that bubble. I could like having sex with Jim, or John, or Jack," she said, naming a long list of people. She reflected that she wished her mother would not sleep around so much. She said, "Once I asked my mom what single people do for sex and my mom answered, 'They do what they can.'"

Ann volunteered that she's worried about her dad because he has ten or fifteen girlfriends and about her mom because she has five boyfriends. She said that she was looking at some *Playboy* magazines, "It makes me almost shiver. It makes me feel like my tongue is going down into my stomach."

Her teacher reported, "Ann is carrying too heavy an emotional load and is escaping into fantasy. She really can't handle reality right now. She's slipped tremendously."

# Chapter 6

# The Child and the Custodial Parent

Mrs. C. described her predicament a few months after she and her husband of eight years separated: "I feel like I'm treading water in a tidal wave."

For the custodial parent and the child the immediate postseparation year is a critical time. Their relationship is highly charged with the aggravated tension of the divorcing period. The newly diminished family boundaries are highly visible. Whether they huddle closer together or pull away from each other, the members of the new family unit have an anxious awareness of each other because each has just experienced the precariousness of human ties. They share in a greater vulnerability and are recurrently haunted by the same ghosts: the ghost of the failed marriage and the ghost of the departed parent.

The extraordinary stresses of these early beginnings of a postdivorce family are not fully anticipated by parents, however, and come as a surprise to most precisely when, ready for it or not, the family must sort out and quickly arrange such matters as work, finance, household routine and child-care arrangements, distribution of household tasks, discipline, allocation of responsibility, and visiting arrangements. Larger issues are also being settled at this time, having to do with attitudes toward each other, toward other new persons in the household, and toward the departed parent. There are questions of how and where the "new" family will live, of adjusting to a lower socioeconomic status, of how to establish standards for personal conduct and morality. They are settled either by drifting or by conscious decision; either way, the custodial parent and the child are moving faster than they are really able to establish the new family unit.

The reverberations of the conflicts and pressures within the parent-child relationship during this crisis were profound and greatly strained the custodial parent's capacity to parent. One immediate consequence was that two-thirds of mother-child relationships deteriorated from the level they had attained within the predivorce family. These worsened relationships reflected lessened cooperation, increased anger (including more open fighting), less trust between child and parent, and greater tension in daily living together. The disorder in the home rose precipitously.

Mrs. S. told us tartly, "If I had my way, I'd pick up only my youngest child and keep on walking and never look back." Women remarked bitterly, "Who wants a woman with three children?" Mrs. G. said, "I feel like a twelve-year-old raising an eight-year-old."

At the height of the crisis the attitudes of many women varied significantly with the age and sex of their children. Young children, especially preschool children, were the chief beneficiaries of their mother's concern, and when there was little attention to go around they got almost all of it. Older children, that is children eight years old or older, often felt the mothering had been almost entirely withdrawn following the parental separation. Children got their own meals, followed their own routines, and sometimes, when they were naughty, punished themselves and put themselves to bed without supper.

Girls were generally treated with greater consideration by their mothers than boys. They had been more protected from witnessing the continuing predivorce parental quarrels, and were being dealt with with somewhat greater sensitivity and affection. Our own observations regarding the difference between the mothers' respective attitudes toward their sons and their daughters were not as apparent to the children as was the preferential treatment meted out to younger children, which was clearly visible. Nevertheless, girls at all ages were parented more considerately by mothers than were their brothers. The one exception to this was the parenting of little boys in the young schoolage group. The open grief of the five- to seven-year-old boys, and their intense yearning for their fathers, may have brought their distress more forcibly to the mother's attention and led to greater maternal solicitude on their behalf.

Sometimes mothers who were not distressed appeared overwhelmingly powerful to their young children, especially when divorce was conceptualized as a fight between two parents in which the one parent had been the victor and, in accord with the rules of the war, had evicted the loser from the disputed turf. Frances, at age five, cheerfully announced, "My mother decided to divorce and threw my daddy out." Little girls who identified with these competent, well-functioning mothers who had taken the initiative in seeking the divorce generally found the separation period considerably less stressful than their brothers.

## Working Mothers and Children

Most of the custodial parents in our study as throughout the country were women, and most of these women were in full-time employment or seeking employment after the separation. As noted, they found the colliding demands of home, work, and children very stressful. While not impossible, their schedules required competence and organizational skill. The mothers also needed a good enough job, a sense of inner balance and humor, and children who could cope with multiple changes in their schedule without undue distress or regression. Only a few women and a few children possessed these capacities or skills in full enough measure at the time of the separation. As a consequence, most experienced a pervasive feeling of high tension and hectic pressure, which became a major component of their relationships.

Mrs. D., who divorced her husband of eight years, reported that she had found working even part time very difficult. She worried about her seven-year-old daughter while she was at work. Yet, she resented having to take off from her job in order to take the child to necessary medical or dental appointments. She explained that she became very upset when the house was in disorder, that she flew into a blind rage, screamed at her daughter, and hit her. She felt very bad about her behavior and often apologized to the child. It was profoundly upsetting to her to think that Dana, her daughter, was afraid of her. Yet, she confessed, she hit the child repeatedly and felt that she could not control herself. She felt that she had failed as a mother, as a woman, and as a person.

Mr. A., a custodial father with young children, reported similar difficulties. He complained of high tension, fatigue, depression, somatic symptoms including headaches, and difficulties in managing. He felt overextended and overworked and intensely dependent on the children. Mr. A. complained that he was unable to sleep on weekends when the children were away visiting with a relative. "I guess I miss their noise," he said.

## Custodial Parents Who Stayed Home

Women who did not work were also stressed, although in different ways. A relatively large number, as we have noted, were agitated or depressed by the divorce and remained at home because they could not yet venture into the marketplace. Others who were financially able to stay home reported a rising sense of disorder and tension, even panic, which seemed to reflect their psychological distress rather than the demands of a hectic schedule.

Mrs. T. presented herself as intensely worried about everything in her life but especially, she said, about the prospect of a summer vacation coming up with no scheduled activities for her children. She explained that she had recently read several books on divorce and children, and had taken a course in parenting which she was thinking of repeating. She conveyed a pathetic, almost despairing, quality. It was as if she had throughout her life tried to do everything possible "that was right." She had read Gesell and Spock. She had consulted her pediatrician regularly and tried in every conceivable way to be a good mother and wife. Ironically, she was now facing the breakup of her marriage and the smashing of her plans to provide the ideal home in which serenity and grace would be dominant life values. Her formerly ordered world was in a shambles, and she had no idea how to begin to put it back together again. Smilingly, she insisted that she was mainly worried about the forthcoming summer and her lack of program and structure for the children. Could we help her?, she implored.

## New Demands of the Parenting Role

Setting appropriate routines and formulating rules for the new family unit were among the more difficult tasks for women newly cast as head of the family. One-half of the mothers found the role of disciplinarian extremely difficult to assume. We were surprised to learn that the father had played the dominant role in setting standards and enforcing discipline in the majority of these divorcing homes. Older boys, especially, had been considered the special responsibility of the father, but in many homes fathers shared disciplinary responsibility for the younger children as well. Therefore, for many children the marital separation signified the departure of the adult who enforced discipline. The children were reluctant to accord the same prerogatives to the custodial parent and reinforced her feelings of ineptitude by their open flouting of her authority.

Inexperience, however, was only part of the problem these mothers confronted. A high number were unable to say no to demanding children or enforce unwelcome rules for fear the children would reject them in favor of the other parent, or the other parent's lover, or the new step-parent. The women's difficulties in setting restrictions were compounded by their inner psychological conflicts, by guilt at having initiated the divorce, by lowered self-esteem during the conflicts of the divorcing period, and by fear of the children's anger. Fearing rejection, women tried to please and placate and, fearing anger, they avoided restrictions. One consequence was disorder in many households during the transition period.

Unfortunately, the disorder tended to worsen. As the fatigued parent felt increasingly helpless, the anxious children raised their demands and the stridency of their voices. Not unexpectedly, the children soon found the center of the mother's vulnerability and took careful aim. They evoked her guilt by insisting they needed two parents in order to grow up properly. They provoked her jealousy by crying for their father when she scolded them and by unfavorably comparing her disciplinary mea-ures with his generosity. They punished her when she punished them by obstructing her halting efforts to establish a new social life.

Many women felt severely threatened by their children's rebelliousness and were reduced to tears, nagging, or screeching. Only gradually, as their fear of rejection by their children lessened, did they learn to stand firm and to assume the parental role and its prerogatives along with its responsibilities. Counseling was very helpful to mothers at this time and was very much appreciated, especially in connection with these issues of exercising controls and governing the household.

The difficulties which so many women experienced often had roots in the past relationship with the divorcing husband. Some had occupied a role more like that of an older sibling in the predivorce family and were newly emerging into their own psychological adulthood at the time of separation. In other families the marital relationship with the power-ful, abusive father had been silently reinstalled in the child's relationship with the custodial mother. It appeared that one or another child could become *pari passu*, the symbolic representative of the abusive parent within the context of the new family. Children cast in this role by family disruption and the psychological expectation of the distressed mother shrilly berated and harassed her. These youngsters, usually older children or adolescents, took on to an amazing degree the direction of their mother. They directed her activities, censured her behavior, su-pervised her clothes buying, criticized her hairdo, and altogether behaved like caricatures of jealous, domineering husbands. The child's conscious or unconscious identification with the departed father and the extraordinarily accurate rendition of the father's deprecating behavior towards the mother, was obvious to everyone except the victimized mother who felt helpless to deal with the child's newly aggressive behavior. Yet it was only when the mother was able to extricate herself from the victimization and assert her adulthood that she was able to help both herself and her agitated child.

Mrs. C. confessed that she was "at the end of my rope" with her ten-year-old daughter, Marian. She complained that she and the entire family were controlled by the child's tyranny. She felt badly because she had just begun to enjoy a limited social life, but had decided that she would have to discontinue even this small pleasure because her daughter made her feel so guilty and also humiliated her when her company arrived.

Marian, who was openly pressing for the reconciliation of the marriage, reminded her mother frequently that she and the other children needed *two* parents to grow up properly. Mrs. C. had begun, as a result, to waiver about the divorce. Yet each time she did so she vividly recalled how her husband had physically and verbally abused her for many years and gambled away their life savings. Finally one day, Mrs. C. stood her ground and explained firmly to Marian that she would on no account, regardless of the child's remonstrations, return to the wretched marriage. Marian screamed wildly for an hour, threatening to run away to live with her father, and then suddenly became very calm and began to cry softly and gently. "Mom," she said through her sobs, "I'm so unhappy." She confessed that she had felt honorbound to represent her absent father with in the new family context.

A few parents continued to be unable to take on the role of authority in the family, and enforcement of discipline was sometimes delegated to the oldest child. This new arrangement could also duplicate the pathology of the predivorce family and particularly the abusive behavior of the departed father. One eleven-year-old girl told us that when she misbehaved her mother instructed her eighteen-year-old brother to spank her. This solution was startling, because central to the mother's complaint against the father was his physical abuse of her and the children. Yet she had arranged for the spankings to continue via her delegation of authority to the oldest boy.

## Increased Dependence

Children and adolescents quickly became aware of their increased emotional and physical dependence on the parent, now that there only was one and, as we already noted, this realization was frightening to many. Younger and older children kept the mother under careful surveillance. They lacked the reassuring presence of a second adult, so the remaining relationship was experienced as more precious and more vulnerable.

Mothers, on their side, relied heavily on the youngsters who were willing and able to take a more active role in the household. Several of these young people worked hard and long, and their contribution was substantial. As mother and child joined together to deal with the problems of life, they were often brought closer together in ways that were at once helpful to the parent and promotive of growth in the child. They shared responsibility and helped each other, and grew to respect each other's contribution to their joint life. Mothers were especially appreciative of the help they received, and the young people were proud of their new importance to the custodial parent and the functioning of the family.

Mrs. S. was bewildered and disorganized following her husband's decision to disrupt their marriage of many years. Prior to the divorce her husband had undertaken full responsibility for the major decisions. The oldest girl, Cindy, age thirteen, had been rebellious. She had refused to abide by curfews or to keep her mother informed of her whereabouts over long weekends, and had contributed to the family tension. It was unexpected, therefore, that almost immediately following the divorce, Cindy drew closer to her mother and began to take very seriously her responsibility as helper, adviser, and even model for the younger children. Expressive of the cooperation between mother and daughter was the shared house-hunting which extended over a year. Mrs. S. informed the startled real estate agents that her young daughter was a full party to her decision-making, and therefore would necessarily accompany her every time she looked at a potential purchase. When the new house was finally purchased, Mrs. S. and her daughter together made all the decisions with regard to remodeling. Cindy was highly pleased with her responsibility within the family. Although much sought after by friends, she was circumspect in all her relationships, especially with young men, and carefully considered her social life in terms of its effect on the younger children. When she left for college she was worried about her mother and hoped that her mother would remarry in order to avoid the loneliness facing her when the younger children departed. Her mother's absolute trust was expressed by naming Cindy in her will as guardian of the children in the event of the mother's untimely death.

The mutual dependency of parent and child was a many-faceted relationship at this critical time, and certain negative aspects to the interaction also emerged. The parent's continued dependence upon the child, especially the young child, was rarely comfortable for the parent or for the child, and there were tensions built into the reversal of roles which occasionally erupted into angry outburst. Although the youngster's help was needed and welcomed, parents consciously or unconsciously also resented the child's competence alongside their own incompetence and felt humiliated by their dependence. Thus the parent-child relationship was newly infused with increased anger, as well as increased affection.

The younger children had varied reactions to the older brother or sister who helped take on the parent's responsibilities. Some of the latter acquitted themselves very well in the caretaking role and were appreciated and adored by their young charges. Fred assured us solemnly that he planned to marry his older sister when he grew up. Other children, however, felt cheated, angry, and deprived of their mother's care. Walter said of his ten-year-old sister, "She bugs me . . . she pretends to be my mom. You should have one mom and one sister, but all I have is a sister who thinks she's my mom and a zero mom."

## The Needy Parent and the Empathic Child

The emotional dependence of a parent on a child is not new although it is little remarked in our society. Most striking, however, was the empathic response which the custodial parent's crisis catalyzed in their children, especially in girls still approaching adolescence. Lonely, dejected mothers were cared for tenderly during this period by children who were able with great sensitivity to follow their moods and to respond with a maturity and tact well beyond their years. The reliance of the parents on these youngsters was profound. Children were helpful in stabilizing parent's moods and anchoring them to the here and now. They seemed intuitively and most remarkably aware of a parent's depression, and attempted within the limits of their understanding not to overtax the parent and to protect her from pressure. Custodial parents told us years later, "I would not have made it except for the children." The children sensed this; they understood that their presence was needed and appreciated, and they regarded their new importance with pride and satisfaction.

The development of empathy *in status nascendi* is evident in the remarks of Lee, at age ten, who with unusual insight described her capacity to understand her mother by putting herself in her mother's place. She said, "I know that my mother isn't ready for the divorce because I can put myself in her place. I can think just like I think my mother thinks. At first she cried a lot but now she doesn't think much about it. At first she wanted dad, but now I don't think so."

The maturity of Ruth, also age ten, impressed us when she said solemnly, "Mom will probably marry, but she's not ready. She just got a divorce and she wants to be settled. I think she has gone through a lot of trouble and sadness and needs more time."

These intuitive children, sensitive to the changing moods and needs of the emotionally distressed parent, also learned early to dissemble in order to protect what they understood to be the fragility of their parent's adjustment. They gauged kindly and accurately the amount of stress the unhappy parent could bear and they shaped their remarks and their behavior accordingly. When they considered it necessary they withheld information or they lied to protect the mother.

Sonya, age nine, told us, "My mom cried, she was so tired of being so strong for the children and she asked us to sleep with her." Sonya and her brother complied. She continued, "It made my mom feel better. Then we got up in the morning and made her breakfast and brought it to her in bed. Sometimes we just tell her, 'We're here, it's going to be alright'."

It is difficult to assess the ultimate effect of such parenting of the adult by the child without following the youngsters into adulthood. And it is also important to note that much of the intense dependence on young children was short-lived and did not outlast the first year and a half. It may be that the empathy and compassion roused by the emotional need of the parent helps to make the child a richer, more empathic person. It is also possible that the empathy that is catalyzed eventually becomes the basis for a life choice, characterized by a wish for service and a talent that has been honed in compassionate service to the mother.

A year later we asked Lee what she might like to do when she grew up. She responded, "You might laugh—a child psychiatrist. You're one, aren't you?" Lee went on to talk movingly of working some day with blind children, or mentally retarded children, or children who "could not speak." We could not help but be reminded of her mother's reliance on Lee's capacity to understand her communication without words.

## Role Reversal

It is important to distinguish the genuine cooperation between parent and child, including the kind of temporary intense dependence of a parent upon a child after separation, from the full dependence of a parent on a child in an enduring reversal of roles lasting over many years. Some of the circumstances in which the children were called upon for help were too demanding; the children were overtaxed by the parent's need and overwhelmed. Several custodial parents shared their suicidal preoccupations with children who were then overcome with worry and would remain sleepless unless and until the parent was safely at home in bed. A few children prematurely took full responsibility for the household and the depressed parent, and were unable to sustain their own development in the process.

Richard, age twelve, decided to live with his father in order to take care of him. The father had told the boy that he was considering suicide following the mother's decision to divorce him. Frantic with worry, the boy would not be dissuaded from his resolve to assume responsibility for the father and himself by setting up an apartment where they could live together. Unfortunately, he was too young to take care of himself and a parent. Although a gifted student, he dropped out of school and spent a restless and aimless adolescence, embroiled in a variety of minor delinquencies. He appeared to have been depleted by the responsibility which he had accepted prematurely, and by his own need for parenting which was unmet by the parent whose care he had assumed.

## Diminished Care of Younger Children

The youngest children had fewer options. The decreased physical and and emotional availability of the custodial parent during the transition period was in marked contrast with the special protectiveness which many mothers had extended to their youngest children during the years of the unhappy marriage. Several of these children experienced greater deprivation during the immediate postdivorce period than they had experienced during the unhappy marriage. Children who lacked older siblings to help the custodial parent with their care were especially exposed to decreased parenting at this critical time.

Jennifer, at age four, had impressed us with her playfulness and charm. She talked happily to the interviewer, offering teasing and affectionate comments about both parents. She played easily and spontaneously, constructing creative play scenes about animals who alternately competed and cooperated with each other. Her view of the world, which she revealed in play, fantasy, and conversation, was that it was an interesting and gratifying place. Following the separation, Jennifer's mother undertook a heavy schedule in which she attempted heroically to combine a career, a new social life, mothering, and household responsibilities. She had married shortly after graduation and entirely lacked the experience of managing a household by herself. During the marriage she had channeled all of her energies into caring for her young children and Jennifer's initial display of good adjustment reflected her mother's devoted care. The mother's new schedule resulted in a breakdown in the continuity of Jennifer's care, a succession of new and different babysitters, and decreased maternal attention.

Within the year, Jennifer's mood became subdued, her spontaneity decreased, her play was more constricted, and she seemed in many ways deteriorated from her previous condition. Her school teacher described her as "waif-like, a *sad* child who needs touching, a child dependent on one-to-one attention for learning, a child who has difficulty in making friends." When we talked with Jennifer's concerned mother, she admitted ruefully that she knew the child needed her attention but, much as she would like to, she simply could not organize herself sufficiently to provide what she realized the child needed.

## The Psychologically Disturbed Parent

Finally, at its most insidious, was the situation of divorce where the custodial parent lost clarity of her own ego boundaries and included the child or children within the orbit of her unhappiness and disorganization. Acute depression in the parent was difficult for the children of all ages, but the older children were able, if they had the inner resources, to distance themselves from the troubled parent. It was the youngest children who were most vulnerable to the parent's disturbance, especially when the parenting deteriorated markedly as well and the mother seemed unable to maintain a distinction between her own needs and feelings and those of the child.

Alex's mother, a young woman of foreign origin with no family in this country, responded to the separation from her husband with acute anxiety and resentment which soon evolved into an immobilizing depression. Her psychological difficulties were reinforced by her social isolation. Alex was three years old when his father left. Initially, he reacted to the separation with mild regression and increased irritability, but he was able to maintain his relationships and his developmental progress for a period of time.

Nearly eight months following his father's departure, Alex appeared severely depressed. He spent several hours daily rocking in his chair while listening to phonograph records left by the father. He continued to make repeated efforts to call his father on his toy telephone. His mother complained of his restlessness and his sleeplessness; often he did not get to sleep before midnight. He had been removed from nursery school and from other association with children his age by his severely depressed mother. She had also rejected our advice and had refused to explain the father's departure to the child, maintaining staunchly that the father was of no importance to the child since he had left him. The child and his mother appeared to be living together in a timeless, structureless household, in a twilight ambiance dominated by the mother's depression.

Sometimes the inability to tolerate the children's dependence, in addition to the other stresses of the divorcing experience, led women to the brink of physical abuse and sometimes over it.

## Combining Parenting and Sexual Needs

One of the more complex tasks which the custodial parent confronted was that of integrating his or her personal life, especially sexual life, with parenting. Although the sexual life of parents within an intact family is by no means as invisible to children as many adults believe it to be, the family system nevertheless provides guidelines for sexual behavior. As we have already noted, one-third of the custodial mothers became involved in an active sexual life immediately after the separation. Only a few had stable relationships at this time; more had a succession of lovers.

There are few conventions which govern the presence of lovers within the divorced family and their relationship with the children of the prior marriage. Many women were uneasy about how to conduct themselves and practices varied widely. Limitations of money and space were major considerations and increased the custodial mother's dilemma. Generally, men were brought home and, although the women considered alternatives and sometimes asked the men to leave before morning, most of the men remained overnight. As a result the children were intensely aware of their mothers' sexual relationships. They formed preferences, made attachments to some, and rejected others. Some of the men were genuinely interested in the children; most were courteous, some were not. The range was wide.

We were interested to find how quickly children made new assumptions regarding family life and how easily they assumed that adults engage in sexual relationships. In several families children soon anticipated that the man who arrived to visit was likely to spend the night in their mother's bed.

Mrs. M., an attractive woman in her thirties, told us that when her eight-year-old daughter did not approve of her date she found the girl asleep in her bed when she returned after a night out. Amused at the child's audacity, Mrs. M. took this as a direct communication from the child that she did not approve of this particular man and had taken it upon herself to tell her this via her behavior. In a similar vein, Mrs. J. told us that once she entertained a man who was approved by her children and they invited him and his child to stay over. As they made up the sleeping arrangements it soon became clear to the somewhat embarrassed adults that the children had, in a friendly way, arranged for the mother to share her bed with the visitor.

Overall, the consideration given to children by the mother and her lover, and particularly the tact of the parent in considering the child's feelings and vulnerability to feeling rejected or displaced by a new relationship, were crucial at this period.


## Resumption of Parenting

Despite their sense of feeling almost overwhelmed at each turn, a substantial number of mothers were able to reestablish their relationship with their children, at the level which they had achieved within the predivorce family, by the end of the first year. Following the drop in parenting in the immediate postseparation period, approximately one-half the children experienced no significant deterioration in this relationship by this time. Some exhusbands were helpful. One father took the children to his home regularly throughout this first year during his former wife's examinations and when her papers were due. Others remained close to their families as financial advisers, handymen, and fixers. Nevertheless, in all of the families the women carried the major responsibility of parenting by themselves, and it was a heavy load.

# Chapter 7

# The Visiting Parent

The relationship between the visiting parent and the visited child of course has no counterpart, and therefore no model, within the intact family. Its parameters, its limits, and its potentialities are new and remain to be explored. Many questions come immediately to mind about the nature of the relationships within the postdivorce family: To what extent and in what ways is the visiting parent likely to maintain his or her earlier role? Under what circumstances is this likely to change? When is the visiting parent able, or willing, to remain a central parenting figure to the child? And for how long, and for which children?

Although different custodial arrangements are emerging throughout the country, the dominant shape of over 80 percent of the postdivorce families is that of a custodial mother with whom the children reside and a father who has visitation rights. A growing number of fathers have successfully sought legal custody of their children, and mothers have taken on the role of the visiting parent. Joint custody arrangements have gained popularity as well, especially among couples with young children, and arrangements for the child to spend several days weekly with each parent, or to alternate weeks or months at a time with each parent have increased. We have, in our study, dealt primarily, although not exclusively, with custodial mothers and visiting fathers. What is crucial in all visiting arrangements, whether the father or the mother is visiting, is that the relationship between child and parent is structured by the constraints and the pattern of the visits. The structure itself sets the broad limits for what transpires between parent and child during the years that follow. Since this is so, the visiting arrangements themselves need to be examined.

As we looked at the various patterns of contact between visiting parent and visited child, we soon discovered that the relation between such patterns and the outcomes were surprisingly varied and often counter to our expectations. These expectations had been based on our knowledge of the intimacy and conflict in the relationships between parent and child prior to the divorce. And, in accord with psychological theory and clinical wisdom, we had assumed that the parent-child relationship would be broadly continuous in the postdivorce period with that which had obtained during the marriage. We did not find this to be so. On the contrary, the greatest change in postdivorce parent-child relationships is precisely that which takes place between the visiting parent and the visited child. At eighteen months postseparation there was no correlation whatsoever between the visiting patterns that had emerged by that time and the predivorce father-child relationship.

These findings were not only relevant to the prevalent arrangement, in which the mother has custody and the father is the visiting parent. In our experience, the role of the visiting parent is not sex-linked. The characteristics of the visiting parent-child relationship appear to be tied in general measure to the visiting role itself, and not to whether it is the mother or the father who is the visiting parent. Thus we have come gradually to recognize the singularity of this new relationship—of part-time parent and part-time child—and we have been led to examine some of its complex psychological workings. Central to the relationship from the start was the children's yearning for their fathers, which not only continued but sometimes intensified in the years following the father's departure.

Yet despite the urgency of the children's requests for visiting, and the strong emotional investment of many fathers in their children we have, as we said, found a striking and unexpected discontinuity between the predivorce father-child relationships and those which continue into the postdivorce period. Some men who had been close to their children during the marriage and had spent every weekend with them as close companions, failed to visit or arrived infrequently and irregularly. Conversely, other previously distant fathers who had hardly acknowledged their children during the marriage or had been frequently irritated by their presence, began to visit with a regularity that surprised both their children and us.

Nor did the mother's attitude towards the father's visiting always appear to be as major an influence as we had been led to believe it would be. Clearly, other factors had entered the father-child relationship and were exercising decisive influences.

## Why Are Visits So Hard?

With the marital separation, father and child both face an abrupt discontinuity in the form of their daily contact. Suddenly, they must adapt their mutual feelings and needs to the narrow confines of the visit. During the years that follow, the father-child relationship rests entirely on what can be compressed into the new and limited form. The difficulties inherent in this compressed funneling process have been insufficiently appreciated. And if anything the courts, and the embattled partners and their respective attorneys, have directed their efforts to imposing restrictions and strict conditions which further encumber a relationship which under the best of circumstances is fragile and needs encouragement.

The parent who moves out of the household begins a new role for which there is no dress rehearsal and no script. A visiting relationship between parent and child is strange by its very nature. The daily events which structured the parent-child relationship have vanished. The roles are awkward and new, no longer defined by sharing meals or family tasks. Neither child nor parent fully shares the life of the other, nor is fully absent.

The part-time parent and the part-time child often begin with a bewildering sense of no place to go and no idea of what to do together. The relationship is from the outset beset by practical problems: by the presence of children of different ages and colliding interests; by the absence of the mother who had often served as an interpreter of the children's needs. To many fathers these practical problems seemed at first insurmountable. What to do with young children still in need of actual nurturing care? Or with older children who appeared to need continual stimulation and entertainment in order to control their restlessness? Some confused men changed their entire routine for the children's visits, others changed nothing at all, and still others, equally perplexed, expected the children to take full responsibility for the agenda. "I feel like a camp director," said one exhausted father.

The broad parameters of the new role are unclear. To what extent is the visiting father a guest, a favorite uncle, or a parent? More explicitly, to what extent does the visiting parent continue to take responsibility for setting behavioral and moral standards? To what extent does he register approval or disapproval, or enforce discipline or even homework, and how can he do so without the built-in safeguards and bedtime rituals of intact family life which lessen disappointment, soften anger, and provide safe channels for alleviating the inevitable conflicts and frustrations of the relationships? Hurt feelings are more likely to continue and misunderstandings are more likely to remain unclarified. Men who were used to commanding their children experienced a new sense of impotence and frustration. All of these complexities combined to keep the father's sense of who he is now unsettled and unsettling.

The sense of time as a component of the parent-child relationship has also changed. For parents and children who share the repeated tasks of daily living together, time is part of the unobtrusive background of family life and provides a steady, muted rhythm which by its very unobtrusiveness conveys the comforting notion that the present will endure. For the visiting parent and child, time is a jarring presence. The constraints of time and space may impose a severe burden or, in some instances, a welcome limit on the interactions of the relationship. But both parent and child must now find time for their meeting, and must part on time. Both meeting and parting have acquired new meanings and accompanying anxieties which may long endure.

Many other factors also generate stress and threaten this fragile relationship. Children, as we have described already, take on special significance at this time: as economic or psychological burdens whose presence is resented; as important sources of self-esteem whose reassurance is sought and whose absence is feared; as friends and needed helpmates and even counselors during lonely, stressful decision-making times; as prizes to be fought over; as the only reliable allies in the marital battles. The complex dependence of adults on children for *their* self-esteem is especially apparent as fathers become vulnerable to their children in new ways that sometimes radically change the balance of the relationship.

One-half of the men were afraid of rejection by their children. They were worried about their children's disapproval and anger because of the divorce. Partly out of these and related concerns, at least one-third of the men were unusually generous to their children, plying them with special treats or money. Playing Santa Claus helped them with their discomfort about what to do and enabled them to deal with guilt about the divorce by making restitution with generous gifts. Their generosity also helped win the children's approval, cooperation, and eagerness for the next visit. This role strained the fathers financially and emotionally and, of course, often angered their divorcing wives.

There were many other problems. Men were uneasy about what to do with their lovers at visiting time. How would this affect both their children and the developing relationship with the woman? They did not know how to arrange for privacy in close quarters, and they often failed abysmally to understand or to be aware of the consequences of their own behavior or to anticipate the children's response.

Mr. A. had a large waterbed in his apartment which he and his seven-year-old daughter shared during her weekend visits. Occasionally, when he invited a woman friend to join them he sent the child for the night to an adjoining room, replacing her with his friend. He was annoyed and mystified by the child's tearful protestations.

Visiting parents also found that the visit itself became an arena which readily evoked in both parents the ghosts of the failed marriage and the fantasies of what might have been. Raw feelings of both marital partners tend to be exacerbated by visits even when there is no actual contact between former spouses or when such contact is fleeting. The visit is an event continually available for the replay of anger, jealousy, love, mutual rejection, and longing between the divorcing adults. In addition, one-third of both parents in our group were in active competition for the affection and loyalty of their children. Unfortunately, therefore, each visit provided a potential second battleground or rendezvous that always involved the children; and although the majority of parents tried to honor the children's visiting time, even those who tried hard often failed. Two-thirds of the women were moderately or severely stressed during the father's visits in the first year following the separation, and the great majority of the men felt much the same. In fact only a small fraction, approximately one-fifth of the men, was not stressed by the visits during this early period.

The fighting between the parents occasionally reached pathological, even bizarre, intensity. One gently bred matron, for example, smeared dog feces on the face of her husband when he arrived to see his children. One father sought a court order requiring his former wife to make herself invisible when he came to the door. All in all, one-third of the children were consistently exposed to intense anger at visiting time. The tension generated by the parents burdened the visits and stressed them and the children. A preponderance of the visits ruined by parents in this way were visits with the older children. Younger children were more protected.

Perhaps half of the mothers valued the father's continued contact with his children, and protected the contact with care and consideration. One-fifth saw no value in this whatsoever and actively tried to sabotage the meetings by sending the children away just before the father's arrival, by insisting that the child was ill or had pressing homework to do, by making a scene, or by leaving the children with the husband and disappearing. In between was a large group of women who had many mixed feelings about the father's visits, resenting the father's excessive gift-giving and his freedom from domestic responsibilities. These irritations were expressed in their difficulties in accommodating the different schedules of the other parent to make the visit possible and to protect the child's access to both parents, in forgotten appointments, in insistence on rigid schedules for the visits, in refusal to permit the visit if the father brought along an adult friend—in a thousand mischievous, mostly petty, devices designed to humiliate the visiting parent and to deprecate him in the eyes of his children.

Sometimes the child's anxiety at crossing the no-child's-land between father and mother spilled into the child's behavior. Exhausted by the ordeal of the crossing or saddened anew at the farewell to the father, children were cranky or poorly behaved after the visit, or they developed symptomatic behaviors in response to the anxiety and fear of angering one or the other parent. They felt that they were in jeopardy between two warring giants and they reacted accordingly.

Unfortunately, some angry women attempted to use the child's symptomatic behaviors as proof that the visits were detrimental to the child's welfare and should, therefore, be discontinued. Attorneys were called by aggrieved mothers who blamed their husband for the child's lapses, thus distressing the unhappy children even more.

The custodial parent's continued presence alone made her an available target for the child's unhappiness and resentment around the visit. Thus, for example, since she was available, whereas the visiting parent was present only intermittently, it was not unusual for children to behave splendidly with the visiting father and to return home cranky and petulant with their mothers. Their behavior often reflected their greater concern that their father might abandon them and their judgment that the custodial mother was more reliable. Mothers, however, rarely appreciated this and felt that they were being treated shabbily as compared with their husbands, who carried so much less responsibility in the care of the children. Not unexpectedly, they blamed the visit for the child's sulkiness or his different behavior upon return, and they threatened to discontinue the visitation.

Contrary to our expectations, parental friction at the time of the visit of the kind just described, although profoundly disturbing to the children, did not necessarily result in fewer visits. The mother's angry opposition strengthened the father's perseverance as often as it discouraged visiting. Friendliness between the parents and the mother's interest in maintaining the father's visits did, however, encourage visiting, and fathers who were encouraged to visit were more likely to continue to come regularly.

## What Internal Barriers Discouraged Visiting?

Parallel to the external complications besetting the visiting arrangements were subtle psychological forces that had a profound inner influence on the nature and frequency of the visiting and contributed to

the fragility of the relationship. Both the father's own psychological conflicts and, more importantly, the father's feelings about the divorce were
involved here. The father's role in the decision to divorce—his eagerness
for, or vigorous opposition to, ending the marriage—were crucial influences in determining the future of the visiting relationship. Unlike what
many children inevitably feel, the pattern of visiting immediately following the separation is *not* an accurate reflection of the father's love. On
the contrary, what makes the visits difficult are the many psychological
dilemmas of the father. Infrequent as well as frequent visiting immediately following the parental separation was affected very much by the
key emotions of the father following the divorce, and such emotions
were not at all necessarily related to the child or the children.

## Depressed Fathers

Men who were depressed following the divorce found it painful to
visit their children. Often they visited irregularly or not at all.

Fathers rejected by wives who had sought the divorce often expected
to be rejected by their children as well. They were preoccupied with
their own shame, grief, and lowered self-esteem. Some were preoccupied
with their expendability in the family system and talked bitterly about
how little they were needed, how quickly they would be replaced by
"male role models," by the new lover or stepfather.

These men found the visits to their children painful because they returned for the visit to the home they had built and then relinquished,
to the children they missed and longed to be with, to places which
evoked memories of happier times, or of the marriage and its downward
course. Some depressed men lacked the energy to mobilize themselves
for the stresses and demands of their children. Or the visit occasionally
brought a flare-up of somatic or other depressive symptoms.

The children, in turn, were profoundly disappointed when the expected father did not arrive. They were hurt and angry, and sometimes pretended that they had other interests or that they didn't really
care. Lack of communication soon burdened further the unhappy relationship, until it was sometimes difficult to uncover the true feelings of
child and father under the many-layered excuses. Tragically, the fathers
who were most likely to be depressed following the divorce were those
who most loved or needed their children to restore their own faltering
self-esteem. Yet the children were rarely able to appreciate the root
cause of the father's inconstancy and they experienced his not coming
as confirming his lack of interest in them.

Mr. H. had been a devoted, shy, and undemonstrative father to his
young daughters. When his wife of twelve years decided on divorce
she asked him to leave the house and invited her lover to move in with

her. For Mr. H. it soon became an impossible task to fetch his two daughters at the home which he had built for the family he had lost and continued to long for. He could not bear to stand at the threshold and wait for the children, painfully conscious that another man was occupying his place. His humiliation was compounded by the fact that the children seemed well and happy and *not* overwhelmed with longing for him. Although he loved his daughters, Mr. H. did not visit *at all* for six months following the separation. Neither his wife nor his children understood this conflict and they assumed that he was not interested in seeing his children. His oldest daughter became depressed as she continued to await his arrival and was repeatedly disappointed.

Fortunately, we were able through counseling to help Mr. H. reinstitute regular contact with his children. His former wife, who had not wished to keep the father away from the children, readily agreed to bring them to a neutral place to meet him. Mr. H. continued to visit frequently and regularly during the four years that followed.

## Guilty Fathers

Men who felt consciously or unconsciously guilty at having ended the marriage had great trouble in initiating and maintaining visits with their children. This group also included fathers who had been devoted to their children, and where, in fact, the preexisting father-child relationship had been of special importance because the deprivations within the marital relationship had brought father and children together to share many activities. The father's guilt was profound at having left an especially close, loving parent-child relationship. Others felt very guilty at leaving their children with a psychologically disturbed or otherwise incompetent mother, or to pursue a different lifestyle, or lover. Several men were ashamed to face their children.

The father's guilt had a two-fold effect, leading either to a decline in visiting or to a guilt-ridden flurry of visiting—which was rarely sustained—immediately following the marital separation. When the father's guilt led to a decline in visits this further reinforced the guilty feelings and led the father deeper into his impasse.

Often unaware of the psychological meaning of their reluctance to visit, these men sought to explain their behavior by a variety of pretexts that strained credulity. It was not uncommon for guilty fathers to project their self-blame onto the children, to magnify moderate misbehavior of the children, and to find in this behavior justification for discontinuing or at least reducing their visits.

One such father who reduced his visits drastically referred with irritation to the "bourgeois values" of his five-year-old daughter. This was a child he had cared for tenderly during the years of the marriage when his wife worked and he remained at home as her primary caregiver.

The little girl wept daily for her father and perceived his behavior as a cruel rejection of her.

The extraordinary rejection of children with whom the father had enjoyed an intimate relationship during the marriage was also evident as a repeating pattern among fathers who took on a new lifestyle, or men who remarried and found children close to the age of their own children within the new family unit.

An affable, attractive man, Mr. I. had a cordial but distant relationship with his wife for many years. He would habitually spend entire weekends with his children. He and his three adoring sons who idolized him, enjoyed many hobbies together, and the children, who were personable and competent youngsters, were the envy of their friends because of their exciting weekend activities and the time and devotion of the wonderful father. There was no overt friction in the marriage, and the mother and children were startled when the father sued for divorce and shortly remarried a divorcee with children. Soon after the separation, Mr. I. almost entirely stopped visiting his own children, and by the end of the first year he had seen them only twice during the preceding six-month period. The children's anguish and bitter rage were boundless and continued for many years.

### Provocative Fathers

Some visiting fell in the shadow of the divorce-engendered conflict and was designed in part to harass the mother. She, in turn, raged helplessly or tried overtly or covertly to disrupt the pleasure for child and visiting parent. The visiting parent sought primarily to anger or to establish continued access to the family turf; the visits tended to drop off and often these relationships ended abruptly.

Mr. A. spent little time at home during his marriage of eight years. An impulsive man, who ran many businesses simultaneously (some legitimate, some otherwise), his relationship with his young daughter had always been fairly limited. When he decided to divorce his wife, he suddenly became interested in his child and visited her regularly, to his wife's chagrin. He enchanted her by taking her to museums, consulting her opinion, and treating her with gallantry and a gentle courtesy.

This new relationship between father and daughter lasted a few months, until Mr. A. withdrew as impulsively from the relationship as he had entered it. He broke appointments and disappointed the child regularly. The little girl was preoccupied for many years by her brief period in the sun with her charismatic father.

Sometimes we were able, through counseling, to modify the attitudes and behavior of guilt-ridden or impulsive fathers, and to bring about greater regularity and/or frequency of visiting. Sometimes, of course, we failed.

## What Factors Contribute to Visiting

These factors in the father's response to the divorce, which were reflected in the visiting patterns, were counterbalanced by the passionate, persistent yearning of the children, especially those below the age of nine, by the commitment of many fathers to their children, which held despite their fear of hurt and rejection, and by the interest of about half of the women in maintaining the visits. Thus, the visiting relationship which successfully outlived the marriage reflected not the relationships of the predivorce family primarily, but the father's motivation, the child's motivation, and the psychological capacity of fathers, mothers, and children to adapt flexibly to the new conditions of the visiting relationship. Men who could bend to the complex logistics of the visiting; who could deal with the anger of the women and the capriciousness of the children without withdrawing; who could overcome their own depression, jealousy and guilt; who could involve the children in their planning; who could walk a middle ground between totally rearranging their schedule and not changing their schedule at all; and who felt less stressed and freer to parent, were predominantly among those who continued to visit regularly and frequently.

### Fathers Who Welcome Limits

Some fathers who regularly visited their children welcomed the limits of the postdivorce relationship, claiming it was easier to visit their children within a circumscribed period. In a number of families these limits enabled fathers to get to know their children better, to express greater affection, to concentrate on their parenting in ways not possible during the marriage when the children's needs were burdensome. We found this especially true among fathers of preschool children and adolescents.

Mr. B. was a critical, ill-tempered man during his marriage. At the time of the separation his adolescent daughter openly expressed her anger at him.

Following the divorce Mr. B. insisted on a rigid visiting schedule which his daughter resented, but with which she nevertheless complied. Away from home in a more relaxed setting and without the presence of the mother, father and daughter began to converse without rancor. Out of this association they gradually achieved a friendship. Four years later his daughter decided to follow her father's demanding professional career.

Tina said of her father, "He has a heart of gold, but he's impossible to live with, especially for me because I have a temper, too, and we fought all the time. As long as we don't live together we get along well."

## Other Factors that Contribute to Visiting

The concern of men for the children left in the care and custody of depressed or psychologically troubled women led some to visit more frequently if the men were not overtaken by their own guilt. Fathers who were lonely, psychologically intact, and not depressed visited more. Fathers who were economically secure and educated visited more. Fathers whose children were not angry visited more. And fathers and families where the relationship between the parents had calmed down or was no longer marked by intense animosity tended to visit more, *although* the mother's negative attitude toward the visiting was a factor of *fading* significance over time.

Finally, it is reasonable to assume that the interventions of our project played a significant role in encouraging the fathers to visit more frequently and in facilitating the development of better relationships with the children. As we learned subsequently, the interventions were influential far beyond our modest expectations. A striking discovery of the study was how fluid father-child relationships appeared immediately after the divorce when the new visiting relationship leaves behind its predivorce form, and how appreciative fathers are of advice at this crucial time. The relationship between visiting father and child is at its most malleable immediately after the father has moved out of the household and as the visiting pattern emerges. The foundations of the new visiting relationship are laid down during the immediate postseparation period. If weakened at this time, the relationship may be more difficult to restore. But visiting parent and child also have a second chance at this critical juncture, a chance to break free of past unhappy relations and establish a new bond between father and child.

# Chapter 8

# The Child's View of Visiting

Throughout the session Andy kept returning to various plans he envisioned for visits with his father. Since the separation, Andy's mother had placed increasingly severe constraints on the father's opportunities to visit, and the number of contacts had dwindled. Andy had been alert to the change: "It's been *three* weeks since I've seen him!" Andy fantasized things he could do with his dad: "We could buy a basketball." "Maybe I could stay overnight." "Sometimes we get a hamburger." Listening to Andy, the interviewer was struck by his sadness and the wistfulness of his open longing. When Andy learned that his father was coming in to talk the same day, he asked urgently, "Can I come in the office with you and see him, too?" Without hesitation, Andy agreed he wanted to see *much* more of his father. The reason was uncomplicated and obvious: "I *like* him." Being six, Andy failed to understand why this disturbing deprivation now dominated his life.

Andy's voice joined a rising chorus of youthful protests that indicates a reexamination of society's accepted notions of visiting is past due and urgently needed.

It has been customary in recent years for courts to assign "reasonable visitation rights" to parents who no longer have legal and physical custody of their children. When parents formally disagreed on the timing of visits, the pattern was decreed by the court. Most often a twice-monthly overnight or weekend visit was ordered with exact times specified for the beginning and end of each contact.

In the absence of a formal legal dispute, "reasonable visitation" has been left to the parents to establish. And, it appears, parents turn more than we might have expected to their attorneys for advice on this issue. They hear, not surprisingly, that "reasonable visiting" is considered to be the customary pattern of twice a month overnight or weekends.

Mr. B., a teacher, was asked how he arrived at his twice-monthly visiting schedule. "Well, I asked my attorney what I should request . . . he said every other weekend is what fathers usually get." Did Mr. B. feel that twice a month was enough? "In fact, now that you mention it . . . no, it's not good. I miss the kids terribly. . . . Sally says she misses me all the time . . . and my youngest one, the three-year-old . . . I feel like he's slipping away from me."

Like judges or mental health professionals, attorneys have simply re-flected the traditions of society, and until recently none of us has challenged this arrangement.

Where did this standard pattern come from? There was, of course, the cultural tradition of this century that placed primary responsibility on the father as sole wage earner and on the mother as parent. These changes, instigated primarily by the industrial revolution, relegated to secondary importance the father's ongoing role in parenting. And until the past decade, many fathers accepted this delimited role without thinking to push beyond its established boundaries. Thus, the majority of fathers quietly accepted twice a month visiting as representative of the lessened importance of their relationship with their children. And, similarly, the majority of women expected to continue in their primary role as full-time mothers, and were reluctant or afraid to view them-selves as anything less than a full-time parent.

Above and beyond tradition, one also sees in the nature of the divorce proceedings themselves some of the reasons for the continuation of cus-tomary visiting patterns. The adversary nature of the proceedings by definition implies that each client, through his attorney, anticipates being a winner, not a loser. "Winning" has encompassed not just property set-tlement, but the issue of who shall own the children. Unlike the flurry of activity devoted to plea bargaining in criminal cases, exploration and compromise have rarely been expended on the issue of a parent's access to his children. In fact, quite the opposite. Attorneys are bound by training, legal ethics, and in some cases personality to protect and fight for their client's rights and desires. Often what the client wants has little relationship to the child's needs or expressed desires, particularly in bitterly contested divorces. And attorneys rarely ask what the chil-dren think about various proposed arrangements; it has not been con-sidered one of their functions. "The best interests of the child" have more often been a matter of the perceived best interests of each parent, as negotiated by his or her attorney.

With the issues of community property settled, the division of spoils, insofar as children are concerned, seems still to come down to a matter of weekends. In a field that relies heavily on precedent for decisions, it has been convenient and comfortable to recommend what has gone before. And the precedent of twice-monthly weekend visits became not just customary, but somehow developmentally correct, morally right. Fathers pressing for weekly and midweek contacts, or more recently for joint custody, were viewed with suspicion by legal and mental health professionals alike. "It just isn't done." "It won't work." "It will cause more fighting." "Children need one toothbrush, one home." Until recently, society thought it slightly odd for a father to want so much time with his children. And mothers who wanted to accommodate such interested fathers were warned not to give up too much. Some were made to feel guilty for wishing to turn part of their sole parental responsibility over to the father. And so the custom of alternating weekends, twelve days with mother and two with father, has continued despite a vastly changed society that by 1979 saw more than 60 percent of single mothers joining the workforce. A rethinking of visiting issues must include the concept that both parents remain centrally responsible for and involved in the care and psychological development of their children.

During our initial interviews, children expressed the wish for increased contact with their fathers with a startling and moving intensity. An average of five months after separation, in our study, two-thirds of the youngsters were seeing their fathers at least twice a month. Their visits were thus at a level deemed "reasonable," and yet there was great dissatisfaction. Complaints about insufficiency of parental visits were heard not just from those youngsters who rarely saw the absent parent, but from many who were being visited rather frequently as well.

Aside from pleas to reunite their parents, the most pressing demand children brought to counseling was for more visiting. A part of this eagerness for more parental contact stemmed from anxieties over the divorce and related wishes to restore the marriage, but only a small part. The intense longing for greater contact persisted undiminished over many years, long after the divorce was accepted as an unalterable fact of life.

## How Often Did Parents and Children Visit?

Other than an expectation that a substantial number of children were seeing the out-of-home parent twice monthly, we initially started with little real knowledge of visiting parameters. No one seemed to know how often or how long children actually visited with their estranged parents subsequent to separation. And once divorce settlements became final, no one knew the effects of the passage of time. Did fathers see more or less of their children than was initially decreed? Our first interest, then, was to determine the overall frequency patterns of visiting for the youngsters in our study: how often, for how long, and with whom did they share said visits. Although such external dimensions of the visit do not capture the quality of the parent-child relationship, they nevertheless provide a baseline for observing the extent of continuity or change over the years. As will be seen, the patterns of visiting found in this study do not support the widespread community expectation that contacts between fathers and children in the postdivorce family are relatively infrequent and diminish precipitously over time.

At the time of our first interviews, 40 percent of the children and adolescents were seeing their fathers at least once a week. Surprisingly, almost half of this group were visiting two and three times weekly. Most often, these were young school-aged boys whose fathers lived nearby and who were not hampered in their access by angry mothers intent on limiting the father-son relationship.

Doug, age seven, told us he certainly didn't like the divorce and missed having his father in the house. He guessed, though, that it would turn out okay for him because "I can see him when I want." Doug was one of those few youngsters who could, without risking parental disapproval and anger, take the initiative in visiting by pedaling on his bicycle to the nearby residence of his/father. The sense of frequent and free access possessed by such youngsters was enormously important in their efforts to cope with the changes and disappointments of the divorce. They had some feelings of control over an aspect of the divorce that affected them most—the visiting relationship—and seemed to feel less hopeless than their more restricted peers. But even among the group of youngsters with the most contact, we heard some complaints about insufficient visits, constraints on time, and difficulties in setting up the visits with flexibility.

Slightly more than a quarter of the youngsters were visiting with their parent two or three times in a month. While this was the group participating in "reasonable" and traditional visiting, the majority were not initially staying overnight on a reliably regular basis. It is important to recognize that twice-monthly contact may involve a full forty-eight-hour weekend each visit, or may only add up to a few sparse hours in a given month, depending on what is desired and allowed by each parent.

Jane, age six, eagerly looked forward to her father's sporadic Saturday visits. Each time she fantasied a long and fun-filled afternoon of activities, maybe followed by a trip to McDonald's before returning home. More often, the father soon tired of the venture, returning Jane prematurely to her home after several hours. Jane's mother became angry that she could not carry out her own plans during Jane's visits; she felt trapped by the need to be home to handle the father's early return. Once when she attempted to force the father into a lengthier visit by staying away from home until the designated hour, she found Jane sitting morosely at the neighbor's house when she returned.

One-quarter of the children were visited infrequently and erratically. We defined "infrequent contacts" as any occurring less than once a month, and these occasional visits turned out to be erratic in their pattern as well. Not included in this group were the children of one family separated by substantial geographical distance from their father, necessitating vacation or holiday visiting. The youngsters involved in vacation visiting increased slowly over the course of the project; but, in our observation, they experienced a very different psychological situation from that of the youngsters whose fathers were nearby and inconstant. Children with infrequent visits typically had no idea when the next visit might occur. For some, the agony attached to not knowing was sad to observe. A father might see his child two times in three weeks, then not call or visit for three months.

Todd saw his father regularly in the summer following his parents' separation. When school started, the schedule became increasingly sparse. He thought surely his father would call and plan something for his eleventh birthday. When the day passed without a phone call, a present, or a card, Todd observed sadly that it had been six weeks since they had last met. "He must be forgetting all about me."

The scheduled visits of these youngsters sometimes did not materialize, as children waited vainly at the window for the familiar car. For the girls, the erratic visiting was like an unsatisfactory love affair, reminiscent of sitting by the phone for the date that never calls.

The nine-to-twelve-year-olds experienced infrequent, erratic visits significantly more than any other age group. Almost half the children in this age range had erratic visits and this was particularly true for boys. The anger in these youngsters, described earlier, seems to be one potent force in contributing to the diminished visiting. It may be that the fragile and tenuous nature of the new visiting situation requires a child who is, for the most part, pleasant company. And where visits diminished, whatever the reason, these youngsters' anger was continuously refueled by the absence of regular contact. When the inconstant father then did attempt to visit, a feigned indifference or outright hostility lessened the father's already faltering intention to maintain contact, which further deepened the youngster's anger and sense of rejection. What was created swiftly, sometimes irretrievably, was a circular response by which infrequent visits and the child's discontent locked a poor situation firmly into place.

Aside from the nine-to-twelve-year-olds, the preschool and kindergarten girls were the only other group to experience a significant amount of deprivation in their visiting pattern. Initially, girls were generally visited less than boys. It may be that the fathers' anger toward women who initiated the divorce spilled into the beginning of the visiting situation with daughters and diminished their willingness to visit initially. We also observed a tendency for fathers, once separated, to feel their boys needed them more than the girls whose needs they assumed were more readily met by their mothers.

Yet in fact three-to-five-year-old girls, in particular, suffered from significantly diminished visiting. The pleadings of these bright-eyed bouncy children for more visits had a quality all its own, and its expression contrasted sharply with the quieter longing of the young school-age children.

Mary called her daddy several times daily after the separation. "I *love* you, daddy . . . I want to see you *everrry* day!" The seductive tone of the pleading, the sadness, the eager possessiveness—all could have combined to stir up painful memories within the father of a marital relationship fallen apart.

And, finally, there were a small group of youngsters (5 percent) who were not seeing their fathers at all. Four of these children, all girls, were refusing to visit despite the interest and urgent pleas of the fathers.

Alice's father left the marriage after a violent argument, one of many, in which the mother ordered him to leave. Soon thereafter, the mother's paranoid rage at being left became even more irrational and was openly shared with all the children. Their father was a "bastard" and a "liar" who did not care for any of them. Initially, Alice visited the father, but as the mother continued to rail against the father, Alice became increasingly resistant to going unless the father promised an expensive gift, which he could ill afford. When the sad and nearly desperate man did promise a gift, more often than not the mother quickly bought the desired item for her daughter before the father's next visit and the child would then refuse to go. Alice's parents became locked into deadly competition to buy this ten-year-old's affection, a battle the father essentially lost within six months.

Refusal to visit a parent by youngsters of preteen years was linked in each case to issues other than the predivorce relationship with that parent. The mothers of each of the girls refusing to visit had powerful holds over their daughters, and the girls' own sadness and anger at being abandoned by the father resonated and meshed with the mothers' outrage at being similarly abandoned, creating insurmountable barriers for their fathers.

Two other youngsters in the same family were not visiting with the father but, unlike the children who actively refused, these preteens had no choice in the matter. Their father left the house after a protracted and frightening period of total silence, punctuated by violence, and never contacted them again. They had no knowledge of his whereabouts for the next six years although he was, in fact, nearby and sent support checks regularly.

## How Long Did Visits Last?

Although two-thirds of the youngsters were visited with "reasonable" frequency, the duration of a single visit disappointed many. Nearly three quarters of the preschoolers and half of the nine- and ten-year-olds, for example, were spending only a few hours on each visit. Initially, overnight and weekend visits occurred with only one quarter of the youngsters, most often the six- to twelve-year-olds.

Brief contacts were valued by youngsters only if there were many of them and they included midweek meetings as well as overnight weekend stays. This more approximates the fleeting but satisfying interactions of many two-parent households. Fleeting, *infrequent* visits, however, tended to arouse hopes and resentments, especially in those below the age of twelve.

## Obstacles to Gratifying Visits

The children's interest and enthusiasm for frequent contacts with the out-of-home parent existed despite a variety of barriers which burdened the actual visits, or rendered the scheduling of visits a troublesome process.

### Planning the Visiting

Many older children were unhappy and insulted that the visiting schedule had been planned without their prior consultation. Children and adolescents were rarely asked to express their desires. Further, few felt comfortable about advancing their preferences at a time when intense angers, volatile tempers, or outbursts of crying characterized their parents' reaction to any aspect of the divorce. They were afraid to stir things up, but harbored many private ideas about how visiting should be handled.

For a small number of youngsters (10 percent) the visiting schedule was established by the court and rigidly enforced by at least one parent. Ten-year-old Sean, a gifted child, talked anxiously and eloquently of his feelings about the visiting schedule which was being contested in court. "I don't want to visit as *often* as my father wants . . . I don't get to see my mom enough. But I don't want to say that . . . he'd get really angry. My dad thinks that because we spend the weekdays with my mom that he should have all the weekends. But we're in school every day until 3:30, then we have all this homework, and I do like time to play with my friends. Actually, I just see my mom a few hours each day, and we *never* get to do fun things together, like go to the beach, or go for a picnic. I don't think that's fair. What I want to tell the court is every other weekend and *flexibility* . . . if mom wants to do something with us, we should be able to do it and then see my dad the next weekend. Isn't flexibility what I want?"

Many youngsters felt helpless and victimized by the rigidity of visiting schedules. They saw them as extending indefinitely into the future, governing and shaping their lives in powerfully restrictive ways.

One independent-minded adolescent firmly delivered her opinion about such court orders. "I'm not going to let the court tell *me* what to do. It's ridiculous that the court can decide how often I see my dad. They said we get to visit every other Wednesday and every other weekend. That puts our relationship in a box. On Wednesday I have to stay at school for cheerleading and on our scheduled weekend he often has to work. It's just not working out." Tina then attempted to modify the schedule on her own, with only limited success. Each parent, angrily intent on maintaining his or her prescribed right to the girl, refused to yield to the other and to her stated needs. Four years later, Tina vividly remembered hating her court-ordered visiting schedule; the inflexibility usually conflicted with her own social activities. "I would *never* subject my kids to anything like that. It's tough when you're an adolescent."

Even in those families where the parents decided the visiting pattern, the children felt little power to modify the schedule when important social activities came up. Indeed, changes in the days or weekends for visiting were made almost entirely in response to adult needs or wishes, and many youngsters perceived this with a startling clarity.

## Visiting with Sibs

Two-thirds of the children visited their fathers jointly with their siblings. The younger the child the more likely he or she was to visit in a group. Where this meant different ages and interests, it became difficult, if not impossible, to find activities of interest to everyone. And, because the father's time was limited, the children were presented with an all-or-nothing dilemma. Going to a sporting event or selecting a movie could mean frayed tempers and hurt feelings when a father tried to accommodate a six-year-old son and a ten-year-old daughter. Group visits became less common as the older children went their separate ways; their increased capacity to say "no" created new visiting arrangements.

When young children in families managed to visit the father alone, their sibs often viewed this with envy and some distress. When the total number of visits was limited to begin with, feelings of being deprived were heightened.

Peggy's father rarely took the children out on visits, seeing them instead on occasion in the family home. Peggy, age twelve, told us: "I don't see my father much. When he does visit, he spends all his time talking with my mom or playing ball with my little brother. Sometimes I feel he doesn't care about me." What does she do when he comes? "I wait around and then I go out to play." What are you waiting around for? "I'm waiting to see if my dad is going to talk to me." Sadly she reflected, "I don't think my dad's going to change much. . . . I guess I'll just have to get used to the situation."

Some mental health specialists have advocated a "separate visit" policy to accommodate youngsters' separate needs and interests. We have, ourselves, occasionally suggested that a parent spend some separate time with one of his children. But such a policy requires that a parent be able and willing to devote considerable time, and psychological energy, to maintaining ongoing relationships with all his children.

### Sharing Visits with Others

Another source of frustration for one-third of the children was the need to share their visits with father's dates, fiancees, or new wives. Children more often disliked, or remained carefully neutral toward, new partners than approved them. For some youngsters, the actual existence of a girlfriend was irritating, most often when attached to the parent that the child or adolescent held accountable for the divorce. But many youngsters were content to let the father enjoy a new relationship. It was the inclusion of dates on visits that caused the difficulties. Youngsters resented sharing the father's time and attention with a date; many felt neglected or unwelcome. "He can see *her* all week long . . . why does he have to bring her along on *my* visit?" Such resentment was strongest in the older school-age children, particularly those least visited. Where approval was achieved, it most often came from the preschool children who enjoyed having an additional source of attention.

A succession of many different dates also created a greater sense of neglect and disapproval. Some older youngsters felt like window dressing, like props used in the attempts of a few fathers to create good impressions with their dates. When relationships became stable over time between father and friend, many youngsters accepted what was perhaps the inevitable and became more graciously neutral. This was more likely to happen when the adults allowed youngsters to determine their own pace in becoming closer, rather than pressuring for instant intimacy.

For those who stayed overnight at fathers' houses at the same time as lovers, sleeping arrangements were a potential source of anxiety. The older youngsters' embarrassment or discomfort sometimes mounted in advance, occasionally to such an extent that some attempted to put off the valued visit rather than worry about who would sleep where with what degree of discretion.

Sean talked with great ambivalence of a forthcoming camping trip. Normally he liked this sort of thing, but this time he said, "I just don't want to go so much." The anxiety of this ten-year-old mounted as he disclaimed knowledge of any reasons for his reluctance. "*Most* of it will be fun, I know, but . . ." Knowing Sean well through a series of extended visits, the therapist wondered aloud if he was worried about where his father and steady girlfriend would sleep. With great relief, Sean said, "Yes, I *certainly* am! . . . I don't want to sleep in the camper with them . . . all *week* I've been worrying. But I'm afraid to sleep outside on the ground and I don't think they'll want to. So I just don't want to go."

Fathers who anticipated their children's discomfort and anxiety defused it by reserving intimacies for private times. Even hand-holding and kissing were intensely scrutinized, and the children often reacted strongly with anxiety, excitement, and sometimes disgust. One ten-year-old expressed his dismay clearly: "They hang all *over* each other. . . . It's really disgusting!"

## Hostilities Surrounding Visiting

Perhaps most distressing of all the barriers interfering with smooth visiting were the parental conflicts which either preceded or brought each visit to a close. As we indicated in the preceding chapter, nearly half the children had witnessed intensely antagonistic exchanges between parents at the time of visiting. Not surprisingly, many youngsters were also anxious about the phone calls needed to negotiate the specifics of each visit. Just the phone contact between father and child was sometimes enough to precipitate a barrage of hostility from some enraged mothers.

In general, the opportunities for hostile exchange were legion; it seemed to some youngsters that crossing a mined field was the prerequisite for reaching their absent fathers.

Ben twisted a rubber band nervously as he talked about his father. "I can see him any time," Ben declared too bravely. Asked what happens when he wants to see his father, Ben forced a casual air. "Oh, it's okay. It's usually not important." Quietly, painfully, he described their unlisted phone number, obtained by his angry mother to prevent his father from calling. Without free communication, mishaps in visiting plans increased, as did his misery.

Ben remembered the time his father failed to hear him calling at the apartment gate. He returned home to telephone his dad. When he arrived at the house, his mother raged at the father's "irresponsibility" and Ben decided not to call. But the mother, by then yelling, called Ben's father herself and vented her fury. His father arranged to pick him up a block from home but Ben, by now completely distraught, started to cry and refused to go. His mother made a scene, angrily insisting that he had no choice and must go anyway.

About one-third of the youngsters were fortunate to have parents who restrained their hostility in front of the children, but the majority of children, like Ben, felt cheated and betrayed by the prelude of hostilities between parents. They came to expect it, but they respected their parents less for it.

Despite all the hostilities between parents, most of the youngsters managed to shake off the bad or anxious beginnings and enjoy the actual visit itself. But a small number (15 percent) considered their visit absolutely ruined by being placed in the crossfire of parental animosities. Older youngsters whose parents pumped and pried for information about their former spouse could not relax. Their wish to remain loyal to both parents created a corresponding need to monitor their responses vigilantly. Nine- to twelve-year-old boys most often felt their visits were ruined. More than girls this age, they seemed to be particularly vulnerable to the mother's anger. They experienced her anger at the father personally, as a direct attack. With firmer identification with their fathers, these young boys were perhaps more profoundly affected and could less easily shake off such hostilities.

## Children's Feelings About Visits

We have repeatedly described the dissatisfaction of so many youngsters who felt they were not seeing their father often enough. If custody and visiting issues are to be within the realm of the "best interests of the child," then such widespread discontent must be taken very seriously. Only 20 percent of all the children and adolescents were reasonably content with their individual visiting situations during the year following the separation. Such feelings of satisfaction did not imply approval of the divorce; most of these same children still earnestly wished for a reconciliation. But given their understanding that reconciliation was unlikely, these youngsters felt they had a fairly good deal. As one eight-year-old put it: "I'm lucky . . . I get to see my dad pretty much when I want to. My friend only gets to see her dad twice a month."

More boys than girls were content with the visiting, particularly adolescent boys, as well as those youngsters who could bike over to their dads frequently during the week. The adolescents' sense of satisfaction derived not so much from numerous contacts, which they did not feel they needed, but from a sense of casual openness about scheduling visits mutually convenient to both father and son, and responsive to the needs of both.

Gary's father called at the spur of the moment to ask if his son wanted to go hiking. Because Gary had already made arrangements to meet some friends, he declined the invitation. We asked how his dad reacted. "Oh, it was fine. He knows I'd go if I didn't have other plans. We agreed to go sailing next Sunday." Gary and his father both felt comfortable in continuing the kind of easy relationship they had established before the separation. And Gary's age (sixteen) was a considerable asset in ignoring or shrugging off his mother's angry attempts to regulate the visits more to her liking.

A different feeling, one of intense excitement and eagerness for the visit to occur, was observed in nearly 40 percent of the children. Such obvious eagerness occurred almost exclusively in the cases of the younger children, those from two to eight, and surprisingly was not related to how frequently the child actually saw the father, or to how well the father had treated the child before the divorce.

Nell's excitement as she talked of seeing her dad was intense. She described the things they did together last time: "Sometimes he'll take me to Great America." When did she see her dad last? "It was last week." In fact, it had been quite awhile since her father called to arrange a visit, but the enthusiasm of this five-year-old remained unbounded.

Some youngsters talked of their disappointment over erratic visits, but with the preschool children these feelings seemed not to blunt their excitement when visits did occur. The willingness of the young children to give their inconstant dads yet another chance was touching, and much in contrast with the older youngsters. Some fathers of younger children instituted a stable visiting schedule for the first time after the counseling. When this occurred, they found delighted boys and girls willing to resume a closer relationship, some even after months of little contact. It was much more difficult to accomplish this with the older youngsters, who, with longer memories and more intense feelings of rejection, harbored suspicions and mistrust.

Sheer disappointment with regard to visiting characterized the feelings of more than a third of the youngsters. Saddened by the father's apparent lack of interest, these boys and girls waited pensively for him. Seen most often in the two-to-eight-year-olds, disappointment dominated their reactions to the divorce and was not covered or replaced by anger. It was with these youngsters that the yearning for the father was most open and poignant. Disappointment was most intense when the visits were, in fact, few and far between or when a father failed to keep a scheduled appointment.

Bobby got dressed for his visit two hours ahead of time, an unusual act of early preparation for this four-year-old. Half an hour before his dad was to arrive, Bobby started listening, and checking outside, for his car. "*That's* dad now . . . I know that's my dad." Two hours later Bobby was still checking, but more slowly, with less certainty. With mounting anger at the pain she saw in her son, Bobby's mom tried to distract him with games and toys. Finally, two and a half hours late, Bobby's dad arrived: "Let's go, Bobby!" No apologies, no explanations. Bobby's mom angrily expressed her opinion of the father's thoughtlessness; Bobby cried as they argued.

Where there was preferential treatment given to siblings the hurt and disappointment was exacerbated.

An articulate nine-year-old, Gwen, talked freely yet sadly of her "problems with the divorce." "The second big hurt," she said, "is that my dad doesn't want to see us now. He never took us out much when we lived together, but now that he is gone he takes my brother out alone." Gwen's face clouded over: "He has never taken me out alone . . . I want him to so much." Just once since the separation did her dad take them both to a place chosen by Gwen. "That was our very best time." Gwen said she'd be "scared to talk with him about important things." "I want to tell my daddy to see us more often."

We found considerable conflict about visiting in one-fifth of the children, almost exclusively in those from nine to eighteen years of age. In these youngsters the wish to see the father remained strong, but became compromised and intermingled with anger at him. Such internal conflict was especially strong in the nine-to-twelves and had several different roots. First there were those children who had expected to see much of their fathers and who felt let down by the father's inconstancy. These children, initially strongly disappointed, felt intensely rejected by the father. But unlike the younger children who maintained goodwill toward the father in similar circumstances, the older youngsters defended against their feelings of rejection and sadness with an open anger. Hurt and puzzlement was quickly covered with a counterrejection of the father: "Who needs him?"

Six months after the separation, Marty talked angrily about his father and how the visits were always "screwed up." "It's not worth going anymore . . . I don't have any fun anyway." From his mother we learned that Marty not only used to anticipate visits eagerly, but was the primary agent in setting up the visits. He called his dad often to suggest get-togethers, but his father always had excuses. Marty told us of the day his father arrived to take him on an eagerly awaited trip some distance away. The meeting time had not been clearly set, and Marty was playing at a nearby friend's house. In a rage, the father blamed Marty's mother for sabotaging the day's outing and left without him. When Marty came back ten minutes later and learned his dad had taken his sibling and departed without any effort to call for him, he was devastated. He sobbed for fifteen minutes, receiving little comfort from his outraged mother. Soon thereafter Marty developed his protective veneer, acting noncommittal whenever the father called. In talking with us, Marty's interest in seeing the father was evident, but equally strong now was his need to save face by pretending it all did not matter.

A second group of conflicted youngsters were those who had developed with the mother an alignment whose central feature was an intensely shared, hostile excoriation of the father. As we have described earlier, most of the boys so aligned were initially overwhelmed by their father's decision to leave and begged him to return, to no avail.

Paul was nine when we first saw him. He stated firmly that he never wanted to visit his father ever. This seemed to be an unshakeable opinion; his anger at the father's desertion was clear. "He calls us *far* too much on the phone." Only as fantasy material was elicited did we hear the evidence for genuine conflict about seeing his father. Speaking of his three wishes, Paul said: "First, I want my mom and dad to get along better, but I *don't* want them back together. Second, I want to be rich. And third, I wish I lived on a desert island with just my mom and sisters, with a very long telephone cord so that I could talk with my dad, and a speedboat so I could visit him." Paul risked disrupting the comforting relationship with his mother if he expressed any greater desire for contact with the father, but even though slim, his wish was present.

For a small number of youngsters their conflict about visits was especially difficult for parents to understand. The reluctance to go stemmed primarily from anticipation of painful feelings evoked by the visit itself, a phenomenon noted more often in visiting fathers.

Ten-year-old Natalie had willingly visited her father immediately after the separation. As a highly charged and inappropriate relationship between mother and daughter became more tense and frightening, Natalie became increasingly reluctant to visit. Although fond of her father and eager to win his approval and respect, she now hated to visit because it was sad and painfully difficult for her when the visit ended. Contributing to her reluctance was the presence of father's new girlfriend, perceived by Natalie as interfering with the father's attentiveness on visits. Natalie continued to talk frequently and eagerly with her father on the phone, but put him off whenever he tried to arrange visits.

Few youngsters were neutral in their feelings toward visiting. A few girls in early adolescence seemed to have extended into the visiting situation the mostly unenthusiastic predivorce relationship they had with their fathers. They had not felt their fathers were terribly interested, nor did they view them after separation as offering much to meet their own needs. Most often, the fathers had devoted more attention to a male sibling, and these adolescents seemed, with calm resignation, to accept this differential treatment as a fact of family life. They visited with their fathers when it was mutually convenient, but not often, did not seek out extra visits, and invested most of their energies in school, social life, and extracurricular activities.

Genuine reluctance to visit occurred in 11 percent of the children and adolescents. Unlike the very few noted earlier who refused to visit, these youngsters, mostly preadolescent girls, did in fact keep their visits. Some went dutifully, with little outward complaint. Others complained bitterly but felt coerced to go.

Darlene, eleven at separation, was immeasurably relieved at having the father out of her life. While an obedient and quiet girl, she had disliked his overbearing, rigid, and frightening manner. The weekly overnight visits were too often for comfort, but she meekly went because the father had obtained a court order enforcing the schedule.

A few adolescents perceived that the financial support for their college education would be forthcoming only if they maintained contact with fathers they tended to dislike.

Anne readily shared her feelings about her father: "He's selfish and mean, and he has a bad temper. I can see what he's like now that we don't live together. I don't like visiting—it's boring—but I'd better be nice or he won't pay for college. I hate to depend on him for anything. If my mom or grandparents had some money, I'd stop seeing him."

# PART 3

## IN TRANSITION

# Chapter 9

# Parents
# in Transition

## Family Circumstances—
## Eighteen Months Postseparation

Eighteen months after the separation—a year after our first extended contact—we reestablished contact with fifty-eight of the original sixty families in our study (see appendix A for details of returning sample and follow-up procedure).

### Extended Changes for Parents and Children

By this time the divorce was legally completed for four fifths of the families, while bitter and draining property disputes were prolonging final settlements for the remainder. Except where divorce actions dragged on in the courts, many parents took little note of the actual date their divorce was legally final. Not unexpectedly, they regarded the termination of their marriage as psychological rather than legal.

In all families but one, the women continued to have sole legal custody, and most children continued to live with their mothers. Only three children lived regularly with their fathers. A few adolescents went back and forth between households, sometimes under duress, sometimes with the full assent of each parent. None of the youngsters lived with grandparents or relatives, although several spent entire summers in other states with grandparents. In each of these cases, the mother was working full time, and both custodial parent and children welcomed the change.

Half of the maternal grandparents, and fewer paternal grandparents, maintained considerable interest in and regular contact with their grandchildren, although many lived at some distance.

More than a quarter of the youngsters and their mothers had moved to more suitable, usually less expensive, housing. A few of these families had already moved twice in the eighteen months. Yet more than half of the children continued in the same school they had attended prior to the family disruption. Parents seemed acutely aware of the youngsters' need for stability in school and with peers, and some paid more for housing than they could reasonably afford in order to achieve this. Very few parents had moved away from the general vicinity, so the vast majority of parents and children lived within an hour of each other. This unexpected stability and continuity for the youngsters, in a region (the Bay Area) known for the high mobility of its inhabitants, may have several causes. More than a few fathers told us of their intent to stay close to their children, and their fervent hope their ex-wives would stay put. And some of the more sensitive women, although yearning at times to flee familiar surroundings and start anew elsewhere, recognized the importance of geographical closeness to their children's father. In the intervening year, one father accepted a transfer out of the state, missed his children more than he imagined possible, and by the time of this follow-up had begun to make arrangements to transfer back.

Undoubtedly another factor contributing to the geographical stability of our families is the desirable weather and beauty of the area and the availability of low-cost, high-quality, post-high school education.

Twenty percent of the men and 17 percent of the women had remarried. Thus, 13 percent of the children now lived with their mother and a new stepfather. A similar number shared their home with mother's live-in male friend or another single-parent family. But three-quarters of the children continued to live with just their mothers.

## Economic Characteristics

The harsh realities of socioeconomic change following separation, described earlier, continued unchanged for the majority of families. Remarkably, 85 percent of the men were still paying child support, although not always regularly or in full amount.° It was the women in

---

° This finding is at variance with other studies investigating payment of child support in California and elsewhere in the United States. In these studies, one year after divorce, "less than half the men are still paying support at all for their children." [See Lenore Weitzman, *The Marriage Contract: Couples, Lovers and the Law* (Englewood Cliffs, N.J.: Prentice-Hall, in press).] Yet even the payment of regular child support did not ensure financial security for many women. A recent study of a sample of California awards in 1972 and 1977 found that "the average child support provided significantly less than one-half of the cost of raising children during those years" [See Lenore Weitzman and Ruth Dixon, "Child Custody, Legal Standards, and

our study, more than the men, who sustained the difficult impact of substantially changed economics. Slightly more than a third of the women
lived with an extremely erratic financial situation. They were unsure of
continued support, anxious over mounting expenses, and frustrated that
their own employment did not adequately contribute to any increased
sense of financial security. Further, in a decade that saw spiraling costs
due to inflation, child support payments did not keep pace with increases
in cost of living. Only if a woman was able to afford the legal fees entailed in going back to court for a cost-of-living adjustment in child support was any change possible, and even then, there was no assurance
that such a request would be granted. Most women could neither afford
the legal fees nor did they relish the idea of entering into battle once
again with their ex-spouses. And so, many women lived on considerably
less income than their ex-spouses.

As the major economic changes sifted into place, we noted that three-
fifths of the women and two-fifths of the men had experienced a substantial decline in their standard of living as a result of the divorce. The decline was most serious, the financial picture most erratic and unsettling,
when both the father and mother were in the lower socioeconomic class.
And when this cluster of economic variables appeared, there was, as
well, a significant link to household chaos and instability on an everyday
basis. From the children's vantage point, everything seemed to have
fallen apart.

Slightly more than half of the men, however, and a third of the
women had not been aware of much change. Among these were both
wealthy men (and one woman), and men and women who to begin
with, had been in the lowest socioeconomic class or on welfare. In a
small group of men and women there had been an improvement in their
standard of living, either through remarriage or because two parents now
worked instead of one.

## Employment and Child Care

The number of women working had changed little in the intervening
year; most of those who had gone to work as a consequence of the divorce did so immediately after the separation and stayed employed. Of
those women (two-thirds of the group) working full or part time, the
clear majority enjoyed their work and the increased self-esteem that resulted from feeling competent and independent. This was especially true
of the younger women. A smaller number accepted the necessity of
working but regarded their jobs as tedious or fatiguing, and derived no

---

Empirical Patterns for Child Custody, Support, and Visitation after Divorce," *Univer-*
*sity of California, Davis Law Review*, vol. 12, Summer, 1979.]. Further, it is estimated
that fewer than one-third of California women receive alimony payments after
divorce.

satisfaction from their employment. A small group (8 percent of those working) bitterly resented the necessity to work imposed on them by their husband's decision to leave the marriage. One-fifth of the women were enrolled in some vocational training or educational program, mostly part time and in combination with their work schedule, in order to prepare for more meaningful and financially remunerative employment.

Household help was rare and available only to the few professional women in the group. Only one mother had a fulltime housekeeper. Usually, young children were carried to babysitters at the beginning of the day and retrieved by mothers on their way home. For many the pace was dizzying and they seemed unable to slow down. Several mothers with young children who returned to work full time reported that they regularly worked past midnight to complete household chores.

Among the women who did not work and remained at home full time, as noted in our findings at the time of separation, about half suffered with moderate or serious depressions, or other serious mental illness. Some among the group that remained at home suffered from serious recurring physical ailments such as severe arthritis or asthma, which periodically incapacitated them for one or more weeks at a time. One consequence of the inability of physically ill or emotionally troubled women to successfully enter the full-time job market was that the number of women who spent more time in the company of young children contained a higher percentage of persons with psychological or physical illness, a serious constraint on their caretaking capacities.

Overall, among the men there was little change in employment. There was a slight increase in those working in full time and continuous employment, and in the number essentially unemployed. Several men who had reduced their work schedule at separation in order to reduce income, and thereby have their support payments to the family reduced, were back at work full time. Some who had quit work as part of a lifestyle change which precipitated or accompanied the divorce had returned to their original occupations. But a few men, seriously troubled and depressed by the divorce, were unable to resume functioning and reenter the work force.

## How Parents Looked Eighteen Months Postseparation

### Attitude Toward the Divorce

Both the men and women were beginning to come to terms with the divorce; there was now more approval than disapproval. Whereas before, only a third of the men favored the divorce, now three-fifths were generally satisfied with the turn of events, and some of these men were quite pleased with their newly changed lives. The remainder continued to have mostly negative feelings, expressed either as considerable misgivings, reluctant resignation, or continued bitter and strident opposition (for 9 percent).

More women than men looked back wistfully to the marriage which they had left. Whereas originally, two-thirds of them had held quite positive views toward the dissolution of the marriage, this number had decreased, and at eighteen months, nearly one-half the women expressed some negative attitudes and feelings about their divorces. That is, nearly one-quarter were unhappily resigned to their divorced status, 13 percent had considerable misgivings, and 9 percent remained bitterly opposed to divorce. The immediate postseparation period had taken its toll on some of these depleted women. In some cases, the psychological positions of the husbands and wives were reversed.

Mrs. C., a dependent and depressed woman, originally insisted on the divorce in the face of her husband's steadfast opposition. At that time she described him as "compulsive, domineering, and autocratic." Nineteen months after the separation, Mr. C. had recovered from his severe divorce-engendered depression, had a better job, and a new gratifying relationship with a woman friend. He remained concerned about and interested in his children. In the interim, Mrs. C.'s psychological health deteriorated. She became disorganized in her parenting, swinging from skimpy contact with her children to tyrannical crackdowns. Depressed and lonely, with no gratifying social life, no gratifying home life, and a miserable job, she maintained a fantasy of her independence, which failed to match reality. She complained bitterly: "Now I have to be the father *and* the mother. I'm turning out to be the bad guy in the divorce."

Slightly more than half of the women, however, were pleased with the direction their lives were taking, including some who had been shocked, frightened, and depressed by their husband's request for divorce.

Mrs. I., in her mid-thirties two years after the separation, demonstrated remarkably the ability, seen in both men and women, to cope with an unwanted major crisis and move into a more rewarding phase of her life. She told us: "I don't regret the divorce now . . . I've really grown and changed. I feel like I ought to thank him!" she laughed. "Now I'm having a much happier life. I'm more aware and can appreciate things about me. The ego thing was important. I'd been shot down and my self-esteem was really bad. I've built it back up again. I feel that since I've handled this, I can handle the whole world."

## Interactions Between Parents

The bitter, passionate, agitated interaction between the parents which characterized the escalating events of the separation and its aftermath had gradually subsided. On the whole, the former marital partners were more circumspect and restrained in their dealings with each other. The men, more than the women, would openly acknowledge friendly or warm feelings toward their previous partners. A small number admitted that they still loved their former partners and would choose the same marriage again.

Mr. M. openly expressed his sadness at the failure of their marriage, accepting now his share of responsibility, whereas before he had been unable to. In the interim he had experimented with various lifestyles without much gratification and described as well his failure to obtain much lasting satisfaction with a series of younger girlfriends. He was a sadder, lonelier, and more mature man. "I really regret the divorce . . . I've lost a good woman."

Forty-five percent of the men and one-third of the women had essentially left all bitterness about the divorce behind them. One of the fortunate consequences of this change was the improved ambience for the children, half of whom now were not aware of any conflict between their parents. These same parents had managed, as well, to cease most, if not all, negative talk about the other parent in the presence of their children. In general, more women than men hung onto the anger they felt toward their ex-spouses. Half of the mothers continued to make extremely critical, or disparaging, remarks about their husbands, whereas only one-fifth of the fathers were so intensely critical in front of the children.

### Parents' Psychological Functioning

As a group, the men and women were still in transition, struggling with the process of adapting to their newly divorced status. Although the vast majority of divorces were legally completed, the parents gave evidence of a certain amount of unfinished emotional business, and not all of this was by any means the result of continuing to share parenting responsibilities.

If we can talk of "averages," then we can construct a composite of the average man and woman in our study, eighteen months after the separation.

The average father was very close to fully reestablishing his psychological equilibrium. Gone was the regressive behavior, the angry and sometimes wild outbursts, the vast fluctuations in mood. Life was moving forward again, albeit changed in many ways. But the fathers were moderately lonely (excluding here the remarried fathers), somewhat more than mildly depressed, and feeling less sense of freedom than the stereotypical expectation in our society for divorced males.

The average mother was moderately depressed and often lonely. But she had experienced a moderate increase in an overall sense of well-

being and general happiness—more so than her former husband. With
the practice of the intervening year, she now felt capable of managing
alone and experienced a new measure of competence. The resultant rise
in self-esteem was an important aspect of her adjustment, but was by no
means yet consolidated and secure. Unlike the average male, life had
not yet stabilized; psychological equilibrium was a sometime thing.
Glimpses of a secure, gratifying, and maybe peaceful life were there,
but not yet the whole of the picture. She continued to feel some anxiety
about her responsibilities as single parent, and living alone was still somewhat unsettling. The sense of freedom toward which she aspired had
not yet been achieved. It was often compromised by her discouraged,
sometimes hopeless, feeling about the future.

A high number of men and women had sought some form of therapeutic support or intervention in the year between the initial counseling
intervention and the first follow-up. While we had recommended various
forms of therapy to one-third of the women and somewhat fewer men, a
larger number of both actually sought help. One-fifth of the men sought
therapeutic interventions, mostly in the form of individual therapy, but a
few in group counseling. The length of contact varied for both men and
women from brief interventions to more prolonged therapeutic relationships. And 44 percent of the women sought help, half of them in individual therapy, the other half in parent counseling groups or group
therapy.

## What Problems Remained?

Some of the central problems that remained were shared by men and
women alike; others were more unique to their newly different roles of
full-time versus part-time parent.

DEPRESSION. Although both men and women continued to experience
more depression than we had anticipated, the women at eighteen
months were significantly more depressed than the men. And while
initially the older women had been feeling significantly more despair
and hopelessness than the younger, this difference had disappeared by
this first follow-up. The depression of some women remained from their
predivorce state, although in some instances it had begun to lift. But
others were newly depressed or had experienced an exacerbation of an
existing depressed state. Some of these women felt more anxious, more
overwhelmed, and more disorganized than when we first saw them.
Overall, close to one-half of the women were depressed to some considerable degree, 17 percent of them severely so. Some of these were
occasionally preoccupied with suicidal thoughts. And while the total
number of men experiencing some depression was comparable overall,
what differed was the degree of severity. The women's depression centered more on continued feelings of abandonment, or being over-

whelmed by day to day living and parenting responsibilities, and the failure to achieve the more gratified, happier state they had envisioned in seeking the divorce. The men's depression was more often expressed as a profound sense of loss of marriage and family life, particularly the absence of the children on a daily basis, and related for some to a continued struggle to cope with rejection and abandonment. For both men and women, continuing depression was not related to socioeconomic status.

LONELINESS. The pervasiveness of profound loneliness among men and women was striking. Two-fifths of the men and two-thirds of the women described themselves as lonely, about half of them painfully so. Social life for those not remarried had been difficult and largely ungratifying, especially for the women who felt they had no control over their lives in this regard. Social activities involving other adults were increasingly common, but a central complaint focused on the absence of meaningful relationships which had some continuity. In dating, only a tiny number of men had not ventured forth. But eighteen months postseparation, nearly one-fifth of the women had not yet had a date, and two-fifths had had no sexual activity (as compared to 14 percent of the men). An additional 20 percent of the women described some sexual experiences although, to the chagrin of some, not within the context of an ongoing relationship. Among those men and women dating but not yet settled into a remarriage or steady relationship, there was a weariness with the superficiality of the social scene and the succession of individuals who had passed through their lives.

CONTINUING INTENSE ANGER. There remained a substantial number of men and women who continued to rage at their former partners, seemingly unaffected by the passage of time. For this group, nearly one-fifth of the women and slightly fewer men, the divorce had not yet been made final, had brought no comfort, and the humiliating incidents of the marital conflict were as fresh as if they had occurred yesterday. These were the parents whose total opposition to and rage about the divorce continued unabated. Outrageous behavior continued, including threats and acts of violence, threats of court battles, and renewed efforts to engage the children on their behalf. Children were still being co-opted as allies in spying on former spouses or in various revengeful subterfuges. Even when children were not actively recruited for combat, these embittered chaotic parents made little, if any, effort to shield their youngsters from witnessing or overhearing angry confrontations, either in person or over the phone. Thus, for a protracted period of time the ambience remained essentially unchanged for the children of these parents.

Mostly, these men and women were disorganized in their psychological functioning. Where the embittered-chaotic stance remained undiminished over time, we observed a significant relationship to a prior history of serious psychological difficulty. Some were warding off severe depressions with their rage; others were consolidating paranoid-like systems centering around their former spouse so that the merest mention of the partner's name triggered the entire narrative of perfidy, betrayal, and abandonment. Some were beginning to include all men or all women in their indictment and often warned their children that "men (or women) are like that." There was no tranquility for the youngsters of these parents, particularly if he or she were a custodial parent. For these troubled men and women, divorce had torn asunder a fragile system of coping with the world, and restabilization was nowhere in sight.

### Positive Changes After Divorce

The counterpart to the continued rage and depression we found were the instances of other men and women giving evidence of adaptation, consolidation, and positive change. Divorce for them, including some who originally opposed the marital disruption, became an opportunity to start anew, to write the outline of the next chapter in their lives with some degree of thoughtful reflection and control. They looked backward with soberness, learning from the failed relationship what personal changes were necessary to enhance the quality of their lives. For these individuals, more men than women, there had been closure on the divorce experience which made some feel as if they were new individuals living in a new world.

Mr. J. described his new sense of self: "I've learned a lot of things about myself I never knew, some of them not so pleasant. But mostly, I've become so *aware*! I feel like I'm sensitive to things I'd never even noticed before, as if all my pores are open now to sensing and feeling. It's exhilarating! I just wish I'd been able to do this ten years ago."

Mr. J. poignantly expressed the feelings of about one-quarter of the men, slightly fewer women, for whom the divorce in a variety of ways had become transformed into an experience of personal growth. The intervening year had brought about significant increase in the sense of well-being and inner contentedness in these individuals. Although sometimes reached via different avenues for men and women, the pleasure in having notably matured was evident. The women in particular experienced a greatly enhanced self-esteem, a feeling readily articulated that they were now more competent, more capable of handling themselves as adults and as parents.

Already accustomed perhaps to feeling competent, at least in work, fewer men experienced such exhilarating increases in self-esteem. Their greater happiness or sense of well-being related sometimes to a growing realization that they were capable of relationships with other adults that could be mature, intimate, and gratifying, or pleasurable and rewarding for their children.

With these men and women positive feelings had also accrued from the realization that they had disentangled themselves from a marital relation that had been mutually destructive, debilitating, or completely ungratifying. Sometimes, but not often, this increased maturity, happiness, and self-esteem was evident in both parents.

Mr. and Mrs. T. independently characterized their marriage as "bad from the start," agreeing that the wife's pregnancy was the sole reason for marrying. Mr. T.: "We were both immature . . . there was a lot of fighting. Her housekeeping was awful. . . . When she gained all that weight she was repulsive to me." At the initial contact he detailed his plans for further schooling and promotions at work, but admitted he had been passed over previously because of his "problems getting along with people."

Mrs. T. described herself as "immature and irresponsible as a teenager. I got married to get away from my family, too." They argued continuously; "He put me down constantly" and always carped at her slovenly ways. There was no love, no communication. Mrs. T. recalled being furious that her spouse put all of their money into his hobbies. "We were both self-centered." Mrs. T. began to mature in the marriage but especially after the separation, when she realized, "Now it's either sink or swim." When we first saw her for the extended contact, Mrs. T. was seeking to better herself by intense schooling and part-time work, but was burdened by poor self-esteem, was considerably overweight, and felt angry and overwhelmed by her children's fighting and demands.

Slightly more than a year later, Mr. T. happily outlined his plans to remarry. "I feel like I've grown up since I last saw you." He related with pride how he and his future wife were able to communicate and work things out well. He was pleased, too, that his ex-wife was happy. "She deserves it. If she could be as happy as I've been the past three months, it would really be nice."

A slimmer, more attractive Mrs. T. was similarly bubbling with happiness a year later. About to be married, finished with school, and with a responsible, gratifying job, Mrs. T. exclaimed: "I can't believe it. Everything is going so well. I never thought I'd find a guy I could love, live with, and still want to marry. Sometimes I have to pinch myself and say this is all really happening to me."

## Improved Parenting

From the standpoint of the children, positive adaptation and maturation in the adult parent is a desirable outcome. And yet, unless the changes have as part of their focus the interaction between parent and child, the child may not be the beneficiary, at least not immediately. The developmental process for young children in particular moves forward at a rapid and increasingly complex pace, and its successful course is dependent in part on the assistance of attentive, nurturing parents. Children cannot mark time for an extended period while parents integrate their own lives if such integration excludes, or fails to take seriously, the youngsters' needs for continued support.

Thus, of interest to us were those parents who focused after the divorce not just on the resumption of their own lives but had hopes and expectations for their children as well. Despite the fact that so many parents had not yet achieved a firm postdivorce stability and had yet to close the psychological door on the marital disruption, things had settled considerably. Within parent-child interactions on a daily basis, the stormy passions connected with the divorce itself were subsiding or had disappeared. And as this occurred, some parents began to note real changes in the quality of the interactions with their youngsters. As an example, women previously uncomfortable with the role of disciplinarian were no longer anxious in setting limits. Men and women initially unable to share appropriate feelings and inner thoughts with their youngsters found that such sharing brought closeness, respect, and true affection. The flow of daily events took on a smoothness never before experienced and parents, men and women alike, discovered that being a parent could be quite pleasurable as well as a responsibility.

Fifteen percent of the men, and twenty percent of the women significantly increased their gratification in being a parent. A large number of individuals experienced more modest changes in this direction, but of particular interest here were those for whom important shifts occurred. These adults not only felt considerably more gratification in their role as parents, but in reality functioned better as parents and were much happier with their lives. The men and women whose comfort and pleasure in the parental role were most enhanced over the intervening year were, as a group, the more psychologically stable, reasonably well-integrated individuals. None of the parents whose rage continued undiminished appeared among this group of better-functioning parents; nor did parents with significant psychological disturbance.

There was a significant link between an initial view of the divorce as representing a "new chance" for improving the quality of life for oneself and one's children and actually functioning significantly better in the parental role a year later. The intention to enhance parent-child interactions from the start seemed to provide an important focus for these parents in the turmoil after separation. When all else seemed bleak or upsetting, these "new chance" women clung to the notion that the divorce was undertaken for—and in fact provided—fresh opportunities to improve the emotional clime for their children. They addressed parenting tasks with vigor, asked for and put to use guidance, and gradually reshaped their capacity to parent.

One year after the divorce, Mrs. N.'s depression was lifting, she was less anxious and better organized in her role of single parent. While she remained socially isolated, her relationship with both children was more secure. No longer afraid of their anger, Mrs. N. was able to set limits firmly without worrying that her daughters would cease to love her. With her growing sense of competence as a parent, Mrs. N. felt stirrings of real pleasure in being a parent, gratification that had eluded her in the marriage and early separation period.

But not all of the parents who greatly improved their parental functioning in the intervening year did so by conscious intent or by pursuing a sense of renewed opportunity. For some individuals, particularly the men, the role of parent took on new dimensions previously unrealized, and the resultant gratification came as a surprise.

# Chapter 10

# Children in Transition

## Children Eighteen Months Postseparation

An attractive high school senior, Tammy had matured considerably during the year since her parents' divorce. She was poised, warm, and responsive. She volunteered that the divorce "seems like years ago." She saw her dad several times monthly and their relationship was good, surprisingly better than before the divorce. "He doesn't get upset as much. . . . I guess I'm seeing him more as a person than as my all-important daddy."

Tammy talked of both parents with compassion. She recognized the marriage as *their* problem and the divorce as *their* failure. She asserted that she was more her own person these days. Happily she described her interests, her goals, and her relationships with friends. The drama and the high intensity that were evident in her early expressions of anger and distress a year before appeared to have been constructively redirected into her own life.

David on the other hand had suffered a decline in his learning and his social adjustment during the postseparation period. He had experienced the new family—his mother had remarried a man who himself had custody of three children—and described his life as less gratifying as he complained of less food (though the family certainly had enough food), greater anger, and diminished care.

A gifted ten-year-old boy, David was seriously handicapped in his academic and social relationships as he came to this first follow-up. His teacher had complained that David rarely finished his assignment, had great difficulty in concentrating in the classroom, and showed little capacity to stand up for himself in his relationships with his peers.

Throughout the interview, David was tense. He complained, "There are three more people in the family now and less to eat . . . and less tolerance for each of the children, and there's a lot more anger. A lot of problems spring up every day." He described his stepfather as quick-tempered and his mother as "less tolerant than she used to be" and more irritable. "She gets even madder than he does."

The divorce, he stated emphatically, "is their choice, not mine. They had their reasons. My dad doesn't like to talk about it. My mom says that she and dad are different kinds of people. I guess my mom just didn't like my dad. I think this is better now, but I'm sure not positive. My mom was active and my dad wanted 'a plain old housewife.' My mom wanted to move around and do plans. Mom doesn't like to do stuff for us so we have to cook for ourselves." About the divorce David commented, "I think the reasons they gave, then they should have divorced. I don't like them having the divorce, but they should have it." "I wish," he added wistfully, "they were still together, but they just weren't getting along." Talking about his own plans for the future, the boy said he wasn't sure whether he will ever get married or have children. "Mom says it's a big bother to have so many children." Finally, we asked whether he would like to have anything different. David shook his head, "No, things are fun," he said unsmilingly.

## How They Appeared—an Overview

One year later most of the children and adolescents looked different. The acute psychological disruptions precipitated by the dissolution of the family were ending. As the crisis subsided, the crisis-engendered responses which we have described—the widespread fears, the grief, the shocked disbelief, and the new symptoms—faded or disappeared altogether. The perspective now at the eighteen-month mark following separation—or a year after our own first extended contact—revealed the efforts at mastery that had been taking place. A majority of the youngsters had resumed their earlier developmental pace. Some, like Tammy, had accelerated well beyond their achievements in the predivorce family. A significant minority, like David, were failing and appeared to be under continuing, or even greater, stress than previously. The complex patterning of the children's efforts at mastery as reflected in their changing attitudes and feelings could be examined in process.

Some of the more striking changes from the way these youngsters presented themselves to us at the time of parental separation were evident in the behavior and attitudes which we had considered marks of the children's crisis. Thus, whereas previously over one-half of the children had been preoccupied with the parental separation, hardly able to think of anything else—whether to concentrate at school, to enjoy friends, or to pursue prior interests—the number who felt overwhelmed had been reduced to 15 percent of the group. The majority of the children had resumed their usual schedules at school, developed new routines at home, and had consciously put the divorce to one side. Anxiety had also decreased during this period; whereas earlier about one-half had been acutely anxious, this number had now declined to one-fifth of the group. Although some worries remained, the acute fear of possible abandonment by one or both parents and the diffuse sense of unease had clearly subsided. And whereas earlier over half of the group had been intensely worried that their future plans would be disrupted or would never materialize, less than 10 percent felt so intensely by follow-up. All of these changes together reflected a turnabout in outlook and a more realistic, less fear-dominated view of the divorce and its consequences. Earlier, at the initial assessment, one-third of the children had been unable to accept the reality of the divorce. A year later all but a handful of the preschool children had given up the fantasy that the divorce would suddenly disappear. Even little girls who confused their wish-laden dream life with the waking world—such as the four-year-old child who told us several weeks after the father's departure from the household, "My daddy sleeps in my bed every night"—had accepted the divorce by this time and, although half of the children still wished their parents to reconcile, they also recognized that the divorce was likely to remain firmly in place.

And finally, most of the acute symptoms which had erupted during the early separation period had become muted or entirely disappeared. Sleep disturbances were half of what they had been following the separation and were now present in only one-sixth of the group. Acute phobias, regression, acute anxiety, whimpering, fear of being lost in the shuffle or of being forgotten by the worrying parent, precipitous drops in school learning—all of these were no longer so visible and had mostly disappeared or had been mastered by children with or without adult help.

One six-year-old child conquered his fear of going to sleep with the help of a placard which he made for himself and on which he wrote, "Robbie, don't be afraid, go to sleep." His mother no longer put him to bed as she had during the predivorce period, and he no longer waited anxiously and sleeplessly for her to do so. Placing the placard at the foot of his bed and reading it aloud, the child put himself to sleep.

These changes, especially in light of continuing intense conflicts between the divorcing parents which cast a shadow over the lives of one-third of the children, led us to conclude that by one and a half years postseparation most of the children had passed through the acute stage of the crisis. The improvements were particularly striking because they were not necessarily accompanied by comparable improvement in the parent-child relationships.

Although both mother-child and father-child relationships, as we have said, were improved from their level of functioning at the height of the divorce crisis, and a few were strikingly better, the changes in the children even surpassed the changes in the parent-child relationship. The improvement evident at this time may well have reflected the resiliency of children in general or the resiliency of this particular group of children who had been selected initially from a normal population and had managed to maintain their adjustment within the conflict-ridden marriage.

## Conceptual Framework at Follow-up

Duration over time is a significant dimension of behavior. Acute responses to stress are likely to be short-lived and are different in their implications for development from responses which endure. At what point relative fixity is reached is not always clear. With children the transition from acute to chronic is particularly difficult to establish. Nevertheless, the coping behavior that derives from the child's inner resources, including courage which flares momentarily and succeeds in maintaining the child's equilibrium at the time, is significantly different in its implications for the child's future development from coping behavior which extends over several years and which may have kept the child moving successfully along a developmental course. Similarly, an acute depression at the time of the separation is much less grave in its implications for the future development of the child than a depression which has lasted a year and a half, although a picture of the symptoms may look quite the same.

A year-long depression will have affected the child's development and learning during that year. He or she may have fallen behind in school and lost ground in relationships with friends. Children who are still depressed a year and a half after parental separation are likely to be in trouble and to need psychological or psychiatric help quickly since every month that passes will probably further consolidate the symptoms particularly the helplessness and hopelessness they feel. Similarly, the child who has coped well, becoming strengthened in this process, may have succeeded not only in solving the immediate problems, but also in sprinting ahead because of the independence and maturity acquired in the successful struggle.

Thus, the responses that have endured and that are visible at one and a half years have a different connotation from those that were reported initially, and can be understood within the context of attitudes and behaviors that have been maintained beyond the acute phase or are newly emerged with the postdivorce family. These behaviors and attitudes that lasted require a special look. They have, by virtue of their persistence, acquired special importance in the developing personality of the child.

## Differences Between Boys and Girls

One major theme which emerged during the first follow-up was the widening gap between the sexes. Girls predominated among the children who looked well. Nearly twice as many girls as boys improved in their overall adjustment and functioning at this time from the way they had looked at the initial assessment, but this striking difference did not appear among the adolescents.

At the time of the marital separation, we had observed only a few sex-related differences among the children in regard either to their overall adjustment or their initial response to the family crisis. The girls had appeared somewhat more intact at that time, although not significantly so. On some measures they came out ahead of their brothers. They were judged by us more able than their brothers to establish good relationships with adults and with other children. They were more empathic, more psychologically sensitive, significantly more independent, and generally more able to enjoy play and to make use of fantasy. They were also somewhat angrier at their mothers for the divorce.

Taken altogether, however, at the initial assessment there were greater similarities between the boys and the girls than there were differences. No significant differences were noted between the sexes along a great many measures, including the sense of being distressed by the divorce, the longing for the departed parent, the fear of abandonment by one or both parents, feelings of being rejected by one or both parents, degree of anxiety, intensity of unhappiness, school-related problems, anger, loss of self-esteem, loneliness, or the incidence of depression. Along all these dimensions, initially there were no significant differences. As we have described, children reacted in ways that appeared consonant with their developmental achievement.

Nevertheless, at the first follow-up the differences between boys and girls were striking. Boys were significantly more opposed to the divorce than their sisters; they felt significantly more stressed within the postdivorce family and more of them had remained intensely preoccupied with the divorce. More boys longed intensely for their father. More boys felt rejected by their father. More boys were preoccupied with fantasies of reconciling the broken marriage. More boys were depressed.

The girls, by contrast, were happier; they were more likely to see the divorce as an improvement over the earlier, perdivorce family. More girls had friends, and more used their friends as a support system. On a wide variety of measures they appeared to be coping more successfully than their brothers.

These findings are surprising and lend themselves to various interpretations which are not mutually exclusive. It may be that girls are generally more resilient than boys in their psychological functioning. And indeed, there is evidence for this in the fact that the girls had weathered the storms of the predivorce family better than their brothers.

Or, the greater resiliency or faster recovery by the girls may be related to the different relationships with one or both parents within the postseparation family. There are indications that girls were treated somewhat better by teachers and by mothers than their brothers. Some mothers did, indeed, vent their wrath on their sons as representatives of the father or of men in general. When the mother's handling had deteriorated, the boys were more often the target than the girls. Furthermore, girls were more often protected than their brothers from witnessing family quarrels and parental misbehavior.

Nevertheless, most of the difference in mothering we observed was age related and not sex related. By and large, women (and men) treated their younger children of either sex with more care and compassion than they treated the older youngsters. The difference in the mother's attitude and parenting of boys and girls does not emerge with enough clarity to account fully for the larger differences which emerge between boys' and girls' adjustment a year and a half following the marital separation.

Fathers' relationships with their daughters following the marital disruption showed a greater consistency than their relationships with their sons. This factor may be of importance in explaining some of the boys' greater decline. Thus, girls who had had good relationships with their fathers prior to the divorce were more likely to experience continuity following the divorce. Similarly, girls who had poor relationships predivorce experienced less change later on. By contrast, many of the boys who had close relationships with their father during the unbroken marriage were abruptly confronted with a changed response by the father. And boys who had had limited relationships with their fathers during the marriage sometimes experienced greater interest in maintaining relationships with him following the divorce. In all, therefore, the boys needed to adjust to greater change in the father-child relationship than did their sisters.

In some important ways there were no differences between the sexes. There were no sex-linked differences, for example, in the amount of order or chaos in the respective households of the boys or the girls. There were no significant psychological differences in the functioning of the parents that might shed light on the different outcome. Although in a few instances little girls were very much loved and supported by teachers, this support did not stave off the child's decline, and overall girls of all ages were not treated significantly better by teachers.

We were also interested to find that the children did not *feel* differently treated by either the mother or the father. Boys or girls did not, as a group, feel more or less rejected by either parent. There were no sex-related differences among the children in their worries about whether they would be taken care of or in their trust of the parent to care for them.

The finding that the girls had recovered their equilibrium earlier than the boys is not necessarily a clear indicator of their future psychological well-being. These findings a year and a half following the separation do not rule out the possibility of a delayed response among the girls, or a response that appears within a much later context of events which may reawaken the original conflict.

### Developmental Spurt

An important subgroup consisting largely of little boys made exceptionally fast progress during this year. Although the children whose development accelerated in general included twice as many girls of all ages as boys (except adolescents), a significant number of younger boys were represented among those who progressed with renewed energy. These were little boys with psychologically disturbed fathers and well-functioning custodial mothers. Young boys separated by the divorce from a psychologically ill father and placed in the care of a well mother were sometimes able to make extraordinary progress during the year following the marital separation.

Larry, who was four when he was first seen by us, was a sad, whiney little boy who felt very much rejected when his father departed from the household. There were several indications of a history of sexual play between father and child. Among the child's symptoms was a restless searching out for men and a climbing into strange men's laps. Larry had troubled relationships with children and teachers at school and appeared to be trying to make contact and push people away at the same time.

A year later, Larry seemed happy, bright, and very much improved. The teacher described him as an "outstanding child . . . happy and the best reader in the class. Feels good about himself. He is no longer easily frustrated." Following the remarriage of the mother Larry had made an excellent attachment to his new stepfather. There had been a dramatic change in the child. Although Larry continued to see his father at regular intervals during the intervening year, the father's destructive influence on him had clearly diminished or discontinued entirely.

*Children's Attitudes and Feelings*

During this year a considerable mellowing had taken place. The mood of the children was less intense, their feelings about themselves and the many issues related to the family had become more moderate, and a modulation in negative attitude and criticism of the parents appeared more widespread at the one-and-a-half-year mark. Within the mellowing process, however, it was the feelings of the children that appeared to have changed rather than their attitudes; in fact, the continuity in attitudes toward the divorce was striking.

Only about half of the children, including the majority of the boys, did not approve at all of the divorce at this time as compared with three-quarters who were opposed initially. One-third of the children, however, had gravitated toward the middle ground, whereas hardly any middle ground existed at the initial assessment. An even larger number of the group, two-thirds of the entire sample, continued to feel that the divorce was no improvement over the predivorce family and, in fact, an exceedingly small number (less than 10 percent) found the change in family to their liking. It is striking that one and a half years after the separation we found that only one-fifth of the children fully approved their parents' decision and that so few found the divorced family to be an improvement. We conclude that, although most children appeared to be coping well, they had maintained their loyalty to the predivorce family and were not at all convinced of their parents' wisdom in seeking the divorce. Their adjustment, which was really quite good in many instances, reflected in large measure their pragmatic acceptance of the new conditions of their lives, imposed by parents whose decisions they continued to question or to oppose. Capturing the salient mood of these children as they appeared at their first follow-up, one ten-year-old commented in her clear-eyed perception of reality, "Knowing my parents, no one is going to change his mind. We'll just all have to get used to the situation and to them." Perhaps such acceptance of the limits of their power to bring about change in the parents is an important component in successful coping by children of divorce.

But their feelings *had* changed. Most of the children were no longer unhappy. The number of unhappy children had, in fact, diminished by half from the initial assessment. Over one-half of the group had muted feelings that were now located within the middle range, combining moderate stress and moderate happiness, framed on each side by one-quarter of the children who were very content and the other one-quarter who were intensely unhappy.

Most of the children were no longer feeling deprived or needful of adult attention or physical contact. We had been concerned earlier with the number of children who appeared needy, a term which we employed to designate the desire to be nurtured that was expressed by children who climbed too quickly into strange laps and reached out for physical contact with teachers, or appeared in a random, regressed manner to search for physical contact. This emotional neediness, although it had not entirely disappeared, had diminished. And over one-third of the children seemed well nourished psychologically.

Most of the children were no longer intensely lonely. At the time of the separation children had felt peripheral to the preoccupied, distressed parents and unsupported by other adults. Many had felt that they could not share the family secrets with friends out of loyalty to the family and their parents. Therefore, the decrease in this intense loneliness is significant: It reflects the children's sense that the family's supportive network had been restored and that they feel protected by the structure of the postdivorce family.

The diminution in crisis-related behavior and symptoms and the greater modulation of emotional responses failed, perhaps, to catch the still very sober, even sometimes somber, feelings these children projected. Many of these youngsters had obviously just come through an ordeal. They had some intense awareness of the storm which they had just left behind. Their feelings were at midpoint and changing, and their dominant mood was neither grieving nor spontaneously joyful.

The children's soberness was reflected by Ruth at age eleven. Speaking of the future, she said, "I'd like to get married but I'd want to make sure that he loves me and I love him. I'd want to make sure, but of course you never know. I would rather not get a divorce." She added, "It used to be that Mom set a good example for all of us, but now with her working I have to be the good example so the two other children will follow me . . . so I have to be good."

### Symptomatic Behavior

Most of the symptoms the children had newly acquired at the time of the marital separation had diminished or disappeared. The most widespread remaining psychopathological finding was depression, which we shall discuss later. Aside from this, the symptom that was observed in a considerable number of the children and that remained constant at the follow-up was that of "manipulative behavior." Approximately one-fifth of the children were described by their teachers as manipulative of other children on the playground or in their social relationships.

Gwen, age nine, was described by her teacher: "She thinks she's queen of the hill." The teacher went on to detail the many clever ways in which Gwen, who was quiet and well behaved at home, was manipulating the other children on the playground and skillfully playing one against the other.

Manipulative behavior is difficult to observe in the consulting room.

It stands to reason, however, that the ability to manipulate one's parents may be adaptive behavior for children at the time of divorce. This behavior may also reflect the child's sense of powerlessness and feelings of having been moved around without consideration of his or her feelings; feelings the child then reverses on the playground by victimizing another child. The learned manipulation of others may well emerge as a divorce-specific symptom which endures.

The incidence of other symptoms was low. Stealing had not increased during the intervening year. Of the ten children between the ages of six and ten who had become involved in stealing at the time of the separation, most had decreased or given up this behavior. Truancy was low. Hyperactivity and misbehavior at school were negligible. Fighting with peers and siblings had lessened since the time of separation. Physical illness and psychosomatic symptoms had decreased in the intervening period as well and were found in 10 percent of the group. Sexual acting-out, however, which a small group of adolescent girls began at the time of the parental separation, remained essentially unchanged.

## Depression

The main psychopathological finding was childhood depression, which we diagnosed in one-quarter of the children and adolescents. Severe depression was found in seven children, moderate depression in twenty-two children—a total of thirteen girls and sixteen boys. A high number of the moderately depressed boys and girls had been between seven and ten years of age at the time of the initial assessment one year earlier.

Depression in childhood and adolescence has many manifestations. The behavior and symptoms include pervasive sadness, poor self-esteem, school performance well below potential, difficulty in concentrating, preoccupation with the parental divorce, play inhibition, social withdrawal, self-blame for the divorce, some petty stealing, compulsive overeating to the point of obesity, chronic irritability, and sexual promiscuity.

Edward, a bright eight-year-old, was depressed at the first followup. He was learning well below his capacity at school and was socially withdrawn. The interview, which we report in detail, showed a child in the process of sinking into a depression. Although he had some poignant awareness that this was happening to him, he felt unable to rescue himself and unable to get help from his mother or stepfather. The boy expressed his loneliness, his confusion about his family, and his sense of being intruded upon by noise at school and by daydreams which he could not control. His loss of pleasure in play and learning came through clearly in his preoccupation with the destruction of Playland.

Contributing significantly to Edward's distress was his mother's re-

fusal to permit the father to visit his son and her unremitting anger at
the father which she expressed frequently and which the boy felt to be
directed at him as well as at his father. It is of interest that, although
Edward was clearly depressed and his learning had markedly declined,
he had not been referred by the parents or the school for help.

FOLLOW-UP INTERVIEW WITH EDWARD, AGE EIGHT. In response to our
question about friends, Edward said that he didn't have many, that he
daydreamed most of the time. He daydreamed about antigravity paint
and about a spray gun that will make him invisible. His mother and his
stepfather got mad at him because he daydreamed so much of the
time. "It just takes a week to get into the habit," he confided. "In a way,
it's a good habit because it helps you get to sleep and, in another way,
its bad . . ." because he spent too much time doing it. He thought daydreaming was a better way to sleep than pills because one could get ad-
dicted to pills. He was worried, he said, that Playland (an amusement
park) was being torn down. He wondered whether there was any way
that they could stop the destruction of Playland.

When we asked about his stepfather, he sighed and said, "They don't
have as many problems as they used to." But lots of times when he
wanted to talk with his mother and asked his mother a question his
stepfather told him to stop. He said that school presented problems.
Everybody in school made so much noise. He didn't like that. The only
thing he liked to do was read or daydream. He volunteered that his
dog was a father now and that it was very complicated because there
was a mother dog that had two husbands. One of them belonged to him
and the other belonged to somebody else. As he left, he said it would
probably be better if he didn't daydream so much. On the other hand, he
thought he would spend much of the summer daydreaming. On this discouraged note the child left the consulting room.

The depression of these children appeared to be frequently associated with the triad of intense anger, a profound sense of rejection by
one or both parents, and strong disapproval of the divorce. These feelings appeared in different combinations, sometimes accompanied by self-
blame. The 10 percent of the children who held themselves responsible
for the divorce at follow-up were found largely among these depressed
children. As we have noted earlier, we did not find continuing self-blame
as a fantasy which persisted in psychologically intact children.

Children who were clinically depressed included those who were depressed during the predivorce family, those who became depressed at
the time of the marital breakup and then continued, and a third group,
in whom the depression was not evident at the time of the initial assessment but appeared at follow-up.

This last group had become depressed during the postseparation year.
On the basis of school and family history, and our own examination we

estimated that the majority of the depressed children in the initial assessment had not been depressed during the marriage despite the marital conflict.

Depression among these young boys was linked to recent developments in the family.° Their depression was significantly tied to infrequent visits from the father and the continued disappointment by the father, to anger at both parents, and to their feeling of being rejected by the mother. There was also a significant link between depression in younger boys and the reduced social and economic circumstances in the postdivorce family. Most of the depressed younger girls had poor relationships with their mother and had experienced a severe decline in parenting during the intervening year. The little girls appeared more affected than the little boys by the psychological disturbance and agitation of the custodial mother, and there was a significant tie between their depression and the mother's psychological illness. The younger boys seemed to be responding more to the father's absence and their sense of rejection by the father. The younger girls seemed to be reacting more to their sense of being rejected by the mother.

The older depressed boys seemed to be particularly sensitive to their exposure to embittered, chaotic parents who continued to battle with each other. We were interested in the acute reaction of older boys to the turmoil of the household. Depression in the older boys was related, as well, to feeling rejected by their fathers and relatively unsupported by their mothers. And finally, the older girls appeared to fall into two groups: those who felt rejected by their mother in the postdivorce family and those who felt rejected by their father.

The great majority of the children whom we had initially judged to be depressed had improved. Therefore most of the children who were depressed at this first follow-up, especially the younger ones, had become depressed during the more chronic stress of the postseparation year.

Among the troubled children, the core of the most highly stressed of them consisted predominantly of preadolescent boys. Most of these boys had been centrally preoccupied with the divorce initially and remained so a year and a half later. They remained preoccupied with sorrow over the departure of the beloved father, the continuing distress at insufficient visiting, the distress at being co-opted by vengeful mothers in the continuing parental struggle. Little boys who had enjoyed good relationships with their fathers during the marriage were particularly vulnerable and unable to master their grief. There was a significant link between the poor condition of these children and the continuing battle between the parents.

---

° See appendix A for age groupings used in statistical analyses at the first followup. "Young" children refers to those two-to-eight at the initial contact.

## Angry Children

At first, anger at one or both parents was a major response among almost one-third of the children, and over a quarter had given vent to explosive outbursts at one or both parents at the time of the separation. A year later, the intensity of the children's anger and the number of angry children had both decreased. Nevertheless, one-quarter of the youngsters continued to be intensely angry at one or both parents, blaming them for the divorce and the marital failure. The anger was most visible and most maintained its initial force in the case of the original nine-to-twelve-year-olds and among the adolescent girls. The children's anger at their mother and at their father were much the same. Some children in the nine-to-twelve-year-old group seemed angrier a year and a half later than they had been initially.

I asked Robin, age eleven, if things were better or worse since the divorce. She said emphatically, "They're worse." She went on to describe in detail how "mean Mother is . . . she's always yelling." Robin described how she was hit by her mother and the mother's boyfriend. She added, "Things are never good with my mom; sometimes medium, sometimes bad, but never good. We have a big fight once a day. She makes me do a lot of work around the house. She's against me because I like my father."

The anger of the children and adolescents appeared to have considerable staying power. We had expected that it would dissipate as the children became acclimated to the postdivorce family and as their fears of abandonment and other disasters proved groundless. Although the intensity had diminished and fewer children were angry, the one-and-a-half-year interval had not brought about the diminution that we anticipated. Patterns of control of anger had shifted somewhat during this period. But close to one-fifth of the children, mostly boys nine-to-twelve-years at the marital separation, had frequent explosive outbursts at their parents.

One of the more unexpected findings is that the children in the nine-to-twelve-year-old age group appear especially vulnerable to depression and that the anger that emerges as a divorce-specific response at this time remains fairly constant during the first year postseparation. The persistence of the anger may have important implications for development. Unfortunately, little is known of the long-term effects of continuing anger at one or both parents during these developmental years.

One visible consequence of the anger was the diminished relationship with the visiting parent. Nine-to-twelve-year-old youngsters were visited less because they were angry, and they in turn became angrier because they were less visited. Their relationship with their fathers thus deteriorated more than it had in any other age group. Children in this age group were also exposed to greater bitterness between the parents and were more involved in parental fighting and alignments.

Roger, age nine, said, "I don't mind any more about the divorce; I don't even care. It's made and I just want it to be final. I just wish they would behave like grownups and not like children. They fight every day. It makes me mad when I remember that they fight."

## Attitudes Toward Parents

The children's attitudes toward their parents had begun to reflect their experiences during the intervening year and a half. The respect for the custodial mother had risen and their trust in her had increased. Some of their initial anger at her had begun, gradually, to dissipate as well. We began at this time to see new, more affectionate relationships emerging between mother and children, combined with the ability to maintain distance from the family quarrel. Some of these youngsters, like Tammy, perceived their mother's struggles with compassion. A good number of the children, one-third of the group, continued to worry about the mother and particularly about her capacity to manage as sole head of the family. And in general, although many parents worried a great deal about being rejected by their children, there was considerable evidence that the children continued to love both their parents.

At the same time, both parents were regarded with increasing disenchantment and some wry amusement. This may result from the children's negative reaction to their custodial parents' greater reliance on themselves—young school-age children—for counsel and emotional nurturance. Some of the increased disenchantment was clearly a consequence of the children's jaundiced view of continued fighting between the parents, as well as to the frenetic social activity they witnessed. As one seven-year-old said disdainfully, "My parents are so silly. They fight over everything . . . even me." Eunice, age twelve, said, "If my parents were right here they would argue over the color of the table between us, like two little kids."

Unlike mothers, most fathers had not earned greater respect or trust during the intervening year, but the extreme attitude of the children had eased and most of the children had come to a more moderate view. Children's concern about the father's capacity to manage had also diminished markedly and only a small group of older girls continued to worry about his general welfare and happiness.

Fathers had become much less acceptable role models for their children. The number of youngsters who openly rejected conscious identification with their father rose steeply with the age of the children, especially among the boys. Approximately half of the nine-to-ten-year-old boys openly rejected their father as a model. The younger school-age boys also appeared to have begun to pull away from their strong initial identification with him. A high number of the nine-to-ten-year-old boys were consciously identified with their mother and spoke glowingly of her remarkable capacities and her loyalty to them.

Both parents had been scrutinized by their adolescent youngsters and sometimes found wanting in morality and decorum in their divorce-related behavior with each other and in their new relationships. One twelve-year-old boy remarked emphatically, "I want to know if my father is a good man." Children and adolescents who witnessed their parents continued fighting following the divorce decision were increasingly irritated and embarrassed by their parents' behavior.

Parents remained the subjects of their children's careful, anxious scrutiny for possible remarriage plans or relocation. The children shared the tense preoccupation with the possibility that the new family arrangement might be changed again. They all nervously, if secretly, believed that family disruption could happen again.

Sally, age eight at the time of separation, had been a pixieish little girl with straight dark hair. She had a lot to say at follow-up. She sat throughout the whole interview with considerable poise, legs crossed, talking rapidly.

Sally reminisced about the year, "My mommy was really sad. She should have a man around the house. She might get married in a few years. My mommy cries sometimes and we hardly ever get in trouble and she hardly ever yells, but when we talk about my daddy she starts to cry and says she still loves my daddy and she does. We go over and hug her and say, 'Please don't cry'; when she cries, we start crying." Asked whether her parents might get together again, she replied, "I don't think so. My daddy got married and has a new house and a new wife. We like her. My mommy asks me if we like her more than we like my mommy and I say no because we don't. We go to visit every two weeks. But if mommy gets married we'll move away so we won't visit my daddy." She presented her problem. "I *want* my mommy to get married and I *don't* want to move far away. I want to visit my daddy and I love him and I like to visit him. But," she added thoughtfully, "I don't think mommy wants us to visit daddy." She added, "I would mind if I couldn't visit. I would like to see him at least every four weeks."

About her parents she said, "They don't fight so often now. It's better to get a divorce because they were fighting so much. Daddy broke stuff and hit Mom. We weren't around when she did stuff to him." "I think my mom should have a man," she said thoughtfully. "If she would, then she wouldn't have to work." Sally also had comments about working. She said, "I help my mommy at home," and she went on to enumerate her chores and said that her brother doesn't do his chores. She said,

"When we were younger we didn't do any work; Mom did it all. But I'm nine now so she puts us to work and I like working." She complained that she thought they were too old for babysitters, but they did need, she agreed, someone to watch them at the pool. About her father she commented, "He's nice to us but when we fight he hits us." Remembering the time when she was trying to decide whether to live with her mother or father she said, "I live with Mommy because she borned me." Asked about her future, Sally said, "I want to marry a man and help him get rich. I want a boy and a girl."

I reminded her about her fears last summer and she said, "Last summer I got pains and had dreams and I had to have a grown-up sleep with me." But she said she didn't have any pains or fears this summer or any bad dreams. She said that the shadows of the trees used to scare her and make her think of a burglar, but she wasn't scared any longer. "I'm nine," she said proudly.

I asked if there were some way her mother could be happier since she had expressed some concern about this, and she said, "If she got married, she wouldn't cry as often. Most women need a man around the house, and love." How often did her mother cry, I asked. "She cries at the dinner table and sometimes upstairs and sometimes she cries on the phone with her boyfriend."

Sally had weathered the crisis well. Despite the pressures placed on her by the mother and the tension between the parents, her psychosomatic symptoms and sleep disturbance had disappeared, her capacity for empathy and compassion had increased, and her anxiety and tension had diminished. She was intact and well functioning in school and at home, a charming, socially facile child, who appeared to have matured a great deal in the intervening postseparation year and a half but who still had a great deal on her mind. She typifies many youngsters who looked well at the first follow-up in spite of many unresolved and still painful issues in their relationships with their parents.

Sally discussed many subjects that are of great concern to children from divorced families at the end of the first year. She touched on her mother's unhappiness, her own role as comforter to her mother, problems of visiting, the burden of the mother's jealousy, Sally's chronic gnawing fear of separation from her father, her awareness of the continued bitterness, of her mother's need for help, and her continuing loyalty conflict. Finally her pride in her own mastery of the divorce crisis came through with clarity.

## Summing Up

The immediate postseparation period was an extremely critical time for these children. Enduring conflict between the parents, which outlived the marriage, and the many changes and distresses of the extended readjustment period combined to produce a continuing stressful environment for children. Nevertheless, despite the impact of continued stress and the persistence of diminished support from parents, the majority of the children improved from their acute response to the separation and resumed their developmental progress.

A number of the children, as we have described, experienced an important developmental spurt. Some of these youngsters were separated from daily contact with a psychologically disturbed parent who had included that child within the orbit of the disturbed parent's functioning. Other children came to the divorce with a history of successful coping and good psychological health which they seemed able to maintain after the dip in functioning following parental separation. Still others recovered after the stress of family disruption had subsided. The widening gap between the sexes, which was insignificant in the initial responses, was a recurring leitmotif at follow-up. Girls predominated among the children who functioned well at outcome, as well as those who improved between the initial assessment and the first follow-up.

One-quarter of the children and adolescents were very troubled and complained of their unhappiness in the postdivorce family, their sense of being unloved by one or both parents, and their loneliness. The major psychopathological finding was depression. These depressed children were learning well below their capacities at school and experiencing difficulties of various kinds in their social adjustment. Some were acting out becoming involved in promiscuous or delinquent behaviors. A smaller number of this group, an estimated one-sixth of the entire population, were those for whom the divorce was a stress that they seemed unable to surmount. This smaller group of children still appeared overwhelmed by the divorce itself and centrally preoccupied with its impact, unable to master their own anxiety and suffering or really able to give their full attention to matters unrelated to their intense yearning for the visiting father, or the sense of deprivation with the custodial mother. Of the children who had declined in their functioning, younger children outnumbered the older children almost two-to-one.

From a developmental point of view, it appeared that almost half the children made appropriate progress during the year intervening after an initial serious dip in their adjustment and overall functioning. The center group of half the youngsters who resumed expectable progress following the time of high stress was accompanied on the one hand by a quarter of the children who were considered to have suffered a moderate or severe developmental inhibition or regression during the same period. This group included the depressed and troubled children. Finally, on the other hand, are those youngsters who experienced a significant developmental spurt consequent to the divorce. In the main, this group consisted of those children we described who were separated by divorce from psychiatrically disturbed fathers and whose custodial mothers were competent and psychologically stable.

# PART 4

## *FIVE-YEAR FOLLOW-UP*

# Chapter 11

# Parents After Five Years

## Introduction

Four years after the initial study began we again called the sixty families for a second follow-up.* By then the majority of families had been separated at least four years, and some more than five. Far-reaching changes, some unrelated to the actual divorce itself, had occurred in the lives of these children and parents during the intervening years. The passage of time and events introduced many new factors which made it increasingly complicated to assess the overall impact of divorce. There were remarriages and redivorces, there were illnesses and tragedies, there were moves, new separations, new work situations, and new schools and neighborhoods. Because of these many changes, we recognized the hazards of attributing a direct causal relationship between divorce and the eventual outcome for parents and children. And yet, it would have been equally remiss to overlook an opportunity to understand the family nearly five years after separation in terms of the factors associated with divorce and its aftermath.

Our second reassessment was designed to understand the experience of the children and their parents within the relative stability of the postdivorce family structure in its varied forms. The intent was to con-

* For a detailed analysis of both the population and structure of the five-year follow-up study, see appendix A.

trast and compare attitudes and feelings, overall individual adjustment, and parent-child relationships with related observations from earlier phases in the study. The initial observations, shortly after the marital rupture and separation, occurred at the height of the divorce crisis when parents and children alike were under high stress. The first follow-up a year later was designed to assess the divorce experience as the crisis diminished, as life gradually moved into a more organized, less hectic tempo, and new family arrangements became more stable and predictable. At nearly five years postseparation we expected the divorced and remarried family structure to be an accepted part of life.

The findings reported in this last section are thus likely to reflect more stable situations than those described earlier. The successful, healthy responses and outcomes are no longer linked to the courage evoked by the crisis, and the strengths they reveal are more likely to be enduring. The more pathological responses and developments are not linked now to acute stress and are therefore more likely to be chronic. All that we know about the mercurial changes in children in the normal course of development will continue, of course, to be relevant, and many of these families are likely to be changed radically by the remarriage of one or both parents. Nevertheless, the observations at this time are drawn from a more stable family structure and can no longer be considered to reflect the divorcing family in transition.

## Family Arrangements

We anticipated, nearly five years after the parents' separation, that geographic change and altered relationships would constitute one of the hallmarks of the lives of these adults and children. Surprisingly, we found as much continuity as change. For some families life remained very much as it had been immediately after the separation. Others were called upon to adapt to many new situations, including new neighborhoods and schools, the advent of stepparents and stepsiblings, and new losses, including the move away from a noncustodial parent. Sometimes these events happened sequentially, but just as often they occurred in one stressful (or pleasurable) package.

There had been few changes in the custody arrangements. Seventy-seven percent of the youngsters continued to live in the custody of their mothers with no further changes anticipated. Eight percent now lived with their fathers; another 3 percent shuttled back and forth from one home to the other, not in a joint custody arrangement, but usually under duress when a parent-child relationship became unbearably strained. Eleven percent of the adolescents were now living on their own, essentially as emancipated older adolescents or young adults.

In those families where the father had newly assumed custodial responsibility, it was in large measure with the assent and cooperation of the mother.

In the two or three years after the first follow-up, almost two-thirds of the youngsters had changed their place of residence, and a substantial number of these had moved three or more times. One child moved five times in the year prior to the second follow-up. Thus, among the divorced families in our study there was more geographical stability in the first year after separation than in subsequent years. Parents seemed to wait until the acute phase of financial and psychological instability was ended before moving. When there was community property to divide, many parents waited to find out how much money they would receive. In many cases the move was precipitated by the necessity of selling the family home as part of the final financial settlement. For some youngsters, moves to new locations were undertaken with some anticipation, as part of a desired remarriage. Others were glum about leaving friends and familiar neighborhood schools, even if the remarriage was welcomed. But many moves were tied to economics, to the need for cheaper housing, better jobs, or more adequate child-care arrangements. Mostly the moves were within a radius of thirty miles; very few families left the region. Almost five years postseparation only six mothers had moved out of state, of whom five had custody. (We interviewed three of these six mothers and their children in their new locations.)

The fathers, too, had made many moves, but they, like their ex-spouses, tended to stay close by. Indeed, one-half the noncustodial parents continued to live within the same county as their children, some still within biking distance. An additional 30 percent were within a one-hour drive from their children. Only two fathers lived out of state. Thus, while there was considerable mobility within our sample of divorcing families, the mobility was confined to a small geographical area, enabling parents and children to remain in contact with each other if they so chose.

Remarriage brought change to the lives of many adults and children. Twenty-four (43 percent) of the fathers had remarried in the intervening four years. Among these men, five were then redivorced, and two of them subsequently remarried again. Thus at the second follow-up, 44 percent of the youngsters had a father and a new stepmother, and in the majority of these reconstituted families there were stepsiblings as well. Half of the remarried men described their new relationships as happy and gratifying, and were pleased that they had been able to establish a marriage that worked well for them. They talked of intimacy and the ability to communicate, of sharing and of pleasure. Even when stepchildren and reconstituted families created stress, they felt on balance that the marriage was solid and reflected a move toward greater maturity. The other men felt varying degrees of dissatisfaction with these new marriages; some seemed to have replaced one unsatisfactory situation with another.

Mr. S. had been married two years when we saw him again. Asked how the marriage had been, he shrugged, "We've had our problems." While first he attributed most of these difficulties to his ex-wife, his children, and his stepchildren, it became apparent that one of his major problems was his new wife's resentment of his children and what she viewed as their continued intrusion into her married life. "It sticks in her craw" that she had to work to support Mr. S.'s children. Mr. S. was unhappy that his wife deprecated him for this: "She sees my ex-wife as my lord and master. . . . that I jump when she snaps her fingers. I don't feel that way. . . . My ex-wife deserves the child support; it was hard for her when I couldn't pay very much."

Worse yet, his new wife disliked having the children visit: "She won't let me invite them for overnights. Unfortunately, she is demanding, she can't let me spend a few hours with my children because she wants my undivided attention." Throughout the interview Mr. S. was close to tears.

One-third of the mothers had remarried in the intervening years. Two of these women were then redivorced, and two were widowed. Thus, at this follow-up, nearly a quarter of the children lived in the family home with their mother and a stepparent. The women who remarried were significantly younger than those who remained single. Remarried women were, on the average, thirty-five years old when we saw them; the women who had not remarried averaged forty-one years of age. Thus, the younger children in our sample were more likely to be a part of remarried or reconstituted families.

While one-fifth of the youngsters had, through their father's remarriage, stepsiblings who lived with the father, only 11 percent lived with stepsiblings who moved in with the mother's remarriage. Only one couple had had a child within the new marriage, although several others were considering having children.

Overall, the remarried women were more enthusiastic than the remarried men about the success of their new union. Despite formidable obstacles, more than three-quarters of the women were content. Their motivation was high and they seemed committed to the concept that sustained and mature effort would make the marriage work. As a group they were realistic in their expectations of the remarriage and assumed some of the financial responsibility as well. All but two of the women worked full time outside the home.

## Economic Factors

The majority of the fathers (68 percent) had made their child support payments with considerable regularity. An additional 19 percent paid some support, but irregularly and in varying amounts. Only 13 percent were completely delinquent. Fathers were significantly more likely to be delinquent in child support payments when their own psychological functioning was not stable. In fact, the psychological stability of the father was a more powerful predictor of continued child support payments than socioeconomic status, although lower-class fathers were more often delinquent than middle- or upper-class men.

The socioeconomic class distribution of the adults was not markedly different from that seen at the previous follow-up. The socioeconomic slide of the women seemed to have stopped and their position had stabilized. Half the men continued to be solidly upper and upper-middle class. With few exceptions the women were poorer than they had been during their first marriage and appeared likely to remain so. One-third of the women were enmeshed in a daily struggle for financial survival. The absence of adequate support seemed particularly disturbing in families whose economic situation before separation had been reasonably secure.

Mrs. B. and her three daughters lived in a run-down, working-class neighborhood. Inside, their house was clean, but the furniture and rugs were threadbare. The children's clothes deepened the feeling of poverty: they were out-of-style, ill fitting, worn thin, and unmatched. Mrs. B. wearily talked of the chronic financial struggle. Her job as a vocational nurse paid only $520 a month, and this income depended on the extra hours she put in on ward duty to supplement her pay. She carried no car or health insurance and worried about neglecting the children's varied health problems for lack of money. Food stamps helped some and her parents tried to send a few dollars whenever they could. Mr. B. was in arrears on support payments many thousands of dollars, despite his well-paying job. Mrs. B. sighed as she recalled the large sum of money she had borrowed to pay for litigating child support actions. "It was an empty victory . . . nothing has changed." Previously quite angry at Mr. B., Mrs. B. is now resigned to a chronic state of near poverty, but spoke sadly of the effects on the children. "They don't understand why they don't get birthday and Christmas presents. I told them we just don't have any money."

One-half the women were neither destitute nor particularly secure financially. They managed to maintain a modest standard of living but expressed continuing anxiety about big, unexpected expenses.

Three-quarters of the women in the study were employed but many expressed dissatisfaction with their pay. Many women continuously checked around for better-paying jobs. Those able to find better jobs in the city had to spend more for child-care and commuting expenses. Only one-fifth of the women were in an economically secure position, either because a remarriage improved their position or because the child support payments were generous, regular, and were combined with an adequate salary from the mother's job.

But while more than twice as many fathers as mothers were in a financially stable situation, there were men, 25 percent of the group, whose economic outlook was as unstable as the women. Without professional training, unable to achieve higher job status and pay, in some cases chronically unemployable, these fathers had little to live on. Some were employed full time and conscientiously paid small amounts of child support; others, employed and unemployed, paid none. Sometimes a remarriage spread a salary so thin as to result in two impoverished families.

One-fifth of the women and a slightly lower percentage of the men had initiated litigation between the first and second follow-ups. The common focus of almost all the renewed legal battles was money: litigation to terminate alimony or reduce child support, litigation to increase child support or recover payments in arrears, and litigation that sought to link payment of child support directly to visiting rights. Since litigation is extremely costly, it was most often initiated by those who could afford it, who were still angry, and who felt they had a good chance of winning. One of the central failings of the legal system remains its unavailability to those most desperately in need of legal assistance. Except for those on welfare, none of our families qualified for Legal Aid (their income exceeded $3,000 per year), and few could afford hourly rates of nearly $100. The great expense of legal proceedings denies many men and women, who have legitimate grievances, the opportunity to seek redress.

## The Parents' Adjustment

Because we accept the fundamental hypothesis that divorce is an appropriate social remedy for serious marital distress, it is reasonable to ask if the divorce has succeeded in its social purpose or if it has failed. If it has succeeded, then for whom, and after what period of time? If it has failed, for whom, and in what ways? Central to our inquiry, then, is an understanding of the parents' attitudes and feelings about their divorces after four to five years, their overall psychological adjustment, and their functioning within the ongoing role of parent.

## Attitudes About the Divorce

Two-thirds of the men and slightly more than half the women viewed the divorce as beneficial, feeling it had enhanced the quality of their lives. Interestingly, the issue of who initially wanted and pressed for the divorce became increasingly irrelevant. Some men and women who vigorously opposed the divorce came to recognize, with the passage of time and a restabilization of their own lives, that it had been rewarding to them.

Mrs. C. reflected on the meaning of her divorce: "When I look back, I wish I had gotten out earlier, before things were so desperate, and didn't wait until the breaking point. I felt diminished, betrayed, and hurt. He forced me into the divorce by humiliating me. When a person does everything to make you let go, it's time to let go." She described her reluctance to advise anyone else to get a divorce because of the pain, the loneliness, and the difficulty in being a single parent. But she added, "staying in a morass is worse." "My divorce was a necessity—it was sad and painful. But it turned out well for me. . . . I was fortunate."

Mr. R. felt, as he had from the outset, that the divorce was a good idea. "I should have done it a long time ago. I didn't love her and didn't like her erratic moods. We only stayed together because of guilt and a sense of responsibility constantly laid on me by my mother. It's much better now. I love the kids and like being with them."

And Mrs. D. said, simply, "It was the smartest thing I've ever done!"

Men and women who generally approved the impact of the divorce on their lives relegated the divorce to the past. The divorce no longer consumed undue amounts of psychic energy; it had become essentially a dead issue, a door closed. Though this attitude was observed in two-fifths of the men and less than a third of the women, it was unusual to find both parties to the divorce having achieved this same state of psychological closure. More often, for one ex-partner the divorce was still very much a live, ongoing issue, while for the other, despite what may have been a hard struggle in the intervening years, the divorce was over. The women who had achieved a sense of finality about the divorce no longer experienced great stress in their parenting. Most often, these men and women for whom the divorce was a closed issue had little if any hostility toward their ex-spouse.

Social class was not a determining factor in achieving such closure, although interestingly, women previously married to men in the lower classes were more likely to consider the divorce over than women previously married to men in the upper classes. Some women had been assisted in achieving closure by psychotherapy, even though in some cases the experience had been brief.

Mrs. I. looked exceedingly well and expressed pleasure at seeing the interviewer again. With quiet pride she told us she was doing just fine. Initially shocked and depressed at being left, Mrs. I. now gave evidence of a considerably increased self-esteem. "I still find myself doing a lot of growing. I don't date very much, maybe because I'm afraid of getting sucked into a relationship that would obliterate my identity. I'm still in the midst of establishing my own identity and I don't want any of the growth to stop. Hopefully I'll find a relationship that will allow me just to be me." But in the meantime, "I'm really content with the way things are at this stage of my life."

Close to one-fifth of the men and women continued to have very mixed reactions to the divorce. With no sense that their divorce was an unqualified success, these adults looked backwards to the benefits of marriage as often as they looked ahead.

Mrs. K. expressed pleasure with her new job, recently obtained after hectic years of full-time work and schooling. She felt her life was better since the divorce because she was freed of the responsibility for the unpredictable and sometimes illegal behavior of her psychologically disturbed husband. But throughout the interview, a sense of sadness and resignation about her life prevailed. There were few gratifications. Worries about the children and keeping up the house created chronic low-grade anxiety; her social life was practically nonexistent. Admittedly, "There just isn't much pleasure." But she was coping well with her responsibilities and derived satisfaction from knowing that she did.

Most sobering were those men and women, close to one-fifth of each, who viewed the divorce as deplorable and as a negative experience. For some, the primary feeling that remained was of anger or righteous indignation. Others looked back with regret, longing, and a sense of opportunities lost.

Mrs. V. openly admitted that she still very much regretted the divorce, "especially now that I have to go out into the real world and work." Mostly she regretted the loss of the role of the married woman and lost financial benefits. While she had enjoyed some experiences many married women wouldn't have, she clearly preferred family life. "At times, I wish he [Mr. V.] were still part of the family and that we were married again." She regretted as well a loss of social relationships that she felt were closed to her after the divorce.

For most of the men and women who felt the divorce was bad, the divorce continued to be of central importance in their thinking and in determining their actions. For these parents, little had changed. The passage of time had not dulled memories; their feelings remained as fresh as if the divorce had occurred just the week before.

Seen six years after his divorce, Mr. H. appeared to have lost his somewhat haunted look. Not many changes had occurred in his own life: he held the same job, lived in the same house, was not married, indeed was very much alone. His central relationships were still his attachment to his child and his hatred of his former wife. Mr. H. recounted the story of the marriage and the divorce as if it had happened yesterday. His feelings were intense, his anger undiminished, and he remained preoccupied with his former wife and her "mistreatment" of him. Mr. H. acknowledged his anger, saying it was there because he was so entirely innocent and had been ruthlessly, shamelessly used by his former wife. "If I felt I had done anything to contribute to this, maybe some of my anger would go away."

## Parents' Communications with Each Other

Two-thirds of the parents continued to communicate with each other, half of them frequently. But frequency of contact did not imply friendliness. Indeed, nearly five years after separation, 29 percent of the children were party to intense bitterness between parents; an even larger group continued to be aware of limited friction or anger. Actually, only one-third of the children were completely freed of burdensome hostilities of the marital interaction. The parents who communicated divided into two groups: those with some feelings of comradeship, usually resulting from continued parenting responsibilities, and those who felt no friendship whatsoever. The women continued to be significantly more angry than the men and were less friendly than men to their ex-partners.

## The Psychological Adjustment

Many of the adults looked well when they came for their interview; they appeared lively, self-confident, and poised. Some looked younger, slimmer, more attractive. It was forcefully and clearly brought home to us that our earlier contacts had occurred at a very low ebb in the lives of most of them.

RESTABILIZATION. The average woman was well into her third postseparation year before life assumed a new coherence and stability; the average man accomplished this restabilization earlier, within the second year. Age was not a predictor of the years required by the women to gain a sense of stability, but was for men. The older men, forty-three years and older, restabilized more quickly, some within the first year. These men more often had initiated the divorce, and often had successful professional careers.

The strongest predictor of length of time for restabilization was the overall psychological status of the adult. The more intact men and women restabilized significantly earlier than the more disorganized or disturbed individuals, regardless of who sought the divorce. Other factors combined as well to prolong the period of unsettled living: poverty, excessive litigation, and extreme anger.

One sobering finding was that almost five years postseparation, 31 percent of the men and 42 percent of the women had not yet achieved psychological or social stability. For some, this resulted from a more chronic lifelong state of disorganization, one exacerbated by the divorce and in no way improved by the divorce.

Mr. M. violently opposed his wife's initial decision to divorce. To his sons he threatened suicide if Mrs. M. continued with her divorce plans. The violence and chaos that riddled their marriage continued into the separation period. In the next few years they were in court fourteen times, fighting over custody and child support. On their frequent visits together, father and sons shrieked at each other for hours. The household was disorganized. When Mrs. M. remarried, Mr. M. screamed that he would no longer support his children, and ordered that the word stepfather never be used in his presence.

For some people life had been very difficult and they had acquitted themselves with courage and determination.

Mrs. N. seemed younger than her thirty-six years as she padded about in her bare feet and long peasant dress. For well over two hours, she recounted the story of the past four years, including details of her remarriage and second divorce. The years had been hard: the children's father harassed them all continually (and was in arrears for $14,000 in support payments), they lived on the edge of poverty, trying to make do on her new husband's GI bill. They moved several times, she had been ill and lost her job, and since the second divorce the family had lived on welfare. There had been little opportunity for this woman to achieve stability during this four-year whirlwind of change and hardship. In addition, her own considerable physical problems remained a deterrent to further schooling. Despite the fact that life had been difficult, she had coped remarkably well and was glad that she had divorced. As the interview ended, she said, "If it hadn't been for the kids, I don't think I *ever* would have grown up!"

With some women, stability as an adult and single parent seemed still almost within reach.

Mrs. T. expressed considerable anxiety about finding a good job. In school for the past five years, she continued to look backward with longing to the security of her marriage. Nearing the end of the interview she said, "I wish this follow-up could have been next year. This is a transition year . . . my work plans are up in the air. I don't know how things will turn out."

PSYCHOLOGICAL HEALTH AND WELL-BEING. The greater number of adults appeared to be functioning reasonably well. There had been important shifts in the intervening years in the direction of healthier psychological functioning for both men and women. As described in appendix A, we determined in our initial diagnostic assessment that one-third of the men and women fell into the broad category of adequate to excellent psychological functioning. Nearly five years postseparation, this group had expanded to include one-half of the men and 57 percent of the women. Many of these adults were, in fact, in good shape psychologically. Most of the men and women whose psychological health had been sound in the immediate postseparation period continued to function well. Characteristic of those whose mental health notably improved in the intervening years was a reduction or disappearance of disabling, neurotic symptoms, including severe depressions, alcoholism, and somatic disturbances.

Notable among women in particular in this group was greatly enhanced self esteem, and for both men and women a greater sense of contentment with life than when initially observed. Thus, for these individuals, divorce, and in some cases remarriage, seemed to have offered not only a workable solution to an untenable marital situation, but an opportunity as well to recover or achieve better psychological health. For these men and women, many of whom we describe throughout this last section, we can state that divorce was successful, despite ongoing problems of loneliness and marginal income.

Corresponding to an increase in the ranks of well-functioning individuals is a decrease in that group of men and women previously considered to be moderately troubled. Whereas before half the men and slightly fewer women were in considerable psychological difficulty, now one-third of the men and one-fifth of the women were in this category. Some of these continued to be severely depressed, suicidal, alcoholic, occasionally erratic with poor impulse control, or had substantial difficulties in relating to other adults and children. The separation and divorce had stressed their limited resources considerably.

Mrs. Y. arrived for her interview dressed entirely in black, looking slimmer but worn out. Though she had originally sought only a temporary separation from her verbally abusive spouse, he had angrily forced a divorce she didn't want. Depressed and suicidal during the marriage, she remained severely depressed for five years after the divorce, unable despite sporadic therapy to disengage from the pathological relationship, or to get on with restructuring her life. While her relationship with her sons improved considerably and remained perhaps the healthiest part of her functioning, her anger at her ex-spouse continued undiminished and consumed disproportionate amounts of psychic energy. She had made slight, tentative progress in the direction of leading a more active life, but found the effort difficult and often unrewarding. Essentially little had changed since the divorce. Some of her former husband's clothing was still in the wardrobe.

And finally, the group of men and women previously identified as seriously troubled or disturbed was unchanged. None of these individuals, with histories of mental illness, bizarre behavior, poor reality testing, and unusual thinking, achieved a greatly improved psychological status in the intervening years. Tragically, they responded to the escalating marital distress or separation with greater disorganization in their thinking and behavior. As we have described earlier, a few sought the divorce as a result of their own deteriorating mental status, but most often these men and women had been left by a healthier spouse. While they had actively contributed to the marital misery, they essentially had no choice about the final divorce decision. Thus, divorce may create the potential for a healthy outcome for their ex-spouse, and perhaps for their children, but will not improve the psychological functioning of the disturbed partner.

A few individuals, precariously held together in their psychological functioning by the routines and structure of their everyday life as spouse and parent became more seriously disturbed after the separation and remained so by the time of the second follow-up.

Mr. and Mrs. E. lived in a loveless relationship characterized by violent beatings, alcoholism, tauntings, and frequent divorce threats. Mr. E. threatened to "put out a contract on your life" if Mrs. E. divorced him. Mrs. E. impulsively left one day, a decision she described as representing "the sanest thing I've done."

At the time of the first follow-up, Mrs. E.'s psychological condition had deteriorated. Engaged in wild, frenetic behavior with much heavy drinking and sexual behavior, Mrs. E. viewed herself as a minor social celebrity and tossed off the possibility that things might not be going well. The relationship to all three of her daughters had become dreadful; she had bruised one of them several times during violent outbursts, and threatened to kill them all while drunkenly speeding in the car. The situation was grave for the youngsters. They were at considerable risk either staying with the mother or living with their alcoholic father.

Several years later, after many unkept appointments, Mrs. E. was seen again. She flamboyantly offered herself as an interesting case history. Her thinking was scattered, and seemed loose and delusional. Only gradually did fragments of information emerge about numerous run-ins with the police for violent behavior, psychiatric hospitalizations, several evictions, and the repeated truancy of the children. Mrs. E. refused to be serious, saying laughingly: "I've fired at least eight or ten shrinks. . . . I told you that before, didn't I?"

To sum up, the majority of the adults felt better than before. One-half of the men and two-thirds of the women were more content with life than when we first saw them, and their self-esteem had risen notably. And for half this group their life was very much improved. Another group, more men than women, seemed to remain at the earlier level of contentedness with their lives, that is, things were neither better nor worse on balance, although the arena had changed. Finally, a significant minority which included one-third of the men and one-fifth of the women were troubled and unhappy.

LONELINESS. The absence of a comfortable, reliable social life created an on-going loneliness for many men and women. Most of the parents who had not remarried spoke openly of their loneliness. More women than men seemed affected by their social isolation, in part because they had little control over initiating social engagements. Long since disillusioned by their experience in the "singles' scene," most women were not as acutely lonely as before, but quietly, longingly, wished for someone with whom they could talk, share, and be affectionate on a daily basis. "I get sort of tired of talking to kids all the time," was the complaint of one mother.

Mr. O. started the interview by saying that "it took me two full years to get over the divorce." Now he realizes that the divorce was inevitable. Near the end of the session he shyly and hesitantly said that he had been dating a woman he'd known for a long while. After several months she put him off, saying she wasn't willing to get involved. "Now," Mr. O. said painfully, "I'm in limbo again. I was happy while I had her, and sad now to have lost her." He said he'd like to marry again, adding, "At times I am very lonely." Mr. O. thanked the interviewer for seeing him but commented as he went out the door how draining it had been "to go back into the sadness again with you."

Where there was severe and acute loneliness, it occurred significantly more often for those men and women whose psychologic functioning was troubled. The acutely lonely men were more likely to be in the lower socioeconomic group. In many instances, they relied entirely on their children as their source of emotional support. Women, too, who experienced acute loneliness nearly five years after the separation were significantly more likely to be psychologically troubled. But unlike the men, many had been previously married to an upper-class husband and continued to feel lost without their former social roles and privileges. These women perpetuated bitter interactions with their former spouses, perhaps, in part, to fill the emptiness in their lives.

BROAD IMPACT OF DIVORCE. One way of determining the longer-range impact of the divorce was to consider whether serious problems were mostly resolved or changed for the better by the divorce, or conversely, whether the divorce created new and/or different sets of problems for the men and women involved. Viewed in this perspective, the divorce served a useful purpose for many adults, but particularly for the women. More than half of the women arrived at better solutions for living their lives, and half this group had undergone striking and significant positive changes that appeared to have lifelong implications. Fewer men seemed to have utilized the divorce experience to bring about positive change in their lives, perhaps because fewer men actually sought the divorce initially.

Nonchange was more characteristic of the men. More than half marked time; their manner of addressing life and relationships was similar to what it had been before the divorce. For them, divorce had not created serious problems, nor had it led to living their lives in an appreciably more productive and gratifying manner. Unlike the men, however, the majority of women tended to achieve a substantially more gratifying way of leading their lives, or they struggled with new or more serious problems.

In assessing the impact of divorce, our conclusions indicate the need to consider the impact separately for each family member. What was a successful solution for one parent was not necessarily so for the other. And if the divorce worked for one or both parents, this did not necessarily portend a successful resolution for all of the children. Sometimes the reverse was true as well, when the divorce created significant positive change for the children, but continued to be overwhelmingly difficult for a parent. As one woman said, "The kids are great, Mama's a wreck!"

# Chapter 1

# Children and Adolescents Reflect on Their Parents' Divorce

Danny, who was eleven at the five-year follow-up, said thoughtfully, "Divorce is not as bad as you think . . . not near as bad as it looks in movies or on television!" He had thought a lot about what divorce was and had just recently figured it all out. "It's something like if you break a glass and pick the pieces up right away they will fit back together perfectly, but if you take one piece of glass and sand one side of it, it will never fit again." He thinks that's what happens with divorce. Danny added, "Mom is not so sad as she was, she's much stronger." "Dad was unhappy during the marriage and he's much happier now." Danny thought his mom would probably find a boyfriend. Mainly he was not worried about them anymore. He didn't see anything wrong with having his parents divorced.

For Danny the divorce had finally acquired permanency. He had arrived at the conclusion that repairing the marriage was as impossible as repairing broken glass. At the first follow-up at eighteen months, Danny was still searching for ways to restore the marriage. Several years later he had given the divorce his approval; he was no longer worried.

When we invited the children to return to meet with us five years later we explained candidly that our wish was to learn from them in order to help other children and parents benefit from the experience of their counsel. We asked many questions, including several hypothetical

we found to be richly productive of the children's re-
tudes. For example, each youngster was asked to sug-
child described as being close to the age of the child
. We asked for advice for the child whose parents were
vice for the parents at that time. Their opinions were
ng to us because it was possible to compare their current perspective and opinions with those which they had expressed
earlier, and to note the consistencies and the changes that had occurred
over the years.

The purpose of the follow-up, as we have already indicated, was not
to assess the conditions and attitudes of the children and to attribute
these in some simple-minded way to the events of the divorce. A great
many physical, psychological, and social changes had occurred during
the five years which were unrelated to family change. There had been
some tragic events. We learned, to our sorrow, that a mother of three
children was struck by a fatal illness. We also knew of many happy
events—of academic honors and other achievements which were also unrelated to the family change.

Nevertheless, we agreed that it would be equally simple minded *not*
to attempt to understand the family five years later.

What was the outcome for the children? For which children had life
improved? And for which children had the divorce failed, and in what
ways? To what extent had the divorce been relegated to a distant past
and to what extent did it remain an immediate presence? And what
factors are linked to a happy or unhappy outcome?

Therefore, we assessed each child individually and the group in its
entirety along many measures comparable to those which we had employed at the two earlier checkpoints of the study. We sought to compare each child against his or her earlier appearance to note continuities
and change in the individuals and within the entire group. Our good
fortune included the continued availability of the same clinical staff.
Most of the children recognized us and many spoke to us as to friends of
long standing. They remembered our earlier meetings and our conversations together in a detail which we found both extraordinary and
moving.

## The Children's Perspective of the Divorce

As a group they were strikingly aware of their family and its vicissitudes. They had many opinions about many divorce-related issues. And,
in fact, it soon became clear that one of the consequences of the divorce
was that the family itself, its strengths and its deficiencies, had become

a focus of their conscious attention and frequently thoughtful consideration. Many continued during the postdivorce years not only to be more aware of the processes of family life, but also to make continuing comparisons of the present with the past.

Another aspect of their lives which emerged was that they had dealt with the issues raised by the divorce on many separate occasions over the years. As the youngster matured in intellectual capacity the divorce was looked at anew, and the maturing child made an effort to explain the march of family events in ways consonant with his or her enhanced intellectual capacity. Therefore, his or her understanding of divorce was likely to change. Similarly, as the child matured emotionally, he or she was more able to separate the needs of the two parents and to regard each parent's needs separate from his or her own needs in the present, and to understand the divorce with greater or less sympathy over the years. In this way, the intellectual and emotional efforts of the youngster to cope with the family rupture were also reorganized at each developmental stage and extended throughout the growing-up years that we have followed.

The views of the children and adolescents reflected a point of view different from that of their parents. They had different observations and they had their own criteria for improvement or failure to improve. The consensus among the children about the significant measures for good or bad outcome was amazingly high, almost as if they had conferred with each other and reached common standards. Thus, most children were intensely aware of the level of friction in the household and took careful note of continued conflict and its expression by the adults. They observed the mood and psychological well-being of custodial parents with care. And most continued to monitor visiting patterns and relationships with the visiting parent and to keep scrupulous count. Past and present along each of these measures were continually compared by these superb, highly motivated, young researchers.

Over and beyond the individual measures which they used, and which they had some trouble defining, they responded to a global feeling about the postdivorce family itself. They described, and we conceptualized, an experience of sufficiency versus insufficiency, or a sense of deprivation. A sense of sufficiency enabled the youngster to deal with the divorce events within the context of a balanced understanding. In contrast, the sense of deprivation placed the divorce in a perspective of continuing unhappiness. This sense of sufficiency versus deprivation was a composite of many factors, but especially reflected the continued parenting by both parents within the present, and underlay the mood and attitudes which they expressed. Essentially, they took the measure of the current family and compared it with their memories of the past. By and large, their gratification within the present governed their feelings about the divorce and affected their view of the past.

As we studied the children's response as a group, it was evident that many of them had modified the views which they held at the time of the parental separation in regard to whether or not they approved the divorce decision and whether they experienced the post-divorce family as an improvement. The changes in attitude had been gradual and reflected more consistency with their views at the eighteen-month mark than we had expected, and more loyalty to the predivorce family than many parents would have found welcome.

Thus five years after the separation, 28 percent of the group strongly approved of the divorce, slightly more disapproved strongly, and the remaining 42 percent were somewhere in the middle, accepting the changed family but not taking a strong position for or against the divorce. Although this represents a major shift from the initial count when three-quarters of the children strongly disapproved of the divorce, it is noteworthy that the five years that had elapsed within the postdivorce family had not convinced at least one-third of the children of the wisdom of their parents' decision to divorce.

Similarly, the number of children who regarded the divorced family as an improvement over the predivorce family had changed, although not as dramatically. A year and a half after the separation about two-thirds of the youngsters did not regard the postdivorce family as an improvement over the predivorce family. This number had eroded by five years. Nevertheless, we were most surprised to find that five years after the separation 56 percent of the children and adolescents continued to find little or no improvement over the predivorce family; 22 percent were highly gratified with the postdivorce family, and the remaining 22 percent expressed the cautious view that the divorced family offered a modest or moderate improvement.

## Those Who Approved

The older group, now between seventeen and twenty-four, was significantly more approving of the divorce than the younger children. These older adolescents were able to conceptualize the needs of their parents separately from their own. Over the intervening years these young people, in the process of their own maturing, had either confirmed their initial view that the divorce was a wise move or arrived at an understanding that the predivorce family had provided a different experience for them than it had for their parents. As they grew older they became more able to separate the perspectives of the divorce in its effects on them and on one or both parents. On balance, they had concluded that it had been helpful to one or both parents and on this basis they understood and approved the decision. Many of the youngsters who were able to approve were older, their capacity for rational thinking was increased, and they were, in a sense, on their way out, no longer as much in need of the protective structure of the family.

Cindy, a senior in high school, thought that the divorce was good for her parents. She said that she, personally, didn't like it but, knowing that they were unhappy together, it was much better that they were divorced than if they remained married. She recalled that she used to hear her parents arguing in the adjoining room and "what a nuisance that had been." She was relieved when they decided to divorce, although she would, of course, have preferred it had they been able to get along together. Now she saw that they are both happier since the divorce. She hoped that she won't divorce when she becomes an adult, and she planned to be very careful in her choice of a marital partner.

Several of the adolescents made astute observations about their parents. They called attention to the ways that the divorce had helped the parents' psychological growth and recognized their increased happiness.

Florence, age seventeen, said that she never wanted to see her parents back together because "Mom was stifled for so many years. My father probably should never have married or had a family; he was not that kind of man."

Tina, age sixteen, said, "The home is running better now that Dad is out." She saw a big improvement in her mom. "She's more open . . . more energetic and more giving."

Children and adolescents also approved the divorce when there had been conflict in the home, and the youngsters had been frightened for themselves or one or both parents. They approved the divorce which had led to diminished fighting between the parents.

Dana, age thirteen, said, "My parents fought a lot. The fighting was terrible, to be exact. It was exasperating. I'm glad that's over."

Ann, at thirteen, said she's glad about the divorce: "That's for sure!" "They are enemies . . . they hold each other in contempt." "Mom says, 'I hate that man.' Dad tells how bad Mom is, how she can't manage money." The fighting, Ann said, had been impossible.

A large number of the children who expressed satisfaction with their life emphasized their continued contact with both parents. Several children volunteered that they saw each of their parents as much, or even more, than they had during the marriage.

Dorothy, age thirteen, volunteered that her life was very good. "Nothing has changed." She sees more of her parents separately than she did when they were together and they are all much happier. She wished her mother were home a little more, but she had given up on that ever happening. She liked her mom's new boyfriend and thought it would be good if they were married. She said both her parents seemed happier being divorced.

Nancy, now in the second grade, said, "When they first divorced I was kind of sad. My sister and me, we tried to stop them. We didn't want them to divorce because at Christmas we were used to coming down and seeing what we got for presents." But, she added, she tried to stop them from divorcing by interrupting them when they were talking. Then, she said, she found out it was still fun, like it was when they were married because, "We get to see Daddy in his house. There are lots of good things to do . . . Things are not so different. . . . You can meet a lot of new dogs and new people when you go to visit him in his house. I see him Saturdays and Sundays . . . Sunday is his day off."

Nadine, now age ten, said, "I knew he was divorced but I didn't take it so hard because Daddy lives just down the street. We were happy to go to his house and spend the night there."

For many children who were nine to twelve at the five-year follow-up the relationship with the father appeared to be the bellweather of their attitude toward the divorce. If the relationship with the father was good and they were pleased with the frequency and the patterns of visiting, they opted for the divorced family or they agreed with one child who said, "It's not any better but it's not any worse."

A number of the youngsters who enjoyed good relationships with stepfathers also approved the divorced family. This was especially so when the relationship with the father had been poor or exploitative of the child in the predivorce family. Several of these youngsters, as we have noted, especially the little boys, appeared to spurt ahead with excitement and new growth in the fresh relationship with a stepfather whom they grew quickly to love.

Larry, at age eight, advised us that having a stepfather was fun. "We go to parties and stuff." "With a new marriage come new people. Now I have five kids in my family."

His brother, age twelve, said, "About divorce, in the long range it's good; in the short range it isn't." "Now everyone is pretty much settled down and there are good things. It benefits the kids a lot . . . sometimes more than the parents. Parents have to start over. . . . Kids float along." He went on, "If parents get married again there's benefit from it—there are two families instead of one. And if you're tired of one family you can always go see the other."

One subgroup of youngsters who approved the divorced family were those who were pleased to be away from a disturbed and cruel parent. These youngsters benefited considerably from the physical distance that the divorce established between them and the disturbed parent when it also led to psychological disengagement from a relationship that was corrosive of the child's self-esteem or destructive of his psychological and/or physical health.

Thus Amy, age sixteen, said that she now got along well with her dad and did not want a reconciliation. "He used to be harsh and drunk and strict. He raised his voice and we marched. I felt badly at first when he left but I wouldn't change the present situation for anything. I like visiting him but never to live with him."

Another group of youngsters who approved the divorce were those who worked through their grief at the loss and rejection of a beloved parent by espousing the cynical idea that all relationships were expectably limited in time. They said they believed that an expectation that relationships would endure was unrealistic, perhaps foolish, and embraced the notion that no relationship would last.

We were particularly interested in the evolution of the opinions as expressed by Ken, age thirteen, because he had been very close to his father prior to the divorce and the father had rejected a continuing relationship with him and did not visit.

Ken's parents had not quarreled during the marriage. The divorce request from the father took his mother and Ken by surprise. The boy was temporarily grief-stricken because his father not only left, but hardly visited. A close relationship between father and son disappeared almost overnight when the father remarried. Ken enjoyed a close relationship with his competent and devoted mother.

Ken, at the five-year follow-up, was cool. He explained with great composure that he and his mother "get along just fine." He'd like her to remarry or at least go out more, but otherwise he was "entirely content." He expected that he would see his dad when his father had more time. Regarding some of the sadness that he had experienced immediately following the father's departure, the boy offered that "it sure was not pleasant in the past." In explaining the divorce, Ken said, "Dad got tired of Mom." He could make no further sense out of it, nor would he try. He volunteered that he thought there was nothing unusual about people getting bored with each other. He had girlfriends and would have others. "I get tired of one and there're others. Groups are more fun."

Ken seemed to have identified with the values indicated by the divorce-related behavior of his father and, particularly, with the notion that the expectation that relationships continue was unrealistic and, perhaps, undesirable. It is, of course, hard to know whether the boy's cynical view reflected his adolescent bravado and denial of upset or whether his attitudes were more profoundly incorporated within his character.

His brother Todd's adjustment was entirely different. At the five-year mark Todd refused to come for an interview, but his mother reported he had done poorly at school, and had been arrested for breaking and entering. Ken was very critical of Todd, accusing him of being "a thief and an addict." He talked frequently at home of his wish to "beat the s—— out of Todd." It seems likely that the older brother's delinquency represented a threat to Ken's poise, his "cool," and his continued mastery of his own feelings. And it may well be that Todd's behavior expressed the anger at the father which Ken had kept carefully hidden under his casual acceptance that relationships are short-lived by their nature. The long-range implications of the different paths chosen by Ken and Todd are of considerable importance and grave concern. Although the boy seemed content, his view of human relationships was disturbing, as was his anger.

### Children Who Disapprove the Divorced Family

By contrast, the children and adolescents who disapproved of the divorce and looked back longingly at the predivorce family were largely unhappy with the present. Many had impoverished relationships with the custodial parent. Others yearned for their father and continued to feel deprived of his daily presence. Some of these yearning youngsters were visited several times monthly and others were visited erratically. In the main, these children were lonely and unhappy and felt rejected by one or even both parents. The initial vulnerability which these children experienced following the breakup of the marriage had continued and their sense of being in jeopardy had not dissipated.

Predominant in this group were the younger children, and the boys in mid-adolescence between thirteen and sixteen years old. There was a trend for boys to disapprove more as they grew older, with disapproval peaking in early and mid-adolescence, whereas girls approved more as they grew older.

Jenny, at age eleven, volunteered that everything was fine except that she didn't see her daddy enough. I asked if she had asked him to visit more often and she said that she had, but he always had an excuse. Asked for her three wishes, Jenny wished that her parents had never gotten a divorce, that she could see her daddy more, and that he would take her on a trip with him. She could hardly think of anything else. Asked for her advice for parents who were considering a divorce, she said, "Tell the parents not to do it. . . . Tell the children that it would be bad."

Sara, age seven, said that she didn't get to see her daddy very much anymore. She's sad about that. She often wished there had been no divorce. She remembered she used to think when she would grow up she would marry her daddy. She said, "I was cuckoo, but then my sister used to think the same thing, too." When she saw her mother and dad together sometimes she felt like she was back at home, like they were together. She wished that they would get back together, but then she didn't feel that they would.

Occasionally, at follow-up, a simple question set off an acute episode of crying in a child. This was especially distressing and unexpected as we recalled that the divorce was now five years old and the question was put gently and phrased with a careful neutrality. Clearly, for some children even the simplest issues were not satisfactorily resolved. When the experience of being left in the custody of an unsupported or troubled parent was combined with rejection by the other parent, the child clearly viewed the divorce as a continuing disaster in his or her life.

Mary, age seven, whose father rejected her and preferred her brother, was very upset by a question about the divorce. When she came, she remembered the office well but not any of the content of what had been discussed earlier. As we began to recall some of the events of the past, Mary left hurriedly to go to the bathroom and upon her return she said she was sick and her tummy hurt and, indeed, she looked ill. I said, "Mary, do you think our conversation about the divorce upset your tummy?" The child started to cry and then, tearfully, in a high, whining, sometimes despairing, tone, she talked for forty-five minutes about her family and her problems and how awful it all was. Poignantly she said that her father didn't love her, that he preferred her brother, that he ignored her requests and wishes. His yelling frightened her. She had always tried not to whine, to please him, to be good, but he was never loving toward her. She didn't want to see her father because he didn't love her and his anger frightened her. The best parts of her visits to him were the times she got to pet his dog. She felt lonely. She would always be lonely on her visits to him.

Throughout the marriage, and throughout the postdivorce years, Mary had felt rejected by her father and insufficiently supported by her depressed, severely troubled mother. Essentially, she was rejected by both parents during the marriage and the divorce, but the father's rejection of her and preference for her brother were made more evident by the divorce. During visits he welcomed the brother and neglected Mary. The unhappy child insisted on visiting her father, hoping in the face of all evidence to the contrary that her father would show her some affection.

Some of the children who complained about the divorced family and looked back longingly on the predivorce family included boys who complained that their masculinity was threatened when they lived with their mother and one or more sisters. We heard this particularly from boys entering adolescence, in the nine-to-thirteen-year-old group. Even where there was regular visiting contact with the father, several of these boys experienced this contact as insufficient to their needs.

Roger, age ten, said, "I wish sometimes that they were together like married. I don't have a father to see very much. Once a week is when I see him and I want to see him more. It's hard to grow up without a father or someone who acts like a father. I'm a boy, living with a mother and a sister, that's hard."

Jeremy, age fourteen, commented, "I have lived without a father during five of the most important years of my male life."

Several children who disapproved of the divorced family were troubled because the divorce had not markedly, if at all, reduced the fighting between the parents. Instead, in many cases quarreling between the parents continued over the years and the children were used as messengers of the conflict.

Ann, age twelve, told us, "I get so pulled that sometimes I feel like a rubber band going back and forth. Mother sometimes says she couldn't care less, and says go live with your father but that's the last place we want to go. She wants to move, but we don't want to move away from Dad."

Roger also was troubled at being a messenger between warring parents and said, "Our parents say opposite things of each other. If you do anything wrong, one parent says, 'You're turning out like your mom (or dad.' Or Mom says, 'You do that like Dad—that's one of his bad qualities.'" "We feel funny," said the child, "but we love them equally as much but it's hard to take that. Sometimes I wish they were together like married."

Several children remained caught up in the wish of one parent to reestablish the marriage, and refused to accept the divorce as final. They seemed able to maintain this expectation firmly in place for many years.

Gretchen, age ten, told us that it was not only her hope but her knowledge and firm belief that her parents would remarry. "Prayers and God's will are powerful." She, herself, would not be responsible nor in control of their reunion. Her task would be to be a Christian and to practice love, kindness, and forgiveness. She was pleased that her mother and father had returned to the church. She said, "We were all hurt by the divorce." She was greatly opposed to divorce and disdainful of the mother's "immoral behavior." She felt that both her parents had matured and very likely would reunite. Gretchen's views were reinforced by her father who had maintained his active campaign to win the mother back.

Finally, children who felt rejected by their mother looked back longingly and sometimes unrealistically on the predivorce family. For some of these youngsters the anger at the mother was intense and unremitting.

Connie, now fifteen, said, "I never did anything bad while my dad was there. I was afraid of him. But after he left my mom couldn't stop me." Connie was ten years old when she was first brought to juvenile hall. "My mom couldn't handle me. She didn't want me." "My dad loved me . . . he would show me off to his friends . . . he would let me sit on his lap. . . . he told me he loved me." Regarding the divorce, she said, "If you have kids, divorce is a bad thing. In my situation I had no parents . . . I had nobody that really loved me and it was very lonely. I could have gone crazy. It was all my mother's fault. The divorce wasn't the bad thing, although it was bad enough. The bad part was after. I could die tomorrow and it wouldn't be any different. . . . I never had a mother."

In summary, the children's approval or disapproval of the parents' decision to divorce reflected their experience of several years within the postdivorce family. Their agenda for family life emerged as clear, consistent, and conservative. It called for a stable life with minimal friction between the parents; adequate contact with both parents; the approval and love of both parents; and freedom from economic worries. Those children who lacked these components of their view of the good life felt deprived in some significant way.

# Chapter 13

# Children and Adolescents: The Outcome at Five Years

No single theme emerged in the lives of all those children who had enhanced, or consolidated, or continued in their good developmental progress following the divorce. Nor is there a single theme that appears in the lives of those who deteriorated, moderately or markedly. Rather, we confronted a set of complex configurations in which the components came together in varying combinations in the individual life of each child. Some of the components are the family relations, others are those in the social surrounding, and all react on the resources or the frailties of the particular child at a particular time in his or her growing-up period. As in a kaleidoscope, the design shifts; the same components appear together in different combinations, sometimes in especially pleasing patterns, and sometimes in disharmony.

To add to the complexity, all these different components are intricately interrelated. Thus children turned to the noncustodial parent for support and yearned for him when the relationship with the mother was troubled and when they were lonely in the divorced family, as well as when they missed him for himself alone. In this way, the attitude of the child toward the father was both separate from *and* inseparable from the child's feelings toward the mother. Or for a further example, the child's capacity to rely on friends and to turn to them for help was dependent on the child's relationships within the family. We soon learned that children with good relationships at home were those likely to make friends more easily and to sustain these friendships. So that once again factors which appeared, at first glance, to be operating independently often had intertwined roots which might be invisible. And we deal therefore, in all these outcomes, not with independent components of the design, but with complexly determined relationships among the different components, which enter into the configuration of final outcome for each child.

Unlike the initial responses of these youngsters, which in so many instances were governed by the child's age and stage of development, or the response at the first follow-up which seemed to reflect significant sex differences, the more enduring responses at the five-year outcome, although still related somewhat to age and less so to sex, were linked primarily to other factors. Briefly stated, those components which seemed centrally to affect outcome in varying combinations of importance at the five-year mark included: (1) the extent to which the parents had been able to resolve and put aside their conflicts and angers and to make use of the relief from conflict provided by divorce; (2) the course of the custodial parent's handling of the child and the resumption or improvement of parenting within the home; (3) the extent to which the child did not feel rejected in relationship with the noncustodial or visiting parent, and the extent to which this relationship had continued on a regular basis and kept pace with the child's growth; (4) the range of personality assets and deficits which the child brought to the divorce, including the child's history within the predivorce family and the capacity to make use of his or her resources within the present, particularly intelligence, the capacity for fantasy, social maturity, and ability to turn to peers and adults; (5) the availability to the child of a supportive human network; (6) the absence of continuing anger and depression in the child; and (7) the sex and age of the child.

Conditions which were present in the lives of the children who coped successfully were not only present in different combinations, but they were sometimes different for children within the same family. It was not uncommon to find that two children in the same family took different paths, for one child to improve and the other child to decline in behavior within the same general milieu. In many of these situations it was possible to discern substantial differences in the relationship between parents and children that could reflect a difference in age (which was a significant factor in adjustment in the remarried family), or a real or fantasied resemblance of the child to the other parent, or individual differences among the children. Sometimes, however, the differences in parental handling were not obvious to the observer, and the factors which distinguished the different developmental courses of the children within the same family remained obscure.

Furthermore, we discovered that absence of the components conducive to good outcome did not necessarily result in poor outcome. The combinations that led to deterioration were not simply the reverse of those which promoted progress. Rather, the configurations differed for each step along the spectrum, ranging from very good to very poor. Thus, children who were not visited by their fathers usually grieved and a significant number of them became depressed and were troubled with low self-esteem and a gnawing feeling of having been rejected. Yet, children who were visited regularly were not assured of good psychological health and were, in fact, also likely to be troubled if the custodial mother was failing to provide adequate care. It became clear, therefore, that it was important to examine poor outcome and good outcome separately and not to assume that the one is the dark side of the other. Accordingly, we have reported these separately in the following pages.

Past and present have both surprised us in this study. One of our more interesting and perhaps more important findings is the significance of the relationships within the present in determining outcome at the time. Thus children whose ego functioning was good or very good at the five-year mark were those supplied with the things required for good development at this period of their lives. The parent-child relationships of previous years appeared not to be sufficient to maintain good functioning within the present. By the same token other supports were needed in the present for the maintenance of the child's progress. Because of the discontinuity in many parent-child relationships following divorce, the importance of the present relationship is especially great.

Unfortunately, and here we return to the differences between negative and positive factors, trauma and loss may be long-remembered. The children from families where there had been a close-knit, warm feeling and good communication between the parents and the children (although not with each other) pre-divorce, had great difficulty for many years in accepting and adjusting to the divorced family. These children were burdened for a very long time by feelings of loss and by their inability to understand the reasons for the divorce.

Finally, it is important to keep in mind that the child is not a bystander in the process of his own adjustment. He or she is an independent actor as well as a recipient of support. Thus, identification with the happier parent was not a universal occurrence among those children who improved. Good feelings of parents following the divorce were not necessarily mirrored in the children or even shared with the children. Sometimes the child's psychological health declined despite a better functioning and happier custodial parent. Moreover, each of the children we described and followed for so many years contributed to the interaction and the outcomes which emerged. The supports which the child used must be available, but the child needed to be able to grasp them and hold on. Sometimes the supports were available and the child failed to use them. Children who made use of others to maintain themselves had to help create these relationships. Sometimes those children who needed people the most were unable to venture. The children who found their support in other adults in the neighborhood or parents of their friends or teachers had to make their plight known before they could be aided. Others who withdrew into themselves increased their own deprivation. Out of all of these complex interactions, the outcomes we found emerged.

## Children Who Coped Successfully

Earl, age eleven, a handsome boy in jeans and well-worn tennis shoes, talked about his plans for the future. His main interest currently was sports, but he had reluctantly concluded that this was not a good career choice and that he would become an architect, like his father, "Because it's more worth my time and it's easier to get a job." He confirmed that he liked school because "I like to learn and I like physical ed."

About the divorce, Earl offered, "A long time ago it was really bad, but it's better now. I see my dad every weekend, as much as I used to before the divorce." But, if he had a problem, he went to his mother. "It's easier to talk to her because I know her longer."

Earl's teacher described him as a gifted student. She added that he was especially sensitive to other children's feelings. Sometimes he would say to his teacher, "Have you noticed that Susie is sad today?" referring to one or another child. The teacher had been impressed with his tactful leadership and his perceptive remarks. When he suggested an idea to a group, he would say, characteristically, "Why don't we try it this way?" Earl had close friends and was popular with his classmates. His teacher said, "He seems aware of both adult and peer levels and can relate accordingly."

When we met Earl shortly after his parents separated, he was profoundly hurt and frightened. He refused for several years to accept the divorce as final, despite his father's almost immediate remarriage. By the time of the second follow-up, Earl had recovered his very good developmental pace. His sensitivity to other people may well have been enhanced by his own successful mastery of the family travail.

Thirty-four percent of the children and adolescents appeared to be doing especially well at the five-year mark. Their self-esteem was high and they were coping competently with the tasks of school, playground, and home. There were no significant age or sex differences among these resilient youngsters. The boys appeared to have caught up with their sisters in the years since the first follow-up, which found the boys lagging behind.

These youngsters were a lively and engaging group, interested in many aspects of the world around them, with the capacity for commitment and the use of their imagination and intellectual potential. They were relatively sensitive and socially mature in their relationships. A goodly number had some special clarity in regard to adults' relationships with each other, which may have had its roots in their mastery of the family crisis and their observations of their parents' distress and attempts to resolve their difficulties.

Even among this group, we detected some lingering reservations about the parents' decision to divorce. At times, these youngsters still felt unhappy, lonely, and sorrowful in regard to the divorce. These misgivings, however, did not appear to affect their overall adjustment. It was gratifying for us to observe these children, since many of them had been unhappy and discouraged at the time of the acute family crisis. These youngsters had stabilized and moved ahead impressively, perhaps strengthened by their mastery of the many stresses of the unhappy marriage, the divorce and the postdivorce period.

## The Unhappy Children

The interviewer recorded:

Barbara, age eleven, looked pretty, but still painfully thin, almost emaciated. Throughout the session, her neediness was striking, as it had been on the earlier occasions that we had talked. And as we parted, she kissed me, clung to me tightly, and asked me to return to see her, begging to know exactly when I would do so.

"As Barbara entered the playroom, she busied herself with a dollhouse and began to construct a fantasy story which could have been a childish rendition of *Waiting for Godot*. She arranged the family dolls around the dinner table, which was set with careful attention to detail. The dolls in all their finery sat quietly awaiting the imminent arrival of the daddy doll who never appeared. It soon became clear that 'waiting for daddy' was a central fantasy which was repeated endlessly as if frozen in time."

"Barbara moved rapidly after this from game to game. Her attention span was short and her restlessness approached hyperactivity. Once she asked for a piece of clay to take home with her and she smelled it repeatedly. She spoke openly and sadly of her loneliness and her great yearning for her father. She dictated a note to him which she asked me to deliver, which read, 'Dear Daddy—I love you. Please, please come to see me.' Barbara described her relationship with her mother as improved. She explained that her mother's anger had diminished and that she was no longer as frightened, 'She doesn't throw things anymore.' Barbara said that she was against divorce because, "It is bad. I will never, never, never divorce.'"

Barbara was poorly parented in the postdivorce period by a father who visited capriciously and made dazzling promises he failed to keep, and by a mother who was herself slowly recovering from an agitated depression precipitated by the father's infidelity and his remarriage to a much younger woman. Barbara seemed unable to integrate the divorce and the separation from the father, or to find sufficient nurturance in her relationship with her depressed mother, whose life was additionally burdened by economic problems, her lack of economic skills, and her ambition to make her way as a creative writer. We considered the child very troubled, in urgent need of psychological intervention, supportive parenting, and a stable life arrangement.

A substantial minority of all of the boys and girls were unhappy and emotionally needy, and many of these were failing in significant areas of their adjustment. We have assessed these children along a great many measures which yield sometimes different, although not conflicting, results.

We found over one-third of the children to be consciously and intensely unhappy and dissatisfied with their life in the postdivorce family. Although the number of unhappy children was highest at the time of the parental separation, the unhappiness had declined at eighteen months and risen again by the five-year mark. Youngsters felt unhappy within the postdivorce family and in one or both of their relationships with parents. Seventeen percent felt rejected and unloved by the mother and 39 percent felt rejected and unloved by the father. Almost one-quarter of the children continued to be very disappointed with the visiting relationship, either because of its infrequency or because of its increasingly shallow emotional quality, which emerged over the years despite regular contact. The yearning for the absent father continued high and was very intense in 20 percent of the group.

We found 37 percent of all the children and adolescents to be moderately to severely depressed. As at the eighteen-month check point, depression was the most common psychopathological finding and was manifested in a wide variety of feelings and behavior, including chronic and intense unhappiness (at least one child with suicidal preoccupation), sexual promiscuity, delinquency (drug-abuse, petty stealing, some alcoholism, breaking and entering), poor learning, intense anger, apathy, restlessness and, as exemplified by Barbara, a sense of intense, unremitting emotional deprivation.

We were interested to find that the moderate depressions did not interfere with the youngsters' developmental progress in all aspects of their functioning. At least half of the depressed children were able to move ahead age-appropriately in several important parts of their lives. These islands of relatively unburdened development in unhappy, troubled children may be characteristic of these youngsters, particularly among those who had functioned well or reasonably well during some period of earlier development. Thus even Barbara, although worried, anxious, and unhappy, was learning at grade level in a special school where the classes were small and where she received individual attention from her teacher. She had one or two playmates and was clearly very responsive to the relationship with the interviewer. She remained, however, in our judgment, at high risk without further psychological intervention.

We were struck as well by the high incidence of intense loneliness which, while less than in the separation period, was observed in 27 percent of the children, once again higher than at the eighteen-month mark. These children complained of coming home to empty houses after school to await the return of the working parent. On weekends, these youngsters often felt ignored because of the social life of both divorced parents. Several also complained of loneliness following the remarriage, while recognizing ruefully that the newly-married adults wanted privacy and time away from curious children.

## Children Within the Middle Range: Adequate and Uneven Functioning

The interviewer recorded: "Sonja, age eleven, said that she was now getting over the divorce. She doesn't think about it as much as she used to. She said, 'Before I wasn't right. I was all mad and yelling at Mom because she wouldn't let me see my dad for a couple of weeks, but then she let us.' 'Usually I still yell at her. I tell her I don't mean it, but I can't control myself.' Sonja said that at first she had blamed her mother for the divorce and now she thinks it's her father's fault too.

"As Sonja talked about her relationships with adults and with peers, there was a continuous threatening undercurrent of 'they don't mess with me,' which we found disquieting. She talked with considerable pleasure about hurting and slapping people. She laughed excitedly as she recounted several stories of people, adults and children, getting into difficulties. She explained that she never wants to get married in the future. She wants to live by herself and she doesn't want to have any children. Asked who comforts her when she is upset or troubled, Sonja said she never talks to anyone. She never thinks about things like that. She added that she is still angry about the divorce. Asked for her advice to divorcing children, Sonja said, 'Try to live with it. Try not to think about the past.'

"Sonja was described by her teachers as learning below her capacity at school, but maintaining her grade level, except in one or two subjects. She had close friends and was popular among her classmates. Her teacher described her tendency to play one girl against the other. Recently, Sonja was caught stealing some things from the shopping center and also from the school. Sonja's mother indicated that the child is not as demanding as she used to be and that overall her behavior is improving. A private tutor is helping the child with her school work and she is expected to catch up within the near future."

The adjustment of 29 percent of the children was within the middle range. Generally age-appropriate although uneven in their overall ego functioning, they were learning at grade level at school and showing reasonably appropriate social behavior and judgment in their relationships with adults and with children. In the main, they had recovered from the unhappiness of the marriage and the stresses of the divorce sufficiently to move ahead on many fronts. And they were considered average by their teachers.

Nevertheless, accompanying their continued progress, these youngsters in the middle range continued to show significant residues of their continuing anger in their persistent emotional neediness, unhappiness, and somewhat diminished self-esteem. Although these youngsters had resumed their developmental progress, islands of unhappiness or anger continued to demand significant portions of their attention and psychic energy and to hamper the full potential of their development.

Although they seemed to relate reasonably well to adults and their peers, the dominant mood of these children who maintained the middle ground in their ego functioning was in marked contrast to the sense of sufficiency and self-confidence which we observed among the children who were doing very well.

## Continuity and Change

There was considerable change in the children and adolescents over the five-year period and not many held to their original level of adjustment during these years.* There was greatest stability among the older

* See appendix A for details of the assessment of the youngsters' ego-functioning at the initial contact.

youngsters, especially among the older girls, and very much less among the younger children. In general, those who came to the divorce with solid developmental achievements were better able to weather the storm. Nevertheless, the stress of the postseparation years and the complexity of life's challenges during these years was such that it was not possible to predict accurately, based on how the child had functioned before, how the child would emerge at the end of this stressful period. There were boys and girls in all age groups who had been able to maintain themselves during the conflict-ridden marriage who succumbed in the postseparation period. Similarly, as we have already noted, many vulnerable, troubled children improved if they broke free of unhappy relationships with their fathers and from an unhappy marriage that had hampered their growth and their self-confidence. Nevertheless, it seems clear that the most unpredictable change, upward or downward, occurred among those children in the middle, who came to the divorce with a mixture of successes and failures.

More specifically, as we followed the course of the children whom we had placed initially within the ranks of the very well-adjusted children, it appeared that two thirds of these successful copers were still functioning well five years later. Those who lost ground in this group did so, in the main, after the first eighteen months, after maintaining their functioning well during the initial period of high stress.

At the other end of the scale were those vulnerable children whose ego-functioning was originally impaired, who came to the divorce battered by the conflicts of the unhappy marriage, or neglected by unhappy, troubled parents. Over 75 percent of these children improved. Approximately half did so with the help of psychotherapy, but most were helped as well by the termination of their parents' unhappy marriage. Most of these youngsters had begun to show improvement by the eighteen-month mark. The most troubled did not appear improved until after this first follow-up.

Very few of the boys and girls who stood at the midpoint of the scale at the initial assessment remained there five years later. These youngsters underwent considerable change in opposite directions during the years and deteriorated or improved in equal measure. They were quicker to change; the incidence of change was very high but the direction of their change less predictable.

It is not surprising to find that well-adjusted children during the failing marriage remained, for the most part, in that category. And it was gratifying to find that youngsters who came to the divorce experiencing difficulty had a good chance to recover and move ahead especially when aided by individual psychotherapy. It is important to note that the children and adolescents who were most likely to be affected unpredictably by the impact of the separation and the postseparation period were those who fell initially within the middle range of adjustment. For these youngsters, particularly, the postseparation period of several years represented a critical and highly vulnerable time. They are the ones who most need watching.

## Configurations in Good Outcome

All in all, the factors that after five years appeared to promote good adjustment in children of the divorced family are similar to those which make for good adjustment and satisfaction in the intact home. Ironically, both the conflict-ridden family and the divorced family face rather similar difficulties in providing conditions in which children can grow and realize their emotional and intellectual potential. It seems reasonable to propose that divorce is not likely to be beneficial to children unless the parent-child relationship, separately or jointly, can be maintained at the level of gratification and guidance which existed earlier within the predivorce family, or unless these are improved. The families in which the children had a good outcome at five years were able to restabilize and restore the parenting after the initial, or sometimes extended, disorganization of the transition period. Custodial and noncustodial parents of the children who did well, separately or in cooperation with each other, retained their commitment to their children. In other families where children did well, one or both parents improved following the divorce and this was reflected in the parent-child relationship; or a third configuration was present where the divorce separated the child from a psychologically destructive parent. Finally, of course, some children benefited from a remarriage.

### Continuity with Both Parents

Successful outcome at all ages, which we have equated with good ego functioning, adequate or high self-esteem and no depression, reflected a stable, close relationship with the custodial parent and the noncustodial parent. In such cases the friction between the parents had largely dissipated. The visiting pattern was likely to be regular and dependable, and encouraged by the custodial parent and related to the child's age and interests. In these arrangements the child or adolescent essentially enjoyed the supports of the intact family. Occasionally, the child's self-esteem was enhanced in that he or she felt especially valued in recognition of the obstacles to maintaining the relationship which needed to be overcome in the divorced family. Children and adolescents were aware of the ease with which appointments could be forgotten, or plans post-poned by the visiting parent. Similarly, children were often aware of the burdens of the custodial parent. They were appreciative of the efforts required to maintain the household, and the demands of working and carrying sole responsibility for the family, and they were sensitive to the worries and responsibilities that the custodial parent carried alone. They saw the custodial mother's attitude, as well, as indicating the special place which they held in her affection. Many of these youngsters were likely to be socially mature, self-confident, and independent beyond their age. And partly as a result of this very self-confidence, they were able to acquire a wide circle of secondary supports and the encouragement and interest of teachers and friends.

DOROTHY. Dorothy's parents separated when she was eleven years old. She was one of five children. Her mother was a devoted parent with relatively few other interests. Her father had been close to his children during the marriage and, although he remarried shortly after the divorce, he maintained his home within a half-hour's drive of the children. He maintained his interest, his regular visiting, and continued to support the family in relative comfort. The mother, who worked part time during the years, had restabilized her life as a parent within the first two years after the separation. It took her almost four years, however, to begin to think of her own needs as an adult separate from her mothering responsibilities, and at that time she finally began to establish an independent social life and to think of returning to school. The children had a sense of the parents' strong emotional investment in them. Birthdays were celebrated twice, once in each household. And the children were consulted in planning Thanksgiving, Christmas, and other family occasions.

At sixteen, Dorothy was an engaging, pretty high-school sophomore. She expressed satisfaction with school, extracurricular activities, and friends, and described her interest in science which she expected would develop into a career. She impressed us as an intact fifteen-year-old who was enjoying her adolescence.

Dorothy talked freely and easily during the follow-up interview. She considered herself fortunate because there had not been many changes in her life following the divorce. She noted that her relationship with her nearby father had not changed much. She saw him about the same amount of time as she had earlier: once a week and often during the week as well when something came up. The arrangement was informal and easy. Dorothy was not crazy about her new stepmother, and on occasion she thought her father dogmatic and hot-tempered but, nevertheless, she got along well with father and stepmother. She and her father both shared a passion for the out-of-doors, which the stepmother did not, and she and her father went camping together.

Dorothy confessed that she had worried about her mother shortly after the divorce and was concerned about whether her mother could manage and what would happen to them all. Now she worried less. She would like her mother to get married because her mother would have many years ahead after the children left.

For the fortunate children like Dorothy, the postdivorce family provided the same supports which had been provided by the intact family after the initial period of instability was over, even though the mother was less happy than she had been during the marriage. Children usually forged ahead under these conditions, strengthened by their ordeal during the separation and their pride in their own capacity to weather the acute crisis.

### Relationship with the Custodial Parent

For all the children and adolescents a good relationship with the custodial parent was the key to good functioning in the postdivorce family. A close, nurturant, dependable mother-child relationship was highly related to the youngster's competent ego functioning, to successful performance at school, social maturity, empathic relationships with adults and peers, and to feeling good about oneself in the world. Forty percent of the mother-child relationships were considered adequate to very good at this point, with an additional 20 percent at the adequate mark, although marred by the intrusive difficulties of the mother at intervals. Mostly the younger children until the age of eight, and girls until twelve, enjoyed better mothering than did the older children. For girls, the tie between their overall adjustment and the relationship with the mother was very strong at each checkpoint in the study. For boys, the relationship was significant as well at each point that we observed, but was less stable over time and became less important (although not unimportant) as the boy entered adolescence. Even in mid-adolescence, at age thirteen to sixteen, the quality of the relationship with the custodial mother remained significant for both boys and girls. And for younger children to the age of eight, the child's relationship with the good or good enough mother was the touchstone of their ego functioning.

A significant subgroup of these children who did well depended almost entirely on the relationship with the custodial mother and drew their nurturance from that relationship. If the relationship was sensitive and sufficiently caring it was possible for these children to do well. These youngsters included the youngest group, those at the five-year mark whose relationship with their father had been brief in time and emotionally limited before the separation. This group included, as well, those younger and older children who had been poorly parented by an indifferent father who had been emotionally or physically unavailable to them throughout the marriage and during the postdivorce years, and for whom the children continued to feel no deep tie. This group that depended on the mother, also included children who had been poorly treated, verbally or physically abused, or sexually misused by fathers they feared, as well as children who had frequently witnessed the father's cruelty to the mother.

These, and other such relationships which we have described elsewhere, were freed from the psychopathology and burdening of a corrosive relationship with the father. They surged ahead and maintained their progress at the five-year mark within the framework of a good mother-child relationship. Others, as we have also described, when they reached adolescence consciously and thoughtfully counterrejected their father as undependable and unloving. In a true sense, they consciously disidentified with the father. For these children the father's appearance and disappearance at intervals in their lives did not seem, at the five-year mark, to profoundly disturb their adjustment and their good functioning if sustained by a rich, sensitive relationship with their mother, their own resources, and a devoted stepfather.

Yet, even in these rich relationships which the child enjoyed with the custodial parent, the relationship with the father played a significant part. Although the children who did well did so within the context of the mother-child relationship, their good adjustment remained conditional on their not feeling rejected by the noncustodial father. The children who felt rejected by the father were burdened in their psychological functioning despite the presence of a good mother. And therefore, although the children and adolescents who did well were likely to have a good or good enough relationship with the mother, the significant link was conditional, and carried the proviso that the same child not feel rejected by the father if the adjustment was not to suffer despite the excellent mother-child relationship. Thus, the seeming dyadic within the postdivorce family appeared in this way to be deceptive, because the child continued to be aware of himself in regard to both parents and the two-parent perspective remained significant despite legal and geographical separation and the passage of years.

## The Noncustodial Parent

The role of the father was two-fold in its potential effect on the child's psychological and social development. The negative effect of irregular, erratic visiting was clear. The father's abandonment, relative absence, infrequent or irregular appearance, or general unreliability, which disappointed the child repeatedly, usually led the child to feel rejected or rebuffed and lowered the child's self-esteem. We soon learned that the unvisited or poorly visited child was likely to feel unloved and unlovable, nor did anger at the rejecting father always undo the child's unhappy conclusion about his or her essential unlovability.

The father's direct contribution to the child's psychological health and competent coping was not so clearly discernible either at the time of counseling or at the eighteen-month follow-up. At five years, however, this positive contribution of the father's role emerged with clarity. Specifically, good father-child relationships appeared linked to high self-esteem and the absence of depression in children of both sexes and at all ages. We were interested to find this significant link in both sexes up to and including those in the thirteen-to-twenty-four age group.

In the youngest children the good father-child relationship was closely related to a regular and frequent visiting schedule and to a visiting pattern that included continuity and pleasure in the visiting. For most children, this meant overnight and weekend stays. As the child entered mid-adolescence the significance of the frequency in contact faded, as expected, and it was the quality of the relationship that appeared to grow more central.

It is noteworthy that the divorce appeared not to diminish the importance of the psychological link between father and child. This connection was especially obvious at the five-year mark in those children who were between nine and twelve, or entering adolescence. Children in this age group took intense pleasure in the visiting and when they were not visited they grieved. It seemed possible, in fact, that in this nine-to-twelve-year-old group the visiting father might sustain a youngster even in the care of a disorganized mother. Beyond this age, for the thirteen-to-sixteen-year-old mid-adolescent group, the connection between self-esteem and a good father-child relationship was still important, although somewhat less than for the younger group. This link between father-child relationship and self-esteem did not disappear even among the oldest group but became less significant as the youngsters entered young adulthood. The trio of good father-child relationship, high self-esteem, and absence of depression appeared, however, to hold for all age groups.

The relationship between father and child was susceptible to change and improvement, and the results of this were evident in the child's adjustment at the five-year mark. For example, we found that boys and girls of various ages who had been doing poorly at the initial assessment were able to improve significantly with increased visiting by the father. Similarly, visits by the father which increased after the first year diminished loneliness among the older youngsters and adolescents. Those children who had been fortunate enough to enjoy a good father-child relationship on a continuing stable basis over the years were more likely to be in good psychological health.

## Sex and Age Differences

Sex differences were of less influence than we had anticipated in the continuing relationship of boys and girls to both parents. Boys relied for their overall good adjustment on a good mother-child relationship at all the checkpoints of the study. But, the relationship between the overall ego functioning of the boy and the father-son relationship emerged more clearly at the five-year mark and was not as evident earlier. The father-son relationship appeared to have grown in importance to the boys' self-esteem as the boy matured.

The strong tie between the good mother-daughter relationship and the psychological functioning of the girl became stronger over the years. The significance of the girl's relationship with her father was more clearly linked to good ego functioning at the five-year mark, but this connection was still less strong than its age-related counterpart among the boys. Thus, although boys and girls continued to depend for their good psychological adjustment on their relationship with both parents, the boys' good adjustment correlated more highly with the father-son relationship and the girls' good adjustment correlated more highly with the mother-daughter relationship for youngsters above the age of nine. These sex differences were not evident among the younger children, whose good adjustment correlated more highly with the quality of the mother-child relationship.

More of the younger children had good relationships with both parents. Younger children were visited more frequently and more regularly, and the pattern of the visiting was likely to be more beneficial for the younger child and, especially, for those below the age of eight. Thus, although the initial vulnerability of the younger children was high, in the long run these children emerged as better parented by both parents than their older brothers and sisters. In accord with the concepts of the configurations which we have suggested, the better parenting which the younger children received may have offset their initial greater vulnerability.

It would appear that the importance of a good father-child relationship does not diminish in the divorced family for boys or girls and may, in fact, increase as the child approaches early adolescence. This finding carries social implications, especially since it is also our finding that older children do not attach readily to stepfathers and that older children often resented the stepfathers' presence in the family.

*Peers*

The children in the group of adequate or well-adjusted youngsters had good friends and did well at school. As noted, they were generally empathic boys and girls who related well to adults and to children their age. Their relationships on the playground with friends and playmates were not, however, as we soon discovered, separate from the events and relationships within the family. Among the older boys there was a close tie between their being independent young people, performing well at school, and their ability to make friends independent of their relationships within the family.

At the height of the divorce crisis older boys, more than girls, had been able to go off with friends and put useful distance between themselves and the household. They did not usually confide in their friends but they succeeded via their friendships in putting the home situation out of their minds and gaining perspective. The older girls, by contrast, showed a different pattern. The girls' relationship with the custodial mother and identification with the mother entered significantly into both their school performance and their capacity to make friends. There was a high correlation between the girl's good relationship with her mother and her good relationship with peers. For the young children who did well, both boys and girls, the same connections were apparent. Those who made friends readily were identified with a psychologically intact custodial parent or had a stable, relatively unconflicted, home environment.

Thus, for children and adolescents in all groups except for the older boys, children did not use their friends to escape from an unhappy, conflict-ridden household. Instead, they were free to make use of friends when the conflicted home was relatively quiet and when the relationships within the family were good and supportive of their efforts. At the five-year mark and earlier, peer relationships did not compensate for the poor home situation. In this sense, friends are not "instead of" but "in addition to." The child in the conflicted home, the worried child, and the troubled child, had a hard time both at home, at school, and at play.

Little girls age five to twelve showed the strongest connection between good peer relationships, a conflict-free home, and a reasonably content mother who was not lonely. This finding suggests, dramatically, that when the little girls find that their mother is troubled and lonely they are likely either to remain at home and abstain from friendships in order to keep their mother company and comfort her, or they themselves feel constrained to enter into relationships with friends when the mother is unhappy and lonely.

These findings are interesting and cause for concern. If children whose lives were relatively conflict-free and whose families were supportive were those best able to turn to friends, then the friendship group cannot be thought of as a resource that is likely to help the troubled child. Several youngsters and adolescents who turned to groups when the situation at home had deteriorated became caught up in delinquent behavior and gangs. As a secondary gain and a support for the children who were doing well when the home situation had eased, it appears that friends were helpful and expanded and enriched the quality of the child's life, but as a source of support when the home situation was trying they were of limited help to most of these youngsters.

### Other Supports

Those children who had extended families, especially grandparents, who were close by or who kept up a continuing interest from a distance were very much helped by this support system. Several children, when asked about what had helped them the most, told us about loving, devoted grandparents who kept them in mind and provided summer vacations for them, telephone calls at frequent intervals, and an ongoing relationship attentive to the needs of the children.

Asked what helped her through the divorce, Amy, age sixteen, said, "A lot of people. My mother helped me in so many ways. My stepdad, once we adjusted to each other. . . . Grandma, I really love her. My friends . . . a couple of teachers." She added, musing, "I kept my mind open and was looking for help. My life has never been bad. . . . I have learned from everything. I like where I am now."

With the exception of the school and teachers which we describe later, the other supports that these youngsters received was meager or serendipitous, and available to few—a neighbor, the parents of a good friend, occasionally a minister or rabbi, an older sibling, a young cousin who came frequently to visit. Essentially, aside from school, the children who did well used their family as the major support system, and within that, relied most on their mothers, their fathers, and their own resources.

### Psychologically Stable Parents

The parenting capacity of both mothers and fathers was related to their psychological intactness and stability as individuals. Women who had more psychological stability were more likely to bring the divorce crisis to an end earlier and to reestablish continuity and order in their lives and in their households within the first year or two postseparation. Consequently children whose mothers were psychologically in good health suffered a shorter period of disorganization within their family and less chronic stress than their less fortunate peers. Little girls seemed especially vulnerable to the psychological disturbance of the mother, and their overall adjustment was significantly related to the extent to which the mother was not depressed or disorganized in her functioning over an extended period of time.

But all children, girls and boys, with a psychologically healthy mother or a mother who was not depressed or continually angry were less likely to have been employed as messengers or allies in the ongoing struggle between the parents. They were less likely to have been frightened by depressed or suicidal parents. Psychologically stable mothers were more likely to cooperate with fathers to facilitate or encourage visits. The psychologically stable fathers were also more likely to reorder their lives more quickly than those who were severely disturbed. They were likely to visit, more likely to maintain a dependable or regular visiting schedule, more likely to keep their promises and not to disappoint their children. They, too, were less likely to continue the friction with the custodial mother or to burden the child as a messenger or an ally. Also, there was indication in our findings that the psychological intactness of the father was directly relevant to the good psychological adjustment of older adolescents, both boys and girls.

It is important to note, however, that the greater psychological stability and higher self-esteem in the parent did not always eventuate in better mothering or fathering for the child. Men and women alike who felt that the decision to divorce had been wise, and who considered themselves happier and the quality of their life enhanced since the divorce, were not always more sensitive, more caring parents, nor were they necessarily more available to their children.

Still, the diminution of conflict between the parents was related at all ages to the child's capacity to cope with the divorce. Most children and adolescents developed little immunity with the passage of time and continued to be troubled and distressed by the ongoing overt conflict between the parents, or the continued sense of strain at being placed in the middle. Friendliness, at least absence of conflict, between the parents was an important component of good outcome for the children.

### Sense of Sufficiency

We have observed earlier that the ambience of the home, and particularly the child's sense of not feeling deprived, was a significant factor in the good adjustment of many children. This feeling of sufficiency was a composite of many of the child's perceptions and feelings, including the child's sense of the economic stability, standard of living in the household, and quality of the parenting. Money and economic concerns were discussed frequently within the divorced family and occupied a major part of family life and concern for many families. Girls appeared sometimes more sensitive than their brothers to the economic conditions of the family. Young children were especially responsive to the economic security of the custodial parent and their good adjustment often reflected a connection between this sense of security and stability in the family. For some of the younger children, and especially the younger boys, the child's good adjustment was also associated at the five-year mark with the mother's not working. Unquestionably, the greater economic security of the parent, the stability of family, and the availability of the mother combined to make the experience of the divorced family one of a safe and comfortable place to be.

Finally no single child experienced all the beneficial factors we have enumerated, but these factors turned up regularly and significantly as we studied the lives of these children who adjusted well. As a result, these fortunate children were able to achieve a sense of closure about their parents' divorce. Most had considered the divorce thoughtfully, each in his or her own way, and arrived at an understanding of the family events which suited the individual's need for clarity and coherence. With this done, they were able to close the door and move on.

## Configurations in Poor Outcome

### Failure of the Divorce

A central cause of poor outcome for the children and the adolescents was the failure of the divorce to result in a reasonable adjustment to it by the parents. When one or both parents continued to be distressed, or when the divorced parents continued to fight with each other as bitterly as they had during the marriage, or when the bitterness following the divorce even exceeded the bitterness of the marital conflict, children felt unable to master the resulting stress and the psychic pain.

We were startled to discover that 30 percent of the children were aware of intense bitterness between their parents five years after the divorce. This continued fighting was not only distressing to the children, but also correlated significantly with their poor psychological adjustment.

Continued friction between parents who had long been divorced was significantly linked to psychological instability, psychiatric illness, and, most particularly, to the loneliness of one or both adults. Therefore, children in these troubled families were adversely affected by the continued quarreling and psychological disturbance and the lonely, unhappy feelings that exacerbated the long-standing anger of the adults.

For these families the divorce had failed, as had the marriage, and the children were bewildered, angry, and unable to understand or to justify the continued difficulties in their family. Moreover, they were deprived as well of the adult help they needed in coping with the postdivorce family. Thus, children who were unable to obtain closure by five years were those for whom the stress continued or for whom the postseparation family was less gratifying, less supportive, and more stressful—or as stressful, although perhaps in different ways, than the intact family had been.

### The Stressed Custodial Parent

Boys and girls of all ages were in trouble when the mother-child relationship was conflicted or impoverished, or overburdened by the mother's social and economic overload, her loneliness and discouragement, her psychological or physical ill health, or her loss of interest in parenting. Many of these children were sad, lonely, and worried. Often they were pathetic in their vulnerability and pervasive neediness or worrisome in their intense anger. The primary cause of decline in children who had been able to maintain reasonably adequate or good functioning during the conflicted marriage was the insufficiency of the parenting following the divorce, which combined with the child's disappointment that the divorce failed to produce relief or improvement, or even continuity of care.

For 40 percent of the mothers the relationship with the children had deteriorated or remained poor following the divorce. One-half of this group had been poor parents during the marriage and did not improve following the divorce. One-quarter of this group had been reasonably good or very good parents during the unhappy marriage but were unable to maintain or reestablish their parenting at the same level within the divorced family. The remainder declined even further in their relationship with their children, from what had been a marginally satisfactory relationship during the marriage.

One-third of all the women continued at this time to experience considerable stress in carrying out the demanding tasks of the single parent. The stress was a composite of economic, social, and psychological factors, impinging in different combinations upon each family unit. The effects, which made themselves variously felt, usually led to heightened tension between mother and child.

## Mother-Child Relationships that Declined

Mothers who regretted their decision to seek the divorce—who viewed their current lives as drab, economically insecure, and socially unfulfilled, who looked back wistfully at the marriage and blamed themselves or their former husband for the current dilemma in their lives from which they saw no exit—had difficulty in maintaining their parenting at the level they had earlier achieved. Their chronic dissatisfaction was communicated daily in various verbal and nonverbal ways to children who worried about them and felt insecure about much in their own lives.

The postdivorce family in which the custodial parent is profoundly unhappy can burden the child with overwhelming worries. The children's worry about the adult soon becomes a chronic part of the child's life. Children worry about the fighting which continues, and the rebuffs to one parent, as well as the mother's state of mind. They take responsibility for "marrying mother off" or for anything else that would ease her pain. Sometimes they feel responsible for the mother's unhappiness. Their chronic worry reflects a general unease and the instability which they experience in the family. They live in fear of additional changes which might further upset the precarious balance of their lives. And they especially fear being removed from the supports they lean on and so desperately need.

Kevin's mother had changed her mind about the divorce. Although she had initially sought the divorce to the despair of her husband who loved her, several years later she wanted to reconstitute the marriage. She was an attractive woman who held a reasonably good office job. Her husband maintained child support and regular visiting. Nevertheless, her unhappiness since the divorce had remained unchanged. Her wish to divorce had followed the traumatic loss of a major parenting figure in her own life; her decision to seek divorce appeared primarily to reflect her own psychological turmoil at that time. She had complained of her loneliness within the marriage. Unfortunately, the divorce had not brought relief for her loneliness. The new man in her life was less reliable, less supportive than her husband had been. And the postdivorce family was much more ridden by psychological difficulty and deprivations for mother and child than the intact family. In the meantime, the father who had vigorously opposed the divorce was remarried. There were no children in the new marriage and the father maintained his staunch commitment and love for Kevin. Nevertheless, the family ambience was too unstable for Kevin. His mother was an unhappy, troubled woman and Kevin was caught in the web of her distress. The child's teacher told us, "Kevin just doesn't do *anything* at school. He just sits there; he doesn't even try to do his work."

## Poor Parenting that Continues to Be Poor

One half of the women whose relationship with their children was poor in the postdivorce family had been anxious, restless, or indifferent mothers during the predivorce family years. Most of these women did not entirely reject their children and maintained a fluctuating interest in their care and welfare. Nevertheless, they were driven during the marriage, and even more so following the divorce, into a series of unstable relationships which absorbed the major share of their interest and time. Their preoccupation with their own social and sexual activities led to a crowded schedule which left little time for attention to the children or to the home. None of these women sought education or careers, and their own conflict regarding parenthood did not reflect the colliding pull of motherhood versus an interest in a profession or another career. Most were eagerly in search of remarriage.

The children had been neglected during the conflicted marriage and were more neglected following the divorce when the attention of the parent was further diminished both by full-time employment and a more frenetic social life. Many of these youngsters lacked the inner resources to deal both with the family rupture and the chronic psychological and

physical instability of their environment. This group included a significant proportion of the children who were psychologically in trouble at
the five-year mark. They felt depleted from within and insufficiently
loved and supported from without.

When Valerie was twelve her parents decided to divorce. She was
an unhappy, lonely, overweight youngster who was barely getting by at
school and, except for occasional violent fistfights on the playgrounds
which alarmed her teachers, she seemed sunk in fantasy most of the day.

She expressed her disdain for both of her parents at the initial interview. Complaining bitterly of their selfishness and their neglect of her
and the other children, Valerie explained that her only comfort was in
spinning fantasies about her toy animals, which she depicted as infinitely
kinder and more loving than people.

Seen at the five-year mark, Valerie was heavily made up and looked
years older than her age. She explained frankly that she had smoked a
great deal of pot and said, "I was stoned most of my freshman
year." She became involved during that year with a high-living, fast-
running group, "smoking four or five reefers a day." She had been sexually active for several years. As Valerie contemplated her own future,
she said that she did not plan to marry because she did not like commitment. She would enjoy having a child, but she would prefer "a kid
without marriage." Although she reasoned that "this might be hard on the
child," she concluded: "It's harder on the child if the parents get divorced." Once again, as she had earlier in our contact, Valerie vehe-
mently expressed her anger and her disappointment at both her parents and talked of their selfishness and how unhelpful they had been to
her since the divorce.

## The Psychiatrically Ill Mother

The vulnerability of the child to the psychological difficulties of the
custodial parent is far greater in the divorced family. The multiple demands of the divorced household are likely to have a more disorganizing
and longer-lasting impact on the parent who comes to the experience
with a history of psychological instability. Therefore, from the standpoint of the child the divorce-related experience is one of greater disorder in the family and greater instability in the immediate environment, which is likely to be enduring. The psychologically disturbed
parent is also more likely to be lonely and socially isolated, even in the
presence of an extended family. Unhappily, as we have already noted,
divorce was sometimes actively sought by the ill parent for reasons that
seemed to reflect that parent's disturbed thinking rather than any severe
difficulties within the marriage. The divorce, therefore, was less likely to
make sense to the children or to bring relief. The troubled parent often
leaned heavily on the children for care and nurturance, or clung to them

for protection against further regression, or to maintain a slipping hold on reality. Finally, the buffering, protective, countervailing presence of the other parent in shielding the child emotionally and in providing an ongoing corrective perspective to a distorted view of reality was no longer available following divorce. As a result, the relationship between the remaining disturbed parent and the child carried a very grave potential for intense pathological interaction and psychopathological identifications.

Thirteen percent of the mother-child relationships at the five-year mark were considered by us to be seriously flawed by the mother's severe psychopathology. An additional 5 percent were considered very poor relationships, marred by the mother's narcissism. The severe disturbances included recurrent depressions which required periodic hospitalization, chronic depression, paranoid schizophrenia, and alcoholism. Half of these extremely troubled women had husbands whose relationship with the children also reflected profound disturbance. Sometimes the presence of the two severely disturbed parents reinforced the psychopathological ambience of the family. In one such family each parent was violent, drank too much, and regularly fought with the other until someone was in grave danger and a frightened neighbor or child called the police. Such parents did not play a separate role in protecting the children and their behavior together intensified the difficulties the child faced. This mutual reinforcement was not always evident, however, and sometimes two very troubled people became disturbed at different times and in different ways, and one parent was able to maintain the household at the height of the other's crisis.

In at least half the families in which the mother suffered with severe psychiatric illness, the father was not psychologically disturbed but took a central role prior to the separation in the care of the children at the time that the mother was in crisis. Men whose wives struggled with disabling depressions often stood by to help. It was not uncommon for the husband to arrange his schedule to enable him to leave his office at quick notice and return home to the children. One mother telephoned her husband at his office immediately after she ingested sleeping pills during each of her several suicide attempts, and he was able to respond promptly, to rescue her, and to protect the young children.

Men also often played a significant psychological role in the lives and functioning of the children. Several fathers, prior to the divorce, had undertaken this responsibility thoughtfully as they had come to recognize the tragic illness of the mother. They acted to cushion and to buffer the impact of the mother's psychopathology. They counteracted the reality distortion of the mother who insisted that "all men are beasts." They provided emotional supplementation and participated in the physical care of the children, especially, but not only, when the mother went into periodic decline. They exercised a braking effect on the children's intense overinvolvement with the one parent. In myriad ways, they safeguarded the emotional, intellectual, and moral development of the children by providing a model of a loving, responsible, and steadfast adult who was there when needed.

The children who remained in the care of a psychologically disturbed mother looked very troubled at the five-year mark. They had not only been left in the care of the more troubled parent, but they had lost the mediating influence, support, and major buffering contribution of the more stable parent, which had kept them from being drawn into the orbit of the mother's illness. Some of the youngsters appeared to have few inner resources to help them withstand the family disruption. And it may be that while their resources had been strained to the utmost during the marriage, they had been sustained by their relationship with the stable, committed parent.

The divorce sent these children into a tailspin which at five years appeared to be consolidated into severe psychological illness and a major skewing of their development. Perhaps we should note that fathers in these families, despite continuing grave concern, did not feel able or willing to care for the children and did not attempt to seek custody. Sometimes men who had carried heavy responsibility during the marriage were relieved to be free of these burdens and maintained minimal contact after the divorce, especially following their remarriage.

This tragic situation was epitomized for us by Cora, who at age eleven told us that she was not sure how old she was and could barely manage a game of checkers. When first seen at age seven, Cora had been considered a gifted child and had begun to master chess.

Cora's parents were married in their teens and divorced nine years later at the mother's sudden insistence and in the face of the young father's strong opposition. During the marriage the young mother suffered with recurrent severe depressions. On at least two occasions she made serious suicide attempts. Her other symptoms included excessive fatigue and somatic complaints, combined with an apathy which kept her in bed for extended periods of time. Occasionally, her thoughts seemed disordered and she would confuse her own needs and even her own self with one of her children. In between these bouts of severe depression, Cora's mother was intelligent, thoughtful, and sensitive, a lovely looking woman who was devoted to her children. During the marriage. He loved and respected his wife, and did not blame her himself available for parenting the children and maintaining the household during the illnesses of the mother. He had been devoted both to the children and his ailing wife and was entirely willing to remain in the marriage. He loved her and respected his wife, and did not blame her for her severe illness.

Shortly after the divorce the mother's mental health began to deteriorate. She married quickly and her new husband, although a loving man and a gifted poet, had no economic skills. The family suffered under severe economic hardship although the father maintained his support of the children at a generous level. The mother suffered a series of depressive episodes which required hospitalization. The family also moved away from the father to the eastern seaboard.

The children, both parents, and the stepfather were seen by us several years later. We were dismayed and saddened by the change in the children and the decline in the mother. The interviewer recorded, "I was very troubled at the way the mother looked and became more troubled as the interview went on. Her face was chalk white and her expression was almost flat. Her voice was monotonous and droning. Gradually, she told me about her recent hospitalization and suicide attempt. She expressed considerable satisfaction with the children's progress, which in no wise matched by impression or the report from the school."

"When I saw Cora, whom I remembered well, she remembered me and I asked among other questions how old she was now. Cora looked quite startled and said she didn't know whether she was eleven or twelve and then began counting from her last birthday and seemed to be in considerable trouble in putting this together. I was taken aback with the changes in her because I remembered her as a very bright girl, who had impressed me as unusually creative, charming, and agreeable when I had seen her at the time of the initial assessment. Her intellectual functioning had deteriorated seriously, as had apparently her social and school behavior. The child was spending much of her time alone and she seemed preoccupied with her own fantasy world."

The disruption of the divorce, the critical psychological illness of the mother, and the geographical separation from the loving father were all overwhelming for Cora and her brother and sister. Although the stepfather was loving and supportive of his wife, he was less conscious of her severe illness than the father had been. Moreover, he did not assume the same protective role with the children, whose reality testing, cognitive development, and emotional progress had been sustained by their daily relationship with their father.

## The Economic Stress

Mothers' relationships with their children were burdened by the economic pressures of the divorced family. As we have already described, many mothers were gravely strained by financial worries, by their need to work hard and long hours in order to maintain themselves and their children, by a gnawing, ever-present sense of having more to do than they could achieve in the allotted time, and their feeling that whichever way they turned some important aspect of their life or their children's lives was being neglected.

The children's response to the economic pressures in the family was mediated through the mother-child relationship. Their adjustment was not directly affected by the economic circumstances alone. Overall, a relatively good standard of living and the positive effects of economic stability were very evident in the mother-child relationship, and reflected in the child's good adjustment. These emerged more clearly than did the deleterious impact of economic deprivation considered by itself.

Even when there was no grave economic hardship in the family, the combination of the role of economic provider, mother, and full-time manager combined to present seemingly unresolvable problems to women who were trying to advance themselves economically by supplementing their full-time work with education or special training. Lacking both sufficient funds for adequate help and a supportive network in the community which would have eased their life, mothers ironically felt defeated and their children experienced diminished care as a result of their very wish to improve their lives and the lives of the children. The mothers whose parenting had been good or very good during the unhappy marriage and declined during the divorced years mostly fell within this category. By and large, these women were highly motivated, upwardly striving, and continued to feel taxed by their crowded agendas and multiple responsibilities in ways that did not seem to lessen over the years.

An important aspect of the ambiance of the divorced family is that the economic status of mother and children does not stand alone, but is frequently, and sometimes continually, compared with the standard of living which the family had enjoyed earlier, as well as with the present standard of living of the husband, or the husband's new family. Where there was little change, even when the standard of living continued from the marriage into divorce was marginal, the mother and children were able to deal with the situation as they had earlier. Sometimes they coped with courage and resourcefulness and considerable psychological intactness. Or, when the father earned very little money and (as happened in a few families) remained at the periphery of the family life of his former wife and his children in a psychologically and economically depressed condition, the former wife and most often the children protected him and tried compassionately to help him.

When the downward change in the family standard of living followed the divorce and the discrepancy between the father's standard of living and that of the mother and children was striking, this discrepancy was often central to the life of the family and remained as a festering source of anger and bitter preoccupation. The continuation of this discrepancy over the years generated continuing bitterness between the parents. Mother and children were likely to share in their anger at the father and to experience a pervasive sense of deprivation, sometimes depression, accompanied by a feeling that life was unrewarding and unjust.

### Children Who Could Not Understand the Divorce

Among the children we found to be troubled at the five-year mark were a subgroup whose parents had divorced for reasons unrelated to marital unhappiness, and who thus could not understand what had disrupted their families. We have earlier suggested that the decision to divorce could occur as a kind of ricochet phenomenon following a death or similar tragedy in the family, or as a symptom in the aggravated psychological illness of one marital partner. Children in such families continued over the years to have difficulty in making sense of the family rupture. They remained bewildered, and their adjustment continued to be burdened by their inability to make sense of their experience. The divorce-related lacunae in their thinking were strikingly inappropriate and at odds with other parts of their cognitive and emotional functioning. We were concerned that their intellectual functioning seemed to have been held back and marred by the childishness of the explanations they had accepted in lieu of age-appropriate understanding.

Stanley, a bright thirteen-year-old, was asked what he thought was the cause of his parents' divorce. He offered the bizarre explanation that his father had been baking bread and that his mother had burned it and this had precipitated the divorce. Stanley's mother had five years earlier suddenly sought the divorce, in the face of her husband's opposition, following a tragic accident.

### Anger and Depression

Adolescents psychologically in trouble at the five-year mark were likely to be angry or depressed. The anger of many of these youngsters appeared related to an underlying depression, although it was fed from many sources and sometimes kept alive over the years by the continuing conflict between the parents.

Anger played a significant role in the psychological life of twenty-three percent of the children and adolescents, and was significantly linked at the five-year mark to poor adjustment, school failure, and acting-out behavior of various kinds. Sometimes the anger was directed at both parents, but most frequently the anger was directed at the father. There was unexpected continuity in both the incidence and the intensity of anger which dominated the relationship of youngsters with the father, especially for the older boys who had reached mid- and late adolescence by this time. We have been impressed with the divorce-specific emergence of anger with parents in so many youngsters at the time of the marital separation, and we were surprised now by its endurance.

Angry youngsters were observed at each check point in the study. At the initial assessment, the clustering of angry children occurred in the nine-to-twelve-year-old group and, in fact, appeared as the characteristic response to marital rupture of youngsters at this age. By five years, these youngsters, especially the adolescent boys, were a subgroup distinguishable by their intense anger. There was, in fact, some indication that the children who had been angry earlier had become angrier as they moved into adolescence. And it is reasonable to assume that the earlier divorce-engendered anger of the preadolescent youngster which had remained unresolved had then joined the characteristic rebelliousness of the adolescent as the young person entered that developmental stage. In this way, the initial anger was fueled by developmental progress as well as by the initial family crisis.

The behavior of these youngsters took many forms, including explosive temper outbursts, repeated rejection of the parents' overtures and offers of friendship, delinquent behavior, including arson, drug involvement, stealing, breaking and entering, and school failure which included poor learning, truancy, and dropping out. Girls as we have said, were more likely to become involved in early sexual activity and promiscuity, and some drug-taking and school failure as well.

Initially many of the older youngsters had been angry at both parents for their role in the divorce. Their anger at the mother, however, appeared to peak at eighteen months after the divorce, and gradually fell away, whereas the anger at the father was more likely to be maintained by the older boys and the adolescents, resulting over the years in a gradually deteriorated relationship.

The anger of these young people had many tangled roots. We found only a weak correlation, for instance, between the anger of children and the quarreling of their parents; and the influence of an angry parent as a role model did not appear to be of major importance. Much, although not all, of the anger was defensive and we believe reflected the underlying anxiety and sense of powerlessness of these youngsters who were standing at the threshold of adolescence at the time that the family structure was weakened by the parents' decision to divorce. The estrangement of these children from the father began at this crucial time and continued during the postdivorce years with hurt feelings on both sides and much expression of anger.

We were particularly interested in the attitudes and behavior of youngsters who had earlier formed close alignments with one parent, which were designed to harass and humiliate the other. These alignment relationships, described earlier, had sanctioned and even encouraged expression of aggression against the other parent within a protective, affectionate, close parent-child relationship. Initially, twenty-five of the 131 children we began with had joined in alignments with one or the other parent. By the five-year mark, no child was aligned with the father and only three remained aligned with the mother. All of these other very intense relationships had calmed or totally disappeared. Most of these youngsters had resumed reasonable, although not necessarily friendly relationships with the parent whom they had earlier rejected.

Paul was still unhappy and angry at his father on his own and on his mother's behalf; however, there was little indication of his being in difficulty at the time. He was doing well in school, had good friends, and had thought seriously about the issues relating to the divorce and decided on balance that he strongly disapproved of his father's behavior. Paul had successfully confined his anger at his father and kept it from spilling into his other relationships.

Other youngsters were not as fortunate or as able to confine their anger and were doing very poorly indeed. Their stance, vis-à-vis the entire world, was angry, and they were sullen and hostile toward their teachers, toward adults in general, and toward all but a few of their chosen peers. They were failing badly in almost all spheres of their life.

Brian, at seventeen, was described by his teachers and his father as sullen, irresponsible, and devious. He was in serious trouble in school and he had flunked all of his high school classes for several years, although he was considered to have average or better intelligence. The principal said, "He rarely spends a whole day at school and when he does, he does no work at all." He added, "Beneath his sullen affect, he is a very angry boy. He has strong resentments against his parents." Brian was also of concern to the school because of some fire-setting and other dangerous pranks. His peers were considered marginally adjusted kids who "hung around," who were "less aggressive actor-outers." His father said of him, "There is nothing he is interested in. When he wants something, he wants it, but he is not willing to wait for anything or to work for anything."

Brian had been involved in an alignment with his mother against his father, and had for several years refused to see his father except when encouraged by the mother to visit in order to spy on the father's activities and report back to her. By the fourth year following the separation, the mother requested that the boy leave the household, and he joined his father, whom he had earlier rejected. Brian by the five-year follow-up was preoccupied with his anger against men *and* women, referring to women as "whores" and tending to take an unmodulated, sarcastic view of people in general. "He sulks, he sits, and he does nothing," said his father in despair.

# Chapter 14

# Father-Child Relationship at Five Years

The relationship that evolved within the constraints of visiting was diminished in its power and influence as compared with that in the intact family, but its importance to the child remained over the years. Whether the father maintained his presence by regular visiting or attenuated his contact to the vanishing point, he continued to influence the thoughts and feelings of his children and, most particularly, their self-concept and self-esteem.

The passage of several years brought changes to the children's feelings and attitudes about their father. The painful, passionate feelings of yearning evoked by the marital rupture had become muted. The early fears of over half the children that they would be abandoned had mostly not materialized. Time had dealt differently with different children, and for some had not softened the hurt or diminished the pain of loss and separation.

## Visiting After Five Years

Although there were many new patterns in the father-child relationship, most fathers and children had maintained contact with each other to a greater degree than we had expected. Five years after the separation most of the fathers continued to visit their children and to maintain interest in their welfare and progress. Although the overall trend had been a gradual decrease in visiting frequency, there had been no sharp decline, and some youngsters experienced considerable consistency. For more than one-third there had been no change at all in the visiting frequency since the first follow-up, and 20 percent of the group actually experienced an increase in visiting frequency.

Nearly one-quarter of the youngsters continued to see their fathers weekly, if not several times weekly. An additional 20 percent of the fathers visited two to three times a month. Thus, 45 percent of children and adolescents, as compared to two-thirds seen after separation, continued to enjoy "reasonable visitation" nearly five years postseparation. The once-a-month visit became more common (now 20 percent of the group), as did vacation and holiday visits for geographically separated fathers and children. But the number of youngsters who were visited erratically continued to decline to 17 percent, and the same percentage as before (9 percent) had no contacts. Thus in general, it appeared that gratifying visiting patterns which were established and endured throughout the first year following separation held the potential for remaining remarkably constant.

At the second follow-up, there were no significant age or sex differences in visiting frequencies. What did vary was the amount of time spent on any given visit. The youngest children spent overnights and weekends with their fathers significantly more often than did the older youngsters. With increasing age, visits were briefer, and adolescents clearly viewed a few hours, or most of a day, as adequate to sustain the relationship with their father. In this regard there was little change from the first follow-up.

Now several years older, all youngsters increasingly shaped both the pattern of visits and their duration. Those who most enjoyed visits saw the visiting arrangement as mutual and flexible. Visits occurred often enough to provide a feeling of sufficiency and a conviction that the father cared. Most of these youngsters appreciated their father's relaxed and thoughtful planning and felt comfortable in requesting a change in visiting plans if special events conflicted.

Mary shared with us her contentment with the visiting situation. "Sometimes we invite friends over, and that's fun, or people come to visit." Occasionally her dad let her go horseback riding with a friend.

Now Mary watched her dad interact with his new wife with great interest. Central to Mary's pleasure in the visiting was its parallel to what life would have been like were her dad still in the family home. Being with her dad "feels good, like it used to in the old days."

More than one-half of the youngsters were pleased with the visiting. The younger children, in particular, regarded the visit as a central and exciting event in their lives. But, at the other end of the spectrum, almost one-fifth of the youngsters did not find the visits pleasurable or gratifying. Most often these were adolescents or young adults who were disappointed and angry at their father's lack of interest and sharply rejected the father and his values.

Sandra, age eighteen, said her father was always busy. She talked about her disappointment when he came because he was always in such a hurry. She noted that he had forgotten her birthday, and had even been visiting a few days before and not wished her a happy birthday. She told him he was a "creep." She described some of her other complaints about her father: his selfishness, his preoccupation with his new wife. But then she added softly, "I worry sometimes about my dad. I feel he'll end up being weird."

With a few youngsters, their reluctance to visit the father was a remnant of an earlier intense alignment with an embittered mother. Now entering adolescence, these boys and girls were unforgiving toward the father.

But more often children remained disappointed with the infrequency of the father's visits. One-half of all the youngsters responded to the father's neglect or indifference with keen disappointment, a large number chronically and intensely so.

The younger children were steadfast in their loyalty and longing, seemingly capable of waiting indefinitely for the nurturant, loving father. Most often these faithful youngsters did not counterreject their errant fathers, but forgave them again and again for disappointing them. Several of the youngest girls lived like Madame Butterfly, keeping alive a vain hope that he would return and their relationship flourish, despite all evidence to the contrary.

The older unvisited youngsters, now into adolescence, continued to deal with feelings of rejection by angrily counterrejecting the father. Described in earlier chapters, these youngsters were mostly unforgiving, and yet unable to erase the father from their lives. For the most part, they were unable to recognize or understand that it was the father's failings which accounted for the thinness or meagerness of the relationship and continued to feel that they were in some measure not worthy of his continued love and interest. This was a powerful conviction, difficult to dislodge even in psychotherapy. (A few adolescents did manage to gain a sad insight into their father's failings and this erased their anger and enabled them to respond with compassion.)

One sixteen-year-old told us of her reaction to the most recent letter from her dad, one of only three in a year, and the only contact he had made with her. "I cry every time I get a letter from him. It's very depressing. He's a lonely man. He doesn't know what he's doing . . . he's not stable. It's not a good situation."

When we observe the sadness, disappointment, and anger of the infrequently visited youngsters, and contrast their pain with the enhanced self-esteem and pleasure of the children and adolescents whose fathers gave continual evidence of their interest and love in the postdivorce family, we reacted positively to the advice of one such father given five years after separation. "If you're concerned about the kids—and you should be concerned about the kids—spend a reasonable amount of time with the children. I can't imagine seeing my kids only on vacations. I talk to them on the phone almost every day and see them very often. Frequent contact is really important to stay in touch with what my children are doing and thinking."

## Changes in the Quality of the Father-Child Relationship

Neither the frequency of the visiting nor its regularity fully reflected the quality of the father-child relationship five years later. Earlier, at the one-year mark, there had been a close correlation between the amount of contact between visiting parent and child and the quality of the parent-child relationship; both rose and fell together. With the passage of the years, as more youngsters moved into adolescence and young adulthood, the amount of contact revealed less and less about the relationship. The quality of the relationship was increasingly governed by the mutual feelings and attitudes of parent and child rather than by the structure of the contact though during the immediate aftermath of the divorce, it had been the latter which had provided the foundation for the emerging relationship between parent and child.

The great majority of the father-child relationships had become emotionally limited over time. They declined despite the fact that the majority of fathers and children continued to see each other fairly often. By the five-year mark many relationships offered little help to the child in dealing with the complex tasks of growing up. Only 30 percent of the children and their fathers were able to build and maintain a mutually rewarding relationship which successfully outlived the marriage for the five years that followed. The remainder were emotionally insufficient to promote or even facilitate the growth and development of the child. The most impoverished father-son relationships were with boys in the thirteen-to-sixteen-year-old group; the next most impoverished were with the older boys aged seventeen to twenty-four. The poorest father-daughter relationships were with the youngest girls between five and eight years old.

Some of these visiting relationships could even be considered detrimental to development, because they infantilized the child or hurt his feelings or exploited the relationship to help the adult. Nevertheless, they played a significant role in protecting the child against the pain of loss and the psychological impact of that loss. Even in these poor relationships the father's presence kept the child from worrying about abandonment and total rejection and the nagging self-doubts which followed. The father also provided a presence, however limited, which diminished the child's sense of vulnerability and aloneness, and total dependency on one parent. And finally, the father's presence muted the intensity of the child's conflicts and feelings which otherwise focused on the mother. The maintenance of some continuity in the father-child relationship, unless the relationship was psychologically or physically destructive of the child's well-being, appeared preferable to complete loss of contact, even though the relationship may have been impoverished from its conception or gradually deteriorated during the years.

## The Frozen Father-Child Relationship

One peril of the visiting relationship, even when it is well maintained, is that it may fail to change with the evolving developmental needs and interests of the growing child. Visiting relationships have by their very nature a potential for remaining frozen or fixated in the modes which prevailed during the preexisting marriage or at the time of the marital rupture and which were appropriate to that time in the child's life. It is as if the divorce has caused the clock of the relationship to stand still, and child and parent continue ever after, as in a fairy tale, to perceive each other as each appeared years earlier, and to respond to each other's needs in accord with these earlier perceptions and expectations. The repetitious pattern of many visits and their rigid scheduling of time and place may contribute to the fixed, rigid quality of the relationship. Within the artificial setting of the visit—the restaurant, the father's apartment, and other non-home-based places—the visiting parent may be less sensitive to the growth and change of the child. Moreover, conscious and unconscious wishes and needs may impel both child and parent to deny the passage of time. Both may wish to repair the ruptured marriage in fantasy, to strengthen the child's dependency, to resist the adolescent separation.

Whatever the motivation, 15 percent of the parent-child relationships remained frozen in their dominant cast at the time of the divorce and an additional 30 percent progressed more slowly than the rate of the child maturing. Thus, almost half of the father-child relationships lagged behind the child's development and reflected in this regard the special difficulties and discontinuity of the visiting relationship and the effect of the visit on the vitality of the relationship. For by their unresponsiveness to change fixated relationships contributed to infantilizing the ties between father and child.

Four years after the marital separation Mr. S. still held his eight-year-old daughter in his lap at the dinner table during her weekly visits to his home. This had been his custom when she was four years old at the time the marriage had been disrupted. He was surprised and amused when we brought this behavior to his attention and he offered smilingly, "I guess Laura likes to think of me the way we used to be. It's hard for *her* to change." Mr. S.'s tone and expression clearly conveyed his pleasure with the child's wish to be his "little girl." Had this behavior occurred nightly during the life of the intact family Mr. S. would probably have become aware of its inappropriateness since his overall relationship with the child was not neurotically bound. As a once-a-week occurrence he regarded the same behavior as appealing and charming, and was reluctant to introduce change. For the child, however, the lap sitting reflected an inappropriately infantile relationship with her father which the stepmother perceived, all too clearly, but was reluctant to mention for fear of angering the father and provoking an accusation that she was jealous.

### Eroticized Relationships

Fixated relationships can all too easily become infused with erotic feelings and fantasies. The erotic components, of which neither the father nor the child is fully aware, combine with the visiting structure, which outwardly resembles a date, and may result in freezing the child's passionate attachment to the father and diverting psychic energies which would be more appropriately invested in friendships with peers.

The absence of the mother whose presence might have had a moderating influence on the intensity of the relationship between father and child increased the excitement of the meetings. Moreover, some of these relationships which were fixated at the time of the divorce had already been infantile and regressive during the marriage. In this way the needs of father and child moved like a cogwheel to combine and shape a relationship which was emotionally gratifying to both and yet, despite its pseudoadult flavor, exercised a regressive pull on both child and parent. Although contact was frequent and visiting was regular, these parent-child relationships which failed to keep pace with the child's development burdened and infantilized the child.

Paradoxically the intimacy of the visit can offer the mature adult the extraordinary opportunity to develop a special closeness with the child in a one-to-one relationship of a kind not readily available within the busy life of the ongoing family. People without sufficient maturity may miss this opportunity and consolidate relationships which not only infantilize the child but are devoid of real intimacy and friendship.

Mr. C. began to visit his nine-year-old daughter, regularly and frequently, immediately after the marital separation which had occurred amid loudly voiced accusations of infidelity by both parents. The father was partly motivated to visit by his genuine concern that the mother's capacity to parent was limited. Regarding the mother as scattered and impulsive, Mr. C. resolved to exercise a stabilizing influence on the child's development. Accordingly, during the five years following the separation he visited every weekend without fail.

Seen at age thirteen, five years later, Pat, who was overdressed and chubby, referred to her father with much giggling as "my daddy." She said, "He's so sweet, he's a cutie. I adore him. I could eat him up. He's just perfect in everything he does. I do everything for him." She volunteered that she loved being "coaxed and spoiled" by her daddy and her daddy's girlfriend, "so I won't object if she and my daddy marry."

The child looked forward with excitement to the regular Saturday visits and gourmet restaurant dinners which had become the main event, and often the only gratifying one of the week. We were concerned because despite good intelligence the child was doing poorly at school, was lonely, unable to make friends, immature in her general deportment, and becoming increasingly obese. Her visiting relationship with her father, although faithfully maintained by both, and despite his commitment and interest, was inappropriately infantile and eroticized, and did not serve her needs or take cognizance of the very real difficulties which she was experiencing. Unfortunately, her relationship with her mother was troubled as well. Although the relationship with her father was not contributing to her emotional progress, to have deprived the child of her father's visits or diminished their frequency would have generated acute anxiety and grief.

## Relationships that Exploit the Child

There were other high-contact relationships between visiting parent and child which were not helpful to the child. The visiting pattern sometimes became impoverished and stereotyped and was locked into a rigid pattern which was predicated solely upon the needs of the adults. Such relationships, which took little cognizance of the child's wishes and changing needs, exploited the child, and contributed little to his or her development. Children caught in these exploitative relationships often resented their demands but felt helpless to break free, fearing that the other parent would be penalized for their rebellion. Others felt, not unrealistically, that the price of continued contact with their father was their continued submissiveness. Despite the anger which these youngsters felt and their sense of being exploited by the parent during visits, they did not reject their fathers and often continued to feel both affection and pity for the men who were exploiting them.

Mr. H. insisted that his adolescent son visit regularly throughout his high school years. The youngster, an obliging, somewhat timid boy, regularly did the household chores for his father and spent the long weekend, from Saturday morning at 9:00 to Sunday evening at 6:00 in activities ties selected by the father. This visiting pattern, which contiued unmodified until the boy graduated from high school, served his interests poorly. The court had ordered the visiting pattern and its frequency at the time of the divorce when the boy was eleven years old. Neither the shy child nor his conservative, rigid parents had been informed at that time by the court about the likelihood or desirability of change as the boy matured. It is, of course, unlikely that the judge had expected that the boy would accede to the father's threats to withdraw child support and that the boy would continue this visiting arrangement until he was eighteen years of age. Nevertheless, this arrangement persisted as ordered by the court. As a result, the boy's adolescence was severely burdened. He was very lonely and felt that the arrangement kept him from closer associations with peers. Sometimes he begged for special permission to attend a school game or dance. Often the father refused.

We were interested to find that although the boy resented the father's exploitation of him, he also felt sorry for his father and pitied his lonely condition. The boy said, "My dad gets so angry. He screams and carries on and says that I didn't have to walk out with my mom at the time of the divorce and that I could have stayed with him. I guess he is lonely and I feel sort of sorry for him. He really has nobody else."

### Relationships that Declined Gradually

Among the father-child relationships which diminished in contact and emotional sustenance over the years were some which had been good enough or average when structured by the intact family and reinforced by the myriad events of a shared daily life. Without the concrete tasks to unite parent and child, and without the continuing physical presence of the children to jog the father's memory, these father-child relationships survived poorly outside the family. Men in this group did not reject their children overtly; they continued in a general, somewhat diffuse, way to be concerned with their progress and to feel some measure of responsibility for their welfare. Nevertheless, the emotional quality of the relationship declined and their psychological investment diminished in ways perceived by the children. In some of these families the mother had played an intermediary role between father and children during the marriage and without her presence and her continued interpretation to the father of their children's needs and wishes the relationship eroded.

Fathers in this group were of different kinds. Some were shy and tended to withdraw from involvement in all relationships unless encouraged to participate. Other fathers in this group were impetuous and impulsive and were likely to think of the children only when the children were present. Others had turned their attention to a new family. Still others were feuding with their former wives. Many of these men found that a regular visiting relationship required a resourcefulness and the capacity to plan ahead, which was alien to their way of thinking and personal lifestyle. These men also had difficulty in understanding and conceptualizing the changing needs of the children over the years. As a consequence, many of these father-child relationships rested increasingly on the initiative of the children and on their capacity to evoke and maintain an affectionate, interested response from the father. This responsibility for holding the father's interest was experienced as a heavy burden for the children, which some resented and others feared.

Children who felt unhappy and deprived by the custodial mother tended to cling to the shreds of their relationship with the father and were often additionally burdened by their sense of having to maintain the father's interest in them. When the father disappointed them or came infrequently they, therefore, not only grieved but attributed the father's decreasing interest to their own incapacity to maintain his commitment to them. They felt rejected and the father's declining visiting or nonvisiting was directly tied to the child's self-image. If the father failed to visit, the child felt depreciated by the father's failure. And conversely, if the father visited, the child felt that his or her lovability had been affirmed by the father's visit.

Unfortunately, father and child often came to the relationship with widely different expectations and needs. Nor did the children's feelings reflect the mother's attitude, except when mother and child were aligned together against the father. The children's responses reflected the history of the relationship between father and child, joined with the child's current needs, which were often intense.

Robert, a sensitive, intelligent boy of twelve, lived with his mother and two sisters. His father, a personable and impulsive man, had remarried and lived in a nearby city, two hours from Robert's home, with his new wife and her children. The father had been a sometimes attentive, sometimes unreliable parent during the marriage. Typically, he broke important promises. For example, on one occasion he had offered to take Robert on a very exciting trip and after the boy had spent considerable time preparing for it, the father suddenly decided to take his new family in his son's place.

Father and son had been close during the marriage. Robert was exceedingly proud of his father and boasted of him frequently and proudly to his friends and teachers. Robert had also continued to grieve over the divorce. He wished profoundly that his parents would reconcile. He longed to see his father more frequently than the once-a-month visit which was arranged by the parents and spoke movingly to us of his hope that his father would some day love him. Robert also complained of his difficulties with his mother, of her tension, of his feeling that his mother was angry at him for loving his father. Robert's mother agreed that life was difficult for her; that she was frequently angry at Robert. She would have liked him to live with his father, but the father and stepmother had no room and were not interested in the boy.

The school confirmed Robert's unhappiness. They described him as a child who was not learning, who rarely did his homework, who was disruptive in class and irresponsible in his work habits. None of the adults, despite their efforts, had been able to develop a relationship with him at the school.

Robert's father was cordial but guarded in his discussion of the situation. He expressed concern about the boy, indicating that he was interested in continuing the visits. While the father's concern seemed genuine, it appeared unlikely that he would maintain a more active role in the boy's life. His history was that of a man who promises and forgets, and the boy knew this and felt trapped. Much of the time at school Robert daydreamed about reunions with his father.

A subgroup of little girls whose fathers left at the height of their oedipal fantasies was also particularly likely to maintain a steadfast loyalty to them for many years, despite a chronic pattern of disappointment. Some of these men were flirtatious and charming with their children, but they had been unreliable during the marriage and remained so following the divorce. During the postdivorce years they tended to pop into the child's life at irregular intervals. Although the visitation pattern often started with frequent visits, these diminished over the years. The sporadic visits of the men were very exciting and stimulated romantic and erotic fantasies which occupied the children's psychic energies. These sporadic appearances kept alive the child's hope for a stable and enduring real relationship which never materialized.

The erratic patterns and limitations in the relationship imposed by the father were distressing to most, but not all, the children. Reaching adolescence, a small group of the youngsters markedly reduced their investment in the fathers who visited them irregularly. These young people, who were usually independent and perceptive as well as socially mature for their age, were able to take a realistic measure of the father and to accept the limitations which they perceived clearly. They were pragmatic and realistic, and emotionally able to deal with the disappointment, to resolve it and to look elsewhere.

We were interested to find that several of the youngsters in this small group had enjoyed a good relationship with the father during the marriage and had opposed the divorce. They did not share a history of poor relationships with a father, but rather a capacity to perceive clearly what the father's likely behavior would be and to relinquish, or to work through, their longing and to turn elsewhere. These youngsters, usually adolescent, had a support system which helped them to turn away from their father. Sometimes youngsters who were able to deal realistically with the limitations in the father were separated from him geographically. This distance from their fathers made it easier for these youngsters to deal with the increasing emotional distance and not to interpret the infrequent visiting as a rejection or to be hurt by the lack of interest that they perceived.

Marion, at age twelve, was an attractive and mature youngster for her age. She was described by her teacher as "outstanding in her charm, wit, and openness." She told us that her relationship with her mother was reasonably good. "I don't have trouble with Mom anymore. We all don't like her overprotectiveness and temper about broken rules, but she's not all that unfair. There are ways to humor her and most of the time it works because she's usually just under a lot of tension." About her father, Marion explained that she saw him very little, but she added, "It's fine. We get along fine. . . . I don't want to live with him, and we do have fun when we are together. Actually, I don't see him that much and I don't miss him that much." Marion added that recently her parents had considered a reconciliation and it hadn't worked but she was not disappointed. She doubted that they could really live together amicably.

The attitude which this youngster conveyed represented a major change. She had been deeply attached to her father during the marriage. Since the divorce she had grown away from him. He lived in a distant city and she saw him on holidays and vacations. She had grown in self-confidence and maturity and her need for his presence as a parent had diminished considerably. Perhaps it was also a mark of Marion's good social adjustment and use of other supports, especially her peers, that she brought along her best friend to remain in the waiting room while she was interviewed. She also announced airily to several of her friends just prior to our interview with her that she was "helping the people in the divorce project"—a reference to our staff.

## Poor Relationships that Remained Poor

Another subgroup of father-child relationships did not change during the postdivorce years. They had been poor during the marriage and remained so during the divorce, and seemed on the surface hardly affected by the divorce, continuing for many years the same general pattern. To outward appearances, these fathers had played a minor role in the household activities and routines associated with the children, or their discipline, or in providing guidance. Many of these men appeared to have defined their responsibilities as providing economic support for their families and had, indeed, attempted to carry them out. Beyond this they envisioned little interaction with their children and they experienced little. Nevertheless, the continuity of these relationships following the divorce is of interest and reflects strengths which may not be apparent. Considering the long-standing limitations and impoverishment in these relationships, it is noteworthy that they did not deteriorate further or fade away—as it was originally noteworthy to us how keen had been the sense of loss which many children in these families experienced at the time of the marital disruption.

During the years following the divorce these men remained in the background, maintaining sporadic, irregular contact with their children. The relationship was such that they could neither be counted on nor entirely discounted in the event of acute need. In some families the father appeared to be assuming the role of an uncle or of a distant relative rather than that of a father. Nevertheless, it soon became apparent that these men held a continued place in the children's affection and interest. And, in some way, their presence in the background conveyed to the children a vague sense of reassurance, of potential support, of not being alone. The children, in turn, were concerned for and interested in the father's continued well-being. These fathers offered little to their children and little was expected of them in return. Therefore, whenever they gave something, their gift was received with surprise and real appreciation. The relationship was low key and low contact, and yet was sustained at that level for many years.

Mr. N., an intemperate and occasionally violent man, spent little time at home during the marriage. He worked long hours and spent the weekend away with his friends, and therefore rarely saw his five children. After the divorce Mr. N. continued to provide moderate economic support, but had no formal arrangements for seeing the children and continued over the years to see them sporadically and according to no particular plan. As medical and economic emergencies arose, he was usually asked for help. Sometimes he helped one or another child, and sometimes he refused, depending on his mood of the moment.

Six years after the divorce, Bert, age fourteen, recalled that the divorce had made him "go bananas" and that he still wished that it had never happened. Asked whether he sees his dad, the boy shook his head sadly, saying, "No, not very much." Then he brightened, "Dad came up yesterday and took me out for a prime rib dinner." In the remainder of the interview the boy described his recent arrest and some serious problems which had arisen at school. As he spoke of his difficulties it was clear that at no time did he even conceive of his father as interested, concerned, or helpful with these or other serious problems. Nevertheless, in some way that it is difficult to define the father remained an important factor in the boy's emotional life and the boy valued this. For example, later in the same interview the boy volunteered that his sister had recently told someone that his father had broken his leg. With high indignation and much feeling, Bert exclaimed, "Dad didn't break his leg, he just hurt it. My sister is real dumb for saying that!"

It would be easy for an outside observer to dismiss the emotional importance of this parent-child relationship because of the irregularity of the contact. Nevertheless, the importance seemed high to the youngster and it may be that this partial relationship, with its sporadic, infrequent contact, protected the boy from a sense of abandonment and the nagging questions which follow in its wake.

## Remarried Fathers

Relationships between fathers and children often declined after the father's remarriage to a woman with children, or when children were born within the new marriage. Psychologically and emotionally it was difficult for many men, although certainly not all, to maintain their strong affection for both sets of children and most experienced inner conflict and felt pulled in opposite directions. The men were also concerned, especially early in the new marriage, with assuring the success of the remarriage and tended to defer to the new wife's wishes. Sometimes, therefore, they gave prior consideration to her children. Economic burdens increased following remarriage, and men not infrequently held two jobs in order to meet their obligations to both families. The father's time was limited by many competing obligations. For these reasons, fathers were challenged to the utmost during the early years of the new marriage. Sometimes further complexity was introduced by the new wife's jealousy of the father's continued commitment to the children of his former marriage. Although the stepmother who resented the husband's children rarely played a decisive role in disrupting the father's affectionate tie to his children, her influence might sway a man whose commitment was wavering.

A tragic counterpoint to these themes within the new marriage was the children's acute concern from the start that they would be replaced by the new children or that they would become increasingly peripheral to their father's concern. The children's vulnerability at such a time was high and they looked for and often found evidence of having fallen into the father's disfavor. For some children this second rejection confirmed and reinforced the rejection they experienced at the time of the divorce.

Mr. S., who had been remarried for two years, admitted sadly and with shame that he saw his children irregularly for five or ten minutes every four to six weeks. He attributed his reluctance to his new wife's objections and her refusal to permit the children to visit although they lived a few blocks away.

We expected that his son, Peter, would be troubled at not seeing his father, but were entirely unprepared for the child's misery. The interviewer asked Peter whether he had seen his dad. "The child looked at me blankly and his thinking suddenly became confused, his speech halting. Just then, a police car went by with its siren screaming. The child stared into space and seemed lost in reverie. As this continued for a few minutes, I gently suggested that the police car had reminded him of his father (a police officer). Peter began to cry and sobbed without stopping for thirty-five minutes."

### Children Who Were Not Visited

Children who were abandoned or who experienced repeated rejection of their efforts to maintain a relationship with their father suffered intensely. Often their continued psychological development was severely burdened. At the five-year mark, eleven of the children were not being visited by their fathers and had little or no contact with them, although in three of these instances the father lived close by. This group included four boys and seven girls of varying ages. Although these children showed many different coping efforts to master the psychological pain of the abandonment, most suffered with underlying or overt depression of varying intensity, accompanied by disabling symptomatic behaviors. The most stressed were those children whose relationship with the father during the former marriage had been warm and loving. Where the disruption occurred in what had previously been a good father-child relationship, the blow seemed an impossible one for the child to absorb.

Children at every developmental level struggled hard to explain and understand their father's continued indifference and absence. Some created rich fantasies to fill the emptiness of their lives. Others were bitterly angry, saying of their father caustically, "He has time for everything but us. I'm sure not waiting for *him* anymore."

The most striking, and at the same time most poignant, responses of children to such disrupted relationships were those that led to idealization of the absent or missing parent. These children yearned intensely to reestablish contact and remained for many years unreconciled to the separation and unaccepting of the obvious rejection by the father, much in the same manner that some children refused to accept the death of a parent. In these instances we saw at its most proximate the similarities of mourning and the postdivorce psychological response. Elaborate erotic and heroic fantasies were woven around the absent father which occupied the waking hours of many children, both boys and girls. Such fantasy life was, in part, stimulated and sustained by a limited or impoverished mother-child relationship.

## The Case of Lea

Lea was five years old, the youngest of four daughters, when her parents separated. A pretty and well-developed child who related well, Lea was at age level in kindergarten, where she was well liked by friends and by her teachers. Her capacity to maintain her developmental achievement was particularly remarkable in that, prior to the divorce decision, the household had been in a frightening and sometimes violent turmoil. As the youngest child, Lea had enjoyed some protection. She was identified openly in the family as her father's favorite child.

We saw Lea initially at a time when there was considerable agitation in her home, and she greeted the interviewer with sweetness and charm, reaching out very quickly to be hugged and kissed and held, at her request, on the interviewer's lap. She denied all sadness and worry in response to questions about her life, maintaining throughout an overly bright, cheerful surface and announcing gaily, "Everybody loves me."

A year later, at the first follow-up when Lea was six years old, we learned of a significant fantasy which, in the intervening year, the child had presented to her teacher in daily installments as an ongoing story of her household. In these stories Lea's mother had given birth to a new baby and it had become the responsibility of Lea to help her mother in the care of this child. She described in minute detail how she and her mother regularly rose at midnight to minister tenderly and carefully to the crying baby. Toward the year's end, the teacher made a home visit and was startled to discover that the new baby was entirely the child's invention.

There are many meanings to this rich and poignant fantasy. We may perhaps assume that the unhappy child has represented herself in the newborn baby. The joint caretaking expresses the fantasy fulfillment of the child's unmet need for nurturance and care. Furthermore, the fantasy speaks of an addition to the family, and in so doing ingeniously obscures the real loss. Finally, the fantasied good care of the baby is superimposed by the child over the real figure of the all too busy mother, and represents the child's effort to deny the daily pain inflicted by the real mother who was too preoccupied with her own needs to supervise the child's care.

The child's actual adjustment during the intervening year consisted of increased difficulty in learning at school and gradual withdrawal from relationships with friends. Her teacher described her increasingly frozen, smiling facade and her driven, chattering monologues. During this same year, Lea's mother had reorganized her own life, largely around her own needs. Although Lea's mother was functioning reasonably well in a gratifying job, the central aspect of her life was an accelerated dating schedule with a great many boyfriends. The mother's hectic schedule allowed little time for the care of little Lea who at age six was responsible for getting herself to school in the morning, as well as providing for her own meals and bedtime routines. Lea's father had, during this time, left for another city in the state and, although he maintained telephone contact, he had not visited at all during the intervening year.

It is important to point out that Lea utilized fantasy resourcefully to make real contact with the concerned teacher and in this way made an attempt to find a substitute parent and friend in order to cope with her loneliness. Nevertheless, at the first year's follow-up, despite the teacher's warmth and concern, the child was having difficulty maintaining herself at an age-appropriate level in school and with her peers, and was showing increasing evidence of childhood depression.

Lea was seen again at age nine and a half, at which time she appeared to be approximately twenty pounds overweight. The interviewer and the child sat companionably on a bed in a room in her house as Lea confessed that she hadn't done too well in school the previous year. She hoped to do better in the forthcoming year. She referred enthusiastically to her many friends and spoke rapidly of a variety of activities that engaged her attention. Not unexpectedly, most of these achievements and relationships were fantasy.

When asked about her father, Lea brought out a box containing all of the letters he had written to her during the past three years. These letters, about fifteen in number, were dog-eared, folded, and refolded, and the interviewer couldn't help but be reminded of a precious collection of love letters that had been read and reread with tears. The father had actually visited only once in the past two years.

Her teacher, a gentle, soft-spoken man, was concerned about Lea's lack of self-confidence and poor self-esteem. "She doesn't believe she can succeed in anything. She's a grade level below in her reading, math, and language skills. She's so cooperative that if I told her to run through the wall I'm sure she'd try without any hesitation. She's always smiling. She is friendly, but harmless. She has a hard time reading because the words don't make any sense to her."

There was much that was discouraging about this child's social and psychological condition. It was impossible to separate the child's neglect by both of her parents from her suffering, which resulted from the loss of her beloved father. Nevertheless, it was clear that the child's fantasy life and emotional preoccupation had crystalized around the father, and were fixated there. And it was not difficult to predict that the child's development was imperiled both by the loss of her father and by her mother's limitations in her capacity to parent.

## Children Who Reject their Father

Not all the youngsters whose fathers broke off contact with them were preoccupied with the loss or depressed. A few were able to draw on their own inner strength to counterreject the father. By so doing they seemed able to break free of the oppressive feeling of having been deserted and to move ahead with increasing confidence in their own capacities. Adolescence provided an opportunity for this repudiation of the rejecting father, and the capturing or strengthening of the sense of being a good person. This establishing of their own core identity as a moral person with socially acceptable goals and the capacity to take responsibility seemed to be central to their successful coping. These youngsters dealt actively with a negative self-image and lowered self-esteem, which the father's abandonment reinforced, by turning against the father as a flawed model. In effect they made a conscious decision to be different from the parent who had rejected them.

They did not accomplish this very difficult task unaided. These young people were able to draw on the available relationships in their environment to help them. Those who succeeded in shaking off the negative self-image and the pain of the father's rejection turned for support and role models to the custodial parent, the stepfather, the steady boyfriend, the teacher, or the school institution, itself. They sought people whom they could love and whose values they could accept as worthy of esteem, and whose view of the world they found both praiseworthy and congenial. Youngsters whose relationship with the deserting father had not been close, or had been marked by conflict or the father's cruelty, were able to accomplish the task of counterrejection with greater ease than those whose relationships had been close and loving during the marriage.

All of these young people—those who succeeded in overcoming the loss and those who remained depressed and troubled—struggled hard. The price they all paid was that their psychic and intellectual energies throughout their growing up years were sapped in the reexperiencing or reworking of the father's desertion at each successive developmental stage. Those who succeeded in overcoming the loss appeared to be consciously working hard toward adulthood, independent in their stance vis-à-vis the world, intensely competitive and relatively or greatly intolerant of siblings or peers or others less successful than they. Those who failed were depressed and angry. Their aspiration level was well below their talents and capacities, and they had difficulty in setting meaningful, socially acceptable goals for their own adulthood.

Joe, at age sixteen, appeared to have waged a successful struggle to integrate and resolve his initially severe response to the father's desertion, which occurred following the filing of the divorce by his mother when the boy was ten years old. At that time Joe appeared to be seriously troubled. His appearance was inappropriate; he wore skin-tight, brightly colored clothing and jewelry; his wardrobe was extensive and he supplemented it regularly by screaming wildly at his mother, insisting that she match each purchase which she made for herself, however modest, with an equivalent purchase of clothing for him.

When we first saw him, Joe's anger was intense and even dangerous;

we were concerned about a possible future delinquent career. He was preoccupied with guns and fantasies of bloodshed and violence. His relationships appeared superficial and empty; he was considered out of control by his teachers and his mother, who felt entirely helpless to set limits for him. Our urgent recommendation for psychological treatment for mother and son was curtly refused by the boy, whose opinions dominated the household.

In view of this frightening picture of a child at high risk, we were interested that at age sixteen, six years later, Joe responded immediately to our letter inviting him for the interview. He was eager to "talk about how things are going." He arrived promptly, still flashily, but not inappropriately, dressed. His manner was entirely changed. He was friendly, open, and poised. As he reviewed the intervening years, he emphasized his good feelings about himself in the present and his current plans. He volunteered that, despite the disruption of the family, he had been sustained over the years in part by the continuity in his residence, in the neighborhood and in the school and he was very grateful that he had not been required to relocate.

Joe reviewed his former difficulties. With impressive candor, he recalled that after the divorce he had lost his interest in school and had "gotten mixed up with a bunch of rough kids." They had become involved in stealing and drugs. Joe remembered his sense of desolation and loneliness at the time of the divorce and its immediate aftermath, his distress at his mother's return to work full time after the father left. He had depended on the group of delinquents. Then, he said, he abruptly decided to quit them. "I just didn't want a court record. I didn't want to be involved in that kind of stuff anymore." On his own, the boy dropped the friends, took a job, found a new social group, and began to set socially acceptable goals for his life. This change, he noted, coincided with "things quieting down at home," by which he meant that his mother had acquired a stable boyfriend who came to live in the same house with them. Joe spoke glowingly of his attachment and admiration for his mother's friend, whom he referred to occasionally as "my dad" and at other times by his first name. Of his father the boy said, "I have no feeling for him. It's not like he's my dad. He doesn't know me and I don't know him. I'm better off than the other kids who are divorced because when you ask them to do something on weekends they say they have to spend the weekend with their dad."

The interviewer observed that, "Joe appears to have put at rest most, but not all, of his longing for his father and has transferred much of his warm feelings to his stepfather. He continues to harbor a feeling of being deprived compared to his contemporaries, but he has reacted to this feeling of deprivation by becoming self-sufficient and more centered on his own economic and emotional independence. He continues," the interviewer went on, "to show a cynicism beyond his years about difficulties in forming relationships and about the need to never depend on other people. In essence, I feel that Joe has come through this whole period better than predicted at earlier times. Perhaps part of this is his fairly unambivalent rejection of his father, his repression of earlier unpleasant memories, both of which have enabled him to relate better to the father-substitute and to identify constructively with him."

Six youngsters refused to cooperate with fathers who sought to maintain contact with them. The fathers were profoundly hurt by the children's behavior. These youngsters had been partners in an intense alignment with the custodial parent, and the anger and rejection of the father was fueled by the angry mother. These children appeared somewhat brittle at times. They showed little modulation in their anger and were pitiless in their condemnation.

As they grew older some of these children modified and softened their antagonism toward the father. The child's willingness to resume visiting appeared to be more likely when the father was able over the years to refrain from contributing to the child's anger and to maintain his composure in the face of the child's rejection. Sometimes a youngster was able to break free of the custodial parent's dominion and to establish more reasonable, even friendly, relationships.

## The Psychologically Disordered Father and his Child

One beneficial effect of some divorce is the physical separation of the psychologically disordered father from daily contact with his child. This separation in itself decreases the psychological hazard to the child's mental health and continued development. Within the ongoing marriage the psychiatrically disordered parent is a powerful, pathological force, especially if the illness is not identified as such or cordoned off from direct involvement of the children. Within the unhappy marriages of our study, which were beset by multiple problems, the pathological behavior of one family member was often not perceived as deviant or not identified as such. Fifteen percent of the fathers suffered with severe psychiatric illness, including paranoid schizophrenia, manic-depressive psychosis, and chronic severe alcoholism. Forty percent of the father-child relationships were profoundly troubled during the marriage and at the time of the initial assessment. Some of these troubled relationships reflected not only the psychopathology of the father, but also the dysfunction in the marriage. As many as 15 percent of all the children were intensely afraid of their father and an additional 10 percent were moderately fearful.

It was not uncommon for one child, in particular, to be selected as the involuntary partner or victim of the father's disturbance. For example, one father had a history of sleeping with his young son several nights weekly when he was drunk. Another father often fondled the genitals of his preschool boy. Others cruelly demeaned their children with a continual stream of verbal and physical abuse. Some used fearsome threats of religious retribution to punish minor misbehavior. Most children trapped into these relationships were markedly immature in their emotional and social development. Several youngsters in this group had been of grave concern to the school because their learning was well below their capacities and they had difficulties in getting along with their classmates.

It is of interest that in none of these situations was the father's openly disturbed, destructive behavior toward the child the significant factor among the acknowledged events that led to the divorce. Only after the divorce decision was definitely made by these women did the pathological father-child interaction, itself, loom as an additional provocation in the divorce situation. Women were often tyrannized by the same disturbed husbands who mistreated their children, and they felt helpless to intervene. Sometimes, tragically, the mother identified with the father's derogatory view of the child. Others did not perceive the father's bizarre behavior as deviant, or even likely to have unfortunate psychological consequences for the child's development. Ironically, therefore, the enormous gains for the child that accrued following the divorce-created release from the pathological influence of the father can, strictly speaking, be considered serendipitous.

For a number of fortunate children, the physical separation itself, combined with good care by the custodial parent, appeared to be sufficient to enable the child to break free of the destructive influence of the disturbed father. Sometimes, however, by the time of the divorce the child's disturbance had progressed well beyond the capacity of custodial parent or other adult in the environment to provide sufficient educational and supportive buttressing to stem the unfolding psychological illness, and psychological treatment was clearly indicated. Several boys in the kindergarten group who were separated from psychiatrically ill parents improved markedly following the divorce, even though regular visiting with the father was maintained.

Steve, age five, the youngest of four children, had always been his father's favorite during the marriage and, alternately, the target of his sarcastic outbursts. The father had been a cruel husband, verbally abusive and demeaning his wife and his children. One factor in the deterioration of the marriage was the parental rivalry for Steve's affection. At the initial assessment Steve emerged as a sullen and immature boy who was anxious at school and on the playground and petulant at home. His temper tantrums, combined with his extraordinary procrastination, tyrannized the household. His social immaturity was marked, and his capacity to learn seemed impaired by his anxiety.

Following the separation, the father began to visit weekly, but his visits were paid to all the siblings together in a fairly formal setting and the relationship between father and Steve necessarily became less intimate and less serving of the father's changing moods and pressing neurotic needs. At the end of the first year, Steve appeared to have made almost two years of growth. When we saw him he was significantly freer to use aggression in play with his friends; he was less fearful; he could compete as a peer. At home his petulance and his tantrums had subsided. He was surging ahead in his academic and social activities at school. At the five-year mark all reports indicated that the boy was doing very well in school and at home and was a source of pride to his mother and his teachers. Throughout these years contact with the father continued, but gradually became infrequent, and the relationship became increasingly attenuated in its emotional significance to parent and to child.

Geographical separation of the disturbed parent and his child was only the first step toward improvement. Beneficent outcomes depended on a variety of converging factors, including, most particularly, the help of the custodial mother. The role of the custodial mother was crucial in helping the child disengage psychologically from the disturbed father, especially in those families where during the marriage the mother had been a silent observer or covictim of the father's abusive or destructive behavior toward the child. And indeed, where the mother proved unable to shake free of the role which she had played during the unhappy marriage, the child was likely to continue to be severely burdened by these influences, and therefore unable to progress developmentally.

Following divorce, the custodial mother often holds the key to the child's ability to separate from the psychologically disordered parent. In the first place, the young child is dependent on the capacity of the custodial mother to perceive the father's deviant behavior and to identify its psychopathology. Moreover, the child is dependent on the capacity of the mother to convey these perceptions tactfully and appropriately, with due regard for the child's age and ability to comprehend, and with sensitivity to the child's attachment to the father. Where the mother fails at these tasks because of her own continued neurotic involvement in her relationship with the father, the child is likely to remain trapped in the divorce as he or she had been during the marriage.

During their years of marriage, Mr. L., a severe alcoholic, was physically and verbally abusive toward his wife and his preschool-age daughter. Showing open preference for his sons, he frequently proclaimed his scorn of all women and publicly demeaned his wife and young daughter. Following the divorce, Mrs. L. remained a tense, self-depreciating, chronically depressed woman who was guilty about having filed for the divorce and was unable to allow herself to experience her own anger and outrage at her husband's treatment of her. Essentially she accepted and reinforced his depreciation of herself and all women, and did not perceive her husband or his attitudes as pathological or deviant.

Mary, a sad-looking, five-year-old child who was closely attached to her father at the time of the separation, identified with his views and was angry at her mother for causing the divorce. She sought pathetically to please him, in many different ways, and was heartbroken that she failed to do so and that he discouraged her visiting. Although he rejected her at every turn, the child insisted on visiting him, crying when she returned home after each visit. Mary soon became increasingly withdrawn and depressed. Her view that little girls were unlovable was further confirmed for her by the divorce itself. In this way the divorce, which ironically could be expected to help the child, had the opposite effect and lessened her already low self-esteem.

One of the thorniest problems presented by the families in which the divorce achieved a physical separation from the psychologically disordered parent was the continuing attachment of the child to the ill parent and the potential for identification with the ill parent by virtue of this emotional attachment. The strength of the child's attachment could easily be underestimated and inadvertently reinforced by the rigid proscription of visiting. Unfortunately, the absolute prohibition of visiting with the psychologically ill parent is as likely to strengthen the relationship as to weaken it, and the well-intentioned strategy may boomerang because children, out of their own intense need, can all too readily idealize the parent they are prohibited from seeing.

We were interested to discover that sometimes children resisted the notion of the mental illness of the father for several years, and then came suddenly to the recognition of its presence. This sudden awakening, which often occurred as the youngster reached adolescence, could lead to a repudiation of the father as a model for identification. But the abruptness of the youngster's perception of the psychopathology was a repeated occurrence.

Marcia, whose father was paranoid schizophrenic, suffered his scorn for many years as she continued to visit him regularly at her own insistence. She had been nine years old at the time of the divorce and during the five years that followed, she lived with her mother but continued to be angry at her mother for disrupting the marriage. She idealized her ill father as a wonderful man who had been profoundly mistreated and misunderstood by her mother and the rest of the world.

Marcia told us that when she reached thirteen she suddenly began to revise her view of her father and the divorce. She offered that she had not understood many things until now, but she had finally begun to believe the many incidents which the mother had described and which she had earlier rejected incredulously.

The turning point came when her mother remarried and her father screamed wildly at Marcia, blaming her for the mother's remarriage. Marcia explained that her father's accusation had hurt her profoundly. She began to notice that the father was a suspicious person, that he disliked most people, and that many of his views were not rationally based. She said, "All of a sudden things began to come together for me. I began to understand the divorce. My dad is strange." She was moving into adolescence with the emerging capacity to recognize the father's psychosis and to diminish her emotional dependence on him.

As we have noted earlier, several children turned to their stepfathers and away from their disturbed fathers. Finding a warm response, they reached out to stepfathers whom they came to love and admire and to consciously choose as a model instead of their father. These fortunate (and usually younger) children moved ahead rapidly in their development and in school, and they derived great benefit from the divorce, which not only separated them physically from a psychologically destructive relationship, but also brought them an opportunity for an experience within a happy family.

On the other hand, we have described a number of children who were caught in a tragic identification with an ill father and who threw in their lot with him in a heroic, although misplaced, effort to rescue him. Several fathers in the study remained in dilapidated condition following the divorce, in the neighborhood of the divorced family, maintaining frequent contact with the children. These men were not dangerous to their children or themselves. Sometimes they worked at odd jobs, sometimes they existed on welfare. However psychiatrically ill and marginally adjusted, they remained close to the family orbit and evoked different responses among the children. They angered some and roused the pity of others. In several such families the relationship with the father continued much as it had during the marriage.

### Father-Child Relationships that Remained Good or Became So

Despite the many obstacles to building a parent-child relationship outside the family structure and maintaining it over the years, we found that 30 percent of the children had an emotionally nurturant relationship with their father five years after the marital separation. Lacking the full authority of the parent *in situ*, these men by dint of sustained effort and commitment had succeeded in winning, or maintaining, a respected place in their children's lives. As a consequence, they exercised continuing influence over the children's psychological development, moral values, and life choices. Moreover, they had throughout the years been able to provide some measure of affection and understanding, a shoulder to cry on or to lean against, a home away from home, a needed place of refuge, and occasionally funds for a special purpose. Lacking both daily contact and direct authority to intervene, their role was circumscribed; in no way could their contribution be comparable to that of the custodial parent. But they maintained a presence which could be used by their children as needed as an additional and separate resource which lent another dimension to their children's lives.

These fathers were a mixed group in the history of their relationships with their children during the marriage. Some had had close relationships during the predivorce family and had successfully negotiated the treacherous currents of the visiting relationship. Others were poorly acquainted with their children at the time of the separation, having spent most of their time away from the household during the years of the unhappy marriage. Their close relationship with the children followed the separation. Still others were galvanized into a new awareness of their children by their own anguish at the time of the separation, especially their sense of the impending loss of a relationship they had taken for granted. A smaller number found the very limits of the visiting relationship more congenial than the constant heavy exposure of the marriage. And a significant subgroup stayed closely involved because they distrusted the parenting capacity of the custodial parent and wished to protect their children.

Despite their differences these fathers were united by their common attitudes toward their children, their general capacity to adjust to changing circumstances, and their particular ability to adapt to the specific demands and constraints of the visiting role. They shared an awareness of their children as individual people and were reasonably sensitive to differences among the children in age and interests over the years. And they tried, sometimes with mixed success, to respond to each child in an individual way.

The capacity of these fathers to deal with their children as individuals was reflected in the flexible visiting pattern that emerged gradually, especially in their relationships with the older youngsters and the adolescents. Sometimes one and sometimes all the children visited together. Occasionally, they came for a weekend or for an overnight; sometimes for a short visit of a few hours. In families with younger children, the visiting followed a more regular pattern. These relationships, however, also made allowances for spontaneous communication during the week: a hurried telephone call or a quick message.

Mr. J. said he was spending more time with the children these days. He saw them regularly every other weekend at his home and he talked to them on the telephone several times between visits. Though occasionally one child would not come because of a prior commitment, generally the visiting had been regular. Mr. J. had tried to keep the visiting structure organized because he had discovered that changes confused his former wife, and also the children appreciated a set pattern. Mr. J. had missed only two weekends of visiting in the five years following the divorce.

These men gave evidence of understanding the importance of continuity in their relationships with their children. They were willing over the years to give the visiting priority and to protect the visit against incursions when demands on their own time fluctuated or increased. They expected more commitment and more maturity from themselves than they did from their children or from their former wife, and they were, therefore, tolerant of the children's sometimes capricious or wavering investment in visiting, and were able to sustain such disappointments without withdrawing from the relationship in hurt or indignation.

Mr. T. said that over the years he had learned to be "sensitive to what develops." He discussed his many efforts to maintain his relationship with the children. This had become increasingly important since his wife's remarriage and the family's move to the country. Mr. T. felt that he had worked hard and now "was over the hump" because he won't "lose the children." Sometimes he had the sense that he had spent more time with them since the divorce than he would if they had remained married. Ruefully he admitted that his efforts to maintain contact with his children had resulted in being excluded from social activities on weekends. Various girlfriends over the years had been angry at him and at times his children did not want to visit him. It was difficult for them, "having to pack up their clothes to come to my house . . . to decide which toys to bring and which to leave."

An additional factor in the achievement of an enduring relationship was the capacity of these men to accept the constraints of their role as visiting parents. This was never easy, and the opportunities for too much or too little involvement were legion and often expressed in extremes. One mother regularly called her former husband four years after the separation to order their son to shower. Another mother objected to her former husband's presence at the hospital when their son underwent major surgery. In addition to crises, the usual occasions that bring the members of intact families together, such as holidays, graduations, and birthdays, created severe strains during the postdivorce years and presented problems that required delicate negotiations and compromise from both parents.

In the face of these conflicts and other potentially stressful situations these men consciously behaved with tact and with scrupulous awareness of the limits of the role of visiting parent. They tried their best not to interfere with the routine of the mother's household or to question her discipline or her decisions. They tried with reasonable success and with some lapses, not to gossip and not to be drawn into conflict with her, and they tried not to compete with the mother or the stepfather for the approval of their children. Mostly they succeeded; sometimes they failed. The difficulty remained.

Mr. D. volunteered, or perhaps confessed, that he had been making an effort not to disparage his former wife to his children but in the last year he had begun to have an uneasy feeling that by not saying anything about her conduct he, in effect, affirmed and condoned it in the children's eyes. Both he and his new wife, therefore, had mentioned to the children a number of things the mother did that they would not choose to do. He confessed further that two or three times during the year he had made negative comments about the mother "just to be negative," but has discovered that when he criticized her to the children they invariably defended her staunchly.

The demands of the visiting role while difficult were not more difficult than the role of custodial parent but challenging in a different way, and stressful. Most of the men who survived its test were not only committed to their children, but had the requisite maturity, psychological intactness, and perhaps even stubbornness to continue in a relatively ambiguous role in the absence of a coherent family structure. They were not, as a group, psychologically astute men or possessed of unusual psychological sensitivity. They were, however, capable of remaining on course and adapting to the needs of the situation and they expected less that others would adapt to them. Most of these men who succeeded were fortunate in their relative freedom from economic worries. Although this group of fathers included blue-collar workers and professional men and many of these fathers worked long hours during the week, none held two jobs and all had some leisure to see their children.

From the viewpoint of the older child and the adolescent, these men were able to build a relationship which, by its very nature, supported the youngster's continued growth into maturity and greater independence. By not binding the child to an earlier dependency, by establishing a relatively new base for the relationship outside the confines of the family home, and by developing a relationship founded on a mutuality of shared interests and affection, the visiting father came to be identified in many youngsters' minds with the next rung in their developmental climb. And the father's emotional significance and his unique contribution lay precisely in the sense of newness that the relationship conveyed and its implied message of greater maturity. This was an important message because the visiting relationship with the older child and the adolescent soon comes to depend on the youngster's interest and active cooperation. The relationship came into its own as the youngster reached adolescence or young adulthood. Several young people chose to follow the professional careers which their fathers had chosen.

Mr. N. had been an absent father during much of the marriage. He dreaded his wife's bad temper, continual nagging, and jealous tantrums. During the many years prior to the divorce he had been a remote parent who worked long hours during the week and pretended to work on the weekends as well.

Interviewed five years after the divorce, Mr. N. said that his two older children visited him several times a week. His relationship with them had grown stronger and closer. He was proud of his son who was now in his second year at college, and he and his son sailed together, discussed may issues of mutual concern, and had developed a close and important friendship. He was very pleased because his son may follow his own career choice or one of equivalent status. Mr. N. also several times weekly saw his adolescent daughter who was in the process of deciding what she wanted to do. Like her brother, she spent little time at their mother's home. She was unhappy there and would have liked to move in with him, but was not sure what she wanted to do. She was fearful of upsetting her mother, and she was struggling with the decision. He would await her decision. If the girl decided to move in with him he would welcome her eagerly. During the divorced years Mr. N. had achieved a rewarding relationship with both of these youngsters which he had not been willing or able to develop during the marriage.

Mr. N.'s son, now age eighteen, presented himself as a personable and poised young man who was doing exceedingly well in his studies and had decided to pursue a professional career. Speaking of his relationship with his father, the boy said that he felt close to his father now. He attributed this to the father's restraint in not burdening the relationship with details of the marital failure. "My dad treats me like an adult; my mom treats me like a twelve-year-old. She's still giving me the details of every single hassle."

Mr. N.'s daughter volunteered that she had decided to move in with her father. She emphasized that her mother continued to be angry about the divorce. "She is not willing to let go of her anger." Mr. N.'s daughter had always adored her father and gotten along well with him. But, especially, she preferred him now because, unlike her mother, "he has closed the door on the divorce."

Some relationships improved following the father's acute, and sometimes terrifying, sense of loss at the time of the divorce. Men who had paid little attention to their children during the marriage were precipitated into a period of profound mourning and sudden recognition that a relationship they had hardly valued, and insufficiently nourished, was likely to disappear from their lives. Their grief sometimes led to a greater maturity and to a consolidating new concept of self as an adult and a parent. The spurt in personal growth, in turn, mobilized new feelings of responsibility and love for the child, which could become the basis for a new and stable relationship.

Mr. O. attributed the breakup of his marriage to his wife's pregnancy, which he had bitterly resented. According to his own admission, he had ignored the child after his birth. Only after the divorce did Mr. O. discover the boy and, although the mother resented the father's visiting and the visits were strained, Mr. O. continued regularly to visit during the six years that followed, despite the formidable obstacles which the mother threw in his path. Gradually, the father learned to put the child to bed, to diaper him, to perform all those parts of parenting he had not performed previously. He began by taking a child he essentially hardly knew but had decided to claim to visit him at his home every other weekend, saying, "I don't want to entertain him. I'm his father." Gradually and **painstakingly, he developed a relationship with his son which he had not** had at all during the marriage. When Mr. O. remarried several years later he made it clear to his new wife that the child of his former marriage was an important commitment. The child's presence at the wedding was of considerable importance to him, and he arranged this in the face of many difficulties.

Finally, some fathers made a special effort to maintain an active role in the lives of their children in conscious recognition of the distress and disorganization of the custodial mother. Their attachment to their children was distinguished by tenderness and frequency of visiting, and the children themselves were keenly aware of the father's affection and concern and they looked eagerly to visits and to their weekends at his home. When the custodial mother was not too distraught, the visiting relationship could be helpful and in a supplementary way strengthen the children or provide them with needed relief. It was not possible, however, for the visiting parent to maintain a role which made up for the failure of the custodial parent.

Mr. B. called, saying he was worried. His nine-year-old son was committed to his mother and identified with her attitudes and, especially, her anger at the father. Mr. B.'s former wife was seriously depressed, drinking moderately, and continued to be angry about the divorce that occurred five years ago. Mr. B. was troubled about whether it would be helpful to his son to take a more active role in the boy's life. He was concerned that his own intervention might create conflict for the boy, generate more anger in the mother and upset the boy more.

Ben, Mr. B.'s son, spoke thoughtfully about his relationship with his parents. He recognized his dad was interested in him and he was pleased by his father's reaching out. Recently, his father had organized a Boy Scout troop and Ben had enjoyed accompanying him on canoe trips and other outdoor outings. Ben said he enjoyed seeing his dad and there was no conflict or worry about disappointing him because, "He understands that I have other commitments." Ben talked about his mother's unhappiness and jealousy. "That's changing;" he said, "she encourages me to do what I want. She doesn't ask me so much about dad and what he does." Ben remembered with sorrow the days when he felt that he was in the middle and felt disloyal to both parents. "Mom seemed to be the most hurt and angry. I couldn't stand to see her unhappy so I stuck by her side and I tried to make her happy." Clearly, the boy was aware of the interest of both parents and his own love and sensitive concern for both of them was impressive.

Men who remained in close touch with the children of their former marriage sometimes experienced profound concern and conflict especially following remarriage. It is fair to state that fathers not infrequently paid a price for their maintaining commitment to the children of their former marriage. Sometimes they were able to resolve their conflicts and hold on to both families with affection and loyalty. Several fathers found this extremely difficult.

Mr. V. said that he thought that his children were probably improved since his last visit, but he felt that his former wife was still very neglectful of their care. He was concerned about the alcoholic record of the stepfather and, although his former wife was calmer she was still a very troubled person, and he (the father) was acutely aware of her difficulties.

He was concerned not only about the mother's inadequate care of the children (he detailed the disrepair of their clothing and his observations that the children were often wet and overtired), but also that he received little information about the school. He knew that his former wife antagonized the school because she had a tendency to blame the teacher rather than deal with a problem. A year ago the teacher sent a note home saying that the child should bathe more often.

Mr. V. has recently bought a house so that the children would have an ample place to spend their weekends with him. He had not remarried although he hoped to do so some day. He had not invited his girlfriends to join him with his children on visits because he wanted to give all his attention to the children. On weekends he drove several hundred miles to fetch them. Mr. V. was often worried about the children, about their lack of accomplishment in school, and about their lack of self-confidence and maturity.

One remarried father, devoted to the children of his former marriage, was reluctant to undertake a new family and found himself in open conflict with his new wife's wishes for children in the new marriage. He said to her, "But, my dear, I already have children."

Clearly, what emerges across this whole group of father-child relationships—those that start well and continue that way during the postdivorce years, or those that out of whatever combination of new-found strengths and motivations become good following the marital separation—is that the fathers as well as the children acquired significant gratifications out of what developed between them. A new bond and a new relationship that had been forged out of the wreckage of the marriage, successfully funneled through the constraints and limited flexibility of the visiting format and, by that token, arrived at as a consciously willed and worked-at achievement, had become all the more rewarding to the participants.

# Chapter 15

# The Child in
# the School Setting

The question of how the separation and divorce experience influences the child and adolescent in their school performance has become increasingly important to teachers, counselors, and parents. Teachers, in particular, are concerned with how divorce affects children in school. Repeatedly they ask what they can do to help the child of divorce.

Recognizing that learning is one of the central developmental tasks for all youngsters of school age, we wished to find out the extent to which the divorce crisis interferes with learning. Temporary interruptions in the learning process have the potential for becoming consolidated into significant academic problems if the child is not able to resume his learning efforts within a reasonable period of time. The anxieties generated in youngsters by a major disruption in their lives can compromise their receptivity to learning, their willingness to experiment with new material, their ability to concentrate, and their overall attitude toward school. The youngest children, in the early stages of mastering reading, may for this reason be most vulnerable to the disorganizing effects of family disruption, but for the older youngsters, a continuing sense of achievement is also critical in determining attitudes toward school.

With full awareness of these various factors, we undertook to study the social and academic functioning of the youngsters in our study in their school settings at each of the three points of contact. With parental permission, teachers were interviewed by a senior member of our staff who recorded the teachers' reports on the youngsters' current functioning and behavior, as well as any changes noted during the year. The interviews, generally lasting an hour, focused on attendance, academic achievement and skills, peer and adult relationships, attitudes toward learning, capacity to concentrate in class, and included any other divorce-specific information the teachers volunteered. The staff interviewer did not have access to other information about the child gathered in the course of the counseling service.

## Teachers and the Issue of Divorce

Children come into contact with teachers at different points in the history of their divorce experience. Except where the separation occurred late in the prior school year or during the summer, the teachers were familiar with the youngsters' usual level of functioning prior to the parents' decision to divorce and subsequent separation. Thus they had the opportunity to observe and be familiar with these youngsters' normal fluctuations in mood, capacity to concentrate, enthusiasm for learning, and interactions with peers and teachers. If a child's behavior changed in the classroom or playground, the teacher had an unusual opportunity to observe such responses. Although teachers are not always objective, they are generally more so than parents. Moreover, they can continually compare the child's behavior with that of other children in the classroom, which gives them an especially valuable perspective. Teacher reports were helpful, therefore, not only as an independent source of information about each youngster, but also for the additional view which they provided in understanding children's school behavior and academic performance in the stressful months following the parents' separation.

Teachers frequently did not know a child's parents were divorcing. It has not been the custom in our society for parents to share matters of a personal nature with the school. And some parents worried about prejudicing the child's teacher against their child by labeling him a child of divorce. More prevalent however, was the failure of many parents to understand that a major crisis in the life of the child could reverberate in behavior and performance in the school setting, and a failure to perceive that a teacher's ability to deal constructively with alarming changes might be enhanced by knowledge of the underlying problem.

For despite teachers' genuine interest in children, their psychological training and knowledge is limited. Many teachers, for example, clearly had not understood that the changes in behavior seen in their children after separation were a result of the youngsters' increased anxiety and tension. Thus teachers are dependent on parents for information which will help them understand and cope with abrupt changes in their students' mood and behavior, and often require the parents' permission to discuss such matters with these youngsters. Conversely, many parents feel that teachers cannot be trusted with such intimate information and confirm the teachers' feelings that perhaps they should not intrude. The end result of these failures in communication is that the child receives less support than he might. For the older youngsters, of course, there is no one central figure to whom they can convey vitally important information, moving as the youngsters do from teacher to teacher each hour of the day. This is important, as no one may notice for months that a youngster's overall academic achievement is foundering.

In general our experience with the teachers was a mixed one. Some were marvelously sensitive to the child's distress and responded accordingly. A significant number were themselves divorced parents, and the increased sensitivity they had gained by observing their own children often enhanced their ability to recognize and meet the needs of students whose parents were divorcing. They seemed especially eager to learn more about divorce and its impact on children. But even within this group, individual experience sometimes influenced sensitivity and the willingness to reach out to the child. If, for example, their own children were coping well, they might expect that other youngsters should also do so, without being sufficiently cognizant of important family differences. A few teachers expected children to continue to function academically as if nothing had happened, even when they knew of the divorce. Their sharp impatience with daydreaming and incomplete work reflected the notion, supported in large measure by society, that, at the very least, children should put aside their distress during school hours. Our own view is that teachers should be informed of major changes in a child's life in order to maximize efforts to create a supportive setting. More than that, we believe that the education of teachers should be expanded to include a more comprehensive, complex view of the psychological development of children, including the effects of temporary and prolonged stress.

Many children drew attention to their needs by sharing the news of separation and divorce with their teachers. The youngest ones openly and naively shared intimate details in "Show and Tell," while some older children more quietly told of their situation, in search of support and understanding. Because only a small number of parents had notified the teacher of the family disruption to alert him to possible changes in their child's behavior, many teachers learned of the divorce only when they were notified by the parent that we would be calling on them for an interview in connection with the clinical purposes and research needs of the project. Quite a few teachers told us they had suspected a divorce but felt it improper and intrusive to inquire. It is ironic that at a time in our society when parents increasingly hold the schools responsible for their child's well-being, these same parents fail to provide some of the important tools for the teachers' effective functioning.

# After Separation: The Children in the Classroom

At the time of our first series of teacher interviews, which took place on an average of five to six months after the youngsters' parents had separated, two-thirds of the children between kindergarten and twelfth grade were doing at least average academic work, and substantially more than half of this group were considered good or excellent students. Some problems in learning existed for the remaining one-third, of whom more than half were doing poor or failing work. We do not have sufficient information to determine if the difficulties these youngsters experienced were primarily a reflection of the tensions of a poor marriage, or more centrally related to substantial deficits in parenting within the conflicted marriage, or both. There clearly are individual differences in the extent to which the academic progress of a youngster is affected by such external factors as marital tension and conflict. Not surprisingly, the very poorest students in our study, usually in the upper grades, were most often from chronically chaotic homes where the behavior of at least one parent or the interaction between both of them was pathologically disturbed and sufficiently open to enmesh the child in the chaos. None of these youngsters was receiving the special educational services available, despite the fact that some, in our judgment, could have utilized such assistance to function more adequately.

The great majority of the youngsters in the study had not been seen as behavior problems in the classroom, were not overly active, and enjoyed an adequate, if not excellent, relationship with their teachers. As we later sifted through the interviews, we estimated one-half of the children were well-liked by their teachers, whose feelings ranged from a general appreciation of the child to genuine enthusiasm and fondness, expressed by one teacher as "I could really take him home with me!" About two-fifths of the students had teachers whose attitudes were essentially neutral, while the teachers of a very small number actively disliked these pupils. Most often these were poor students who had created classroom difficulties.

## Changes in the School Setting

Teacher observations indicated that approximately two-thirds of all the youngsters showed some notable changes in school, subsequent to the parents' separation. While the youngsters differed both in the manner and intensity with which their distress was expressed, responses affecting academic achievement were the most common. For more than half of the students, teachers reported a high level of anxiety. Most often this was described to us as new and unaccustomed restlessness. Children who used to sit and do their work now roamed about the room constantly, and in the process began to interrupt classroom activities.

Not surprisingly, for many students the rise in anxiety and preoccupation with the family dissolution brought new problems in concentration. For nearly one-quarter of the youngsters, their difficulty in concentrating on schoolwork was severe, while for others, the interruptions in attention were evident but not totally disruptive. Sometimes the older youngsters consciously struggled to marshal their attention, but gave indications of the effort involved in maintaining their usual good work.

Saul angrily protested to the therapist that excessive demands were being made on his capacities by his high school teachers. "*How* can they expect me to *do* all this work when I'm so busy thinking of the divorce? It's not fair." Parallel to the rise in concentration difficulties was a substantial increase in daydreaming. As with the observations of anxiety, restlessness, and decreased concentration, there were no significant age or sex differences in the youngsters who began to daydream substantially more after the separation. Many children, preoccupied with their parents' well-being or worried about their own futures, brought these new and intrusive thoughts into the classroom, and at least 25 percent of the youngsters seemed unable to put them aside successfully for some time after the separation.

And finally, teachers noted either considerable sadness or depression in one-fifth of the youngsters. This was more evident in the younger children, who more openly revealed their sadness in the school setting. And the combination of intense sadness, daydreaming, and problems of concentration resulted, for one-fifth of the students, in a significant decline in academic achievement during the several months following the separation.

The onset of the changes in behavior seemed to be unpredictable. Some teachers saw a fairly immediate shift, while others noted more gradual change. There was no relationship between the tempo of the changes in behavior and the child's age, his prior academic achievements, or the amount of conflict between the parents. Children seemed to respond according to their own internal timetables.

Sonia was one of those who responded immediately. She announced with a flourish the family separation the morning after she herself was told, but then proceeded almost immediately to fall apart in both academic work and social relationships. Her distress was painfully apparent to teacher and peers, and continued on for some months.

Carol, on the other hand, had a somewhat delayed response. Initially relieved after her parents' separation, Carol, two months later, entered a very difficult period, marked by whining, frequent crying, and begging for possessions from her fellow students. She would eat all her lunch by ten in the morning, then plead for more food at noontime when she had nothing left. Carol told her teacher she no longer cared about school work, no longer wished to help out around the classroom, and said, "I don't want to do *anything*." While the teacher had noticed some improvement during the period of counseling, the short-term intervention was insufficient to stave off the effects of the frightening battle between her parents for custody and ultimate loyalty. A year later we learned her academic functioning had dropped precipitously, she had lost most of her friends, and she was "a very unhappy child." Her teacher remarked with concern that, for Carol, "the year was a total disaster."

With one child the major response to the divorce, as observed in the school setting, came nearly a year later. In such instances, because of the considerable delay, teachers are bewildered by the appearance of new behavior and mood when "the divorce was such a long time ago."

Becky was described initially to us as above average academically—a quiet but charming child. The teacher had not seen any particular reaction in the months following the separation. But at a follow-up interview, her new fifth-grade teacher described a later reaction, which started soon after school resumed in the fall. For three months Becky sat all day in class without removing her oversized jacket. She never spoke or smiled, was unable to learn or to make friends. By the end of the school year she had gradually recovered—"She was no longer withdrawn, depressed, and resentful"—but her teacher was frankly puzzled by the episode, particularly since she knew that Becky's behavior and performance the previous year had been unaffected.

Some youngsters retained their ability to function academically but lost considerable ground with classmates when their anxiety was expressed in ways that the other youngsters found jarring.

Dana seemed unaware of her increasingly strident voice and, according to her teacher, "screeched at her friends." An only child, her tension expressed at school with peers reflected the anxiety generated by the disorganized and immature behavior of her overwhelmed mother.

One of the unfortunate consequences of the spread of the child's divorce-engendered reaction to peers is that the behavior often alienated, at least temporarily, the very youngsters from whom they normally received solace and companionship. Their friends had no way of understanding the bewildering shifts in behavior, and the teachers nowhere seemed helpful in this regard. While they felt comfortable in calling the child's attention to classroom behavior or were capable often of comforting the child themselves, they never addressed the child's now precarious interactions with peers in such a way that it could be understood and therefore helpful to either the child or peers.

And finally, other teachers described more gradual, often less dramatic changes in students' behavior that, in retrospect, seemed linked to the divorce.

Todd began to feel that his fifth-grade teacher did not like him. Despite a history of good grades and enjoyment of school, school was "no fun" anymore. Initially sad after the separation, within several months he could no longer accept constructive criticism from the teacher, became increasingly irritable, and started many fist fights on the playground. In explanation to us, Todd said, "The littlest things make me mad."

Todd's changed behavior was linked to an emerging depression, a result of severely diminished contacts with his once-beloved father who, though nearby, was withdrawing from his children after a remarriage.

Many teachers described subtle, gradual changes in children which very much paralleled our own clinical observations. They talked of children increasingly seeking them out, needing more attention, wanting in the early grades to sit beside them or on their laps. As one second grade teacher said at a workshop, "These are the kids that are waiting by the gate when I come to school in the morning."

### No Change Observed

For about one-third of the youngsters, the teachers reported no evidence of substantial change that was visible to them at the time of the divorce. Some of these children, as will be discussed later, were showing vigorous response to the divorce at home but were able to continue on basically unchanged at school.

Tom loved school throughout the year, consistently achieved fairly good grades, and was described by his fourth-grade teacher as "an all around student with no problems."

Other youngsters, particularly adolescents with a history of good achievement, increased their school-related activities after the parents separated.

Tina maintained her stride in her high school subjects with seeming ease. We noted a greatly increased attention to extracurricular activities shortly after the separation which seemed to enhance her ability to cope with a difficult divorce, both by expending her energies and doubling the time spent away from her home. Five years later she recalled this period with some pride and amusement, and confirmed our observation of her conscious effort to distance herself from her mother through the somewhat frenetic clustering of activities.

In contrast to those who coped well without much observable change in school were those poor students who remained poor students throughout.

Burt, entering high school, had a history of nearly failing grades, "tough" behavior, and frequent absences from the classroom. Nothing much changed in the intervening year in the school setting, although at home his belligerence began to match that seen earlier at school. The threat of the father's discipline no longer controlled his behavior at home, and now he was belligerent in both places.

## The Intensity of Response at School

Allowing, of course, for individual differences in youngsters and varying sensitivities of teachers to change, our data enabled us to draw some conclusions regarding children who were more likely to show striking alterations in their school behavior and to isolate some factors within the divorcing family which were likely to evoke these changes.

For children in their early school years, the ability to maintain concentration in school without substantial and enduring disruption was very strongly linked to the custodial parents' continued ability to handle the children without serious deterioration and to protect the children from the divorce turmoil. It was additionally helpful if the other parent was able, as well, to be comforting and sensitive to the child's needs. In addition, young boys developed an increased ability to concentrate on academic tasks after their mothers divorced disturbed, sometimes violent, men.

Conversely, children's learning suffered, at least temporarily, when household turmoil continued unabated and the children remained unprotected. Frequently, when a mother's self-esteem was shattered by a husband's decision to divorce, primitive, angry exchanges between parents erupted unpredictably, and the mother's previously good parenting deteriorated. In such cases we found an upsurge in daydreaming in class, along with impaired concentration. This was particularly a problem for the younger boys who seemed less able to isolate such divorce turmoil from their functioning at school than were the girls. The younger boys' capacity to concentrate in the atmosphere of parental hostility was extremely vulnerable to disruption. Younger girls engaged in increased daydreaming and experienced concentration problems when preoccupied with fervent wishes for the return of their adored fathers to the family home.

Further, a detrimental effect on the young child's concentration was evident when either parent actively attempted to use the child to do battle or to forge with that child an active collaboration which excluded the other parent. But on the whole, it was especially the mother's distress that affected the child's ability to learn. Where such disruptions were temporary, there may have been little impact, but the stress and its subsequent effect on academic or social performance often continued for many months, if not for the whole of the school year. With older boys, in particular, we noted a serious decrease in ability to concentrate when the mother was severely depressed and disorganized as a result of the divorce. These boys seemed unable to put aside their acute anxiety about their parent's well-being.

Separate from the marital turmoil, when a child was centrally preoccupied with strong wishes to restore the marriage, the daydreaming that focused on potential words or behaviors that might effect a reconciliation interfered, as would be expected, with the child's ability to focus on classroom activities, lectures, and learning.

And finally, those children whom we had observed to have some prior psychological difficulties, seen often in the classroom in the form of poor self-esteem, frequent academic failures, difficulty in relating to peers, or excessive anger, were more likely to experience a more intense central response to their parents' divorce in general, and for some of these children, regardless of the atmosphere of the divorcing period, there was a spill-over into the school setting.

## Discrepant Responses in Different Settings

The teachers' reports were valuable in allowing a comparison of the children's divorce-related behaviors in a variety of settings. Of interest to us was the absence of a high correlation between children's divorce-engendered behaviors and responses, as expressed in the various settings of school, home, and office. The teachers of more than half of the youngsters reported notable changes in their students at some point after separation, but these students were not necessarily those expressing vigorous response at home or with us in the office. Some angry youngsters, newly irritable and difficult to manage at home, continued their exemplary behavior at school.

Jason's second grade teacher fondly described him as "a highly motivated child, scholastically. He wants to be tops in his class, and he is. Jason has adjusted really well to the divorce . . . he speaks equally of both his father and mother, which I find unusual with children whose parents are divorcing. He's entirely delightful!"

At home, Jason's anger was erupting in frequent temper tantrums, obscene notes left for mother's boyfriends, and disruptive dinner table scenes.

Some of the younger children, perhaps attempting to ensure that yet another parent would not leave, tried to be on their best behavior at home, cooperating with their mother, helping out with chores, and maintaining a cheerful demeanor. Their efforts to cope with stress often fell apart at nursery school or kindergarten, where teachers noted episodes of crying "over nothing," frequent flare-ups with peers about the use of play materials, and what appeared to be an intense need to cling to the teacher for support and direction. Some teachers, alarmed at these changes in behavior, then sought some explanation by contacting the parents.

William's teacher was worried because he seemed frightened and had increasing outbursts of crying, with continued decline in his ability to control his behavior. She sent a note home with William, inquiring as to any home changes that would explain his behavior. "He was too scared to give it to his mother, so later I called, and it was then I found out there was a divorce."

Some children were consistent in showing their upset in all settings.

Shocked and depressed by the divorce, Jim was strongly preoccupied with restoring the marriage. At home and with us, his panic was made evident by his crying and sad recitations of the separation events. At school he tightly contained his feelings but was described by his sixth-grade teacher as "very restless . . . poor concentration . . . doing less well than his potential."

Some of the older youngsters, while upset by the divorce, continued to function at home and school with minimal observable disruptions. This was especially true for those well-integrated adolescents whose capacity to function academically had become reasonably autonomous and therefore less vulnerable to temporary disruption. But even for these students there were personal struggles, not necessarily evident to those teachers whose only contact was one academic period per day.

## One Year Later

The teachers that we interviewed at the first follow-up were, for the most part, different from those we spoke with earlier. They entered the lives of these children between one and two years after the separation and had limited knowledge of what the youngsters were like prior to the family disruption. Unlike the first group of teachers who observed divorce-engendered change *in status nascendi,* these teachers saw youngsters who had by then coped with divorce in a variety of ways, some more successfully than others.

There were encouraging changes in teacher reports of academic functioning and behavior one year later. The percentage of children described as tense and anxious was significantly smaller, and fewer children exhibited behavioral problems. Attitudes toward school appeared to have undergone changes and had become more positive. Whereas previously more than half of the youngsters had extremely mixed feelings and nearly one-fifth actively disliked school, now almost two-thirds of the group felt very positive toward school and only a small number actively disliked it. Similarly, there was an increase in the positive attitudes of teachers toward the children.

Academic functioning, on the whole, had improved, with 55 percent of the youngsters achieving good to excellent grades. Nearly one-third of the youngsters had improved in their academic work to a level more nearly approximating their intellectual potential. There were still some youngsters in trouble, however, some of whom remained so from before, and some who were newly experiencing difficulties in learning. In contrast to those whose school work improved, nearly one-quarter of the children had declined in their performance. In understanding the shifts in both of these groups of youngsters, we observed links to the nature of the protracted postseparation period, to substantial changes in parent-child relationships, and in the child's or adolescent's ability to rely upon school as a supportive network.

### Children Coping Well at School

There was a large group of children whose ability to cope adequately with the divorce experience was reflected as well in a resumption of functioning within the school setting. Of one of these children a teacher remarked, "I didn't know he was from a divorced family." But more often by now, teachers were aware the youngster's parents were divorced, in part because the youngsters were more willing to mention it and in part because divorce and single-parent families were increasingly discussed in the classroom.

Peggy's work had not paralleled her ability when we first saw her. "She wasn't concentrating as well as she might have. She needed and wanted a lot of attention." A year later in sixth grade, her teacher reported, "She's really a great kid. She works up to her potential; she's a popular, good student." The extensive interview with the teacher demonstrated Peggy's capacity to utilize the school experience as a support system while the situation was still difficult at home. Her previously noted need for attention had been subtly transformed into a need for nurturance that no longer created academic or peer difficulties. She often sought out the teacher to talk, "especially to talk of her anger at her mother for not taking her side in anything." (The teacher's observation paralleled our own. At the initial follow-up sessions, Peggy had directly and symbolically complained of her mother's unfairness: "My mother always buys Fig Newtons; she *knows* I hate Fig Newtons!") Peggy also made friends with sensitive male teachers and utilized a creative writing class to express her angry feelings about her father and his girlfriends. Peggy's teacher noted fondly, "She binds her affection for me by leaving little notes or doing small things that assure my verbal acknowledgment."

Some youngsters who recovered academically and socially from their initial distress did so with the residues, both positive and negative, of the divorce experience still evident in their daily behavior. In teacher workshops created to develop curriculum ideas and group activities that would enhance the coping skills of divorcing children at school, we gathered sensitive observations. Teachers reported that many divorced children continued to need a lot of support in the aftermath of the separation. "There's a tremendous demand for a one-to-one situation . . . they want to help and be helped in this way."

Many teachers recognized the extent to which the school setting reflected the continuing efforts of these well-adjusted youngsters to cope with the vagaries of the divorce experience. With the younger school-age children doing well in general, Mondays were often observed to be bad days: "There are readjustment problems . . . sometimes their feelings are really close to the edge." Teachers noted the youngsters' disappointment when visits had not occurred as planned or fantasied.

But less apparent to many teachers were the beneficial effects of the school experience itself as a setting for coping with the divorce by working, producing, and thereby easing the stress of sadness and anger. One teacher noted that older youngsters frequently "work like crazy . . . they tear into their work and then desire more. . . . But sometimes without the structure of all that work they're lost. They don't know what to do with themselves. . . . Those are some of the times I see sadness and withdrawal." It seemed clear, especially in the case of older youngsters, that teachers could be helpful to some of their students in channeling their energies and encouraging sublimation in the service of coping with the divorce experience. Some teachers agreed, for example, that the anger initially demonstrated in hostile one-up-manship with peers sometimes developed into a healthy competitiveness which had beneficial results in academic and athletic endeavors.

And finally, the older students were observed to have a certain flexibility that distinguished them from their peers. "They don't get upset when we change the schedule . . . they roll with the punches!" The teachers' observations of this increased flexibility paralleled our own. We noted that many youngsters were at ease in moving from one parent's house to another and from one set of rules and standards to another.

This was especially so when parents facilitated the moves without intense hostility. The teachers' explanation for the increased classroom flexibility seemed on target: "These kids have to learn to accommodate both parents' schedules." It may well be that in always waiting to see one or the other parent, the youngsters who coped well with the divorce developed, in the intervening year, an enhanced capacity to delay gratification, which also contributed to their ability to be flexible.

### Little or No Change

Some children did not change much from the first contact to the next. While some were poor students for whom nothing improved in the intervening year, others showed the continued effects of a difficult, and by now prolonged, period of adjustment, and they had not yet been able to rally in the school setting.

When we first saw Ben, his third-grade teacher described the boy's restless behavior, noting that he was particularly irritable and disruptive for brief periods following visits to his father. Nevertheless, he was intelligent, mostly happy, and clearly wished to do his best.

In fourth grade he seemed easier for the teacher to handle but his concentration varied considerably, and erratic work was becoming a chronic problem. "Ben could be a much better student but he doesn't have any self-discipline." Easily frustrated, he lost his temper with peers or when school work demanded too much concentration. At home, Ben lived with an embittered mother who continued her rage at the father unabated. Ben wanted to see more of his father, but fearing his mother's anger, was unable to express his wishes to her.

### Children Failing to Cope

For almost one-quarter of the youngsters, the intervening year had been one of a steady decline in academic performance. These children were clearly losing ground, and no recovery was in sight. Some had been holding their own in school when initially seen, but gradually buckled under the continuing pressures of their specific divorce situation.

Jason, described earlier as delightful and well motivated, was now causing considerable concern to his third-grade teacher. Since the school was small, she had known Jason before and also carefully compared notes with his previous teacher. Jason's academic work had begun to slip; he was no longer "top of his class." Causing more alarm to his teacher was Jason's pronounced interest in her body, coupled with stories related to her about his mother's sexy outfits and behavior. His teacher also noticed a loss of spontaneity, one of the things that had earlier caused him to be so "delightful."

A second group failing to cope in the school setting nearly eighteen months postseparation had been experiencing academic difficulties in connection with the divorce when we first saw them and had continued in their downward course in the intervening year. Their further deterioration was disheartening.

At our first contact, Edward's teacher reported increased daydreaming and decreased school performance in the months following the divorce. Edward became "restless, fearful of other boys; his power of concentration went down." His very concerned teacher referred him for psychological testing toward the end of the school year.

One year later, in the second grade, we noted a striking deterioration in Edward's school performance. His teacher observed that Edward "vacillates between coming on as an adult or acting completely like a baby." He was a loner with no friends, and was now prone to temper tantrums. Edward had insisted on having a male teacher this year, and forced the assignment by a series of angry, manipulative scenes. He announced to the whole class, "I don't have a father!" His teacher characterized his functioning by saying, "His intellectual capacities are now marred by emotional difficulties." Educationally, Edward was very much at risk.

His mother's psychological functioning had deteriorated during the intervening year. Her fury at her ex-husband and anger at Edward combined with her deliberate attempts to sever the relationship between Edward and his father. Edward was devastated. He attempted to cope by reaching out in the school setting for a substitute figure (the male teacher), but the badly deteriorated relationship with his mother overwhelmed his fragile efforts to recover.

# The School as a Support

Because so many children and adolescents experience divorce each year and because the school represents one of the most continuous institutions in their lives, a central question is to what extent can children utilize the school as a supportive network in the midst of their crisis. To whom are which aspects of school useful, and in what respects? The school setting served as a "support system" in diverse ways for different children of different ages. As with other support systems outside immediate and extended families, however, a child's ability to utilize the school for support in the midst of crisis increased significantly with age.

First, it was clear that school was useful precisely because it provided structure in a child's life at a time when the *major* structure of his life, the family, was crumbling. Going to school daily, being required to perform certain tasks in and out of school, having routine social contacts, all of these "structural" supports potentially assist a child in his adaptations to divorce. It was evident that many children were supported by school in this basic way, regardless of the quality of their academic and social functioning within the classroom.

Second, there was the support provided those children who enjoyed attending school and whose academic achievements sustained and nourished them. Such children, who worked hard, obtained good grades, and received praise for their efforts, were not in the majority. Our findings suggested that school served as a good support system only to those children who were of above average intelligence, doing well academically to begin with, and who were psychologically some of our healthier youngsters. They were not necessarily dependent upon the teacher to be a supportive figure, although a good relationship was helpful.

And third, some children were supported in school at a time of high stress by their close relationship to, and reliance upon, a friendly teacher. Preschool and kindergarten children climbed into the laps of teachers to receive nurturance and solace. These youngsters stayed close to the teacher, checking often to receive assurance that they and their work were approved. The comfort that the teacher provided was important to those who sought it because it temporarily reduced anxiety and brought a small measure of security. But such nurturance did not necessarily have "staying power" in influencing the child's ultimate capacity to cope with the divorce. The richness of the school experience in some cases was insufficient to stave off the eroding effects of the divorce turmoil at home. It is important for the teacher who observes the continuing need of a child for reassurance and solace to discuss the child's vulnerability with his parents before his progress in learning becomes seriously compromised.

Ironically, with the younger children, their high reliance on the teacher as a "support system" was closely linked to their capacity to use their mother in the same way. Thus, some youngsters received support on several fronts in their efforts to deal with the divorce, while others seemed to have no one to whom they could turn.

With the older youngsters, we most often saw them turn to teachers for support and comfort when they were turning, as well, to siblings and peers. In short, those who were capable of seeking out the assistance or solace of others did so in a fairly wide circle. Some older boys not visited by their fathers turned to extended family and a teacher as a reliable source of support. An interesting observation was the inability of the older youngsters to develop and maintain good peer relationships if they had been frequently exposed to intense marital fighting and violence in their families prior to divorce.

In general, however, fewer children than we had hoped really utilized or were capable of falling back upon the school network. And with the exception of the youngsters, particularly girls, whose reliance upon the school was linked to good intellectual capacity and performance, there was little evidence to suggest that the availability of school as a support system, as currently constituted, determined or shaped the child's eventual outcome. Rather, the course of the child's future was linked much more strongly to the network and quality of support provided him by his parents, and in some cases there was precious little the school or anyone else could do. As described elsewhere, we noted a deterioration in the younger children's psychological functioning when the mother's relationship to the child and her handling of him were poor. For the first year or so, boys showed the effects of this decline in the mother-child relationship more precipitantly in their school work than did girls. But, where the relationship continued poor, the children's depression and growing disorganization ultimately affected the academic performance of both boys and girls.

## School Performance Five Years Postdivorce

Just as the overall psychological functioning of the youngsters was determined five years later by many factors, of which only some were divorce-related, so too was school functioning a product of many intervening variables. In terms of school success and failure, academic performance of the entire group was roughly comparable to what it had been four to five years earlier. Thus divorce did not significantly alter school performance of the group as a group, although there were changes within it in the direction of improved or deteriorated academic functioning. Three-fifths of the youngsters were now doing average or better work, and the majority of this group were, in fact, excellent students. Of the remaining youngsters, nearly one-quarter were performing below average academically and an additional 16 percent had extremely poor grades. Among those youngsters functioning poorly were a significant preponderance of the thirteen-to-sixteen-year-olds. This age difference was not originally present in the sample and emerged gradually in the group we originally described as being quite angry about the divorce. This same group of early adolescents also had significantly more who at five years were having serious behavioral problems at school. Of considerable interest was the finding that academic performance was not significantly related to the father's or mother's socioeconomic level.

## Good School Functioning

Several groupings of youngsters were discerned among those whose academic functioning nearly five years after separation was good, if not exemplary. For all these students, more than two fifths of the entire group, the influences contributing to academic achievement were complex and largely paralleled those described in chapter 13 for youngsters whose overall outcome was good. They are here described as good students because of an ongoing record of consistently high grades, with reading, math, and writing skills at an age-appropriate level or better; none of these students had substantial behavior problems which brought them to the attention of school authorities.

The first group of good students were those whose academic performance five years earlier had also been quite solid. While some of these children and adolescents experienced temporary disruptions in concentration and productivity after the separation, their recovery had occurred soon enough to ensure a continuing history of academic achievement. These youngsters had been psychologically intact initially, and remained so throughout the intervening years. As described earlier, these good students were more likely to rely upon the school setting and their own strong performance as a support and diversion in the midst of their divorce-engendered distress. This was especially true for adolescents.

Michelle was fifteen when we first saw her, liked school very much, and planned to go on to college. Her grades were mostly A's and B's, with some C's in science courses. After the separation, she devoted greatly increased time to school-related activities, managing to avoid being at home as much as possible, but she maintained her grade average.

More than five years later, Michelle was seen during the summer of her junior year at college. Her continued difficulty with mathematical concepts adversely affected her functioning in science courses, but she nevertheless maintained a solid B average in college. Seeing herself as competent, Michelle's intention was to continue on to graduate school in preparation for a professional career.

Michelle was representative of the girls whose continued good functioning in school was significantly linked to a good mother-daughter relationship by the five-year mark, an association that was not apparent initially among the girls who had been good students. Michelle's career aspirations were tied to strong identifications with both parents. For younger girls, especially those in preschool or early primary grades when the separation occurred, their good achievement in school was more closely related to strong identification with a competent mother and a good mother-child relationship, and less dependent on the father's functioning.

With boys whose school functioning continued to flourish five years postdivorce, the mother-son relationship was less of a significant determinant. What was crucial, instead, was that the boy have some capacity for independence and not be depressed. As described in an earlier chapter, this was most often linked to the father's continuing interest in his son, or to the presence of an interested stepfather.

In nursery school when first seen, Frank's reaction to the divorce was intense. Despite the solid achievements obviously attained in his development, the separation represented a crisis for this boy, one demonstrated by his whining, crying, and clinging, and overwhelming fear that his dad would remarry and "find another little boy." His mother, guilt-ridden and fearful of rejection by the children, needed intensive treatment to help her cope with her own enormous anxieties and anger.

At the first follow-up, Frank had recovered from his acute reactive depression and was calm and self-assured. Thoughtful and serious, Frank was doing well in school, had many friends, and was active in sports. His mother's considerable difficulties in adjusting to the life of a single parent were still evident, but were more expressed in the mother's relationship with Frank's sister than with him. Frank's father, now remarried, had become a happier, more relaxed parent, and remained very involved in his children's lives.

Several years later Frank was described by his third-grade teacher as "a very good student" who concentrates well and "is always on top of things." A "very responsible child," "a natural leader," Frank had earned the respect of his peers, with whom he was sensitive and understanding. "A tremendously mature" boy, Frank talked a lot about his father at school and conveyed the impression he enjoyed the support of both father and stepfather. Although somewhat improved in her parenting, his mother continued to be very conflict-ridden and now struggled to maintain her career in the face of a serious illness.

There was a new group of youngsters who emerged as good students only by the five-year follow-up. Most of these were slowly reversing a history of mediocre performance.

When first seen, Roberta was having difficulties mastering reading. Her first-grade teacher described her as a "humorous, generous, and thoughtful child, self-sufficient, yet painfully shy and withdrawn, and unable to ask for help." Her teacher had recommended tutoring, feeling that she would fall far behind in her reading without extra attention.

In the year intervening between separation and follow-up, Roberta received the tutoring she needed and was beginning to do better in school. Now in a remarried family, Roberta was valued by her stepfather and encouraged in her social growth by him. At school the teacher reported that she had matured considerably during the year; that while she was still shy with adults, her relationships with peers had grown easier. Her characteristic pattern of absences had diminished and learning was now approximating grade level.

Five years postseparation, Robert had adjusted to a new school system with more exacting standards. In sixth grade her mother described her as "very, very successful, getting mostly A's and B's. Next year she will be president of the student body, and being very athletic, is a member of each sports team!" Her teacher talked of her as "a conscientious student, who is very definitely working up to her potential. She and her best friend compete for top honors and are both popular."

There were interesting findings, parallel to those reported earlier, which bear further investigation. With the younger children whose formal school experience had begun since the separation, good academic functioning was related in interesting and significant ways to the mother's economic and working status. There were sex differences. Younger boys achieved especially well in school when their mothers did not work full time. These young students were no longer preoccupied with the divorce and were not depressed. Young girls seemed to respond to related, although somewhat different, conditions. They were significantly more likely to be good students if their mothers were assured a certain degree of economic security. The younger boys seemed more dependent on the mother's physical availability to ensure good academic achievement, whereas the younger girls needed a mother reasonably free of the anxieties about whether there was money for the rent, the dentist, or the babysitter.

With boys and girls of all ages, there was a significant link between high academic achievement and good peer relationships. The same factors contributing to good psychological functioning contributed as well to gratifying friendships, and the ability to give attention to school subjects.

## Poor School Functioning

Two-fifths of the children and adolescents were doing academic work which was below average for their grade level at school. Limited intellectual capability, as before, was not a factor in this academic failure. More than half of this group of poorer students were receiving C's and D's for their work; the others were failing completely. Many were behind in their grasp of mathematical concepts, reading, and comprehension skills. Others were completely uninterested and failing in school, either because their chronic failure to achieve academic rewards had diminished any will to make an effort, or because their anger, disenchantment, and depression affected the school experience.

As with the good students described previously, these youngsters doing poorly at school divided into different groups: those who were poor students in the predivorce family and remained so in the intervening years, and those whose move toward academic failure occurred in the aftermath of the divorce.

Of those whose poor school functioning was essentially unchanged since the separation, we saw parallel evidence of troubled psychological adjustment as well. There had been a consolidation of many difficulties, including intense anger, feelings of neglect and rejection, depression, poor self-esteem, and poor social judgment.

One group of youngsters doing poorly at school had begun to fail only in the aftermath of the separation and divorce. For these youngsters who deteriorated in their functioning over time, the events subsequent to, or set in motion by, the divorce overburdened and stressed their ability to function academically, if not in other areas. The deterioration in the relationship between custodial parent and child and the failure of the father to remain interested in his child were significant factors, separately or in combination with each other.

We have described the influence of the father's essential nonavailability to his child, an influence particularly unfortunate when the father-child relationship had been adequate, if not better, prior to divorce. For one group of newly failing students, regardless of age or sex, there were significant links to an erratic, infrequent visiting pattern, depression in the youngster, and a continuing preoccupation with the divorce. Some of these children and adolescents had been good students when we first saw them, so their decline was noteworthy. As described, the hallmark of their distress was a significantly damaged and by now poor self-esteem. Feeling unloved, they developed a futile sense that whatever they did would not be good enough to bring the father's more regular attention and approval. The growing dislike of school paralleled their deepening distrust of their father's intentions. The feeling that no one cared began to show itself with other adults as well, and certainly included teachers.

The second group of youngsters, who became poor students only after divorce, were those who lived with a seriously disturbed parent. In some of these families the chaotic behavior triggered in the parent by the divorce remained a central and disorganizing aspect of the home. The youngsters' school performance was seriously affected, together with other aspects of their psychological development.

Robin's family history was marred by violent episodes between her parents induced by their excessive drinking. Robin's mother was very troubled throughout the marriage and her psychological problems deepened following separation. At school, while her academic performance had been "somewhat erratic," Robin had managed during the years before the separation to do very well in most subjects. Robin was respectful with adults, not a discipline problem, and a good student. With peers, she seemed to be shy, even intimidated: "She can't stand up for herself."

A year later, Robin's school performance had deteriorated as markedly as her relationship with her mother. Her mother's violent outbursts had increased. Several school personnel in whom Robin had confided were fearful for her safety. No longer able to concentrate, Robin hung around the teacher "like a puppy dog who doesn't know what to do with herself."

Robin was forlorn and lonely, upset that her mother had driven her two best friends away, either "by acting weird or by being drunk," or by fighting with the friends' mothers. At school Robin wandered around by herself at lunch time. Her learning declined precipitously.

Five years after the separation, Robin, now an adolescent, passionately hated school. She cut classes regularly, smoked pot heavily, and was sexually active. Robin no longer had any interest in learning. Her mother described Robin as "bitchy, ungrateful, and shiftless." Robin, for her part, saw the mother as hostile, uninterested, sexually promiscuous, and "crazy."

Some youngsters five years after the separation were involved in vandalism, including arson, at the school, which they had come to hate. These have been the children and adolescents historically labeled the products of "broken homes," seen in the school setting as failures and disruptive. They are assuredly *not* the majority of the youngsters who experience the divorce of their parents, but they represent one group of such children desperately in need of a supportive network soon after the separation, both in the school setting and in the community.

# Chapter 16

# Remarriage

Almost half of the children again confronted far-reaching change in their daily lives when one or both of their divorced parents remarried.

These changes were likely to be more marked when the custodial parent remarried and especially when the new stepfather brought children from his former marriage into the suddenly merged new family. The transition was not easy for the adults or the children. Nevertheless, most men and women expressed approval and a sense of increasing contentment which they experienced as a generally enhanced quality of life, particularly in comparison with the divorced family or their unhappy marriage.

Mrs. T. said that her marriage was fine, it was working as well as the earlier marriage worked poorly. She now had someone who loved her and she could now give to a man and felt that it was the right thing to do. "He is good with the children and we are all happier and better off."

Only a small group among the adults had serious misgivings about their second choice at this early stage of the new marriage. Many of the children were reasonably pleased as well, although their adjustment followed a different course than that of the parents, and their approval or disapproval of the new family evolved gradually and cautiously.

The changes required by the remarriage were formidable and went well beyond the family structure and interrelationships. Expectably, remarriage led some families to relocate geographically. The move introduced additional disruptions and discontinuities, including greater distance between the noncustodial parent and the child. Some of the remarried families left the state and others remained within the same general area but at a considerably increased driving distance from the father. Several remarried families moved to rural communities, electing an entirely different way of life, including school systems that were different from those which children had previously attended and peer groups which valued other kinds of social skills and interests. In some families the social and economic changes were outstanding, and the standard of living of the remarried family was considerably lower than that of the divorced husband or the predivorce family. And finally, some of the stepparents adhered to value systems, educational and cultural standards, and childrearing practices which were very different from those that had prevailed in the original household.

## Remarried Mothers

Along the way, between the two marriages, many women had undergone important changes. Their motivation was high and they were, as a group, more willing to devote sustained and mature efforts to make this second marriage work. They were also, as a group, more realistic or perhaps less ambitious in their emotional demands on the partner. And they fully expected that problems would arise, and that these could be addressed within the marriage.

Mrs. S. told us, "The marriage is good. We work at problems on a sound, comfortable basis." She said laughingly, "He puts up with a lot more from me . . . in fact, he probably puts up with more from me than I do from him."

Some were impressively honest in admitting the hurt of the divorce, and pragmatic in recognizing and accepting the limitations of the present. They had lowered their expectations of others and increased their expectations of themselves.

Mrs. C. said that her divorce was both sad and painful, but necessary. Wistfully she added that she would probably never duplicate the feelings and commitment that she had with her former husband. At that time she had said and meant, "I give my soul." She considered herself fortunate that this second marriage had turned out so well. Presently, both she and her husband made a continuing effort to work out their problems together. They were compatible and the marriage was congenial. She had learned, however, that she would not stay in a relationship if it threatened to destroy her. Her new marriage had turned out better than she ever imagined or hoped for and she thought that her husband felt similarly.

These remarried parents were a relatively young group. Several had first married directly out of high school or during their college years. And they had in the interval between the marriages succeeded in exorcising the ghost of their adolescence. After a year or more of frenetic running in the singles' scene they had opted for marriage and commitment. Their values in regard to marriage were surprisingly conservative.

Mrs. H., a very attractive twenty-eight-year-old woman, said that she had enjoyed dating and partying with several guys after her separation. When she was married she had been envious of the freedom of single women to do as they wish. But, "Now it's good to be able to roll over in bed, to reach out, and to know someone special for me is there."

Most of the women worked full time and expected to continue, although few found their jobs interesting or sought a career. They were agreeable to the sharing of financial burdens. During the postseparation years many had acquired a greater sense of competence and an enhanced confidence in their capacity to manage. Several women also felt a sense of obligation at bringing dependent children into the marriage. Many were working very hard both at home and outside the home to make this marriage succeed. They were interested in providing a better life for themselves. They wanted to undo or forget the unhappiness of the former marriage and the divorce, and to provide a better family environment for their children.

Several women, of course, brought the problems they had experienced earlier into the new marriage. Their remarriage did not affect chronic depressive illness or the restless, hungry, driven need to change partners. These remarriages soon began to show the familiar signs of strain and impending failure.

## Stepfathers

Most of the stepfathers were older and had been married before, and had also traveled a lonely road and were eager for a home and a gratifying marriage. By and large, they too were a sober and committed group who were supportive of their wives. With a few exceptions, they expected to assume the role of parent to their wives' children. Encouraged by the women, most men took this responsibility seriously and moved quickly into the role of the man of the household, with the prerequisites, prerogatives, and authority traditionally accorded this position.

The immediate entry into the role of husband and father was not easy for the men, and generated anxiety for them and for the children. Several of the new husbands had earlier lived in the household as lover and companion. Their relationship with the children was different during that time and more inclined to be friendly, casual, or uninvolved. Occasionally, men were especially pleasant and generous with the children when they were courting the mother. The change in their status sometimes abruptly altered their attitude and general demeanor with the children.

Christina, age ten, complained bitterly of her stepfather of several years. "I don't really like him. He was nice and kind before the marriage and we did lots of things together. Since they got married he is mean and strict and not at all loving." Her brother and sister echoed her disappointment.

At the outset, stepfathers were moderately fearful of being rejected by the children, and particularly concerned about being compared unfavorably with the children's father. Several men referred uneasily to the children's prolonged observation of them, to their initial coolness and withholding of affection and approval. Neal, at age nine, confirmed this when he said, "In the early days I watched him a lot to see what he was like and he didn't like that at all." The anxiety which the men experienced at the beginning of the marriage had many sources: the history of their early marital failure, the new marital relationship, the complex feelings at replacing an absent father in the children's affection. Perhaps in reaction to their own anxiety, a substantial number of men assumed a fairly rigid disciplinary stance with the children, especially with the older youngsters. Stepfathers were variously described as "stern," "not affectionate," "when he says something he never changes his mind," "he has a temper, you don't goof off when he gets mad," "when he comes home if dinner isn't cooked and the house is a mess, watch out!"

Only a few men appeared sensitive to the need to cultivate a relationship with the child gradually, and to make due allowance for suspiciousness and resistance in the initial stages. Sometimes parent and stepparent made the mistake of expecting instant intimacy, or instant affection for the new stepfather. Such expectations were disturbing for children who experienced the demand for instant affection as if they were being called upon to betray their love for their father and to substitute the stepfather in his place. Even very young children needed to be reassured the new adult was not being presented as a substitute for the departed parent.

Karen, age three, refused to greet her mother's fiancé. "You're not my daddy," she said tartly. Only after the child was reassured that the man knew that she had a daddy and wanted additionally to be her friend did the child permit the conversation to proceed.

Age was a significant factor in the stepfather's approach to the child and in the child's response to the stepfather. The relationships with the younger children, mostly those below the age of eight, took root fairly quickly and were happy and gratifying to both child and adult. Little girls were especially responsive to the affection and admiration of the new stepfather.

Mr. A. said that his relationships with all the children were improving, but Inge who was seven adored him. She got very upset when he disapproved of her conduct. At first she was stand-offish and would not permit him to hug her, but now she wanted to sit next to him on the couch and to kiss him. And she always kissed him goodbye when he left for work. He sometimes thought he was more of a father to her than her father ever was.

The relationship between the stepfather and the older children followed a more conflicted course. Some of the older youngsters and the adolescents continued to resent his presence and failed to develop a significant attachment to him. Others gradually changed their minds and grew to respect and to love him. Eventually, some youngsters sought to emulate the stepfather and placed him as the central identification figure in their lives. We were told repeatedly, by different stepfathers, about the course of a troubled relationship which took an important turn at a particular moment in time, following an incident or even a confrontation when the balance suddenly changed and the child ceased to withdraw and decided, as if suddenly, to accept the stepfather as an authority and a parent.

Mr. G. described his breakthrough with his stepson Neal, age twelve, who he said had finally begun to trust him a year after the marriage. Apparently the trust began following a strong verbal confrontation in which Neal had talked back to him, he had pushed the boy up against a wall, and they had yelled vigorously at each other. Following this episode the relationship began to change. Mr. G. said he had been very worried about the effect of the tongue lashing he had given his stepson, but then he decided to take the gamble and now he felt that he and the boy were going to make it together. His concern was that Neal was "spoiled" during the years of the marriage.

Mrs. C. described the different relationships her son and daughter had with her new husband. Although there was considerable turmoil and tension in the household in the beginning, the eight-year-old girl managed very well with the stepfather, "and always came to him." But Bill didn't really accept him. He always asked his mother to ask his stepfather for something and this annoyed the stepfather very much. Around Christmas of the second year of the remarriage, the relationship suddenly took a noticeable turn for the better. Bill had spent two weeks with his father and he never mentioned what, if anything, happened during that visit and they didn't ask. But when they picked the boy up he climbed into the car next to the stepfather, patted him on the knee and said, "Well, what are we going to do today, Paul?" Since then Bill had been making morning coffee for his stepfather and they had been planning their days together.

The school teachers commented on the difference in Bill's adjustment and learning and confirmed the sudden change reported by the mother. They contrasted the first year of the new marriage when "he was a smart aleck and was generally lazy." "This year," said the teacher, "is a whole new ball park. Bill is a different boy. He is polite, cooperative, completely trustworthy, completes his assignments on time, is punctual and generally a delightful boy." "He has completely cut out the horseplay of last year and is putting things in order." The teacher added that he really didn't know what happened, except that Bill *suddenly* changed his behavior for the better.

A few stepfathers took very little responsibility as parents and remained out of a direct role in their stepchildren's lives. The relationship which emerged had an entirely different cast.

Mr. C. made it clear that he left all the decisions about the children to their mother. His stepson, age thirteen, said in turn, "I like my stepfather, but he's not my father. We are friendly."

### Children's Attitudes

At the outset the children were eager and very anxious. They welcomed the arrival of a stepfather because of the greater security his presence provided. They were relieved to be a two-parent family, as well as pleased with the mother's greater contentment, which reflected itself very quickly in her management of the household. Several children had urged the mother to remarry since the divorce.

As Neal said, "It is nice to have two adults around." The new marriage was good for them. His mother was happier and it was easier for everyone in the family.

As the children took the stepfather's measure and found him congenial, interested, and sympathetic, they approved.

Doris, age eleven, said, "My dad is unfair and he has a terrible temper, but Bill [the stepfather] is the father I can talk to."

Joe, age sixteen, talked about his admiration for his stepfather. He described his own interest in cars and his decision to become an automobile mechanic, linking this to his stepfather's mechanical talent and interest in cars and motorcycles.

Adolescents learned to respect and value the honesty and fairness of the stepfather. Bill, age fourteen, said, "I like David and I respect him. I don't feel close to him and I get upset with him once in a while, but things are better."

There were, of course, many opportunities for faulty communications, for anger, for divergent agendas, and for conflict in beginning a new marriage with children. And, although the youngsters were eager for the stepfather, they were resentful as well of the new man's special place in their mother's affections and of the instant authority conferred on this new adult in their lives. His arrival was worrisome and led to the children's uneasiness about their own position in the family. They were concerned that they might be shunted to the side and replaced or excluded by the new marital relationship. As they worried, they watched tensely for evidence of acceptance or exclusion.

The newlyweds' need for privacy collided head-on with the children's preoccupation with being excluded or rejected. Whereas adults struggled to find privacy to enhance their understanding of each other and their pleasure in each other's company, the children sought to join the activities. Several children complained bitterly about being excluded by parents who spent evenings together while the children played dispiritedly in an adjoining room.

Terry, age six, complained that she felt shut out by the private goings on between her mother and stepfather. The child described in detail how her parents went into the bedroom and locked the door, or had dinner without the children, or went off frequently for the weekend. Peter, age eight, volunteered, "They tickle and giggle a lot in the bedroom, and they don't eat with us."

Although many children were somewhat threatened by the special privileges accorded to the newcomer, children who had been especially close to the mother during the difficult divorce period and had tried to provide both help and companionship, found their position suddenly changed by the stepfather's arrival. Some welcomed the relief from responsibility and felt freer to go about their own postponed activities. But others were angry and humiliated at suddenly being needed so little, pushed out by the remarriage, and unrewarded for their many efforts. These youngsters sometimes fought back with anger and mischievous behavior and tried openly to break up the new marriage. They succeeded in incurring the joint wrath of the stepfather and the mother. On occasion, the child's bad temper, lack of restraint, and mischief posed a real threat to the new and fragile marital relationship. A few children were sent away to live temporarily, or permanently, with the noncustodial parent, who may or may not have been eager to receive them at this time. One young adolescent girl, who had been very close to her mother and shared the mother's bed prior to the mother's remarriage, outwore her welcome in both homes in her intense need to intervene in the marital relationships of both of her parents.

We were interested to find that although the children felt reassured by the mother's remarriage and by the comforting presence of two adults in the home, they also worried whenever friction developed between the two parents. The new marriage evoked the memories of the earlier experience, and children reported retiring in anxiety to their room or crying at night when the new couple quarreled. Their view of the family friction was sometimes at odds with the perspective of the adults, and the divorce which they had recently experienced was an important contributor to their more anxious perception of the interaction between these adults in the new marriage.

## Fathers versus Stepfathers

The child's relationship with stepfather and father, and the various ways in which this issue was resolved by the child and adults or continued as a source of open conflict, was of central importance in the psychological development and adjustment of the child within the remarried family. The extent to which the child was able to share in the benefits of the marriage depended in large measure on the satisfactory resolution of this conflict by the adults and the children.

Many children were able to maintain and enjoy both relationships. The father and the stepfather did not occupy the same slot in the child's feelings and the child did not confuse the relationship with the two men. Mostly, children enlarged their view of the family and made room for three major figures, all of whom were potentially and actually of major importance in shaping the child's psychological, social, and moral development and ultimately important life choices. The conflict in values between the parents, which often stirred them to great anger, did not pose insolvable dilemmas for the children we observed. Often the children were relatively unaware of, and certainly unconcerned about, some of the differences that most angered the adults, such as differences in sexual mores, in modesty, in nudity, or in manners (barring, of course, seduction or abuse of the child, which raises other issues).

The expectation of many people that the children would necessarily experience conflict as they turned from father to stepfather during their growing-up years was not borne out by our observations. Nor was the expectation that in the happily remarried family the biological father was likely to fade out of the children's lives. The great majority of fathers in remarried families continued to visit, much as they had earlier. Geographical relocation to another state following remarriage was a serious limitation on continued visiting. But the pattern of visiting seemed less affected when the mother remarried than when the father remarried, in spite of wide geographical distance.

The stepfather's influence, in turn, was not undone by the child's continued visiting with the father. Neither divorce nor remarriage ap-

peared to change substantially the importance or the emotional centrality of both biological parents for the growing child. At the same time,
the stepfather's influence was enormous. He, clearly, could greatly enhance the child's development—broadening his or her intellectual hori-
zons, strengthening moral development, and exercising a far-reaching,
beneficial effect on every aspect of the child's character structure
which was still in the process of formulation. Conversely, the stepfather
could constrict the child's emotional life, narrow his or her vision of the
world, increase unhappiness, or decrease self-esteem. But even with this
major potential influence, the stepfather did not replace the departed
father. Only when the child *voluntarily* rejected the father, or counterrejected the father and voluntarily disidentified with the father and
placed the stepfather in the father's role, did replacement occur. We have
described this active choice of the child as a process which we have observed among children with a psychiatrically ill parent or an abandoning
father.

Most of the children in these remarried families made every effort to
conceptualize stepfather, father, and mother together, and their efforts
to make room for all of them were impressive.

Tony, age twelve, whose mother had remarried immediately after the
divorce several years earlier, told us, "The divorce came out pretty
good. My dad is pretty straight; my stepfather is not so straight; I'm a
mix of both. I am like my dad, I am like my mom, and I am like my stepdad. I like rock music and I like western music. I like all music."

Jerry, age ten, when asked how often he saw his dad, responded
"Which dad do you mean?" He would like some day to live in a house
where each day his father and stepfather could alternate as a live-in
father.

Children with good stepfathers whom they loved and admired did
not turn away from fathers, whom they continued to visit. Sometimes
children with good stepfathers held on to or created the image of a father
which was closer in their mind to that of the stepfather, so as to reduce
the discrepancy which they perceived in the two men and to mute the
conflict which they experienced.

Bill provided an interesting example of an attempt by an adolescent to
bring his perceptions of the father and stepfather closer together than
they actually were. Bill's father was a popular man-about-town, who
enjoyed his single life immensely. He spoke contentedly about his many
women friends and about the many pleasures which money and re-
gained bachelorhood made available to him. Occasionally he visited his
son and maintained a relationship with him on the same fairly remote
level that he had maintained during the years of marriage.

Bill's mother was very happily remarried. The stepfather was a personable, committed family man, who was opposite in his behavior and
value system to Bill's father.

In order to avoid the conflict in values posed by the emergence of step-father and father, because of the entirely different lifestyle of each, and to keep a tight lid on his feelings of hurt and anger toward his father, Bill began to attribute to the father the ideals which he had found appealing in the stepfather and the new remarried family.

At age thirteen, Bill told us, "My dad used to be a partygoer. He was always going out and getting drunk with celebrities, but that was because it helped his business. Today he's a changed man. He very much enjoys being at home and he hates to be away that much. Both my parents really want the same things now—a home life and a good place away from the city, a quiet happy place. My dad would like to settle on a farm and be a family man."

Many adults were less successful than the youngsters in defining the different roles. The rivalries between father and stepfather in the re-married families were often bitter and long lasting. And indeed our observation is that, where the child experienced painful psychological conflict which he or she was unable to resolve between the love for the father and the love and loyalty to the stepfather, the adults were likely to be pulling hard in opposite directions. Unfortunately, the relationship between stepfather and father could all too easily become charged with the unresolved angers of the divorce and the aggravated jealousies of the remarriage. Father and stepfather, both of whom needed patiently to exercise restraint and to make room for the continued relationship of each with the child, were all too quickly swept into becoming warring or competing factions.

These conflicts, which brought stepfather and mother on one side against father, disturbed the child and the newly married family. Some-times the conflicts were fueled specifically by the presence of a father who opposed the divorce and hoped secretly for a reconciliation with his former wife. At other times they were caused by jealousy of the re-marriage, or by the remarried family having a significantly lower stan-dard of living than the father or the predivorce family.

Unfortunately for adults and children, these problems of competing father and stepfather were especially difficult to resolve because com-munication was limited, and there was no proper forum for discussion. Feelings were therefore more likely to be exacerbated as both men found new grounds for accusations and counteraccusations. Often the conflict ranged far afield, spreading into differences in childrearing and discipline and attitudes towards work. These differences were easily magnified as each accused the other of serious failings as a parent.

Mr. T., the stepfather, told us, "The relationship between us [referring to the child's father and himself] is 'total hatred.' He comes just like clockwork [referring to the father's arriving promptly after a long-distance drive in order to visit the children], but he doesn't care at all about his children. He's only concerned about his own status, not at all about them." The father, in his turn, referred to Mr. T. as "a man of low intellectual ability and low moral character."

Essentially the child, who needs the adults as role models for a peaceful resolution of conflict and as allies for his own ego in addressing the serious conflicts of love and loyalty within himself, finds himself thrown back on his own inadequate, immature resources to solve the complex problems posed by having several different parental figures in his life. He is doubly handicapped by their fighting, which intensifies the conflict, and by lack of the support needed from the adults to resolve the conflict under the best of circumstances. Although the external fighting does not create the problem for the child, the parental rivalries effectively prevent him from finding a satisfactory resolution, and keep the conflict open and acutely stressful for years.

The most tragic situations for the child were those where mother and stepfather demanded that the child renounce his or her love for the father as the price for acceptance and affection within the remarried family. Such children sometimes bore a physical resemblance to the father. However, the scapegoating of the child also occurred in the absence of physical resemblance and reflected the neurotic needs of the remarried parent to banish the father physically and psychologically from all their lives. The remarried family's anger at the child's father could be maintained at a high pitch and reinforced by their continued anger at the child, who in turn felt that whichever way he turned he betrayed a parent. The anger of these families at the father, and the tenacity of their campaign to root out any vestiges of his existence, bordered on paranoia.

The child who was made the hapless scapegoat of adult anger was in grave psychological danger. His mother and stepfather regarded him as obstinate and perverse for holding to any allegiance to his disreputable father. They were unable to appreciate the child's strength and integrity in maintaining this love for his father, and they attacked the child for holding fast to memories and perceptions separate from theirs. Such children were severely troubled and depressed, too preoccupied with the chronic unresolvable conflict to learn or to play or to develop at a normal pace.

When Edward's mother remarried she encouraged her new husband to relocate in another part of the country in order to avoid visiting with the child's father. Her anger had many sources, but she was especially exercised at his failure to provide child support. When the remarried family was visited by us in their new home on the eastern seaboard they greeted the interviewer with much cordiality and made plain that the new family was very happy except for the parents' annoyance and concern that Edward, age fourteen, continued inexplicably to miss his father, and also to do poorly at school and to have few friends.

"Edward recognized me immediately and we spoke at length," reported the interviewer. "The boy appeared to be under great pressure. He stated at the outset that his problem was his father. His mother and stepfather consider his father a worthless person, a sheik [his words] with many wives, an irresponsible man who never supports his children. Yet, he dreams all the time of hiring a private investigator to find out the truth. 'There must be some good in my father!' the child said with desperation. 'Perhaps a private investigator could find it and let me know.' Edward's voice dropped. He said, 'My problem is my stepfather. Joe hates my dad. My dad is jealous of my stepfather. Both are trying to get me to their side. I think Joe is winning. It's like a tug of war. . . . I'm in the middle and if the rope snaps—wham!, I fall in.' He began to cry. 'I don't know what to do,' he said plaintively. He really appreciates his stepfather who has bought him so many things and takes good care of him. He wants so hard to be like him. He thinks a lot about the divorce all the time and he says to himself, 'Edward, face the facts. Joe has done all this for you.' He used to be like his father but he's changing to be more like his stepfather. He tries everyday. It's hard. They don't even allow him to speak to his father on the telephone when his father calls."

As the interviewer left, the unhappy boy reminded her anxiously, "Please don't tell my mother what I said. It only makes her mad at me."

## Stepsiblings

About half of the stepfathers had children by their former marriage. Some of these youngsters tended to be older and more independent than the mother's children and, not infrequently, drifted in and out of the father's home, remaining for varying, sometimes extended, periods of time. The youngsters often arrived after a fight with the custodial mother, or after they had sustained a crisis in their own lives—school failure, an arrest, or a depressive episode. Among other remarriages fathers brought children with them into the new family. In these instances, the children of both parents were likely to be closer in age and to form a subgroup within the family. One father who held joint physical custody had two children who spent half of each week in his home. As a result of this bringing together of the families, there were in some households, at any given time, five or six children, or sometimes more. The physical work was exhausting and the logistics of feeding and supervising so many lively children were at times staggering. Most of the burden fell on the mothers who generally assumed these responsibilities with energy and relatively few complaints. Aware that their husbands expected them to take over these responsibilities, most of the women kept their misgivings to themselves and worked very hard and often very successfully.

Mrs. H., a young woman of boundless energy, ran a household which for several years included four of her husband's adolescent children and two of her own younger children. In addition, she had a part-time job. She reported that "life is good." She felt amply rewarded and explained that she and her husband go off to the movies and eat out by themselves and try, successfully, to protect their privacy. Laughingly, she added, "Any parent who has two children should go out and adopt three more." She viewed the stepchildren as interesting. They had given her new relationships and her life was more rewarding now.

Another view was expressed by Mrs. C., who had actively disliked the responsibilities of managing a household and taking care of children during her first marriage, when she had only her own two children to supervise. Mrs. C. soon tired of the three additional children and the increased work that the new marriage had introduced into her life. Resentful, restless, she soon filed for her second divorce.

The siblings and stepsiblings usually settled down to friendship patterns which they enjoyed after an initial settling-in period which lasted perhaps a year in most families. Overall, most of the children liked the availability of a larger group of peers within the household to draw from if the parenting was fair and tactful in the initial phase of the remarriage, and if the management of the household was competent. The rivalries seemed somewhat keener in a larger size family, but the friendship patterns were more valued. Several children approved of their new siblings and felt that the losses associated with the divorce had been more than balanced by the acquisition of the new stepsiblings. Tom, age twelve, commented, "Kids have an easier time with divorce than grownups. They get something—a stepmom or a stepdad, more sisters or more brothers."

For those children who were less assertive, less attractive to the parents or the other children, or less able to take care of their own needs, the large group posed serious problems. Such children could easily become lost in the multitude of needs and voices. Four or five children represented a very large group for two parents to supervise, especially when the children were within the same age groups. The responsibility was too much for some adults and they grew to resent all of the children or some of the children, and in some families the children felt needy and rejected. Several children complained bitterly of less to eat, less to enjoy, less of everything, and more anger since the remarriage. Additionally, when the angers of the divorce remained unresolved, the child especially felt passed over or mistreated. The inevitable tensions of living with a larger group of other children lent themselves to becoming sources of new and continuing grievance.

## Stepsiblings and the New Mother

New relationships between the children of the father and a relatively young stepmother generated tensions. Sometimes, as we have noted earlier, they arrived in the father's home following a crisis, when they were feeling troubled and angry at the adult world. Those in mid- or late adolescence were relatively close in age to their new stepmother and frequently not a full generation apart. The young women who had recently entered a new marriage were often unprepared to be mothers to adolescent stepchildren, who brought their rebellious attitudes—which were not necessarily inappropriate to their age—into the arena of the new marriage.

The new wife was likely to feel vulnerable by virtue of the newness of the marital tie, and uncomfortable at suddenly having acquired a teenage child. The responsibilities of parenting a teenager are challenging enough to the parent who has known the child since birth within a stable family. Thrust on an anxious and unwilling parent, who is expected by the husband to take charge and successfully resolve whatever crisis has brought the adolescent to the father's home, they become very difficult indeed. In addition, the situation was often complicated by the adolescent's angry accusation that the young wife had destroyed the father's first marriage.

Mrs. H., a young mother of twenty-eight with a six-year-old child of her own, presented her problem with her fourteen-year-old stepson. He resented her bitterly and considered her a homebreaker who destroyed his parents' marriage. He had refused to accept her authority and treated her with discourtesy and sarcasm. Mrs. H. said, "I'm only fifteen years older than he is. I worry about his truancy and his poor school record and I don't know what to do." "I try very hard to be strict but he won't listen to me. I really need some help."

## Stepmothers

Although more men than women had remarried since the initial separation, their new wives had little direct influence on the lives of most of their children. Stepmothers, as a group, evinced little interest in assuming the parental role for children who remained in the custody of their mother. The relationship between children and the stepmother therefore developed very slowly despite a regular pattern of visiting and, with notable exceptions, remained of limited importance in the emotional, intellectual, or moral development of these children. About half the children had hardly any attachment at all to the new stepmother during the early years of their father's remarriage.

As with the relationship between child and stepfather, age was a significant factor in differentiating the children who established warm relationships from those who did not. Older girls were more likely than younger children to resent the stepmother and to elect not to develop a friendship with her. Younger children were more likely to develop warm, close relationships and to see more of the stepmother.

Stepmother-child relationships could make a particular contribution to the child whose mother was disturbed, depressed, or disorganized. The stepmother who was motivated to do so was able to move successfully into the breach and befriend the unhappy child or children. Stepmother and youngster under these circumstances developed close relationships. Adolescent girls, especially, turned to the stepmother for advice and a role model which they could not find in the depressed mother. Stepmothers in these relationships were valued and loved, and found these relationships rewarding. Their role with the adolescent was more likely to be that of a friend or an older sibling than that of a parent.

The stepmother's influence on the children was exercised primarily through her enormous capacity to affect the father's relationship with his children. The father's commitment to the children of his former marriage, and his capacity to remain steadfast to this commitment, depended significantly on the marital relationship within his remarriage and on the support or disapproval of the stepmother. If the stepmother felt threatened, or jealous of the time spent with the children or of the money spent when the father visited them, she could take a posture of advantage and power to discourage the father's commitment and press him to disengage from the children of the former marriage. Conversely, several stepmothers took it upon themselves to instruct the husband about the importance of fulfilling his obligation to his children. Men who had been indifferent parents during the marriage sometimes changed radically under the tutelage of the new wife. One stepmother in the group was very troubled at her husband's neglect of the children of his former marriage, and took it upon herself to invite the children to their home on birthdays and other important occasions in the life of the child. Unfortunately, her efforts to encourage the husband to be more responsible had little effect on him.

Only four babies had been born within the new marriages by the time of this follow-up, although several of the couples were planning to have children. The babies were generally enjoyed by the children of the former marriage, although the birth evoked all the same conflicted feelings that new siblings evoke in the intact family, sometimes experienced more strongly by the children's jealousy of the fact that the new stepmother was living with their father and they were not. It was, however, undeniably difficult for some men to maintain their love and high initial investment in the children of their earlier marriage and the new baby tended to reduce the father's interest in the children of the former marriage. And as the father became a new parent in the new marriage, and took his responsibility seriously as father to his new children, the time he had available for his own children and his emotional investment in them tended also to diminish gradually.

## Conclusion

Most of the remarriages, while representing only a minority of the adults, were more gratifying emotionally and sexually to the parents than the earlier marriage had been. The remarriage appeared to have catalyzed or accompanied significant psychological growth. As a group the women were happier, both as wives and as mothers, and they worked at both of these roles. The men reported less change.

The role of mother was frequently more demanding because of the presence of the husband's children and the rising anxieties of the mother's children with the entry of a stepfather into the household. The greater demands of the home were usually combined with full-time work outside the home. Although the men were helpful, the greater burden of both roles fell in a fairly traditional fashion on the women. Several women appeared to thrive in this arrangement. Others were more stressed, but most felt less stressed than they had been in the earlier marriage or during the transition period.

Remarriage was likely to create conflict in the noncustodial parent regarding continuing commitment to the children of the former marriage. The resolution of this conflict was very much affected by the attitude of the stepmother and the fragility or strength of the new marital bond, but mostly by the presence of young children living within the remarried household.

The remarriage enhanced the lives of many of the children, particularly those still in elementary school or younger. These children were better parented by happier mothers and by stepfathers who took their responsibility seriously and tried hard to fulfill a parental role. The children were contented when their relationship with their biological father was not proscribed or curtailed by the remarriage, and when the adults did not pull in opposite directions. The children did not experience conflict of loyalty which they could not resolve satisfactorily and, indeed, resolve very well if the parents were not warring with each other and competing for the child's allegiance and affection.

For approximately a quarter of the children, mostly those who were age ten or older at the time of the remarriage, the needs of the youngsters diverged from those of the remarried parents. The remarriage that brought contentment and greater maturity to the mother and the stepfather did not similarly enhance the lives of these youngsters. And although the youngster may have benefited in some important regard from the greater economic stability of the remarried family, the child's psychological needs were sometimes peripheral or antithetical to the new marital relationship, and children were explicitly excluded from its pleasure and its other benefits.

Children acquire new emotional meanings for their parents within the divorced family. Their presence inevitably perpetuates for the mother in some way the prior attachment to the divorced partner, with its balance of gratifications and disappointments, its bitterness and its sweetness combined. The extent to which the adults are able to integrate past and present for themselves, and to deal with the children in terms of the children's needs separate from their meaning within the marital battles, the divorce, and the remarriage, will govern the extent to which the children are able to share in the benefits of the remarriage.

# Chapter 17

# The Implications of the Findings

In his first year at high school, five years after his parents separated, Jeremy chose to write a term paper entitled, *What Is Divorce Like In California Today?* In his preface, he explained, "I was interested in divorce because my mother and father had a divorce and I had a vague idea of what was going on, but I did not fully understand and now I do." "In this research paper," he continued, "I shall examine such aspects of the problem as statistics, causes of divorce, and psychological inferences." He concluded his introduction with, "Some joker has said the major cause of divorce is marriage. However, we all know this joke is no joke, especially when children are involved."

After a scholarly review of divorce statistics, the provisions of family law in California, and various theories of marital disruption carefully footnoted and referenced, Jeremy concluded, "My personal experience has been a sad one. My father picked up his suitcases one day and walked out, because, as he said, he wanted his 'freedom.' We thought we were a close-knit family and it was an unexpected shock. I was only nine and my brother was six and a half. It was the death of our family. Today we see him on visitation day, but it is an artificial situation. He doesn't really know what I'm all about. I have actually lived without a real father for five years; perhaps the most important years of my male life. My luck has been that I have a mother who picked up the pieces. She acted as both parents and made her goal to bring me up as a man with true values. Divorce can destroy. It has not destroyed me. I was lucky. In my case, I think it added to my awareness and comprehension of what people and life are all about. Mainly trying to be less selfish, try to understand, rather than condemn. This is very difficult, sometimes impossible, but all I can do, right now, is to try a little harder everyday."

## Divorce as an Extended Process

Although five years, or one-third of his life, have elapsed since the marital rupture, Jeremy's attitudes and feelings are not significantly changed. His anger at his father, his sense of rejection and betrayal by his father, and his strong attachment to his mother remain relatively undiminished by the passage of time or his developmental progress into adolescence. The carefully researched school paper also represents his active and resourceful efforts at mastery of the divorce experience; efforts which must continue over many years. These youngsters taught us a lot about the extended aftermath to the marital disruption: the staying power of feelings and the repeated and enduring efforts at mastery, which are brought into play at each successive developmental stage throughout the child's growing up years and perhaps into adulthood as well.

It is just this kind of experience, multiplied many times, that has not only affirmed our view of divorce as a process that takes place over time, but has also demonstrated that the timetable of the divorcing process is considerably longer than we initially supposed. The multiple changes in the individual lives of the adults and the children and in their relationships with each other, which were set into motion by the decision to divorce, exceeded our expectations in their drama, their complexity, and their widening effects. As we bring our study to a close, it is obvious that, for many children such as Jeremy, as for many of the adults, the divorce-related issues remain open and still infused with strong feelings. Perhaps this extended timetable is realistic and expectable, and we and others have been naive in expecting quicker integrations of these major changes precipitated by the divorce.

## Divorce as a Several-Stage Process

The five-year perspective of our study enabled us to distinguish several stages in the trajectory of the divorcing process and to report separately on the experiences of the children and the adults during each of these separate, although overlapping, periods. We could follow the participants as they progressed from the initial stage of high stress to the transition period that followed and finally to living within the postdivorce or remarried family.

The initial period, following the decision to divorce and the parental separation, was profoundly stressful for almost all of the children and adolescents and for many of the adults. Feelings ran high in most families, and sexual and aggressive behaviors were no longer constrained by the marital structure. As a result, conflict often escalated and unhappiness was widespread. The children's acute responses to this stress were magnified by the parents' diminished capacity to parent at this time of crisis in their own lives.

By the end of the first year following the separation, the acute responses among the children had subsided or disappeared altogether. Many children recovered their usual functioning faster than their parents. Another unexpected finding was that girls recovered faster than boys. Those symptomatic behaviors of the children that remained after the initial phase were likely to have become chronic. The persistence of the acute early distress responses could no longer be attributed entirely to the stress of the family dissolution, but was now rather to be attributed to long standing stresses prior to the divorce or new ones in the postdivorce family.

The transition period which, in over half the families, lasted two to three years, was marked by many external changes in the social, economic, and family circumstances, as well as by changed relations within the family. Because the adults face a great many decisions which will affect the lives of the family members for many years to come and because of the relative fluidity of the family relationships at this time, we have come to consider not just the early crises but the transition period as well as the optimum time for interventions. We have attempted to capture the ambiance of this transition time in our separate reporting of the families' experiences at eighteen months after the separation, and particularly the shifting patterns in parent-child relationships which were characteristic of this period.

The third stage of the divorcing process that we observed at the five-year-mark and reported is that of the early years within the restabilized postdivorce family or the new marriage. These families were a diverse group. Some of them had succeeded in creating a stable and loving home and in improving the quality of life for all of the family members. At the other end of the wide spectrum, the adults or the children, or both together, were unhappy or were no happier than they had been during the failing marriage.

There are significant differences in the experiences of adults and children during each of these three phases of a divorcing process, which is sometimes overlooked by researchers and obscured by the general question regarding the effects of divorce. Although the initial breakup of the family is profoundly stressful, the eventual outcome depends, in large measure, not only on what has been lost, but on what has been created to take the place of the failed marriage. In full and proper perspective, the effect of the divorce is an index of the success or failure of the participants, parents and children, to master the disruption, to negotiate the transition successfully, and to create a more gratifying family to replace the family that failed.

Perhaps we should add that there might, indeed, be an additional stage. We are aware, and Jeremy's paper reminds us, that the five years of the study represent our own stopping place and not the end of the divorcing process. It may well be that some important, undetected effects, whether beneficial or detrimental, will emerge at some future time, perhaps only when these youngsters marry and become, in turn, parents in their own right.

## Differing Responses of Parents and Children

The troubling divergence between the wishes and attitudes of the children and their parents in regard to the divorce, which we noted at the time of the divorce decision, diminished somewhat by the end of five years, but had far from disappeared. We were surprised at first to find that many marriages that had been unhappy for the adults had been reasonably comfortable, even gratifying for the children, and that very few of the children concurred with their parents' decision or experienced relief at the time of the separation. Five years after the separation, most of the adults approved the divorce decision and only one fifth of them felt strongly that the divorce had been ill-advised. Among the children, however, over one-half did not regard the divorced family as an improvement over their predivorce family. Many of these youngsters, some of whom were doing well, would have preferred to turn back the clock and return to the predivorce family, despite its remembered failings.

Furthermore, most of the adults, especially the women, were feeling better, despite the greater economic pressures and the many stresses of their lives in the postdivorce family. Their self-esteem was higher and their overall psychological adjustment was considerably improved. And, as we have described, many of their somatic symptoms and their psychological dysfunctions disappeared during the postdivorce years.

Unlike the adults who felt considerably improved after the divorce, the children and adolescents did not, as a group, show an improvement in their psychological health during the years following the separation. Only those children who were physically separated by the divorce from a rejecting, or a demeaning, or a psychiatrically disturbed father showed improvement comparable to that of the adults.

At the five-year-mark, one-third of the youngsters were lively, well adjusted, and content with the general tenor of their lives. Matching these in number were youngsters who were unhappy, still angry at one or both parents, still yearning for the presence in the family of the departed parent, still lonely, needy, and feeling deprived and rejected. We have attempted at some length to demonstrate the particular combination of factors during the divorce crisis and the postdivorce evolution that led to these different outcomes.

Perhaps it should be emphasized here, however, that over and beyond the psychological functioning and developmental progress of the children even among those who had made splendid progress and certainly among those youngsters whose adjustment was only adequate or barely holding, that all had the sense of having sustained a difficult and unhappy time in their lives which had cast a shadow over their childhood or their adolescence. For some, this divorce stress eventuated in greater sensitivity and compassion. For others, the continued stress was too great to master and proved overwhelming. But for all, a significant part of their childhood or their adolescence had been a sad and frightening time.

There is considerable evidence in this study that divorce was highly beneficial for many of the adults. There is, however, no comparable evidence regarding the experience of the children. There is, in fact, no supporting evidence in this five-year study for the commonly made argument that divorce is overall better for children than an unhappy marriage or, for its opposite argument, that living within an unhappy marriage is by and large more beneficial or less detrimental than living in the divorced family. Taking the population of the children as a whole, while noting considerable individual change, the distribution of healthy and impaired functioning among children and adolescents within the conflicted marriage when compared to that five years following the marital separation strongly suggests that the divorced family was neither more nor less beneficial or stressful for the children than the unhappy marriage. Unfortunately, as we have noted throughout this book, neither unhappy marriage nor divorce are especially congenial for children; each imposes its own set of stresses.

Perhaps we should add as a cautionary note that the children within our study probably emerged at least somewhat or perhaps considerably better than a comparable group of children from nonstudied divorcing families by virtue of our limited intervention; the fact that we attracted parents with some continuing commitment to their children to participate in the study in the first place; and that the children were a relatively sturdy group of youngsters in that they had not been referred for psychological treatment at any time in their lives and had achieved age-appropriate learning and behavior within the school, despite their experiences and unhappiness within the failing and conflicted marriages. They were, moreover, drawn from a predominantly white, middle-class population and had been relatively protected from economic and social privation. It may well be that there would be considerably greater emotional decline among children in a general population.

## The Continuing Psychological Importance of Two Parents

Within the postdivorce family, the relationship between the child and both original parents did not diminish in emotional importance to the child over the five years. Although the mother's caretaking and psychological role became increasingly central in these families, the father's psychological significance *did not* correspondingly decline. Even within remarriages, at least during the earlier years of these remarriages, though the stepfather often became very quickly a prominent figure to the children, the biological father's emotional significance did not greatly diminish, although his influence on the daily life of the child lessened. It has been, in fact, strikingly apparent through the years that whether or not the children maintained frequent or infrequent contact with the noncustodial parent the children would have considered the term "one parent family" a misnomer. Their self-images were firmly tied to their relationship with both parents and they thought of themselves as children with two parents who had elected to go their separate ways. It should be noted that all of these children, except for brief separations, had lived continuously with both parents prior to the divorce.

Perhaps, given the vicissitudes of divorce and the postseparation years, each parent-child relationship is thrown in bolder relief. Lacking the intact family structure and physical presence of both parents, each parent-child relationship which is taken for granted in the intact family may become suddenly highly visible and may, in fact, be accentuated following divorce and even grow in importance, or at least be maintained in importance, by the child.

Certainly one characteristic of so many of these children was their acute, conscious, sometimes hyperalert monitoring of their parents and their parents' attitudes over the years. The cruel, erratic, openly rejecting behavior—or even abandonment—by a parent did not seem to dim the child's awareness of that parent and often did not diminish the child's compassion or longing. And as we have reported, only a few children when they reached adolescence were able to counterreject a rejecting parent with a conscious resolve to follow another road in their life by choosing to emulate another adult whom they had come both to love and respect.

Regardless of the legal allocation of responsibility and custody, the emotional significance of the relationship with each of two parents did not diminish during the five-year period that we have studied.


## The Special Vulnerability of the Divorced Family


A further consideration is the fact that the developmental needs of children do not change in accord with changes in the family structure. Unfortunately, it appears clear that the divorced family is, in many ways, less adaptive economically, socially, and psychologically to the raising of children than the two-parent family. This does not mean that it cannot be done. The children in our study who made excellent progress attest to its feasibility and to the combination of heroic efforts of parents with the resiliency of children. And, as we have seen, where one or more children were of the age, the capacity, and the inclination to take responsibility for themselves and others and to contribute to the work and emotional support of the household, the divorced family provided not only a "good enough" milieu, but one that fostered maturity and mutual devotion between parent and child. But, the fact remains that the divorced family in which the burden falls entirely, or mostly, on one parent is more vulnerable to stress, has limited economic and psychological reserves, and lacks the supporting or buffering presence of the other adult to help meet the crises of life—especially, as we have shown, the crises of physical or psychiatric illness. Even when two parents share custody and maintain their love and commitment to the children, the responsibility for raising the children usually devolves more on one parent than on the other and rarely, if ever, approaches the mutual support that parents provide for each other within the stable marriage. And, as we have reported, the chronic emotional and economic overload was frequently intolerable for the custodial parent, and the cumulative effect on the children was all too visible in their unhappiness and depression.

Our considerable concern increased over the years as we became familiar with the extraordinary absence of supports in the social surround, which appeared to be characteristic of so many middle-class families within our population. Perhaps the absence of supports places children in white, middle-class families in some ways more at risk during periods of stress than children in other socioeconomic and ethnic groups who have a sense of extended family and community.

Furthermore, our findings reflect the significance of the parenting that is going on within the present. Those children who did well were well-parented by at least one parent at that time. It appears that the nurturance provided during earlier years will hold the child for a while, but that good, or at least "good enough," parenting continuing over time is needed to safeguard and to maintain good developmental progress in children.

More than any other constellation of factors the disrupted or diminished parenting by one or both parents was associated with the dismayingly high incidence of depression which we found at each of the checkpoints of the study and most especially at five years. In fact, the five-year postseparation incidence of depression which was higher than that observed at eighteen months postseparation reflects the stresses and emotional deficits of the postdivorce family well after the acute responses to the breakup have subsided or disappeared altogether.

This ongoing need by the child for competent, nurturant parenting places a continuing demand on the parent who assumes full or major responsibility for the child's upbringing. In order to fulfill the responsibility of childrearing and provide even minimally for the needs of the adult, many divorced families are in urgent need of a formal and informal network of services not now available to them in the community. The first steps toward easing the burdens of the parent and enhancing the quality of life within the family should include, our findings indicate, setting child support payments at a level that reflects realistically the cost of raising children; providing educational, vocational and financial counseling combined with training and employment programs for adults returning to the economic or professional marketplace after a several-year absence; enriched child-care and after-school programs and facilities for children of various ages as well as divorce specific counseling programs (which we will describe later in this chapter). Although it is still not clear whether and to what extent supportive services are able to substitute for lacunae within the family structure, nevertheless, even if we regard such services as supplementary or secondary, the divorced family is at high risk when it stands alone.

## Issues of Custody

Taken as a whole our findings point to the desirability of the child's continuing relationship with both parents during the postdivorce years in an arrangement which enables each parent to be responsible for and genuinely concerned with the well-being of the children. For those parents who are able to reach an agreement on child related matters after divorce and are willing to give the needs of the children priority or a significant role in their decision-making regarding how and where the children reside, joint legal custody may provide the legal structure of choice. (The parents of one-quarter of the children in our study who had been able to maintain a shared commitment and devoted parenting within the conflicted marriage would provide an appropriate pool of candidates for joint custody.) Although the influence of the legal structure on the fabric of family life may be considerably less than many persons believe it to be, nevertheless, there is some evidence that legal accountability may influence and shore up psychological and financial responsibility. Furthermore, there is evidence in our findings, that lacking legal rights to share in decisions about major aspects of their children's lives, that many noncustodial parents withdrew from their children in grief and frustration. Their withdrawal was experienced by the children as a rejection and was detrimental in its impact.

In viewing joint legal custody as a reasonable step, we differentiate shared legal responsibility and shared physical custody. Both concepts require clarification in law and research. Some mistakenly view joint physical custody as requiring a strict sharing of the child's time on an equal or fifty–fifty basis. Actually, joint physical custody can take many forms, and parents can negotiate or modify a division of time in consideration of the needs of the children and of the adults. Central to the notion of shared physical custody is an understanding that it does not mean a precise apportioning of the child's life, but a concept of two committed parents, in two separate homes, caring for their youngsters in a postdivorce atmosphere of civilized, respectful exchange.

There appears to be no compelling legal reason to pattern the divorced family after the married family and to establish one presumptive pattern for all couples. Parents may have little interest in their children; they may demean or exploit their children; they may use the children to establish a permanent foothold in the divorced partner's life. Moreover, joint custody poses many logistical problems because of the mobility of adults in American life and the high incidence of remarriage.

Our findings point, however, to the undesirability of routinely designating one parent as "the psychological parent" and of lodging sole legal and physical custody in that one parent. Such an arrangement has been interpreted by the courts to presume that the child does not have two psychological parents. This finding can be devastating to child and parent when both parents are indeed committed to a continuing relationship with their children.

In taking a position in favor of flexibility and encouragement of joint legal custody where feasible, as a symbol of society's recognition of the child's continuing need for both parents, we offer a view diametrically opposed to that of our esteemed colleagues Goldstein, Freud, and Solnit in their book *Beyond the Best Interests of the Child.*° Although we share a common psychodynamic framework with these colleagues, we have in the course our research, arrived at findings and recommendations which are greatly at variance with their views. Our findings regarding the centrality of both parents to the psychological health of children and adolescents alike leads us to hold that, where possible, divorcing parents should be encouraged and helped to shape postdivorce arrangements which permit and foster continuity in the children's relations with both parents.

## Building Blocks for Constructing Preventive Intervention

We began this work with the conviction that divorce is and should remain a readily available option to adults who are unhappily married. Our findings, although somewhat graver than expected, have not changed our conviction. They have given greater impetus to our interest in easing the family rupture for children and adults alike and in providing a knowledge base in the real experiences of divorcing families for informed parenting as well as for improved legal, educational, and psychological interventions which can prevent, or at least mitigate, unhappy and psychopathological outcomes for the children.

---

° Joseph Goldstein, Anna Freud, and Albert J. Solnit, *Beyond the Best Interests of the Child* (New York: Free Press, 1973).

Therefore, a major goal of our work, which we described at the outset, was to formulate beginning models of expectable response or norms for divorce-related reactions of children and adolescents and their expectable duration following the marital rupture. The unavailability of such formulations or norms has severely handicapped parents and those who undertake to help parents in their efforts to fashion appropriate measures which will provide comfort and relief to the children. Additionally, in the absence of knowledge regarding normative responses and the expectable duration of these responses, it has been difficult to identify those children whose behavior reflected the need for special interventions.

Our study has indicated that divorce is predictably extremely stressful to most children and adolescents and that the physical separation of the parents, which was regarded by most youngsters as the central divorce event, precipitated a wide range of feelings and behavioral changes at home, at school, and on the playground. Despite significant individual differences, the children's age and developmental stage appeared to be the most important factors in governing their initial responses. The stage of development profoundly influenced the child's need of the parents and perception of the stress, as well as the child's understanding, coping, and defensive strategies.

The patterning of response into these four age-related groupings—preschool (two and a half to five), early school age (six to eight), later school age (nine to twelve), and adolescence—may provide the basis for the beginning norms which we have sought. Precisely because we did not start out with these a priori groups and because the patterns which we have conceptualized did not primarily reflect the individual's family experience or the child's predivorce experience, and did reflect the age and developmental achievement of the child, we propose that these groupings are likely to have wide applicability to children in many divorcing families. They may reflect children's responses to acute stress within a more general framework—and not only to marital rupture. Perhaps their usefulness will extend only to predominantly white, middle-class children in communities where the nuclear family is the predominant family structure. Or it may be that we will find that some major experiences, such as loss, death, and divorce, and the feelings that they evoke in children span broad social, economic, racial, and ethnic differences.

As an example of one such formulation, we have suggested that the preschool child, following the marital rupture, is likely to regress behaviorally; is likely to be preoccupied with anxiety about who will provide the continued care which the child feels that he or she requires; is likely to worry about being abandoned by both parents; is more likely than his or her older siblings to feel responsible for causing the divorce and driving one parent away; is likely to be troubled at the many separations of day and bedtime and to find these threatening and distressing; is likely to be tearful, irritable, and more aggressive; and is likely to suffer an inhibition in play. Although the preschool children often suffer more intense fears than their older siblings, and have fewer inner resources to help them, their fears are more easily allayed by concerned parents and their symptoms yield more quickly to appropriate reassurance and continued contact with both parents.

The findings among children within the other age groups can be similarly extrapolated to suggest a particular range of expectable behaviors. There is not enough evidence at this time to suggest that behavior that does not fall within these ranges is deviant. Nor is there evidence to suggest that children who show little or no overt change in feelings are either more or less troubled than their peers who appear more openly distressed. The considerable usefulness of these norms that we have suggested is that they may serve to alert adults toward future behavior of the children and to facilitate sensitive and informed parenting as well as professional advice.

## When to Divorce

Within this frame of reference of beginning knowledge of responses and expectable outcomes, and drawing on our findings at the five-year mark, we can approach the question parents frequently ask, namely, "Should the children's ages govern the timing of our divorce decision?" or, as more frequently put, "Should we wait for the children to reach a particular age before divorcing and what would that age be?"

Our findings suggest that in the long run neither age nor sex are central factors in determining outcome. At the onset young children tend to show more acute and more global responses to the divorce than their older brothers and sisters. And girls, as we have described, tended to recover significantly faster than boys from the initial unhappy reaction to the parental separation. But, by five years, the factors that contributed to good outcome and to poor outcome were related to the configurations of factors which we have elaborated and which reflect primarily the quality of the relationship with both parents, the quality of life within the divorced family, and the extent to which the divorce itself provided the remedy which the adults sought. Neither the age nor the sex of the child were as relevant at this time.

Thus, the age of the child should be carefully considered in anticipating expectable early responses to the parental separation and the average duration of these responses. Further, the age of the child should be considered carefully in providing the appropriate explanation of the parental decision, in supporting the child, and in establishing appropriate postdivorce family arrangements. The readiness of the parents to provide the appropriate supports to the children and to make and implement careful planning on behalf of the children should enter prominently into the timing of the divorce decision.

Perhaps we should add that little is known of the psychological effects of burdening children with the knowledge that their parents remained together within an unhappy marriage on their behalf. Our sense is that this would tax the child heavily.

## At What Age Should Children's Preferences Be Followed

Although the wishes of children always merit careful consideration, our work suggests that children below adolescence are not reliable judges of their own best interests and that their attitudes at the time of the divorce crisis may be very much at odds with their usual feelings and inclinations.

One unexpected finding which emerged serendipitously in our search for norms was the dividing line between those children in the first three grades and those in the fourth to sixth grades in their responses to the family rupture and in their relationships with both parents. Psychological theory, while recognizing the continued developmental progress of the child, does not shed light on some of the significant attributes of children at the threshold of adolescence. The long-lasting anger of children in the nine-to-twelve-year-old group at the parent whom they held responsible for the divorce; the eagerness of these youngsters to be co-opted into the parental battling; their willingness to take sides, often against a parent to whom they had been tenderly attached during the intact marriage; and the intense, compassionate, caretaking relations which led these youngsters to attempt to rescue a distressed parent often to their own detriment have led us to rethink our expectations of these children. Furthermore, their particular age-related propensity to split the parents into the "good parent" and the "bad parent" (which was often at odds with the role of the respective parents over the years and which seemed to be rooted primarily in the children's own acute fears) led us further to doubt their capacity to make informed judgment about plans which would be in their own best interests. These observations, and the fact that several of the youngsters with the most passionate convictions at the time of the breakup later came shamefacedly to regret their vehement statements at that time, have increased our misgivings about relying on the expressed opinions and preferences of youngsters below adolescence in deciding the issues which arise in divorce-related litigation.

## Some Expectable Changes in the Parent-Child Relationships

The many observations about parent–child relationships which we have attempted to report in detail offer another set of building blocks for preventive or clinical intervention and enlightened parenting.

We have reported as widespread a diminished capacity to parent at the time of the family breakup which, while often temporary, may have long-lasting implications and may significantly affect the coping capacities of both children and adolescents and the perseverance of symptomatic behaviors and distressed feelings.

Additionally, a range of expectable patterns of behavior parallel to those which we have proposed for the children's reactions emerges regarding the child's relationships with each parent at nodal points during the divorcing process. We have at some length considered the visiting relationship, spurred on by our surprising discovery that by eighteen months after the separation there was no correlation between the regularity or frequency of the visits by the parent and the predivorce relationship. Recognizing that the part-time parent/part-time child visiting relationship has no real counterpart within the intact family, we have attempted to elicit those factors which promote and foster the continued relationship of the visiting parent and the visited child and those factors which are likely to contribute to its diminution. These and related findings regarding the difficulties inherent in the visiting relationship, its early fragility, combined with its long-term importance for the child and perhaps the father and mother as well, all have many implications for parents, for those who aid parents, and for the courts. Our findings argue against burdening the visiting relationship with severe restrictions of legal constraints which make it more difficult for parents and children to seek out each other's company in response to their own wishes or needs.

Similarly, we have been impressed with the vicissitudes of the relationship between the custodial parent and the child. Such relationships may cause distress and confusion for many parents which decrease their capacity to distinguish the children's needs from their own and which are detrimental to discipline and orderly household routines. However as the changed perceptions that occurred in the wake of the parental separation were accepted, there gradually (sometimes very gradually) emerged improved relationships and a real sense of a "new chance."

The psychological consequences of these changes for the children and for the adolescents have held our attention as we have come to regard these changes as centrally significant—and as expectable components of the divorcing process. Although these changes and their respective outcome reflected age and developmental differences among the children, they also reflected sex differences and sibling order and sibling relations as well as considerably individual variation.

## The Postdivorce Family

A major conclusion regarding the effects of divorce is that the relationships within the postdivorce family are likely to govern long-range outcomes for children and adolescents. Put simply, the central hazard which divorce poses to the psychological health and development of children and adolescents is in the diminished or disrupted parenting which so often follows in the wake of the rupture and which can become consolidated within the postdivorce family. Thus when the divorce is undertaken thoughtfully by parents who have carefully considered alternatives; when the parents have recognized the expectable psychological, social, and economic consequences for themselves and the children; when they have taken reasonable measures to provide comfort and appropriate understanding to the children; where they have made arrangements to maintain good parent-child relationships with both parents—then those children are not likely to suffer developmental interference or enduring psychological distress as a consequence of the divorce. Even though the children may still regret the divorce and continue to wish that their parents had been able to love each other, some of these children may nevertheless grow in their capacity for compassion and psychological understanding.

Alternatively, if the divorce is undertaken primarily as a unilateral decision which humiliates, angers, or grieves the other partner and these feelings continue to dominate the postdivorce relationship of the divorced partners; if the divorce fails to bring relief from marital stress or to improve the quality of life for the divorcing adults; if the children are poorly supported and poorly informed or co-opted as allies or fought over in the continuing battle and viewed as extensions of the adults; if the relationship with one or both parents is impoverished or disrupted, and the child feels rejected; if the stresses and deprivation of the postdivorce family are no less than those of the failed marriage—then the most likely outcome for the children is developmental interference and depression.

The end result of a successfully established postdivorce family can be an improved quality of life for adults and for children. The results of the failed divorce are likely to be low self-esteem and depression, accompanied by a continued feeling of deprivation or continued anger for children and adolescents which can endure for many years.

## Help for Divorcing Parents and Their Children

During the next decade the expectable life cycle of a significant proportion of American families is likely to include divorce and remarriage. Perhaps it is time to take their needs seriously—to provide help which will safeguard the children and provide guidance to their concerned parents. Our findings amply document the freestanding character of the nuclear family at these critical junctures; the striking unavailability of supports for the children, and the absence of resources for information and guidance. Parents who are uncertain about what to do have no reliable place to turn. Most cannot draw on their own personal histories for models in their new situation; there is little accumulated wisdom and the many new roles of the visiting parent, joint custody, father custody, and stepparent are in the process of evolving—and the rules are not clearly defined. As a result, people are thrown back even more on the passions or anxieties of the moment in making decisions with long-range consequences for themselves and their children.

It is a curious phenomenon that family policy in this country has recognized the state's responsibility to offer services in family planning, for prospective children still unborn, but has left parents alone to deal with most of the issues that arise after the children are born. Perhaps the time has come for a more realistic family policy, one that addresses the expectable metamorphoses of the American family and the stress points of change.

Divorcing parents, as we have seen, face a bewildering array of tasks in putting their own lives in new and better order and in shaping the relationships of the postdivorce family. Many will need help in setting up postdivorce arrangements for the children and especially in arriving at the mutual understanding on which such arrangements must be based in order to endure. For people who have decided to separate from each other in sorrow and anger, joint planning is very difficult to achieve.

Many adults will need the skilled help of a neutral counselor or clinician who is well versed in the psychology of children and in the knowledge of the expectable effects of divorce on the child's development and the, parent-child relationship. Such help, we propose, should be made available to divorcing families. We have come to regard the ready availability of such services as a necessary adjunct in a responsible society to the accessibility of divorce. As our experience has convinced us, guidance for parents is needed, welcomed, and well used if offered appropriately at the right time and within the right context. The timing of the help early in the divorcing process is crucial to its success.

Even within our own very limited intervention, two-fifths of the men and a somewhat greater number of the women characterized the counseling which was offered as useful and supportive and were still following suggestions which had been made at the first meetings five years earlier. Long before we knew what we have since learned, one of our first surprises was the avidity with which parents, especially fathers, whipped out pad and pencil and wrote down our suggestions. We wondered then what we had said that they considered worth noting. Gradually, we realized the extent of their perplexity and their great need for guidance which led them to grasp at our sometimes very obvious advice.

People need help as the marriage declines and at the point that they decide to divorce. They don't know how to tell their children and, as we have seen, they often neglect to do so. They need help in providing proper support to the children during the transitional time. They need help for themselves and their children, in preparing for the many changes (economic, social, and psychological) which are expectable in the postdivorce family and in setting up appropriate joint plans for continued care of the children when at all possible. Parents may also need help later on as they contemplate remarriage and wish to prepare themselves and their children for the gratifications and tasks which they are likely to encounter within the remarried family. They will also need help for themselves at each of these junctures. We are hopeful that the findings of this study can provide beginning guideposts at the critical turns along this road.

Finally, it should be noted that divorcing with children requires of the adults who had once been together the capacity to maintain entirely separate social and sexual roles while continuing their cooperation as parents on behalf of their children. This is difficult and requires the kind of commitment that parents have often, but not always, made to their children. Perhaps only a society which values continuity in relationships and steadfast commitment to its children is likely to reward such complex behavior with approval sufficient to enable it to happen.

# Appendix A

# Method and Sample

## Initial Contact

The sixty families who participated in this study came initially for a six-week divorce counseling service. The service was conceptualized and advertised as a preventive program and was offered free of charge to all families in the midst of divorce. Parents learned of the service through attorneys, school teachers, counselors, social agencies, ministers, friends, and newspaper articles describing divorce as an expectable period of high stress. A few families in litigation over custody or visitation were referred by the superior court. All parents came with the understanding that our counseling service was child-centered, preventive, planning-oriented, time-limited, and voluntary.

Two criteria for participation in the project were established at the outset. The separation of the parents was a precondition for beginning, as was the legal step of filing for a divorce. Presumably, both of these actions demonstrated serious intent to divorce on the part of at least one parent.

### Structure of the Service

Families in the divorce counseling service understood from the outset that the brief intervention was part of a larger research project, and that our roles as clinician and researcher were interrelated.

Every family member was seen individually. Our research objective in seeing parents and children separately, and in getting independent information from the schools, was to obtain a complex and rich set of data about each family collectively and as individuals within that family. The potential pitfalls of interviewing just one family member about a family's overall divorce experience were convincingly demonstrated throughout the history of the project. These multiple sets of data enabled us to triangulate often irreconcilable appearing data into a meaningful psychological portrait of the family and its members in the midst of divorce.

Each parent was interviewed weekly over a six-week period; each child was seen for three to four sessions beginning after the first two sessions with parents. Parent interviews ranged from an hour to one and one-half hours; most child sessions were fifty minutes. Families were not excluded because one family member refused to be involved. Generally, the same clinician saw all family members, but occasionally two staff members shared parents and children if time considerations or particular expertise dictated such an arrangement.

The average number of interviews per family was fifteen. Despite our intention to see each parent for six sessions, mothers were seen more frequently than fathers. We observed greater motivation for counseling on the part of the women, in part because their new role as single parent created high anxiety. And the pressing agendas they brought to counseling for handling their upset and angry children required more hours than were needed with fathers. With school and office interviews, detailed dictations, and staff case presentations, the average time devoted to each family at the initial contact was thirty hours.

At the end of the original six-week session, families were invited to return a year later for follow-up consultations and research and were assured of the clinician's availability in the interim should questions or problems arise.

## Obtaining the Data

When we met with parents and children, we had well-formed questions but no questionnaire. Each clinician was familiar with detailed parent and child forms outlining the many things we were interested in learning about family members, relationships, and circumstances.

OBTAINING INFORMATION FROM PARENTS. The first two or three sessions with parents were informally structured to provide us with a basic fund of knowledge about each family before and during the divorce crisis. Sufficient understanding of marital and family relationships was important in assessing the impact of the divorce on children and adults alike. We asked parents to describe the history of the failure of their marriage. We sought details of the balance of gratifications as well as stresses and conflict within the marriage and the shifts over time in this balance. This information helped us understand and place in context the decision to divorce.

Second, we sought specific details regarding the decision to divorce: who made it, and the extent to which the other spouse or children participated in the decision-making process in contrast to being shocked by a sudden announcement. Our interest was in the extent of preparation of each family member for the divorce. And it was critical to determine the events and related psychological ambiance of the actual separation once the decision to divorce was communicated. The divorce-engendered angers, threats, counterthreats, and newly-occurring physical violence often represented an abrupt change for children who lived in families without a prior history of intense conflict.

A third major focus was on family relationships, particularly parent-child relationships, during the marriage. One reason for assessing the quality of these relationships prior to divorce was to determine in a sense what, if anything, the child was losing. The loss of a close-knit, nurturing family was likely to have different meaning to a child than one in which every member had customarily gone his independent way without regard for the others.

Fourth, we were interested in each parent's view of his child, any changes they had noted over time, and the current status of the relationship.

We asked parents what and how they told their children of the marital dispute and divorce, and what responses or changed behaviors, if any, were noted after separation. With the custodial parent, we sought information on stresses, capacities to cope, and the gratifications inherent, if any, in assuming a new role as single parent. We learned their view, as well, of their children's continued contact with the visiting parent. And with the visiting parent a special area of inquiry focused on visiting plans, patterns, and frustrations. With both parents, we were interested in their views of the future for themselves and their children.

And, finally, we noted the parents' current social, economic, and work situations and their plans for the future. We determined whether moves, changes in employment, social life, or marriage were foreseen, and to what extent such plans would affect their children's lives.

All of this basic information, plus that which was unique to each family's history and current situation, enabled us to develop interlocking sets of formulations about the parents' own central psychological responses to the divorce impact and their motivation and available capacities to assume or continue the role of parent within the structure of the postdivorce family. These assessments, combined with comparable assessments of the children, formed the basis of the counseling strategies and agendas.

Perhaps it is appropriate to state here our observation and belief that parents were, for the most part, willing to share vast amounts of intimate, often painfully sensitive, information precisely because they were eager for help and we were interested in helping. Our investment in the well-being of their children was clear from the start as we addressed the parent primarily in his or her parenting role. We began early to make psychological connections between new behaviors and divorce-induced stress; we quickly established ourselves in a direct helping role. The rich and extensive information so gathered is one of the strengths of the project, and we recognize as well that our active participation may have influenced the later adjustment of some of the youngsters.

The quality of the real and psychological relationship that developed between clinician and family was different from the more usual therapeutic relationship, a difference that emerged with startling clarity at the one- and five-year follow-ups. The parents in our project fell into a very special category that we have as yet been unable to describe. They were not subjects, colleagues, patients, clients, or friends, and yet they were all of these. For them, too, we were counselors, therapists, colleagues, conscience-prodders, and friends, yet not exclusively any of these.

SEEING THE CHILDREN. We advised parents to tell their children that we were available especially to help children when their parents were getting a divorce. The younger children raised little resistance to coming and many of them wished to remain or were cross or sad when our time ended.

A few adolescents refused to come. Most of those who came did so reluctantly or out of a sense of obligation to their parents. Not uncommonly, many of them stayed for an hour and a half during their first visit and returned willingly.

We saw children and adolescents alone in office-playrooms that were well supplied with the usual play therapy equipment, including dollhouses and family dolls. After initially exploring and clarifying, if necessary, what the children understood of their visits with us, we invited them to play and to talk. At some point during the sessions each child was asked to draw a picture of his or her family.

With the children, as with the adults, we relied upon the ability to triangulate data from a variety of independent sources in order to form an understanding of the child's experience with the divorce and with each of his parents. We had each parent's observations, independent school observations, the child's own feelings, words, and behavior as expressed with the clinical interviewer, and the developmental-clinical perspective of the clinician for each child.

DIVORCE-SPECIFIC ASSESSMENT. Our major interest in seeing the child was a child-centered, focused assessment of each child's response to the divorce stress. A detailed psychological assessment or developmental profile of each child was impossible due to the constraints of the short-term intervention. What we wanted to establish directly was whether the child or adolescent had achieved the usual psychological and developmental milestones appropriate to his age against which we could then measure the effects of current divorce-engendered stresses. What evolved and was refined in the course of the research project and clinical service was a Divorce-Specific Assessment of Children, described elsewhere by the authors, which incorporated a basic understanding of the child's psychological functioning, but focused specifically on divorce and divorce-related change for each child.

The three major areas of inquiry within this Divorce-Specific Assessment included: (1) the child's unique response to and experience with his parents' separation and divorce; (2) continuity and change in parent-child relationships; and (3) the network of support systems outside of the home available to the child.

The initial divorce experience in its broadest sense included each child's thoughts, fantasies, emotional and behavioral responses to the divorce, the extent to which pain and anxiety were consciously experienced, and the various inner psychological resources deployed to deal with the stress. Throughout, we sought to determine the influence of the child's own developmental position on his response and whether his experience was heavily influenced by conscious or unconscious parental pressures and activities.

We wanted, of course, to explore each child's understanding of his parents' divorce—what he had been told, how he understood the parents' various explanations, and what were his private ideas about the divorce. Determining the youngsters' predominant emotional and behavioral responses to divorce was, of course, a central goal of the initial phases of the project. A further interest was the pervasiveness of the child's responses to the divorce. Was his behavior similar in all settings —that is, father's home, mother's home, school, playground, and office? Or did the child contain and hold inside certain feelings in one place and express them in another?

The child's usual style of coping with life was of interest in order to compare it with his defensive and coping strategies in response to the stress of divorce. In this connection, we looked for new behaviors, specifically the appearancce of new symptoms.

A second aspect of the Divorce-Specific Assessment was the close scrutiny of the *current* parent-child relationship as seen through the eyes of the child. The child's relationships with the custodial parent and the visiting parent must be studied separately at the time of the divorce. Because parent-child relationships are fluid and subject to radical changes in character under such stress, we felt it important to evaluate the extent to which the relationship with each parent was providing support, promoting development, and holding the potential for future growth.

Support systems take on particular significance at times of crisis for children, especially when the crisis may involve an extended period of disorganization. To determine the helpfulness of extrafamilial supports, we studied the nature of support provided by siblings, peers, grandparents and other extended family, the school, teachers, and extracurricular activities.

The processes of obtaining information and providing empathic support and clarification were intertwined. Each enhanced the other. We could not have learned from children what we did without providing a brief, focused intervention simultaneously. The promise of confidentiality was important in gaining their trust, and our willingness to be advocates for them, if needed, was appreciated.

### The Data Analyses

Following each session with parents and children, full process recordings were dictated by the clinical interviewer and then transcribed. With parents, but not with children, copious notes were made during the sessions, capturing whenever possible their comments verbatim. Interviewers reported not only what was said by parents and children, but also their clinical observations of the interchanges.

CODING THE DATA. At the completion of the initial phase of the Divorce Counseling Service, data forms were constructed by the authors in order to encode the large amount of data collected. The Parent Data Form, containing 290 items, included demographic and factual data about the families, their marriages, and separation(s). Each parent's report of the economic stability within the marriage, for example, or the frequency of violent episodes between spouses, or suicidal attempts, was coded. In addition, a large number of scales were devised to assess the psychological functioning and social experiences of each spouse in the marriage and after separation. Most often these were five- or seven-point scales, ranging from the absence or minimal appearance of a variable to its full or extreme expression.

The Child Data Form, with 231 items, encoded basic demographic data for each child, the various changes in his environment, and detailed ratings of each child's response to and experience with the parents' divorce. It was only after we completed the initial phase of research that we knew the range and extent of variables to include in this area. Further, for each child there were ratings of his intellectual, academic, social, cognitive, and psychological status. The quality of parent-child relationships, changes in parenting consequent to divorce, and visiting attitudes and patterns were also given ratings. The various ratings for each child represented, where relevant, a composite score, taking into account all the sources of information available. In assessing, for example, the extent of anger or sadness generated by the divorce, reports from parents, child, and teachers, and the clinical interviewer's observations were jointly considered in making the final rating. Other variables had as their base one or two sources of data, as, for example, the child's own expression to the interviewer of greatly conflicted loyalty between parents that his parents were as yet unaware of.

The authors completed all of these data forms for each family, rating approximately 1,400 items for an average family with two children. The process was then repeated for the follow-up material, using slightly modified, shortened Follow-Up Data Forms at the first follow-up and considerably shorter forms at the second follow-up. The coded data for each family member were then punched into IBM cards for statistical analyses.

ANALYZING THE DATA. In the early stages of the Children of Divorce Project, before all follow-ups were completed, the child data were organized and analyzed clinically by visual inspection. The earliest papers published from this project reflect that effort. Following the five-year interviews, all parent and child data from the three points of contact were analyzed statistically by computer, utilizing a mix of statistical methods and tests.

For purposes of readability, we have opted to report a minimum of statistical data, other than frequencies, in the text of this book. In describing real differences between the sexes or age groups, or in noting important relationships between variables, however, we have reported those that were statistically significant and have reserved the use of the words "significant" or "associated with" for this purpose.

Initially, frequency tables and means were obtained for all adult and child variables. With the children, our clinical observation that some initial responses to divorce were determined primarily by age was tested by dividing the 131 children into the following six age groups: two to four years old, five to six years, seven to eight years, nine to ten years, eleven to twelve years, and thirteen to eighteen years. All child variables were analyzed by these six age groups and by sex of child. These age groupings were retained in inspecting the first follow-up data as well, and analyses of variance were performed to determine which of the age and sex, or age-sex, differences represented statistically significant differences. Later statistical and psychological inspection of this data led us to combine the children in four larger groups for continued statistical analyses: the two to five-year-olds, six to eight years, nine to twelve years, and thirteen to eighteen-year-olds. In general, when we report age differences in these chapters, at counseling and at each follow-up, the results of the analyses of variance using these age groups are reported.

In looking for relationships between variables, for example, the link between the father's own divorce-engendered psychological responses and the frequency and pattern of visiting his children, correlation studies and factor analyses were extensively used. These are among the most effective statistical procedures for analyzing large amounts of raw data. Correlation matrices allow one to examine the degree of relatedness between pairs of variables, and to determine if their correlations are statistically significant. Factor analysis is an extension of the correlation technique in which one can determine the contribution that each variable in a selected cluster of variables makes to a larger factor.

In order to ensure that the correlation and factor analyses yielded data that were statistically reliable, we selected, using previous data analyzing age differences, four larger groups of children when looking for age-sex differences: boys two to eight, girls two to eight, boys nine to eighteen, girls nine to eighteen. Sometimes we looked additionally at all two to six, seven to twelve, and thirteen to eighteen year olds if the data warranted it. Parent data were usually analyzed by sex of parent and sometimes age was also an independent variable.

# The Research Sample

The majority (88 percent) of the families were white, a few (3 percent) were black, and a small number (9 percent) were interracial marriages in which one partner was Asian. The racial and socioeconomic distribution of our sample paralleled that of the suburban county in which the study was located. The distribution of the families along social class dimensions, as determined by occupation and educational level * can be seen in Table 1.

TABLE 1
*Social Class Distribution at Initial Contact*

| Social Class | | Percentage (N = 60) |
|---|---|---|
| I | (high) | 23 |
| II | | 20 |
| III | | 28 |
| IV | | 18 |
| V | (low) | 10 |

## The Parents

WORK HISTORY. Among the poorest families were some where the father and/or mother were chronically unemployable for reasons of emo-

* August B. Hollingshead, "Two Factor Index of Social Position." Unpublished manuscript, Yale University, New Haven, Conn., 1957.

tional instability and a larger group who were frequently laid off in a tightening labor market. A few other men had dropped out of their jobs during the marriage in response to the temptations of a new and more carefree lifestyle.

In the two years before the marital separation, half of the women had worked, a substantial number of them in full-time jobs. Some of these women had worked out of economic necessity, either to complement a husband's low salary or to provide the family's sole source of income. The county in which the study took place has had one of the highest cost of living indices in the country, creating more economic hardship for the lower-middle- and lower-class families. Other women working full time were preparing for divorce and worked willingly to establish economic independence. But almost half of the women had not worked before or during the marriage and, because of their age and lack of job experience, were viewed realistically as unemployable.

EDUCATION. The educational attainments of the parents were considerable (see Table 2).

TABLE 2

*Educational Level of Parents at Initial Contact*

|                        | Percentage of Fathers | Percentage of Mothers |
|------------------------|-----------------------|-----------------------|
| Less than high school  | 5                     | 2                     |
| High school diploma    | 13                    | 22                    |
| Some college           | 23                    | 42                    |
| College degree         | 22                    | 25                    |
| Some graduate work     | 10                    | 5                     |
| Graduate degree        | 27                    | 3                     |

The largest group of women married during their college years and ceased their formal education at that time. The majority had not developed or maintained marketable skills commensurate with their intellectual capacity or interests. Early pregnancies played a significant role in the diminished economic experience for many women.

COURTSHIP AND LENGTH OF MARRIAGE. The average length of courtship was sixteen months; the range was two months to seven years. One-third of the couples were rushed into precipitous marriage by unplanned pregnancy.

These were first marriages for all but 10 percent of the men and 7 percent of the women. The average length of marriage was eleven years, prior to separation, with a range of four to twenty-three years. Those pregnant when married separated sooner (mean = eight years) but did not differ in family size from the overall group. At the time of separation, the mean age of the men was thirty-seven years (range = twenty-five to fifty-seven years), and the mean age of the women was thirty-four years (range = twenty-three to fifty-three years). The marriages in our sample, when compared to a national average of seven years for all couples filing for separation, were of longer duration. The difference may in part be accounted for by the presence of children in the families in our study.

THE MENTAL HEALTH OF THE PARENTS. We made clinical judgments of the general psychological functioning of each parent during the marriage based on parental self-description, cross-spouse descriptions, and our own observations. In some cases our task was made easier by recounts of hospitalization for severe mental illness, suicide attempts, severe psychosomatic illnesses, work histories riddled with unsatisfactory performance, or arrests for assault. Conversely, the predivorce evidence for those who functioned well in occupations, within the family, or in continued schooling, was often obtained and confirmed through both spouses.

We grouped the men and women into three large categories: (1) those whose functioning overall during the life history of the marriage was generally adequate or better; (2) those who were for the most part moderately disturbed or frequently incapacitated by disabling neuroses and addictions; and (3) a group of severely disturbed adults whose erratic, sometimes bizarre, thinking and behavior were a major presence in the family life.

One-third of the men and the women fell into the first category of generally adequate psychological functioning. These adults coped with family, occupation, household responsibilities, and the ups and downs of unsatisfactory marriages in an average, if not at times exemplary, fashion.

In the second group of moderately troubled individuals were 50 percent of the men and close to half of the women. Here were the chronically depressed, sometimes suicidal individuals, the men and women with severe neurotic difficulties or with handicaps in relating to another person, or those with long-standing problems in controlling their rage or sexual impulses.

And finally, 15 percent of the men and 20 percent of the women were found by us to be severely troubled during their marriages, perhaps throughout their lives. These individuals had histories of mental illness including paranoid thinking, bizarre behavior, manic-depressive illnesses, and generally fragile or unsuccessful attempts to cope with the demands of life, marriage, and family.

The psychological status or well-being of the fathers and mothers did not differ significantly by the sex of the youngsters. There was a trend, however, for the fathers of the younger children to be in better mental health than the fathers of the older youngsters ($p < .05$). This difference was not true for the mothers of the children studied.

PSYCHOTHERAPY DURING THE MARRIAGE. More than a third of the men entered therapy or counseling during the marriage. The largest number of these men were involved in conjoint marital counseling with their wives. With a few exceptions these men were those in the moderately impaired or mentally healthiest group. The largest number were in therapy from two to twenty months. Most often for the men the therapy was in the context of attempting to resolve marital difficulties and was of brief duration. It was sometimes undertaken to appease a wife who insisted on joint participation in therapy as a precondition for accepting the husband's wish for a divorce. More than three fifths of the men had not sought therapy prior to their divorce. Among this group were those whose overall mental health was good, as well as some who gave evidence of considerable psychological disturbance but saw no need for any psychological assistance.

More than half of the women had been engaged in some form of psychotherapy during the marriage, but unlike the men, the majority of these were in individual treatment. The women tended to stay longer in therapy, and more often than the men used their individual psychotherapy as the eventual springboard out of the marriage. A large number of these women entered into at least one other form of therapy in addition to their individual treatment, usually group or conjoint marital counseling. It should be noted that the county in which the study was located was rich in both community and private therapeutic resources, and that the community-based therapeutic services were highly visible and available for minimal fees to those with limited incomes.

OTHER SUPPORT NETWORKS. Among the sixty families studied only 10 percent had extended family networks geographically available during the marriage. Most of our families were nuclear ones, heavily dependent on themselves, social agencies, or educational networks for support. The heavy reliance on therapeutic support among our men and women may be a reflection of this relative familial isolation. The dearth of extended family is common to nondivorced families as well in this region. Nearly one-half of the families were totally uninvolved in religious life, despite earlier and more significant ties of some of these men and women to the Protestant or Catholic religions or the Jewish faith. Of the remainder, it was unusual for both parties to the marriage to share a strong religious affiliation or to practice their faith at a similar level of commitment.

## The Children

The sixty families had 136 children, ranging in age from one to twenty-two, and 131 of these youngsters participated fully enough in the project to be included. Forty-eight percent were male, 52 percent female. Slightly more than half of the children were between the ages of two and eight when first seen; the remainder were between nine and eighteen years of age (see Table 3).

TABLE 3

*Age Groupings and Sex of Children*

| Age Groupings | Boys | Girls | Total | Percentage of Total Group |
|---|---|---|---|---|
| The preschool and kindergarten group (two to five years) | 19 | 15 | 34 | 26 |
| The young school-age group (six to eight years) | 19 | 16 | 35 | 27 |
| The older school-age group (nine to twelve years) | 18 | 26 | 44 | 33 |
| The adolescents (thirteen to eighteen years) | 7 | 11 | 18 | 14 |
|  | 63 | 68 | 131 | 100 |

THE SEARCH FOR A NORMAL POPULATION. As stated earlier, we were interested in studying the experience and impact of divorce among a normal group of children and adolescents. Thus, we excluded from our study any families where a child (or children) had a history of psychological difficulty or was currently in psychotherapy for his or her own personal difficulties. Further, we did not accept into the project youngsters whose intellectual capacity or social development was retarded or significantly below developmentally appropriate norms.

Thus, the children and adolescents in our sample had not been identified by their parents or school personnel as particularly at risk or in need of psychological services prior to coming for the divorce counseling service. In fact, our own observations indicated that these youngsters fell along a spectrum of psychological adequacy, ranging from those with significant and serious psychological problems to those who were coping and functioning extremely well. It may be that this wide diversity in psychological functioning that we found is characteristic of all so-called "normal" populations of children. Certainly, we must emphasize that the children in our study had been living in families where the parents were in conflict or had been, as individuals, sufficiently lacking in personal gratification to seek divorce. Little is known about the psychological effects of this experience on children's overall development. Further, as we have described, marriages and families involved in divorce are of sufficiently diverse character to preclude any single, all-inclusive categorization other than the common experience of divorce.

With the youngsters, as with the adults, we arrived at an overall assessment of their psychological adequacy. With the children this was a shorthand psychodevelopmental profile. These ratings of their general state of developmental and mental health were found to be significantly and highly correlated with more discreet, but component, aspects of the child's psychological functioning, including self-esteem, creativity, anger, capacities to sublimate, feelings of deprivation, anxiety, depression, conscience development, peer relations, social maturity, and school functioning.

Grouping the ratings of the youngsters' general psychodevelopmental adequacy into three major clusters, we can describe our "normal" population in the following ways.

Thirty-six percent of our sample faced the divorcing period with well-integrated personalities and successful coping had been a recurrent and gratifying aspect of their functioning. These remarkably intact youngsters (twenty boys and twenty-six girls) confirm our observation that unsatisfactory marriages can still provide an arena for successful parenting and loving relationships between at least one parent and child. Children and adolescents defined by us as psychologically quite healthy had good self-esteem; were not depressed or chronically angry; related well and enjoyed themselves with peers, teachers, and parents; utilized their time in creative, productive ways; tended to be good students; and did not feel excessively anxious or in need of emotional attention.

Another 48 percent (thirty boys and thirty-three girls) came to the divorce with a mixture of successes and failures. These youngsters represented, in a sense, the adequate and average child who copes as best he can, where he can, with a mixture of supports and environmental givens. Some of these youngsters did well academically, for example, but had ungratifying relationships with parents and peers. Others were mildly depressed and had difficulties at school, but were engaging and capable of seeking nurturance wherever they could find it.

The remainder of the youngsters (17 percent) entered the separation period with the serious handicaps of either developmental arrests in functioning or notable psychological problems and a prior history of successive and accumulating failures in coping. We were conservative in rating children at this end of the scale, not wishing to overdiagnose psychopathological behavior which might, in fact, be primarily stress-induced. And yet, for this group (thirteen boys and nine girls), the impairments and failures in psychological functioning were so obviously chronic that the divorce seemed to represent yet another traumatic event in a life filled with trauma, lack of gratification, and failures in mastery at various developmental stages.

There were no significant age differences in overall psychological functioning—that is, the preschool-kindergarten children were no more nor less mentally healthy than the school-age or adolescent groups. Further, among the four major age and sex groupings previously described that we used for correlational and factor analyses, there were no significant differences in overall psychological adequacy. When sex alone was considered, however, there was a trend toward better psychological functioning among the girls ($p < .05$).

In considering the quality of the father-child and mother-child relationships experienced by the children, there were no significant differences between boys and girls. But an age-related trend, not strongly significant, was found with regard to the quality of the father-child relationships. The younger children, two to eight years of age, tended to have better relationships with their fathers than did the older youngsters. This age difference did not hold, though, in considering mother-child relationships, where no differences emerged between the various groups of children.

## First Follow-Up

Contact was reestablished with fifty-eight of the original families. In the remaining two families, both parents either refused further involvement or their whereabouts were unknown to us. Two additional couples had been reconciled in the intervening year and restored their marriages. Thus, the first follow-up population included fifty-six families, with data derived from interviews with forty-one fathers, fifty-three mothers, and 108 children.\* † Forty-five percent of the returning youngsters were boys, 55 percent girls.

The follow-up assessment was an abbreviated version of the initial assessment described earlier. Each family member was again interviewed separately in an extended clinical interview by the same clinician who initially saw them.‡ One of the team members again visited the schools and (with the parents' written permission) conducted extensive interviews with teachers regarding each child's academic performance and classroom and playground behavior in the intervening year. After all family interviews were complete, parents were offered an additional session for informal discussion of our impressions of their children.

---

\* Of the forty-seven fathers seen initially, one moved away, one was not reached, four refused to return, two restored their marriages, and two fathers not originally seen agreed to come for follow-up. Of the fifty-nine mothers seen initially, two moved away, two refused to return, and two restored their marriages. Of the 131 children originally seen, four moved away, four refused to come in, the parents of six children refused to bring the children (but came themselves), three children were not pursued sufficiently by us, and six children were in restored marriages. Of the seventeen children not interviewed, ten were boys, seven were girls, ranging in age from four to eighteen years.

† Race or socioeconomic status was not a factor in determining who returned, moved, or refused to return. Of the reunited families, one was Class II, the other Class IV.

‡ Five of the families originally seen by a staff member who then resigned were followed up by the authors.

# Five-Year Follow-Up

Contact was reestablished with fifty-eight of the original sixty families. In thirty-eight of these families both parents provided follow-up information about themselves and their children. In the remaining twenty families we obtained data from either the father or mother but not both. Two families in the initial study maintained their married status and, although seen four years later, were excluded from the data analyses. Thus, the research sample at five years included fifty-six families with data derived from interviews or telephone contacts with forty-one fathers and fifty-four mothers.* † ‡ One hundred and one of the original 131 youngsters returned for direct follow-up interviews. Five of these continued to live in reconciled marriages and were excluded from further data analyses. Thirty youngsters were not seen personally, but factual data regarding living arrangements, visiting patterns, economic and child-care status, school adjustment, and general attitudes were obtained for twenty-five of this group from one or both parents.** Thus, general information concerning 121 children and adolescents was analyzed and will be discussed in this section. Psychological data, such as specific attitudes, symptoms, feelings, factors in relationships to parents, and variables related to overall psychological functioning were recorded and analyzed only for the ninety-six youngsters interviewed in person.

* Thirty-five fathers and fifty-one mothers were actually interviewed in person; an additional six fathers and three mothers allowed telephone interviews, but either were not willing to be seen in person or had moved away.

† Of the nineteen fathers with whom contact was not successfully reestablished, eight had been unwilling to be part of the project from the beginning and continued to refuse, eight initially came but then refused further participation at either the first or second follow-up, two had moved away with addresses unknown, and an additional father was not adequately pursued. Two fathers who initially expressed no interest in the project came for interviews at the second follow-up.

Six mothers were not seen for the second follow-up, three could not be found, one refused, and two were not properly pursued. Five of these six women had moved, three out of state. The one mother not seen at the initial extended contact willingly participated in the second follow-up.

‡ As before, race and socioeconomic status were not factors in determining who refused to return, who moved out of state, or who allowed telephone contact but not personal interviews. Among this latter group, staff agreed there appeared to be two themes: (1) a strong reluctance to go back to the past for fear such an interview would, as one stated, "open up a can of worms"; and (2) an unspoken, yet detectable sense that things were not going well for the parent or child and that the anticipated scrutiny of an interview would be too stressful.

** The children not seen in direct interviews included nine (seven boys, two girls) who refused to be seen, seven whose parent(s) refused to bring them for interviews, eight youngsters who could not be located, two out-of-state and not available, and four youngsters not adequately pursued by us. There were two families with five children with whom we lost contact. Of the group not interviewed, ranging in age from seven to twenty-three, twenty were boys and ten were girls.

The age and sex of the youngsters seen after five years are included in Table 4.

TABLE 4

*Age and Sex of Youngsters Seen at Five Years*

| Age | Boys | Girls | Total | Percentage of Group |
|-----|------|-------|-------|---------------------|
| 5 – 8 | 5 | 10 | 15 | 16 |
| 9 – 12 | 18 | 17 | 35 | 36 |
| 13 – 16 | 14 | 20 | 34 | 35 |
| 17 – 23 | 3 | 9 | 12 | 13 |
|  | 40 (42%) | 56 (58%) | 96 | 100 |

The structure of the five-year follow-up was similar to that used in the earlier follow-up. Each family member was again interviewed separately by the same clinician in an extended, semistructured clinical interview. Interviews ranged from one to two hours, and an additional consultation was offered to parents interested in receiving feedback on their youngsters. Again, in-depth interviews with teachers regarding each child's academic and social functioning were conducted. Methods of data analysis were similar to those described earlier but with different age breakdowns.*

---

* Looking for group differences in adjustment, analyses of variance for parents compared men and women, and older men and women versus younger men and women. With youngsters, overall, sex and age differences were analyzed for significance, using the major age breakdowns described in Table 4. Factor analyses varied in their age or sex breakdowns, depending on the variables included in any given matrix. In general, however, statistically valid factors were sought using the following division of subjects: (1) all boys, all girls; (2) all five to eight, nine to twelve, thirteen- to sixteen-year-olds; (3) five- to twelve-year-old boys, five- to twelve-year-old girls, thirteen- to twenty-three-year-old boys, thirteen- to twenty-three-year-old girls.

# Appendix B

# Bibliography of Children of Divorce Project

Wallerstein, J., and Kelly, J. "The Effects of Parental Divorce: The Adolescent Experience." In *The Child in His Family: Children at Psychiatric Risk. vol. 3.* Edited by E. J. Anthony, and C. Koupernik. New York: Wiley and Sons, 1974. Also reprinted in: *Childhood Psychopathology.* Edited by S. I. Harrison and J. F. McDermott. New York: International Universities Press, 1978.

Wallerstein, J., and Kelly, J. "The Effects of Parental Divorce: The Experiences of the Preschool Child." *American Academy Child Psychiatry. Journal. 14* no. 4 (1975): 600–616. Also reprinted in *Annual Progress in Child Psychiatry and Child Development.* Edited by S. Chess and A. Thomas. pp. 520–537. New York: Brunner/Mazel, 1976.

Kelly, J., and Wallerstein, J. "The Effects of Parental Divorce: Experiences of the Child in Early Latency." *American Journal of Orthopsychiatry, 46* no. 1 (1976): 20–32.

Wallerstein, J., and Kelly, J. "The Effects of Parental Divorce: Experiences of the Child in Later Latency." *American Journal of Orthopsychiatry, 46* no. 2 (1976): 256–269. Also reprinted in *Family in Transition: II,* Edited by J. Skolnick and A. Skolnick. Boston: Little, Brown and Company, 1977. And in *The Anatomy of Loneliness.* Edited by J. Hartog et al. New York: International Universities Press, 1979.

Wallerstein, J., and Kelly, J. "Divorce Counseling: A Community Service for Families in the Midst of Divorce." *American Journal of Orthopsychiatry, 47* no. 1 (1977): 4–22. Also reprinted in *Parent Education Handbook,* Edited by R. Abidin. 1979.

Kelly, J., and Wallerstein, J. "Brief Interventions with Children in Divorcing Families." *American Journal of Orthopsychiatry, 47* no. 1 (1977):23–39. Also to be reprinted in *Annual Review of Family Therapy, vol. 1,* New York: Human Sciences Press,

Wallerstein, J. "Some Observations Regarding the Effects of Divorce on the Psychological Development of the Pre-School Girl." *Sexual and Gender Development of Young Children,* Edited by J. Oremland and E. Oremland. pp. 117–129. Cambridge, Mass.: Balinger Press, 1977.

Kelly, J., and Wallerstein, J. "Part-Time Parent, Part-Time Child: Visiting After Divorce." *Journal of Clinical Child Psychology*, 6 no. 2 (1977):51–54.

Wallerstein, J. "Responses of the Pre-School Child to Divorce: Those Who Cope." *Child Psychiatry: Treatment and Research*, Edited by M. F. McMillan and S. Henao pp. 269–292. New York: Brunner/Mazel, 1977.

Kelly, J., and Wallerstein, J. "Children of Divorce: The School Setting." *National Elementary Principal* (October, 1979):51–58.

Wallerstein, J., and Kelly, J. "Children and Divorce: A Review." *Social Work*, 24 (November, 1979):468–75.

Wallerstein, J., and Kelly, J. Divorce and Children. *Basic Handbook of Child Psychiatry, vol. IV*, Edited by J. D. Noshpitz et al. New York: Basic Books, 1979.

# Index